IMPERIAL UNITY AND
CHRISTIAN DIVISIONS

CHURCH HISTORY, II

Editorial Committee
ANTHONY P. GYTHIEL
JOHN ERICKSON

General Editor
JOHN MEYENDORFF

JOHN MEYENDORFF

IMPERIAL UNITY AND CHRISTIAN DIVISIONS

The Church 450-680 A.D.

ST VLADIMIR'S SEMINARY PRESS
CRESTWOOD, NEW YORK 10707
1989

Library of Congress Cataloging-in-Publication Data

Meyendorff, John, 1926-
 Imperial unity and Christian divisions.

 (The Church in history; vol. 2)
 Bibliography: p.
 Includes index.
 1. Church history—Primitive and early church,
 ca. 30-600. 2. Church and state—History. I. Title.
 II. Series.
 BR200.M49 1988   270.2   87-31433
 ISBN 0-88141-056-X
 ISBN 0-88141-055-1 (pbk.)

IMPERIAL UNITY AND
CHRISTIAN DIVISIONS

ISBN 0-88141-055-1 — Paper
ISBN 0-88141-056-X — Hard

PRINTED IN THE UNITED STATES OF AMERICA
BY
ATHENS PRINTING COMPANY
NEW YORK, NY 10018

Dedication
and
Acknowledgements

This book is the result of many years of teaching Church history, first at St Sergius Orthodox Theological Institute, Paris, France, and, during the past three decades, at St Vladimir's Seminary, Crestwood, New York. The author is happy to dedicate this work to his students, who, by their questions, their curiosity and their challenges, have contributed to making it what it is.

Much of the additional research has been accomplished in 1981-82, when the author was a Fellow of the Guggenheim Memorial Foundation, to which he expresses gratitude.

The author is also grateful to his colleague, Professor John H. Erickson, for reading the manuscript and making helpful suggestions, and to Professor Anthony Gythiel of Wichita State University for his editorial work. The Index has been prepared by Mr. Peter Hatlie of Fordham University, and the maps were drawn by Mr. Ted Bazil of St Vladimir's Seminary Press. Useful advice and assistance in selecting illustrations was provided by Mrs. Natalia Teteriatnikov, Curator of Visual Resources, Byzantine Center, Dumbarton Oaks.

John Meyendorff

Contents

Chapter IV.

CULTURAL VARIETY AND MISSIONARY EXPANSION IN THE EAST

Chapter V.

Chapter VI.

Chapter VII.

Illustrations

Abbreviations

AB	*Analecta Bollandiana,* Brussels, 1882-.
ACO	E. Schwartz, ed., *Acta conciliorum oecumenicorum,* Berlin, 1927-.
Beck, *Kirche*	H. G. Beck, *Kirche und theologische Literatur im byzantinischen Reich* (Handbuch der Altertumswissenschaft XII, 2, 1), Munich, 1959.
Bolotov, *Lektsii*	V. V. Bolotov, *Lektsii po istorii drevnei tserkvi. IV. Istoriya tserkvi v period vselenskikh soborov. 3. Istoriya bogoslovskoi mysli.* Petrograd, 1918.
Butler, *The Arab Conquest*	A. J. Butler, *The Arab conquest of Egypt and the last thirty years of the Roman dominion.* Ed. by F. M. Fraser. Second edition, Oxford, 1978.
BZ	*Byzantinische Zeitschrift,* Leipzig, 1892-.
Chalkedon	A. Grillmeier and Bacht, *Das Konzil von Chalkedon. Geschichte und Gegenwart,* 2 vol. Würzburg, 1953-62.
CJ	P. Kruger, ed., *Codex Justinianus,* Berlin, 1954.
CN	P. R. Coleman-Norton, *Roman State and Christian Church. A Collection of Legal Documents to A.D. 535,* I-III, London, SPCK, 1966.
CSCO	*Corpus Scriptorum Christianorum Orientalium,* Paris, 1903-.
CSEL	*Corpus Scriptorum Ecclesiasticorum Latinorum,* Vienna, 1866-.
CT	T. Mommsen and D. M. Meyer, edd., *Theodosiani Libri XVI cum Constitutionibus Sirmondianis et Leges novellae ad Theodosianum pertinentes,* Berlin, 1954, 2 vols.
DOP	*Dumbarton Oaks Papers,* Washington, D.C., 1941-,
Duchesne, *L'Eglise*	L. Duchesne, *L'Eglise au IVe siècle,* Paris, 1925.
EO	*Echos d'Orient,* Paris, 1897-.
Frend, *The Rise*	W. H. C. Frend, *The Rise of the Monophysite Movement,* Cambridge, 1972.
GSC	*Die griechischen christlichen Schriftsteller der ersten drei Jahrhunderte,* Leipzig, Berlin, 1897.

GOTR	*Greek Orthodox Theological Review*, Brookline, Mass., 1952-.
Jedin-Dolan, *History*	H. Jedin and J. Dolan, *History of the Church, II. The Imperial Church from Constantine to the early Middle Ages*, by K. Baus, H. G. Beck, E. Evig, H. J. Vogt. Translated by Anselm Biggs, The Seabury Press, New York, 1980.
Jones, *Roman Empire*	A. H. M. Jones, *The Later Roman Empire, 184-602. A Social and Administrative Survey*. Oxford, Blackwell, 1964, 3 vols. and maps.
JTS	*Journal of Theological Studies*, London, 1899-.
LP	*Liber Pontificalis*, ed. L. Duchesne, 2nd ed., I, Paris, 1955; English translation by L. R. Loomis, New York, 1916.
Mansi	G. D. Mansi, *Sacrorum Conciliorum Nova et Amplissima Collectio*, Florence, 1759-63.
Meyendorff, *Christ*	J. Meyendorff, *Christ in Eastern Christian Thought*, 2nd. ed., Crestwood, NY, 1975.
MGH	*Monumenta Germaniae Historica.*
Michael the Syrian, *Chron.*	J. B. Chabot, ed. *Chronique de Michel le Syrien, patriarche jacobite d'Antioche*, 1066-1109, 3 vols., Paris, 1899.
Nov	R. Schoell and G. Kroll, *Justiniani Novellae*, Berlin, 1954.
NPNF	*A Select Library of Nicene and Post-Nicene Fathers of the Christian Church*. Second Series, Grand Rapids, Michigan, n.d.
OCA	*Orientalia Christiana Analecta*, Rome, 1935-.
PG	J. P. Migne, ed., *Patrologiae graecae cursus completus*, Paris, 1844-66.
PL	J. P. Migne, ed., *Patrologiae latinae cursus completus*, Paris, 1844-66.
PO	R. Graffin, *et al.*, edds. *Patrologia orientalis*, Paris, 1907-.
Rhalles-Potles	Γ.Α. Ῥάλλη—Μ. Ποτλῆ, Σύνταγμα τῶν θείων καὶ ἱερῶν κανόνων, I-V, Athens, 1852-9.
REB	*Revue des études byzantines*, Bucharest, 1947-8; Paris, 1949-.
Richards, *Popes*	J. Richards, *The Popes and the Papacy in the Early Middle Ages, 476-750*, London, 1979.
SC	*Sources chrétiennes*, Paris, 1941-.
Stein, *Histoire*	E. Stein, *Histoire du Bas-Empire, I. De l'état romain à l'état byzantin (284-476)*, Paris, 1959.
SVQ	*St Vladimir's Theological Quarterly*, New York, 1951-.
VV	*Vizantiisky Vremennik*, St Petersburg, 1894-1927; Moscow-Leningrad, 1947-.

Bibliographical Note

The author of this volume is indebted to many historians who, before him, pursued the same task of presenting a general picture of the period, or studied more particular issues.

Among the general histories, most useful were—and still are—volumes 4 and 5 of the *Histoire de l'Eglise des origines jusqu' à nos jours* published by Augustin Fliche and Victor Martin (Paris, 1948 and 1947, respectively). The more recent German *Handbuch der Kirchengeschichte* edited by Hubert Jedin, is now available in an English translation by Anselm Biggs. Volume II, entitled *The Imperial Church from Constantine to the early Middle Ages,* as reedited by John Dolan, (New York, 1980) chronologically corresponds to the period covered in the present work.

Among the older "histories," that of Louis Duchesne, frequently referred to in our footnotes, remains invaluable, as is also the case for the *Lektsii* ("Lectures in the history of the ancient church") of V. V. Bolotov, printed posthumously in 1918. Little known in the West, Bolotov's immense erudition and understanding of the doctrinal developments in the Non-Greek East have been often used in the following pages.

For the study of various Eastern Churches in Syria, Persia, India, Egypt, Nubia, Ethiopia, Armenia and Georgia both scholars and students must refer to C. Detlef and G. Müller, *Geschichte der Orientalischen Nationalkirchen* (= *Die Kirche in ihrer Geschichte. Ein Handbuch.* Band 1. Leiferung D2), Göttingen, 1981.

This last work, together with Jedin's *Handbuch* (and its English translation), contains an exhaustive bibliography. The availability of these works convinced this author that detailed bibliographical lists need not be reproduced here. The footnotes, however, refer to various important publications which were used by the author; they can serve as a foundation for further research.

INTRODUCTION

To undertake once more, after so many others, a systematic account of Christian history can be justified only by the ambitious desire to present the facts, the events, the persons and their interrelationships in a new perspective. In the present undertaking, the novelty consists primarily in the author's hope to achieve a fairer balance than can usually be found in textbooks of Church History, between the Eastern and the Western visions of the historical past.

Indeed, it can be said, in general, that modern historians of the late Roman Empire and the Middle Ages either limit themselves to those periods, without discussing later repercussions, or, if they envision the eventual consequences for the subsequent history of Western civilization, consider the latter in a rather limited fashion, as the history of Western Europe only. In contrast to this Western historical orientation, the development, in this century, of specifically "Byzantine" studies has led to the new recognition that a Christian Roman Empire continued to exist after the fifth century until the late medieval period. However, Byzantine studies have generally failed so far to have a significant influence upon the teaching and the understanding of history in most schools and universities of the West, partly because they have remained a somewhat recondite discipline, requiring knowledge of Greek and of other Middle Eastern and Slavic languages, and the study of a civilization which led to no really significant human achievement. Indeed, the modern world, as we know it, was not shaped in Byzantium, in the Middle East, or in Eastern Europe, but by the Western European Renaissance and by the Enlightenment (*Aufklärung*), so that the modern student finds it difficult to relate to Byzantium and to discover its relevance.

But, then, is there really a historical balance to be established? Was not the "East" but the back waters of European civilization, a peripheral area, surviving for centuries, but leading to a cultural dead end? This view, expressed by Edward Gibbon in his famous *History of the Decline and Fall of the Roman Empire*, was indignantly rejected by the earlier generations of Byzantinists. However, it is being resumed by many today, out of reaction against the exaggerated, romantic conceptions which extolled Byzantium as the bridge between Greek antiquity and modernity.

It appears to this author that if one applies to Byzantium and the Christian East the cultural criteria which prevailed in the West during the Enlightenment, one is indeed almost unavoidably led to Gibbon's assessment that the history of Christian Byzantium is not much more than "a tedious and uniform tale of weakness and misery."[1] If, however, one takes a more critical view of the secular society and culture which resulted from the Enlightenment; if one has doubts as to whether Western Christianity has always used the right philosophy and the right methods to preserve the values of the Christian Gospel; one can very well find it legitimate to look back into history for alternative possibilities and lost opportunities, especially to the world of Byzantium, as the other facet of the Greco-Roman Christian legacy.

It is in this sense that this book will attempt to strike a better balance in the historical perception of the relationships between East and West.

It is my conviction that such a balancing corrective will be useful not only to Western historians, but also to Eastern Orthodox authors, whose writings may not be well-known in the West, but whose approach influences the self-awareness and the mentality of Eastern Christians. Defensive against all things Western, these authors—despite their own position of principle which recognizes that ecclesial unity existed between East and West during the entire first millennium of Christian history—tend to identify Orthodoxy exclusively with things Eastern and Byzantine, and to simply overlook not only the historical shortcomings of Byzantine Christendom, but also the authentic and truly Orthodox achievements of Western Christianity.

In other words, the problem of Christian historiography—Western and Eastern—is that authors tend to view the past with a bias acquired by the study of *historically later* cultural and confessional divisions.

---

[1]*The Decline and Fall of the Roman Empire, New York,* Random House, n.d. II, p. 520.

Thus, our concern for balance is actually a concern for authentic Christian catholicity, as it is an attempt to meet the demands of historical method and scholarship

Resulting from the experience of teaching Church History for several decades in Orthodox theological schools, both European and American, the content of this volume is chronologically limited to the fifth, sixth and seventh centuries. These chronological limits require a brief justification. Indeed, history is always a continuum, and datable signposts are unavoidably chosen by the historian to accomplish his purpose and do justice to his conception of the events.

My specific purpose it to discuss that period of Church history, when the Church, with its theology, its institutions, its liturgy and social action, was merged with society at large within the framework of the Roman Empire and the various political structures which had inherited Roman ideology. This period remains crucial for our understanding of the Church today, not only because of the distinctive relations which existed between Church and State, but also because of the decisive doctrinal options taken then, because of the schisms which divided Christians and which have not been solved until today, and because the Church, inseparable of its Tradition, cannot solve its present problems without constantly referring to these decisive, formative centuries.

The chronological beginnings of my account could have been set with the reign of Constantine (305-337), who established religious freedom for Christians, or with that of Theodosius I (379-395), who was the first baptized Christian to occupy the imperial throne, or with that of Justinian I (527-565), who suppressed the last vestiges of paganism and legally sanctioned the existence of the Empire as a monolithically Christian society. In the two introductory chapters, the ideological and legal principles adopted under Constantine and Theodosius are actually analyzed in some detail. Without such an introduction the history of either the Byzantine or the Latin Christendoms would be unintelligible. However, the actual historical account begins with the council of Chalcedon (451). My choice of 451 is based upon the fact that the council of Chalcedon was, in many ways, the first truly "ecumenical" council, with both East and West appropriately represented. It also inaugurated a centuries-old split of Eastern Christendom, pointing very clearly to the problems that were to dominate the future: the division caused by the christological controversy in the East and the more explicit emergence of a new consciousness of the Roman primacy in the West. These problems, nevertheless, did not immediately lead to "final" schism: a strong consciousness of unity was maintained for several centuries, until, in the middle of the seventh century, the Muslim conquest severed in an irrevocable manner, the relations between the Chalcedonian and the Non-Chalcedonian communities of the Middle East. Between Byzantium and Rome unity will survive longer, but issues which would eventually cause the schism can already be clearly defined by studying the events discussed in this volume.

CHAPTER I

CHURCH AND EMPIRE

In February 313, the Roman emperors Constantine and Licinius met in Milan and agreed on a new religious policy. The decision, often described as the "Edict of Milan," was eventually issued by Licinius in Nicomedia on June 15 of the same year.[1] The policy consisted in ending the persecution of Christianity, declaring it therefore to be a "licit" cult *(religio licita)*, in restoring the previously confiscated Christian properties, and in establishing a regime of religious tolerance. Two centuries later, in 528, the period of religious tolerance had already ended! Through the laws of emperor Justinian, not only was Orthodox Christianity established as the sole religion of the State, but Christian bishops had become legally responsible for the forceful suppression of paganism: "We order our magistrates," the emperor wrote, "both in this royal city (of Constantinople) and in the provinces to advance with all zeal, both by their own resources and when by the most God-beloved bishops they have been instructed in such matters, to investigate legally all the impieties of pagan worship, so that these may not occur and, when occurring, may be punished."[2]

In the intervening two centuries, a new society which formally accepted Christianity as its religious—and therefore also moral, cultural and political—norm, came into being, and survived until, in modern times, secularization would lead to such extreme consequences as the outlawing of Christianity (and religion in general) by Lenin in 1918.

Of course, the Christian Church existed before Constantine and

[1] Text in Lactantius, *De morte pers.* 18, and Eusebius, *Eccl. hist.* X, 5, 1-14 (tr. G. A. Williamson, Baltimore, MD, 1965, pp. 401-3).

[2] CJ, I, 11, 9; tr. in CN, III, p. 1026.

5

survives after Lenin, but the relationships to society were different and the opportunities in human terms, limited. During the centuries of the Christian empire and the medieval period that followed, society accepted guidance by Christian principles—though, paradoxically, it also used such methods as law, coercion and violence to impose them. Hence the ambiguity, the Utopian character of the concept of "Christendom," as it existed then.

By the middle of the fifth century, although the christianization of society was by no means complete, the pattern of the alliance between Empire and Church was already clearly defined. This definition did not come about suddenly, but through an empiric evolution to which neither side was theoretically prepared. Emperor Constantine I (305-337), the first "Christian emperor," was originally an adept of solar monotheism. He probably underwent some sort of personal conversion-experience in connection with the battle of the Milvian Bridge against the usurper Maxentius (312), but the change in religious policy was not abrupt. As a result of the battle, he entered Rome, a largely pagan city, at the head of an overwhelmingly pagan army, and was proclaimed Augustus of an empire where Christians constituted a small minority. He continued to invoke the "Unconquered Sun" (*Sol Invictus*) on his coins and official documents and remained the supreme pontiff (*pontifex maximus*) of the official Roman, largely syncretistic paganism. He changed practically nothing in the traditional behavior and political methods of Roman emperors. For example, he ordered the execution of his former colleague Licinius—the co-signer of the edict of toleration—whom he defeated (324), and, later, of his own son, Crispus, and his own wife, Fausta (326). These executions took place at the very time when Constantine was sponsoring and presiding over the council of Nicaea (325). Nevertheless, throughout his reign, as sole Augustus, he increasingly identified the Supreme Divinity, whom he worshipped since his youth, with Christ worshipped by the Christians. At the same time he extended his attention to the affairs of the Church and his favors upon the clergy. It was perhaps his inability to reconcile, in conscience and in theory, the duties of the Roman principate with the personal ethical requirement of a Christian that made him postpone baptism until his deathbed (337). The baptism was performed by the Arian bishop Eusebius of Nicomedia. It is, therefore, perhaps misleading to call Constantine the "first Christian emperor," since he did not share in the sacramental life and the liturgical celebrations of the Church until his last moments. Nevertheless,—and in spite of his Arian baptism—the Orthodox Church has recognized him as a Saint, "equal to the Apostles." Indeed, no single human being in history has contributed, directly or indirectly, to the conversion of so many to the Christian faith.

The gradual transformation of the empire into a formally Christian society continued under Constantine's successors. But this slow evolution was to be full of contrasts and paradoxes. The two sons of Constantine—Constantius II (337-361) and Constans (337-350)—, who reigned in the East and the West respectively, expanded the Constantinian legislation in favor of Christianity and took an active part—especially Constantius—in the affairs of a Church divided by the Arian crisis. Both followed the example of their father in postponing baptism until the last days of their earthly life. In the social consciousness of the time, confession of Christianity was still not seen as a prerequisite for becoming an emperor. Julian, the "apostate"—the only remaining nephew of Constantine the Great, who survived the bloody purges of Constantius—won much public sympathy by his restoration of paganism (361-363). Another pagan, the praetorian prefect Secundus Solutius, obtained unanimous support of the army to succeed Julian after his death. Secundus refused the honor in 363, and again in 364, for reasons of age and poor health.[3] Among the ephemeral emperors of the late fourth century, the case of Valentinian I (364-375) is noted as an exception by contemporaries, because, as a military commander under Julian, he had refused to offer pagan sacrifices.[4] He must, therefore, have nourished strong Christian convictions. However, since his election took place in Nicaea by the same assembly of military dignitaries who had previously chosen the pagan Solutius, one must presume that, by 364—fifty years after the edict of toleration—the religious convictions of the candidate were seen as a rather immaterial factor in the choice of an emperor.

Substantial steps in the direction of the establishment of Christianity were taken by Theodosius I (378-395) and his Western colleague Gratian (379-384). Gratian formally renounced the pagan title of *pontifex maximus* in 381, whereas Theodosius became the first emperor to be baptized at the very beginning of his reign. It is possible, however, that, when the baptism was performed, Theodosius

[3]Stein, *Histoire*, I, pp. 170-172.
[4]Jones, *Roman Empire*, III, p. 25.

conceived of it as a deathbed rite which he solicited from bishop Acholius of Thessalonica on the occasion of a grave illness. Upon his recovery, however, he consciously tried to fulfill the requirements of a Christian life and regularly participated in the liturgy, becoming also subject to the penitential discipline of the Church. The famous incident in Milan, when, in 390, St Ambrose demanded that he submit to public penance after the chastisement he had inflicted upon the people of Thessalonica, would have been impossible under his unbaptized predecessors, who did not go to church and were not canonically answerable to bishops for their private or public behavior.

As a practicing Christian, Theodosius naturally broke totally with pagan cults and gladly approved petitions by Christian bishops to have temples closed, destroyed or transformed into churches. In some areas, violent incidents opposed Christians and pagans on such occasions, as for example, when Theophilus, archbishop of Alexandria, turned a temple of the pagan god Dionysus into a church and had the famous shrine of Serapis—the Serapeum—destroyed. In 391-392, Theodosius issued two decrees banning pagan cults, public or private, altogether.[5] It is at this point that the Empire became constitutionally and legally a Christian state with paganism reduced to the position of a barely tolerated minority. It still survived for more than a century: in the West, the usurper Eugenius (392-394) even favored a pagan revival. In Athens, the old Academy remained open, and vast pagan areas survived in the countryside. However, all the sons and grandsons of Theodosius who reigned until the middle of the fifth century, followed his example in becoming formal members of the Church and in enforcing anti-pagan legislation. Finally, the drastic policies of Justinian (527-565), eliminated paganism altogether from public life.

1. Imperial legislation and the Christian faith

The emperor Theodosius II (398-450), in the year 438, issued a general codification of imperial decrees published between 312 and 437. This collection known as the Theodosian Code (*Codex Theodosianus*), represents the richest and the most reliable source of the social, economic and religious policies of Christian emperors in the fourth and fifth centuries. It allows the reader to follow the gradual

[5]CT XVI, 10, 11-12 (tr. Clyde Pharr, Princeton, 1952, p. 473).

changes in this policy as well as its inconsistencies. Outdated and superseded texts are often included in the collection. On the other hand, the repetition of certain legal provisions clearly indicates that their application was encountering difficulties. Upon its publication, the Theodosian Code acquired immediate force of law in the whole empire. Later imperial constitutions which preceded the disappearance of the Western empire in 476, were issued separately in the East and the West, and, unless received by both emperors, kept regional validity only. Some of these later texts appear frequently in an abbreviated form in the even more monumental, more selective and better edited Code of Justinian, published in 534.

The fact that the Theodosian Code accepted the year 312 as a starting point, indicates that its compilers considered the "conversion" of Constantine as something of a watershed in the history of Roman legislation. One would, therefore, expect that a radical change in the content and philosophy of the law would be consistent with that event. In fact, the texts show quite the opposite: the empire, its methods of government and social principles remained basically the same, with only relatively limited, humanizing Christian influence in some areas.[5a] The real change came primarily in the advantages received by the Church as an institution, initiating a long-term process of transformation in society at large.

Two areas can be singled out as examples of institutional, legal and social permanence, only superficially affected by Christianity: marriage and slavery. Even in these cases, however, it is not always possible to ascertain whether the changes interfering in the fourth and fifth centuries were caused by Christian influence exclusively. Other factors were also important, for instance the ethical principles of Stoicism, integrated into the very syncretic forms of Neo-Platonism, were the prevailing philosophy of the day, and tended to inculcate temperance (*sophrosyne*) and self-discipline. Like Christianity, they were opposed to extreme forms of oppression and cruelty.

The philosophy of marriage found in the imperial laws was based on the old Roman principle of a contract, concluded between freely consenting parties. Like any contract, it could be dissolved.[6] Constantine, however, forbade divorce by simple mutual consent, so that lists of "sufficient reasons" for divorce appear in imperial laws. These in-

---

[5a]On this issue, see B. Biondi, *Il diritto romano christiano,* 3 vols. Milano, 1952-54.
[6]CT, Nov. 12 (July 10, 439, tr. cit., p. 498); CJ V 17, 18 (Jan. 9, 449).

cluded not only adultery, but such offenses as state treason, stealing cattle, robbing graves. Socializing with known prostitutes by the husband was a legitimate reason for a woman to ask for divorce, but the husband could do the same if his wife was going to circus games or the theater.[7] However, it appears that the courts remained practically lenient, so that divorces for simple "incompatibility" continued to be granted. In 421, Honorius forbade remarriage to the party which claimed only "incompatibility" as reason for divorce, but allowed it to the innocent spouse.[8] Some inequality between men and women persisted, particularly in the right of re-marriage after divorce, e.g. an "innocent" husband divorcing a "guilty" wife was allowed to remarry immediately, whereas a wife in a similar situation had to wait one year.[9] A remarrying widow, but not a widower, automatically lost tutelage of her children[10]—a regulation connected with inequality in property management rights.

Obviously, these laws concerned civil marriage, which was contracted before a magistrate (or witnesses) and which was the only available way of contracting marriage for Christians and non-Christians alike. The Church had no competence in the legal aspect of the marriage contract and state legislation did not accept the Christian view of marriage. The Church, however, could apply its own principles and its own penitential discipline to its members. These principles implied a mystical and eschatological view of marriage, as a reflection of the union of Christ and the Church (Eph 5:22-33). For Christians, the norm was one single marriage, with remarriage allowed after either widowhood, or divorce, but only after a period of penance (St Basil). Any form of remarriage, as a breach of Christian norm, was an obstacle to ordination into the clergy. The possibility of divorce was never formally eliminated, but was limited to only one ground— adultery—in accordance with Mat 19:9. But these serious discrepancies between imperial laws and church requirements tended to be minimized in practice, as the Church gradually accommodated itself more and more to state legislation, at least in its *de facto* approach to the marriage of lay persons.

If the Roman state, now Christian-inspired, hardly modified its

[7]CJ V, 17,8 (Jan. 9, 449).
[8]CT III, 16,2 (March 10, 421, tr. cit., p. 77).
[9]*Ibid.*
[10]CT III,17,4 (Jan. 21, 390, tr. cit., p. 78).

philosophy of marriage, it did begin to integrate some principles of Christian family ethics. Thus help was provided to parents unable to feed their children and tempted to abandon them.[11] The sale of children to slavery and their use for prostitution was severely punished. Laws prohibiting celibacy, which was encouraged by the Church, were abolished.[12] Homosexuals were to be burnt at the stake.[13] Earlier, Constantine had condemned pederasts to gladiator's fights,[14] but soon decided to abolish such fights altogether,[15] after also forbidding mutilation, by fire-branding, of a criminal's face because "it bears the similitude of God."[16]

Similar examples of concern for human dignity did also appear in attitudes towards slaves, but nobody challenged the very principle of servitude, as a social institution. The law continued to consider a slave, as property of his master, entitled to occasional acts of mercy, but not to rights of a human being. Thus, since a slave could not give "free consent," he or she could not legally marry. Not even a free man could marry a slave woman, and the children born of such illegitimate unions were to be considered as slaves.[16a] As lacking freedom, and therefore responsibility, slaves could be heard as court witnesses only under torture, and were to be crucified if they denounced their master.[17] They could not be admitted into the clergy without manumission by their masters.[18] Justinian relaxed this rule somewhat by allowing ordination of slaves with their master's consent, provided that they return to him if they were to leave holy orders.[19]

Whether under Christian, or Stoic influence, Constantine forbade immoderate torture and deliberate murder of slaves by their masters,[20] and discouraged the separate sales of individual members of a slave's family.[21] Other laws strictly forbade the sale, or use of Christian slave-women for prostitution and provided, in such cases, for their automatic

---

[11]CT XI,27,1 (May 13, 315, tr. cit., p. 318).
[12]CT VIII,16,1 (Jan. 31, 320, tr. cit., p. 217).
[13]CT IX,7,6 (Aug. 6, 390, tr. cit., p. 232).
[14]CT IX,18,1 (Aug. 1, 315, tr. cit., p. 240).
[15]CT XV,12,1 (Oct. 1, 325, tr. cit., p. 436).
[16]CT IX,40,2 (March 21, 315, tr. cit., p. 255).
[16a]CT IV,12,1 (Apr. 1, 314, tr. cit., p. 92); CT IX,9,1 (May 29, 329, tr. cit., p. 233); CJ V,5,3 (June 23, 319).
[17]CT IX,5,1 (Jan. 320, tr. cit., p. 230).
[18]CJ I,3,36 (484).
[19]Nov. 123, 17 (546).
[20]CT IX,12,1 (May 11, 319, tr. cit., p. 235).
[21]CT II,25,1 (Apr. 29, 325, tr. cit., p. 56-57).

manumission.[22] In general, the Church became an official agency for the freeing (*manumissio*) of slaves. A manumission performed in the presence of clergy could take place at any time, even on Sunday (when courts were not in session) and required no other witnesses or formalities.[23] Christian emperors also took measures to protect the religious convictions of Christian slaves, forbidding Jews, under severe penalties, to circumcise their Christian slaves,[24] and eventually forbade the ownership of Christian slaves by Jews altogether. Similarly, heretics were prevented from forcing Orthodox slaves to convert to their sect.[25]

It remains, however, that Constantine and his successors never even considered the possibility of including in their legislation anything which would reflect St Paul's affirmation that, in Christ, there is simply "neither slave, nor free man" (Gal 3:28). The empire remained an institution "of this world" with its social inequality, with its use of violence, as a normal form of exercising power, with the law serving only as a principle of rational order and moderation. The revelation of a "new creation," found in Christian Scripture, was not understood as an interference with the "normal" order of things, but rather as an eschatological ideal, announced and anticipated in the Church and its sacraments. As far as the empire was concerned, the real change which came about with Constantine, was the support given to the Church in accomplishing its mission. However, this support, which could only take the form of legal or economic privileges within the imperial system, went to the Church, as an institution. Its effect was to provide the entire population of the empire with the possibility of accepting Christianity, but, at the same time, the alliance thus concluded between Church and State implied, on the side of the Church, certain shifts of priorities and compromises often detrimental to the credibility of its message. The gradual acceptance by the Church of the legalistic approach to marriage, which necessarily dominated Roman legislation on the subject, has been noted earlier. On slavery, not only was there practically no opposition to the institution itself, but the Church endorsed it implicitly, not only by using slaves, but also by condoning the State prohibition against accepting slaves into the clergy. St Leo

[22]CT XV,8,1 (July 4, 343, tr. cit., p. 435); CT XV,8,2 (Apr. 21, 428, tr. ibid.); Theodosius II, CT, Nov. 18 (Dec. 6, 439, tr. cit., p. 504).
[23]CJ I,13,1 (June 8, 316); CT IV,7,1 (Apr. 18, 321, tr. cit., p. 87); CT II,8,1 (July 3, 321, tr. cit., p. 44).
[24]E.g. CT XVI,9,1 (Oct. 21).
[25]CT XVI,5,65 (May 30, 428).

the Great (440-461) is indignant of some exceptional cases when
"slaves who were quite unable to gain freedom from their masters
are elevated to the high rank of the priesthood, as if the lowly
character of the slave were the one to receive this honor; and it is
believed that a slave who has not yet been able to prove himself to
his master can be approved of by God. In this matter, of course, the
guilt is twofold, the sacred ministry is contaminated by taking in such
party of low rank, and the rights of slave owners are infringed on
since their possessions are taken from them."[26] It is true that such
statements by some princes of the Church were balanced by the radical
social preaching of a St John Chrysostom, or the generally egalitarian
spirit which dominated the early monastic communities.

It would be impossible to present here a complete survey of
privileges bestowed by the emperors upon the Church, its personnel
and its institutions in the fourth to sixth centuries. These privileges con-
ferred immense power to the Church—a power not to be compared to
the influence exercised previously by pagan priests, who were primarily
ministers of temples and lacked a common organization and sense of
unity.

The new power of the Church was, first of all, economic. The
gifts made by Constantine to the Church of Rome, after his victory
over Maxentius (312), and which included the imperial palace of the
Lateran, became the legendary symbol of imperial *largesse* throughout
the Middle Ages. Similar donations went to other churches, and especially to the archbishopric of the new capital, Constantinople. The
building of immense basilicas in all the major cities of the Empire
implied huge imperial endowments for the upkeep of the buildings
and the clergy attached to them. Of particular, and permanent, significance was a law of Constantine authorizing the Church to benefit from
wills, and every other form of private donations.[27] Ecclesiastical wealth
grew fabulously, although many donations were, in part, earmarked
for charitable institutions, such as hospitals, orphanages and old age
homes. In Antioch, for example, where Chrysostom was a presbyter,
the Church fed three thousand virgins every day, and provided food
and clothing to a large number of persons inscribed on its welfare
roles. It also maintained hostels for travellers and dispensaries for

---

[26]*Ep.* 4, 1, PL 54, col. 611 A (tr. E. Hunt, New York, 1957, p. 23-24); similar
views expressed in the East by Severus of Antioch, *Ep.* I, 35.

[27]CT XVI,2,4 (July 3, 321, tr. cit., p. 441).

the sick.[27a] In fact, throughout the Middle Ages, the Church assumed the practical monopoly of social work, both in the East and in the West. It was inevitable, therefore, that in the fifth century, the major episcopal sees would dispose of immense riches, enhanced by partial tax-exemptions (the lands belonging to the Church were taxed). Thus, pope Damasus (366-384) was known to live in a grand style—"make me bishop of Rome, and I will become a Christian tomorrow," jokes the old pagan senator Agorius Praetextatus—and St Cyril of Alexandria (d. 444), when he was in difficulty after his high-handed treatment of his adversaries at the council of Ephesus (431), was able to offer as much as 2500 lbs. in gold as bribes to court officials in Constantinople.[28] The wealth of the Church was further enhanced by the principle—partly of Old Testament origin—that a gift to the Church was a gift to God, and therefore inalienable. In the fifth and sixth centuries, imperial laws endorsed the principle, reserving only limited rights of the emperor to alienate some church property after appropriate compensation.[29]

Bishops were granted both power and prestige. An average Christian bishop could certainly not compete with the economic power possessed by the great sees of Rome, Alexandria, or Constantinople, but he was their equal in terms of judicial and moral rights. An imperial decree authorized bishops to judge without appeal any case submitted to them voluntarily by the parties involved.[30] Eventually, in 399, such episcopal judicial rights were restricted to causes involving religious issues. Christian bishops, while remaining the only judges of delinquent clergy,[31] gradually assumed a large part of the former competence of civil judges as well. Furthermore, they were given powers to participate in the election of civil magistrates[32] whereas—at least in principle—civil authorities had no competence in the election of bishops (cf. below, pp. 44-5).

This new official position assumed by the Church in Roman society involved imperial legislative and administrative support against all religious dissenters. The laws of Theodosius I had outlawed all pagan cults[33] and the tenacious survivals of paganism among city aristocrats

27aSt John Chrysostom, *Hom. in Mat.* 66 (PG 58,630).
28ACO I, vol. IV, pp. 224-5.
29CJ I,2,24 (530, emperor Justinian).
30CT I,27,1 (June 23, 318, tr. cit., p. 31).
31CT XVI,2,41 (Dec. 11, 411).
32Cf. Jones, *Roman Empire,* p. 758.
33CT XVI,10,12 (Nov. 8, 392, tr. cit., p. 473).

and intellectuals, as well as in wide areas of the countryside, were actively fought by Christian bishops, who relentlessly used all legal, and sometimes violent, means at their disposal. In 392, St Ambrose of Milan struggled against the restoration of the altar of Victory in the Roman Senate. Both Christians and pagans of Alexandria were involved in riots when bishop Theophilus presided over the conversion of a temple of Dionysus into a church and over the forcible demolition of the famous Serapeum (ca. 389 or 391)—himself striking the first blow against the huge statue of Serapis.

It is clear, therefore, that the Christian clergy became willing agents for the establishment of the new, monolithically Christian social order desired by the emperors, and it was natural for a man like John of Ephesus, to accept from Justinian in 542 the mission of a kind of "Grand Inquisitor" in the rural areas of Western Asia Minor, and thus to convert over 70,000 remaining pagans by force. Under Justinian, the disaffection of all remaining pagan temples—whose columns and marble were used to build St Sophia in Constantinople and other churches—and the closing of the pagan Academy in Athens, can be seen as the last stroke over the pagan past. Law required that all pagans receive baptism, under penalty of confiscation of property and exile.[34]

If Roman imperial law eventually prohibited paganism, it continued to offer limited protection to the Jews. Not only was their cultic freedom guaranteed, but the disaffection of synagogues was forbidden[35] and their personnel—like the Christian clergy—were exempt of civil and personal charges.[36] Arbitrary violence against Jews was punishable by law.[37] However, since the very beginning of the Christian empire, drastic measures had been taken against Jewish proselytizing among Christians, and baptism of Jews was encouraged. Conversion of Christians to Judaism was prohibited, and Jews molesting a convert to Christianity were to be burnt at the stake.[38] As we saw earlier, they were not to own Christian slaves, and were deprived of legal protection if they showed disrespect for Christianity.[39] They were also excluded from the army, the civil services and the legal profession.[40] It does

[34]CJ I,11,10 (529).
[35]CT VII,8,2 (May 6, 368, tr. cit., p. 165).
[36]CT XVI,8,2 (Nov. 29, 330, tr. cit., p. 467).
[37]CT XVI,8,21 (Aug. 6, 420, tr. cit., p. 469); 10,24 (June 8, 423, tr. cit., p. 476).
[38]CT XVI,8,1 (Aug. 13, 315, tr. cit., p. 467).
[39]CT XVI,8,21 (Aug. 6, 420, tr. cit., p. 470).
[40]CT, *Const. Sirmond.* 6 (July 9, 425, tr. cit., p. 480).

not seem, however, that—before the reign of Heraclius (610-641)—forcible mass baptisms of Jews were practiced within the Empire, as they began to occur in the barbarian Christian states of the West after the fifth century.[41] The sect of the Samaritans enjoyed a status similar to that of orthodox Jews until the big Samaritan rebellions in Palestine under Justinian, which led to their forcible suppression.

All the legal texts issued by the emperors in favor of Christianity specify that imperial favors were directed exclusively to *catholic* Christianity and the *Catholic Church,* whereas severe prohibitions sanctioned the innumerable groups of heretics and schismatics. We will discuss below the problem of criteria by which heresy and schism were distinguished from doctrinal and canonical orthodoxy; indeed, all groups claimed "catholicity" for themselves. It is clear, therefore, that the lack of unity and the continuous disputes which divided Christians among themselves must have constituted the greatest disappointment for emperors, who considered religious unity as an essential factor of the State's welfare. The absence of a clear and universally accepted method for solving doctrinal controversies by the Christian Church made it inevitable that the emperors would try to devise and impose such methods, using their own approach and initiative. The alternative would have been to allow religious pluralism, which neither the State, nor any of the Christian groups were prepared to accept. Thus, Constantine tried to solve the dispute between Catholics and Donatists in Africa by having bishops agree on a solution which would lead to unity. The failure of the two successive councils of Rome and Arles led to an imperial decision, which was actually solicited by the conflicting parties themselves. However, many other imperial decrees on the faith proved eventually to be failures. The definition of "orthodoxy," as found in the codes of Theodosius II and Justinian, was therefore the result of a complex and painful process of selection, between competing Christian groups. By 451, "orthodoxy" meant the faith of Nicaea, as understood by the Cappadocian Fathers, and the faith of Athanasius and Cyril of Alexandria, as interpreted at Chalcedon (451). Dissenters were legally excluded from the Church and from society in general.

Already with the enthronement of Theodosius I (379) the measures directed earlier by Constantius II and Valens against the orthodox Nicaeans were turned against the various categories of Arians. Arian meetings were forbidden and their churches were transferred to

[41]Jones, *Roman Empire,* pp. 949-950.

the catholic bishops.[42] Similar decrees—frequently repeated, denoting obvious difficulties in systematic enforcement—were directed against Apollinarists (who accepted Nicaea, but were at odds with the orthodox Christology of the Cappadocian Fathers, supported by Theodosius),[43] and the older African group of the Donatists.[44] Heretics were also excluded from all State jobs and in general deprived of civil rights.[45] Some categories of dissenters—mainly sectarians, whose groups went back to early Christianity—were treated even more severely: Quattrodecimans, who celebrated Easter at a date different from the one adopted by the Church were punished with exile,[46] whereas the adepts of Gnostic sects were sometimes subjected to the death penalty.[47] It is clear, however, that practical considerations often dictated tolerance towards large and influential groups of heretics. This was the case of the Gothic troops, predominantly Arian, on which the emperor had frequently to rely for his security, and of the various Gothic rulers, who conquered the Western regions of the empire and were not only invested with imperial court titles but also remained diplomatic partners until the reconquest of the West by Justinian. The empire was also forced to exercise moderation and use diplomacy with the opponents of the council of Chalcedon (451), who constituted at least half of the population in the East. The numerically small, but intellectually influential group of Nestorians was not as fortunate. After its condemnation by the council of 431, it was "deprived of the Christian name"[48] and forced to emigrate to Persia, where, together with the local Syriac speaking community, it began a long history of survival, and also missionary expansion throughout Asia.

While granting privileges to the Catholic Church and protecting it against opposition or dissent, imperial laws also gave official status to its clergy. In addition to the judicial powers granted to bishops— which were mentioned above—the law considered any offense against clerics as a public crime,[49] while clerics themselves were answerable only to episcopal tribunals. This special status of ordained persons soon became legally incompatible with any other professional status:

[42]CT XVI,5,5 (Aug. 3, 379, tr. cit., p. 450); 5,6 (Jan. 10, 381, tr. cit., p. 451).
[43]CT XVI,5,15 (March 10, 388, tr. cit., p. 453).
[44]CT XVI,5,46 (Jan. 15, 409, tr. cit., p. 458).
[45]CT XVI,5,25 (March 13, 395, tr. cit., p. 454); 26 (March 30, 395, tr. cit., p. 455).
[46]CT XVI,6,6 (March 21, 413, tr. cit., p. 465); 10,24 (June 8, 423, tr. cit., p. 476).
[47]CT XVI,5,9 (March 31,, 382, tr. cit., p. 452).
[48]CT XVI,5,66 (Aug. 8, 435, tr. cit., p. 463).
[49]CT XVI,2,31 (Jan. 15, 409, tr. cit., p. 445).

in a *novella* issued in 452, emperor Valentinian III ordered clerics to abstain from trades, or be deprived of their legal privileges. Although this law concerned the Western empire only and does not seem to have been followed very consistently, it clearly shows that not only the episcopacy, but also the priesthood had acquired a sought-for economic standing. This situation led to other state-imposed conditions for admission into the clergy.

We have seen earlier that slaves were excluded, unless they had previously obtained freedom from their masters. Similar limitations were placed, in laws of the late fifth and sixth centuries, on the so-called *coloni adscripti,* or serfs bound to land and working for landowners.[50] Since, on the other hand, members of the senatorial class, or the military, rarely joined the priesthood—unless they were elected to episcopal positions in major cities like Milan (*e.g.* St Ambrose in 374), or Constantinople (*e.g.* Nectarius in 381)— Christian clergy were primarily recruited among the middle class and especially the *curiales,* or city-dwelling landowners, who were subjected by law to some "curial" obligations or "liturgies," in maintaining public facilities in the cities such as water supply, baths, theaters, etc. Since the welfare of the cities depended upon the particular contributions of the *curiales,* or decurions, the emperors attempted unsuccessfully to forbid their ordination to the clergy,[51] for the privileged position of the clergy made it inevitable that clerics and their families be exempt from curial charges.[52] As more and more *curiales* joined the clergy, this privilege had to be restricted: in order to be admitted to ordination, decurions were obliged to abandon their patrimony to the *curia,*[53] or find a substitute able to carry their obligation to the city after their ordination or monastic tonsure.[54] The reiteration of measures directed at limiting conflict of interest between a privileged clergy, constantly increasing in numbers, and a city-government depending upon its taxpayers, shows this to be one of the serious problems presenting itself to the State in its new alliance with the Church.

It certainly would be wrong to believe that the privileged and official position acquired by the Christian clergy within the structure of the Empire profited only the personal welfare of clerics: it also

[50]Cf. Jones, *Roman Empire,* 801-802, 921-924.
[51]CT XVI,2,6 (June 1, 329, tr. cit., p. 441).
[52]CT XVI,5,11 (Feb. 26, 342, tr. cit., p. 442).
[53]CT XII,1,121 (June 17, 390, tr. cit., pp. 359-360).
[54]CT XII,1,63 (Dec. 11, 399, tr. cit., p. 351).

gave them an opportunity to influence and humanize society. In addition to the judicial rights of bishops and opportunities to liberate slaves, emperor Theodosius I gave clerics and monks an official and extraordinary right to intercede for accused or condemned criminals and solicit mercy.[55] Furthermore, it was admitted that bishops could use their moral prestige in public affairs. In a famous episode (387), bishop Flavian of Antioch succeeded in obtaining pardon for the population of his city, following an insurrection provoked by imperial taxation, and which had led to the overthrow of imperial statues by the populace, a crime of *lèse-majesté*.[56] The bold and effective behavior of Flavian convinced many pagans to convert to Christianity.[57] Similar involvement in social issues, e.g. intercession for an over-taxed citizenry, are characteristic of men like the great John Chrysostom, archbishop of Constantinople (398-404), or St John the Almoner, Chalcedonian patriarch of Alexandria (611-619), or, in the West, St Martin of Tours (371-397).

It is rather common among historians to linger on the moral compromises involved in the alliance between the Christian Church and the Roman empire—an alliance which, by 451, was taken for granted by all—and to forget the witness and actions of a dedicated Christian clergy. To doubt the sincerity of Christian convictions held by the emperors, would also be unfair to historical reality. By allying itself to the Empire, the Church ceased to be a sect accessible to only a few. It assumed "catholic" responsibility for society as a whole. But in doing so, it did not renounce its eschatological calling. Throughout the Middle Ages, its history will not only be one of failures, but also of remarkable victories, achieved less by the "system" itself, than by individual Saints who succeeded in using it in the spirit of the Gospel. Neither the economic, nor the social systems of the Roman empire were changed as Christianity became the official religion of the State. The administrative and economic structures established by Diocletian and confirmed by Constantine remained the same, and no Christian leader or movement considered that they could, or should, be challenged. But this weakness of Christian "social witness"—which stands in

[55]CT IX,40,16 (July 27, 398, tr. cit., p. 257).

[56]The main sources for this famous episode are five speeches by the pagan *rhetor* Libanius and twenty-one homilies *On the Statues* by St John Chrysostom, who was then a presbyter in Antioch (text in PG 49), cf. a detailed account in G. Downey, *A History of Antioch in Syria,* Princeton, 1961, pp. 426-433.

[57]Chrysostom, *De Anna,* I, PG 54, col. 634.

such obvious contrast to the conception of twentieth century Christian "activism"—was neither mere passivity nor a lack of concern, but the persistence of an *eschatological* view of the Christian message. Standing before Pilate, Jesus had proclaimed that "His Kingdom was not of this world" (John 18:36). A Christian's main concern, therefore, was not to promote reforms, or improvements of the imperial structures, but rather to witness to the anticipated presence, in the midst of a fallen world, of the Kingdom to come.

The Saints actively lived this paradoxical tension. In some cases their lives and actions had a liberating and, to a degree, reforming influence on society. In others, there was merely a witness to the dualism of the two Kingdoms, well expressed in contemplative monasticism. Most Christians however, were not Saints and simply enjoyed the newly acquired privileges without consideration for the Judgment to come.

2. *Cultural pluralism*

The Roman Empire, which included all of Europe to the West of the Rhine and the South of the Danube, as well as Britain, Spain, Northern Africa, Egypt, and the entire Middle East, had not suppressed local cultures, languages and religions, but had included them all into a single legal and administrative structure with a *de facto* predominance of two languages: Latin, used primarily in administrative and legal procedures, and Greek, preferred by many intellectuals and dominant internationally in most urban centers, not only in the East, but in most of the Mediterranean West as well.

Christian writers, before and after Constantine, almost without exception, and in spite of the persecution of Christianity by Roman authorities, considered Roman universalism as a providential historical fact, which made possible the spreading of the Gospel on the "inhabited earth" (*oikoumene*). While the miracle of Pentecost, when each nation heard the apostles "speak in its own language" (Acts 2:6), confirmed Christian universalism, implying cultural variety, the Church never endorsed any canonical, or organizational division based on ethnic, or cultural differences: all Christians living in the same place were supposed to be united under one bishop, who was himself the member of the episcopal synod of a province. This territorial organization was through the centuries confronted by many strains, but was never abandoned in principle.

Thus, between a Roman Empire, culturally diverse, but united administratively, and a universal Christian Church, equally tolerant of cultural pluralism, but committed to territorial unity, there was a structural affinity which made their alliance even more natural.

However, the fifth century also saw the *de facto* gradual disintegration of Roman universalism. Successive waves of peoples, which were called "Barbarians" because they spoke neither Latin nor Greek, occupied the entire Western half of the Empire. Rome itself, the ancient and prestigious capital from which the Empire got its name (although it had long ceased to serve as imperial residence) was sacked by Alaric the Goth in 410, and permanently occupied in 476, at which date the Western empire ceased to exist.

However, 476 marked neither the end of the Empire as such (since it survived with its capital in the "New Rome"—Constantinople), nor the disappearance of the Roman imperial idea in the West. Although the various Barbarian leaders were politically quite independent, they were conscious of the fact that they were settling on imperial territory. The idea of a permanent and universal Empire had become part of Christian civilization, and the Barbarian nations were either already Christian, or were being, one by one, converted to Christianity. Thus the Church—acting consciously and systematically as the channel through which Roman ideas, Roman law and even the actual authority of the emperors of Constantinople, continued to be promoted in the West—preserved the old Roman and Christian universalism after the collapse of the Western Empire itself. The idea of a Christian world, united as one universal Church, but allowing for cultural pluralism within its confines, remained the ideological basis of society. However, already in the fifth century, the practical application of this ideology was not quite the same in the East and in the West.

The obvious difference was due to both political and cultural factors. With the Barbarian occupation, the Western regions of the Empire suffered terror and social chaos, which were described as an apocalyptic catastrophe by many contempories. Others, on the contrary, interpreted it as an act of divine judgement and providence. Lamenting the destruction of the Roman world, St Jerome, in his correspondence, directly predicts the coming of the Antichrist,[57a] and compares the Barbarians with savage beasts.[58] For the poet Prudentius, the Barbarians were as different from Romans, as quadruped dumb animals are from two-legged and reason-endowed humans.[59] Other writers, however, like the great St Augustine in his *City of God,* attempted to understand the catastrophe in more Christian terms, interpreting it as punishment for the sins of pagan Rome. Going further, Salvian, a priest in Marseille, exalts the childlike moral qualities of the Barbarians, which he contrasts to Roman decadence and immorality; he views their coming as an opportunity for Christian expansion.

Be it as it may, the political and cultural situation of the Christian West was drastically changed by the end of the fifth century. A Visigothic kingdom in Spain and as Ostrogothic kingdom in Italy replaced former Roman rule. Vandals occupied Northern Africa and Mediterranean islands, Burgundian and Frankish kings ruled Northern, Central and Southern Gaul, and there were Anglo-Saxon kingdoms in Britain, not to mention the less powerful principalities of the Suevi in the Iberian peninsula and the Alamans of the Rhine.

As distinct from Attila's Huns—a Mongolian nation, which was finally defeated by the Roman general Aetius, and whose triumph would have probably meant the end of Christian civilization—the Germanic tribes, now settled in Europe, actually *wished to become Roman.*[60] This aspiration towards a superior civilization was facilitated by the fact that the emperor residing in distant Constantinople, could wage no threatening power, being unable to impose and direct political control upon them. Instead, he gladly invested Barbarian kings with Roman court titles, and regarded them as representatives of his own authority in the West. Such formal ties with the empire were actually much more than a fiction. Indeed, with the exception of the Franks who long retained their customs and institutions, the Barbarian kingdoms adopted—at least partially—the legal system, the institutions, the art, and the language of Rome, or Byzantium. The high-quality mosaics decorating the churches of Ravenna, and commissioned by the Visi-

---

[57a]Ep. 123: 15-16, ed. J. Labourt, VII (Paris, 1961), pp. 9-94.

[58]Ep. 9; *ed. cit.* I (Paris, 1949), p. 26.

[59]*Sed tantum distant Romana et barbara, quantum quadrupes abjuncta est bipedi vel muta loquenti, Contra Symmachum,* II, 816-819.

[60]Cf. for example the classical analysis of Henri Pirenne, *A History of Europe, I. From the end of the Roman World in the West to the beginnings of the Western States,* Anchor Books, 1958, p. 9-17.

gothic king Theodoric, witness to that general trend. Of course, in time, the West was "barbarized" to a large degree, but, before that happened, the cultural vacuum created by the disappearance of the secular—and sometimes still pagan—Roman intellectual élite, was filled by the Christian clergy which eventually acquired a practical monopoly of literacy. Latin was the only language used officially by the catholic Church. And since the clergy often looked for guidance towards the one apostolic see of the West, which was also located in the old imperial capital, the Roman bishop gained an increased prestige. Was he not a guardian of the cultural and political inheritance of *Romania*, as well as the source of apostolic authority? The history of the Christian West at the beginning of what is still (rather improperly) termed the "dark ages," is one good example (there are others) of how conquerors can be culturally overpowered by the superior civilization of the conquered. In the case of the Germanic barbarians, the Church played a central role in this victory.

It is true that one factor played a disruptive role in the process of "romanization": the Barbarians, in their majority, were not confessing Catholic Orthodoxy, but Arianism, which hampered their relationships with both the Roman Church and the Empire, centered in Constantinople. The original reason for this situation was somewhat accidental: the Goths who, before the invasion of the Huns, lived in the region of the Dniester river, north of the Balkans, received Christianity from a then-Arian Constantinople. Although we know of some Orthodox Goths during and after the fourth century, the most important role in their conversion as a nation was played by the famous Ulfila (311-383),[61] who had been consecrated bishop, perhaps during the council of Antioch (341), by Eusebius of Nicomedia, a well-known leader of Arianism. His acceptance of Christianity in the East explains why Ulfila, instead of learning to pray in Latin, followed the Eastern practice of translating Scripture and liturgy into the vernacular, Gothic. He was a loyal Arian, however, and was present at the Arian council of Constantinople in 360. We also know that he actively opposed the Nicaean faith restored by Theodosius I after 379. The Goths, pushed away by the Huns, migrated to the West. During those migrations, Barbarian tribes continued to be evangelized by native Gothic, and not Roman missionaries, independently from a now orthodox empire.

[61]On Ulfila and his work, see E.A. Thompson, *The Visigoths at the Time of Ulfila,* Oxford, 1966.

Thus, the Goths transmitted Arianism to the Vandals, the Burgundians, the Alamans and the Lombards. Theological issues *per se* were hardly their major preoccupation, but there is no doubt that Arianism, involving the use of Ulfila's Bible and a vernacular liturgy, was long regarded by them as their own native form of Christianity distinct from Roman orthodox Catholicism. But this native Germanic Christianity would not survive because the gradual adoption of the Nicaean faith by the Barbarians of the West coincided with their "romanization." Even the great Visigothic king of Italy, Theodoric (493-526) —culturally much "romanized," while still remaining Arian—was not able to secure the survival of Arianism much longer.

The eventual disapperance of Arianism in the West will signal the victory of Roman and Latin orthodoxy, and therefore, the end of cultural separatism among the Barbarians. A unified and "barbarized" Romanism will then constitute a basis for the development of the new Latin medieval civilization, which would unfortunately be competing with the hellenized Romanism of Byzantium for supremacy in Christendom.

The issues of cultural pluralism within the Church took a quite different shape in the East. Here a diversity of venerable Christian traditions had existed since the very origins of Christianity, and will constitute a significant factor in the missionary expansion to be studied below. If, as already in New Testament times, the Greek language served as the major tool of intercultural and international communication, Syria and Egypt preserved not only their cultural identity, but also their respective languages, and gave birth to daughter-churches and daughter-civilizations in Armenia, Georgia, Mesopotamia, Persia, India, Arabia, Ethiopia, and Nubia. In all these cases, the model given at Pentecost (Acts 2) of each nation accepting the Word of God in its own language was applied; and Greek—in spite of its being the principal tool of theological creativity and doctrinal debates—was never seen (as Latin was in the West) to be the only available vehicle of civilization.

The Syriac language, being a dialect of Aramaic—the language spoken by Jesus Himself—was used in Syria and Mesopotamia. Serious indications point to direct connections between Syrian Christianity and the original Judeo-Christian community of Jerusalem. In any case, Christian communities in Syria certainly existed before Constantine.[62]

[62]Cf. a brief recent review of the available evidence, based on a very abundant

Syriac versions of both Old and New Testaments were available even then, and a Christian school, similar to Jewish talmudic schools, existed in Nisibis. In the fourth century, Syriac Christianity produced not only theologians like Aphrahat (*ca.* 270-345), but also "the greatest poet of the patristic age," St Ephrem (ca. 306-373). They knew no Greek at all, but this did not prevent St Ephrem from being venerated as a Father of the Church in the East and the West, and from greatly influencing later Greek hymnography.

In Egypt, the educated classes of Alexandria spoke Greek, and, in their midst, appeared the founders of Greek theology—Clement and Origen—as well as the great patristic figures of Athanasius and Cyril. But the Egyptian masses used Coptic, a derivative of the ancient Egyptian language. The Coptic monks, followers of the great founders—Anthony, Pachomius, Shenute—numbered thousands, and provided the Greek-speaking and economically powerful archbishops of Alexandria with the popular support they needed in their attempts, during the christological controversies, to either sway the empire to their side, or to challenge imperial orthodoxy.

The existence of Christian churches, dependent upon Syria or Egypt, beyond the borders of the Empire strengthened the cultural identity of both Syria and Egypt. Until the Muslim invasion of the seventh century, the centralized imperial trends were challenged by these foreign connections, by the necessity to maintain them and, thus, by the need to respect linguistic, liturgical and, even, theological pluralism within the empire itself.

Such cultural diversity did not mean that the sense of Christian unity was lost in Eastern Christendom. The perpetuation of an imperial center in Constantinople constituted a strong factor—both positive and negative—in its preservation. As Rome always was, the imperial government was tolerant of cultural diversity, as long as its political authority was not challenged. However, its role in convening councils, in interpreting their decrees and in enforcing them *manu seculari* necessarily antagonized the dissidents. It has often been stated that the various christological schisms of the fifth and sixth centuries were due less to theological convictions of the Nestorian or Monophysite theologians, than to the ethnic separatism of Syrians and Copts opposing imperial policies. Such a view, however, is only partially

literature on the subject in Robert Murray, *Symbols of Church and Kingdom. A Study in Early Syriac tradition,* Cambridge, 1975, pp. 4-38.

supported by the facts. Not only were Greeks in the majority among the intellectual leaders of the dissidence, but strong evidence shows that initially both Nestorians and Monophysites were consistently loyal to both the imperial idea and the Empire itself, and were using imperial support whenever they were able to obtain it.[63] This was the case of Dioscorus of Alexandria, who enforced Monophysitism with the help of emperor Theodosius II in 449, and of Severus of Antioch, who enjoyed the temporary support of Justinian's government in 513-519. All sides of the christological controversies accepted the standard idea that the Christian empire was providentially set up to assure the universality of the Christian message. Occasionally, one was also confronted by the fact of emperors supporting heresy: such emperors were then *personally* considered as unfaithful to their God-established office. Thus, men like St Athanasius, St John Chrysostom and later St Maximus the Confessor, on the basis of their own sad experience of imperial tyranny, urged that emperors should not interefere with the affairs of episcopal synods, and claimed the superiority of the sacerdotal functions over the imperial.[64] Similarly, for the Monophysite Michael the Syrian, emperor Marcian, convener of the Council of Chalcedon, was a "new Assyrian," *i.e.* in fact, an usurper.[65] But no one challenged the imperial institution itself, or the role of the emperor in church affairs. Thus, in 532 Monophysite leaders addressed another Chalcedonian, Justinian: "Thus, shall peace prevail in your reign," they wrote, "by the power of the high hand of God Almighty, to whom we pray on your behalf that without toil or struggle in arms He will set your enemies as a stool beneath your feet,"[66] because they hoped that the Justinianic "peace" would be a Monophysite one. Clearly, therefore—"for all the rancoeur of the controversy, the anti-Chalcedonians were far from being in intention political rebels."[67]

As late as the seventh century, the unionist efforts of emperor Heraclius, based on "monoenergism" drew significant support, and, in

---

[63]Cf. A.H.M. Jones, "Were ancient heresies national or social movements in disguise?", *JTS*, NS, 10 (1959), pp. 280-298. The only schisms which Jones considers as possibly motivated by nationalism, are those of the Germanic Arians and the Armenian Monophysites.

[64]Athanasius, *Hist. arian,* 36, PG 25, 736AB; Chrysostom, *Hom. in illud, Vidi Dominum,* IV, 5 PG 56, 126; *Acta Maximi,* 4.5, PG 90, 117 BD; tr. G. C. Berthold, New York, 1985, pp. 20-21.

[65]*Chron.* VIII, 14, IV, 5 (II, 122).

[66]Zacharias, *Eccl. hist.* IX, 15; Engl. tr. in Frend, *The Rise,* pp. 365-366.

[67]Frend, *op. cit.,* p. 62.

Egypt, according to a Monophysite author, "innumerable multitudes" were led to accept the imperial faith.[68] Recent research does not condone the view that Non-Chalcedonian Copts welcomed Muslims as liberators from the Roman rule: even then, and in spite of Chalcedonian persecutions, there was widespread loyalty to the Christian empire.[69] It appears, therefore, that it is only under Persian or Arab, and later Turkish rule, when intellectual contacts with Greek theology were lost and every connection with Byzantium was viewed with suspicion by the new masters, that the Non-Chalcedonian Christian communities of the Middle East became close-knit national-churches. As long as they were part of the Roman *oikoumene,* Syrians and Copts remained basically loyal to it ideologically, even if they had, in their majority, rejected Chalcedonian orthodoxy and suffered persecution. In their minds, their struggle was not in the name of national particularism—since neither their culture, nor their language, nor their liturgical traditions were challenged by the empire—but against that which their spiritual leaders (often Greek-speaking) saw as a betrayal of the true faith. Egypt, in particular—the cradle of the anti-Chalcedonian dissidence—was not, Peter Brown remarks, a national enclave within the Empire, but a microcosm of Mediterranean civilization, as moulded by Rome.[70]

In the eyes of the Egyptians, the Chalcedonian emperor in Constantinople was perhaps an "Assyrian" tyrant, but they still hoped for his conversion, not for the creation of an alternate center of Christian unity. Essentially, their view of the empire was still the same as that accepted among Christians at the time of Constantine.

It can be said, therefore, that by the middle of the fifth century, the Roman and Christian idea of the world was essentially the same in the East and in the West, although a modified perspective was gradually taking shape in the form of a "Barbarianized" Romanism. This new Romanism eventually found its incarnation in the Frankish Kingdom, which, in the Carolingian period, challenged the old mediterranean *oikoumene* centered in Byzantium with a political and cultural alternative.

---

[68]Severus of Asmounein, *History of the Patriarchs,* ed. and tr. B.T.A. Evetts, in *PO I* (Paris, 1907), p. 491.

[69]Cf. especially, Butler, *The Arab conquest.*

[70]*The Making of Late Antiquity,* Harvard University Press, Cambridge, 1978, p. 82.

3. The emperor and the Church

No issue in early Christian history has been more thoroughly studied and discussed than that of the imperial role in Church affairs since Constantine. There can be no doubt that the confessional, or philosophical, bias of historians has often influenced their conclusions. Nineteenth century Protestant scholars, condemning "caesaropapism" —the concept that the emperor acted as head of the Church—were implicitly struggling against the regime which was dominant in Northern Europe after the Reformation, and which tended to reduce Christianity to a department of the State (*cujus regio ejus religio*). Roman Catholic historians, on the other hand, generally accepted as normative the Western medieval supremacy of the popes. Consequently, they often tried to apply the same norm to the history of the early Church, and considered the Byzantine East as a victim of imperial usurpations of papal authority. Finally, secular historians were often not attuned to the religious dimensions of Late Antiquity: their interpretation of church history in terms of a cynical imperial autocracy represented a convenient reduction of a complex reality to familiar secularistic socio-political concepts.

The issue cannot possibly be discussed here in detail, except in terms of a few facts, based on textual and historical evidence.[71]

The Roman empire which had accepted Christianity in the fourth century and eventually made it into its state religion, was an Empire ruled autocratically by a person—or persons—believed to be *divine*. This divinization of the emperor had early roots particularly in Hellenism. By the fourth century it was already a relatively old tradition going back to Julius Caesar, and Augustus. It had been promoted by Cicero, Ovid, Horace and Virgil, and had become an integral part of the imperial social fabric. Christians had encountered it during the persecutions, when their biblical monotheism and exclusive allegiance to Christ as the only Lord (Κύριος) forced them to refuse participation in the imperial cult—a refusal which was tantamount to civil disloyalty.

There is no doubt that this Hellenistic, essentially religious understanding of the emperor's role did not disappear overnight, but, on the

---

[71]Cf. especially P. Gaudemet, *L'Eglise et l'Empire romain*, Paris, 1958, and F. Dvornik, *Early Christian and Byzantine Political Philosophy. Origins and Background*, II, Washington, D.C., 1966, pp. 610-850. For translated sources, see *CN*.

contrary, was integrated into a new Christian understanding of Roman society. Was this integration legitimate? Was it consistent with both the Hellenistic conception of kingship and Christian theology? Was it consistent with itself? Are there objective criteria for answering such questions?

Neither the New Testament, nor early Christian literature contain a systematic treatment of political ideology. On the other hand, it is important to note that the New Testament presents at least three different approaches to the power of Rome: the attitude of eschatological estrangement, professed by Jesus Himself during his trial before Pilate ("My Kingdom is not of this world," John 18:36); the recognition by St Paul that State power comes from God, inasmuch as it serves the Good (Rom. 13:1-7); the curses of the author of the Apocalypse against Rome, as a new "Babylon" (Rev. 18). On the basis of these texts alone, it was inevitable that the Christian attitude towards the State—as towards the created and fallen world in general —could only be defined in dynamic, or dialectical fashion, depending on circumstances.

The sudden transformation of the emperor in the fourth century from persecutor to protector of the Church, could only be interpreted by most Christians as an act of Providence. The emperor had indeed become the instrument "serving the Good." However, even earlier Christian apologists had discerned divine Providence in the Empire as unifier of the human race, thus making possible the uniting and universal preaching of the Gospel. In their view, this providential role of Rome had begun with Augustus, under whom Christ was born (Luke 2:1), and with Tiberius, whose reign saw the beginning of His Messianic ministry (Luke 3:1)—not only with Constantine. Even then, at the beginning of the Principate, Rome was providing universal peace, whose true significance and true fullness was being revealed in Christ, born at Bethlehem. The idea is expressed in the second century by Melito of Sardis,[72] but also by the great Origen, whose influence upon the later patristic tradition was overwhelming:

Jesus was born during the reign of Augustus, the one who reduced to uniformity, so to speak, the many kingdoms on

[72]The relevent fragment of Melito's *Petition* to emperor Marcus Aurelius, is significantly preserved by Eusebius of Caesarea, the panegyrist of Constantine (*Eccl. Hist.* IV, 25; tr. p. 187-8).

earth so that he had a simple empire. It would have hindered
Jesus' teaching from being spread through the whole world
if there had been many kingdoms . . . everyone would have
been compelled to fight in defense of their own country.[73]

Origen's view of Augustus as fulfilling a providential mission, is
assumed by an impressive *consensus patrum* of the East and of the
West, including not only Eusebius of Caesarea, but also John Chrysostom and Gregory of Nazianzus, as well as Prudentius, Ambrose, Jerome
and Orosius.[74] In Byzantium, it was included as the central idea in a
hymn sung on Christmas Day.[75]

In the light of this tradition, Constantine was not a revolutionary,
but rather the first emperor to realize the true meaning of Roman
kingship, which others had already exercised before him: the *Pax
romana* was not the creation of Augustus, but of Christ.[75a] In the third
century, Christian apologists indeed considered the persecution of
Christianity by the Roman State as a tragic misunderstanding, a struggle
of the empire against its own divine legitimacy. In the light of this
perspective, shared by most Christians, the empire was not even
expected to undergo any fundamental transformation with the conversion of Constantine, and indeed—as we have seen earlier—it did not,
except in the fact that it granted first freedom and then exclusive
privileges to the Church. Before and after Constantine, the Roman
emperor was regarded as the providential manager of earthly affairs,
following the methods and logic of "the world," a fallen world, where
divine Providence was nevertheless at work. The difference was that
beginning with Constantine, the emperor fulfilled his mission with a
full understanding of the ultimate goal of creation, which was anticipated in the mysteries of the Church. Christians admitted that the
fallen world could not be changed overnight by imperial legislation,
but the ultimate goal—the Kingdom of God—was now common to
both the Empire and the Church. Meanwhile, imperial power was
supposed to provide the Church with freedom and protection, only
gradually humanizing society at large.

[73]*Contra Celsum* II, 30, GCS, 2, p. 158, tr. H. Chadwick, (Cambridge, 1953), p. 92.
[74]References in Dvornik, *op. cit.*, p. 725.
[75]*The Festal Menaion*, London, Faber, 1973, p. 254.
[75a]According to St Gregory of Nazianzus "the state of the Christians and that of
the Romans grew up simultaneously and Roman supremacy arose with Christ's sojourn
upon earth, previous to which it had not reached monarchical perfection," *Oratio IV
(Contra Julianum)*, 37, PG, 35, col. 564 B.

But what about worship of the emperor, so essential to the hellenistic view of kingship, and accepted as a norm since Augustus? Clearly, it could not persist in its pagan form and was indeed suppressed by Constantine and his successors. However, the person of the emperor preserved its sacred character—which was emphasized in court ceremonies—and much of the hellenistic vocabulary in addressing the "divine" emperor and describing his functions was preserved. Conveniently, the Old Testamental idea of kinship was also utilized, so that the Roman emperor could be acclaimed not only in terms familiar to pagan hellenism, but also as successor of David and Solomon— ancestors and images of Christ. Together with many historians who share his view, F. Dvornik is only partially right in saying that it is Eusebius of Caesarea who "became responsible for the wholesale acceptance of Hellenistic political thought by the Christians."[76] It is more probable that Eusebius was not really innovating, but expressing, in his official court panegyric, an approach which most people took for granted. On the other hand, as we shall see below, the hellenistic political theory was not exactly accepted "wholesale," but with important qualifications.

Two specific aspects of the religious outlook of the period have been brilliantly emphasized by Peter Brown, and help us to understand the blending of Hellenistic and Christian elements in the conception of the empire: on the one hand, in the society of Late Antiquity "the invisible world was as real as the visible" and human existence was always understood in reference to the Divine; on the other hand—as distinct from the earlier period, when the individual was seen as destined to a merger into the Divine One—in the fourth century, the human *person* "leaps into focus," and marks an era when people looked for leadership by holy men, prophets, or "friends of God, who find direct personal access to the Divine."[77] This new personalism, which appeared in pagan society, met with the Christian search for personal salvation and personal experience of God.

In reading the famous Oration delivered by Eusebius on the thirtieth anniversary of Constantine's reign, one discovers that it is precisely one of these "friends of God" that the Christian bishop sees in the person of the emperor—not yet baptized, but ready to make the ultimate commitment to Christianity. In Constantine, Eusebius sees the

[76]*Op. cit.*, p. 616.
[77]*Op. cit.*, pp. 10-26.

divinely appointed agent fulfilling the destiny prefigured by Augustus, and able to assure the cosmic triumph of Christianity, i.e. the historical goal of the Incarnation.

"The only begotten Word of God reigns from ages that had no beginning," Eusebius proclaims, "He, (our emperor) ever His friend, who derives imperial power from above and is made strong by being called after the divine name, has controlled the empire of the world for many years. Again, the Savior of all things makes the sky and earth and the Kingdom of Heaven worthy of His own Father; thus, His friend brings those whom he governs on earth to the only begotten Word and Savior and renders them fit subjects of His Kingdom."[78]

On earth, the emperor is, therefore, the image and the agent of Christ: "He derives his reason from the great source of all reason; he is wise and good and just, as having fellowship with perfect wisdom, goodness and righteousness; virtuous, as following the pattern of perfect virtue; valiant, as partaking of heavenly strength. And truly may he keep the imperial title, which has trained his soul to royal virtues after the standard of the heavenly Kingdom"[79] . . . "Hence is our Emperor perfect in discretion, in goodness, in justice, courage, piety, and devotion to God. He is truly a philosopher . . . and imitates Divine philanthropy by his imperial acts."[80] "Like the radiant sun and through the presence of the Caesars, he illuminates his subjects in the remotest corners of his Empire with the piercing shafts of his brightness . . . Bearing the image of the heavenly empire, with his eyes fixed on high, he rules the lives of mortals after that original pattern, with the strength drawn from an imitation of God's monarchy."[81]

Theologian and court-bishop, delivering an official panegyric, Eusebius followed the rules of the genre. Using standard Neo-Platonic imagery, he paints a portrait of the *ideal* emperor, and proclaims that Constantine personally fits the pattern. This *ideal* image was accepted by all in the patristic and Byzantine periods, but everyone was aware that not all emperors were realizing it in practice. In terms of *Christian* theology, the *imperium* was understood as a particular personal charism bestowed directly by God; one which, according to the same Eusebius, granted to the emperor "episcopal" functions

[78]*Praise of Constantine*, 2, GCS 7, p. 199.
[79]*Ibid.*, 5, p. 203.
[80]*Ibid.*, 2, p. 300.
[81]*Ibid.*, 3, p. 201.

"over those outside" (ἐπίσκοπος τῶν ἐκτός),[82] i.e. essentially, the responsibility of administering and, evenutally, Christianizing the pagans in his ideally universal Empire, and the whole world.

But, unity, universality and order, these essential elements of the *pax romana,* were now inseparable from the interests and responsibilities of the universal Christian Church. The Roman emperor could not care any longer for the Empire without also being concerned with the unity, universality and good order of the Church as well: a divided Church would also mean a divided Empire. Of course, the internal affairs of the Church were cared for by the bishops—as was recognized by Constantine in the same passage of his *Vita* by Eusebius—but each bishop was in charge of his local community only: the early Church did not have a central administration preoccupied, in a permanent and institutional way, with universal unity. The emperor's responsibility was recognized immediately, precisely on this universal level. This implied, in particular, his competence in organizing provincial groupings of bishops, granting them facilities to gather in synods and to resolve issues of common concern.

The problem, in this new situation, was that the "external" and the "internal" aspects of ecclesiastical affairs were, in fact, inseparable: the "internal," sacramental and disciplinary life of the Christian communities depended upon their *unity in faith*, which had to be assured by councils, convoked by the emperor and spelled out in clear credal formulas, understood not only by Christian theologians, but also by the Roman officials in charge of organization, procedures and financial disbursements. This is the reason why the theological debates of the fourth and following centuries were so often centered around credal *formulas,* whereas the no less serious theological debates before Constantine (i.e. Gnosticism, Origenism, etc.) were rather debates on substance, with less concern for verbal expression. The new alliance with the Roman empire, whose administrative and legal structures required simplicity and clarity, imposed new servitudes upon the Church including the use of universally agreed upon theological formulae. It demanded constant cooperation, frequently assured by court bishops like Hosius of Cordoba

---

[82]*The Life of Constantine,* (IV, 24, GCS 7, p. 126) reports the famous episode of Constantine attributing this title to himself. On the meaning, see the very conclusive study by D. De Decker and G. Dupuis-Masay, "L'épiscopat de l'empereur Constantin," in *Byzantion* L, 1980, 1, pp. 118-157 (The expression τῶν ἐκτός is masculine and means "those outside," and not neuter, meaning "the external affairs" [of the Church]; cf. the same expression designating the pagans in CT *Sir. Prol.,* 5.

or Eusebius of Nicomedia under Constantine, and, later, the episcopal incumbent of the permanent new capital, Constantinople.

The situation was further complicated by the fact that, throughout the fourth and fifth centuries, the bishops could not agree among themselves. Council succeeded council, issuing formula after formula, so that, in order to assure unity, the emperors were, in fact, forced into *choosing* between ecclesiastical factions and, therefore, interpreting conciliar formulas themselves. There are many occasions showing that Constantine and his successors stepped in with great reluctance into the role of interpreters of Christian theology and church discipline, and that Christians themselves called on them to assume that role. The most famous case in point is Constantine's role in settling the Donatist dispute in Africa. His personal decision in favor of the Catholic party followed lengthy and persistent attempts at having councils—in Rome, then Arles—to resolve the dispute.

But once involved in such debates, the emperor inevitably began to share in "episcopal"—therefore "internal"—responsibility. Eusebius of Caesarea was already fully aware of this inevitability in his *Vita* of Constantine:

> As dissensions had arisen in various lands, he acted like a universal bishop (οἵά τις κοινὸς ἐπίσκοπος) appointed by God, and convoked councils of the ministers of God. He did not disdain to be present at their meetings and to become one of the bishops (κοινωνὸς τῶν ἐπισκοπου-μένων). He took cognizance of the subjects that came up for discussion and communicated to all the benefits of the peace of God . . . He treated with the utmost consideration all those whom he found ready to follow the majority and disposed to work in agreement and harmony, showing that above all he rejoiced for the common concord of all; but those who refused to yield to persuasion he rejected.[83]

Interestingly, the pattern described here by Eusebius and generally accepted since, is not that of a Hellenistic monarch dictating divine revelations, but one of conciliarity: the goal of the emperor is to assure the orderly triumph of the majority. Furthermore, the analogical description of Constantine as "universal *bishop*" presupposed a limita-

[83]*Ibid.,* I, 44, GCS 7, p. 28.

tion on his powers: no one believed in episcopacy as implying infallibility, but as a charism to be appropriated—always imperfectly—by the individuals invested with it. The emperor was a special "friend of God," but, in the company of bishops, he was one among many. Furthermore, no one understood the "episcopal" functions of the emperor in a literal, sacramental sense, but as an analogy. Writing to the Fathers assembled in Ephesus in 431, Theodosius II orders his delegate Candidianus "to have nothing to do with problems and controversies regarding dogmas of faith, for it is not desirable that one who does not belong to the body of holy bishops should meddle with ecclesiastical questions and discussions."[84]

It is, therefore, not so much by virtue of the Hellenistic principle of the emperor's divinity that Constantine and Constantius gave their support to the Arians; that Theodosius I in 380 opted not only for Nicene Orthodoxy, but also against the "super-Orthodox" (or "Old Nicaeans") attitude of Rome and Alexandria; that Theodosius II supported Cyril against Nestorius in 431, and Dioscorus against Flavian in 449; that Marcian and Pulchieria turned the tide again, and sanctioned the Chalcedonian definition in 451; but because such was their—and their episcopal advisors'—interpretation of the mind of the Church which alone was able, in their opinion, to secure the *pax romana* again. The imperial constitutions on the faith issued by Zeno, Anastasius and Justinian went a step further: they tried to impose imperial interpretations of earlier conciliar statements without new conciliar procedures, endeavouring to achieve episcopal consensus afterwards. Such attempts proved to be failures, unless this consensus did indeed occur, as, for instance, in 553, following Justianian's unilateral decrees against Origen and the Three Chapters. Everybody agreed that imperial sanction was necessary for a conciliar statement to be effective, but no one believed in the concept of personal doctrinal infallibility of the emperor (or anyone else): this is why the concept of "caesaropapism" does not match the reality of the early Christian imperial system.

As we have noted above, Christian leaders unanimously admitted the emperor's ideal role in the life of the Church, and had no qualms in formulating it in the familiar Hellenistic terms, even when they had every reason to doubt his doctrinal reliability. Even St Athanasius—a direct victim of Constantine's turn-about in favor of Arius—did not question imperial authority itself, e.g. in convoking councils and remov-

[84]Mansi, IV, col. 1120.

ing disobedient bishops. Furthermore, as late as 355, addressing Constantius II, he used all the Hellenistic imperial titles: the emperor, who was not yet baptized and was giving systematic support to Arianism, is called "very pious" (εὐσεβέστατος), "friend of truth" (φιλάληϑες), a "worshipper of God" (ϑεοσέβαστος) and "beloved of ' God" (ϑεοφιλέστατος),[85] a successor of David and Solomon,[86] for whom Christians pray.[87] A year later, however, Athanasius calls Constantius "godless" (ἄϑεος) and "unholy" (ἀνόσιος): he is not "David" anymore, but "Achab" or "the Pharaoh," worse than Pilate,[88] and even a forerunner of the Antichrist.[89] Similarly, St Gregory of Nazianzus, certainly reflecting the mentality predominant in the mind of the other great Cappadocian fathers, writes of Constantius: "No one surely was ever possessed with so fervent a desire for any object as was that emperor for the aggrandizement of the Christians and their advancement to the crest of glory and power . . . For though he did slightly vex them (a surprisingly mild reference to Constantius' Arianism! J.M.), yet he did so not from spite or insolence, . . . but so that we should become united and unanimous instead of being divided and rent by schism."[90]

Always intellectually honest and less prone than Gregory of Nazianzus to use Neo-Platonic terminology, St John Chrysostom still fully shares the general recognition of the providential character of *pax romana*.[91] But he also lists moral qualities as necessary requirements of "true"[92] kingship. Furthermore, he formally proclaims the superiority of priesthood: "the office that prevails in the Church," he writes, ". . . excels the civil office as much as heaven excels the earth."[93]

Councils also formally recognized the imperial right of convocation and approval. "We therefore, ask your clemency," the fathers of

[85]Cf. *Apologia ad Constantium*, 2, 3, 9 ,14, etc., PG 85, cols. 597, 605, 621, etc. The titles are the same, as in the writings of Eusebius.

[86]*Ibid.*, 5, 12, 20, cols. 601, 609, 621.

[87]*Ibid.*, 10, 17, cols. 608, 616.

[88]*Historia arianorum ad monachos*, 30, 34, 45, 67, 68; PG 25, cols. 728, 733, 749, 773, 776.

[89]*Ibid.*, 46, 76, 77, 80, cols. 752, 785, 788, 792.

[90]*Or. IV, contra Julianum*, 37, PG 35, col. 564.

[91]"Now, those vast spaces the sun shines upon, from the Tigris to the British Isles, the whole of Africa, Egypt and Palestine, and whatever is subject to the Roman Empire, live in peace. You know that the whole world is untroubled, and that of war we only hear rumors" (*In Is.* 2, PG 56, col. 33).

[92]"The true *basileus* is he who masters his passions of anger, envy and lust, and subordinates everything to the laws of God" (*Hom.* 31, PG 63, col. 695).

[93]*In Epist. II ad Cor., Hom.* 15, 4, PG 61, 507.

the Second ecumenical council (381) write to Theodosius I, "that letters of Your Piety should ratify the decrees of this Council. As you honored the Church by your letter of convocation, so also lend your authority to our decisions . . ."[94]

It is often said that "caesaropapism" is a trait of the East only, and that the West had a greater sense of the Church's independence from the Empire. In fact, in addressing emperors, Western councils used a language identical with that of the Eastern council of 381.[95] St Ambrose of Milan praises the providential advantages of the *pax romana* as did Eusebius of Caesarea: "as (the Apostles) spread over the earth," he proclaims, "the power of the Roman Empire followed in the wake of the Church, whilst discordant minds and hostile nations settled down in peace. Living under a world empire, all men learned to profess in the words of faith the authority of the one omnipotent God."[96] Of course, St Ambrose is also famous for his stand against imperial power. When Valentinian II wanted to allow Arian Goths to use a basilica in Milan, Ambrose, in opposing the move, invoked Luke 22:21: "Render to God what is God's and to Caesar what is Caesar's," and challenged imperial right to dispose of a church: "Palaces belong to the emperor, churches to the priest of the Church. Public buildings are under your care, sacred buildings are not."[97] The famous incident of 390 when, in a polite and diplomatic letter, Ambrose refused communion to Theodosius I, demanding public penance for the slaying of 7000 members of the rebellious population of Thessalonica, is a historical fact. However, the story which records the same episode as a spectacular public confrontation between the bishop and the emperor is an edifying legend, which, significantly, appears, for the first time, in the writings of the *Eastern* historians Socrates and Theodoret in the fifth century. A similar, legendary confrontation between emperor Philip the Arab and bishop Babylas of Antioch is reported by Chrysostom.[98]

Among many other examples of Christian personalities, ready to praise kingship in hellenistic terms, while also resisting its encroachments on the Church, one can mention Pope Leo of Rome. On the one

---

[94]Mansi III, col. 557.

[95]Cf. the Synods of Aquileia and Rome gathered in 382 (Mansi III, col. 623-627).

[96]*In Ps* 45, 21, PL 14, col. 1198 ff.

[97]*Epist.*, I, 20, 19, PL 16, col. 1041. This is the first recorded use of the famous passage (Luke 22:21) to describe normal relationships between Church and State.

[98]*In sanctum Babylam*, 5, PG 50, cols. 539 ff.

hand, one reads in his letters to emperors not only formal recognitions of the emperor's right to convoke and direct church councils, but other even more ambiguous statements. For instance, he expresses joy that the soul of Theodosius II "is not only imperial, but priestly"[99]; he wishes Marcian "besides the imperial crown, also the priestly palm."[100] On the other hand, the same Roman pontiff is well known for both protesting the decrees of the Robber Council of 449, approved by Theodosius II, and the encroachment on what he believed to be the rights of the Roman Church by the council of Chalcedon, sponsored by Marcian.

Clearly, therefore, there is no real contrast between East and West in the fifth century in the prevailing understanding of the role of the emperor in Church affairs, but rather the same lack of clear legal definitions and the same inconsistencies. Emperors favoring positions, considered as orthodox, are praised with "divine" and "priestly" titles; by contrast, those who supported heretics and persecuted the Orthodox were considered tyrants. The fact that later relationships between Church and State tended to follow different models, in the East and in the West, was primarily due to changed historical conditions. In the East, the imperial "New Rome" survived for many centuries, whereas, in the West, conquered by Barbarians, the idea of the Roman principate—gradually but unmistakenly—found a new incarnation in the person of the "apostolic" bishop of Rome.

[99]ACO, II, 4, p. 3.
[100]Ibid., p. 64.

CHAPTER II

THE STRUCTURE OF THE CHURCH

The Christian faith is based upon the *witness* of a group of disciples, chosen by Jesus Himself. This unique record of the death and resurrection of Christ has been sealed by the gift of the Spirit, at Pentecost: its authenticity is based on the historical record, but also on the living communion with the Father in Christ, effected by the operation of the Spirit within the community of the Church. This communion itself is an anticipation of the Kingdom of God, already present yet still to come—an anticipation fully realized in the local eucharistic gathering, the *ecclesia.*

The New Testament writings and the early Fathers show that the ministries of the Church were determined by their functions within the local eucharistic gathering: under the presidency of the bishop (or "overseer," *episcopos*), the presbyters (or "elders") and the deacons (*diakonoi*, "servants" in charge of social functions) became the permanent and necessary ministries in every Christian community. Originally, in New Testament times, ministries may have been more diversified, and, later, the requirements of historical development created new functions, but the nature of the Church, and particularly the implications of the eucharistic assembly, kept these developments within the general framework of the threefold ministry of bishops, priest and deacons.

However, even if the *essential* organizational framework was determined by the *local* eucharistic gathering, Christians were always aware of the *universal* unity of the Church and her universal mission. This universality was a universality both in time and in space. Universality in time required that each local Church be faithful to the original message of the "witness" of Jesus' resurrection, to a unique and continuous "apostolic tradition." It was understood that the first bishops received both the context of their teaching and the episcopal ministry itself, from the apostles of Jesus. Universality in space presupposed a concern for mission—hence a certain follow-up of the "apostolic" ministry, with "apostles" being sent by churches, rather than personally by Christ—, and a strong dedication to unity between the local churches. The writings of the Fathers of the second and third centuries (Ignatius, Irenaeus, Cyprian, Hippolytus, and others) clearly reflect all these concerns within the rapidly changing conditions in which the Church had to live. It is they who coined the word "catholic" to designate the Church, both as guardian of doctrinal and apostolic "wholeness" and as carrier of the Christian truth to the entire world.

The conversion of Constantine was interpreted by all Christians as a providential opportunity for realizing this "catholicity" more fully. The Roman emperor himself, as guardian of the *Pax Romana,* volunteered his powerful help in securing unity between the local churches and in promoting the Christian faith in the whole world. No wonder his position was soon interpreted as quasi-apostolic.

But this new alliance with the Empire, which we have already discussed in the preceding chapter, demanded that the Church adapt its institutions, or create new ones, which would respond to the needs of its new dominant position within society. This would be effected by the numerous councils of the fourth and fifth centuries, in a canonical legislation, pursuing a double goal: to establish a parallelism between the institutions of the Church and the structure of the Roman state (and thus make their interaction and cooperation easier), and to maintain the basic, essential elements of the original "eucharistic" structure, without which the Church would cease to be the Church. These two goals were often in tension with each other, and entered in direct conflict especially when emperors supported heresy. Conflicts could be resolved only as long as adaptation to imperial laws and structures was conceived as a means to admit the continuing mission of the Church and assure its unity, using whatever element was positive and helpful in secular society. But conflict was inevitable when the priorities were reversed and the State tended to use the Church as a tool of its own interests.

Understandably, this process of adaptation is judged differently by modern scholars depending upon their confessional or methodological presuppositions. Nineteenth century Protestant historians tended to believe that the "Constantinian" period meant a surrender of Christianity to the principles of a totally heterogeneous legal structure, incompatible with the New Testament concepts of the Christian community. Roman Catholic scholars, visualizing the period in terms of the Western medieval struggle between popes and emperors, emphasized the evils of "caesaro-papism" and were primarily concerned with establishing that Roman primacy has been already the main safeguard against imperial control of the Church. Such confessional attitudes are probably inevitable as long as Christians hold incompatible beliefs concerning what are the essential, "apostolic," unchangeable characteristics of the Church, and how these differ from ecclesiastical institutions which were created, or suppressed in the course of history, without involving the ecclesiastical being itself.

1. *The local church: bishop, clergy, laity.*

In the fifth century, the leadership of a single bishop, helped by a college of prebysters and a group of deacons, was the universally accepted model of local church structure. No authority had ever endorsed, or defined it specifically, and the terminology, describing church ministries in the New Testament and the earliest Fathers, was inconsistent. The fact that the "threefold ministry" of the bishop, the presbyters and the deacons withstood the challenges of Gnosticism, Montanism, Novatianism, Donatism, and, later, Messalianism, which were all movements questioning the objective, sacramental character of that ministry—and particularly the "monarchical" episcopate—is the most convincing sign that Church structures were based neither on arbitrary or disciplinary considerations only, nor merely on custom, but that they were seen as reflecting the very nature of the Church. This does not mean, however, that there was absolute uniformity in the ways in which bishops, priests and deacons exercised their respective functions, or that significant changes did not interfere with the new conditions in which the Church had to live after Constantine. After 320, the original structure was challenged not by charismatic sectarians, as in the early period, but by the temptation to identify church functions with the legal administrative patterns of Roman society.

Already in the third century, bishops, especially in larger cities, had ceased to be the only regular celebrants of the Eucharist—as this was originally the case (cf. particularly Ignatius of Antioch, *ca.* 100 A.D.)—and their leadership gradually lost some of its immediate pastoral and sacramental character, to become a ministry of teaching and government *over* several eucharistic communities. Originally, the bishop headed a single community—like the parish priest today—and such communities were often quite small. St Gregory, as he was consecrated bishop of Neocaesarea in Pontus (*ca.* 240 A.D.), headed a congregation of seventeen people.[1] This original structure—a bishop in each community—even if it was a small village church—remained the norm, even after Constantine, in the African church. One of the so-called "ecclesiastical canons" required no less than twelve adult lay people (evidently an apostolic number) for the election of a bishop,[2] implying that even smaller communities occasionally wanted to have one.

In the fourth century, however, the episcopal function became closely associated with the *city,* which was the administrative and social center, controlling the countryside around it. This development, which was probably inevitable (it began before Constantine), implied a certain secularization of the episcopal office. The new social conditions required higher educational standards to be applied to episcopal candidates. Indeed, they were required to participate in frequent theological debates, and assumed greater responsibilities for the unity of the Church at large. Such new requirements were associated with wealth and social influence. Theodore of Mopsuestia, writing at the end of the century, witnesses to this sense of social importance, newly acquired by the bishops; in the past, he notes, "bishops were ordained not only in cities, but in quite small places where there was really no need of anyone being invested with episcopal authority."[3] A similar concern is voiced by the council of Serdica (A.D. 343): "One should not establish bishops in villages (ἐν κώμῃ), or in small cities, where a simple priest suffices . . ., so that the name and prestige of the bishop (τὸ τοῦ ἐπισκόπου ὄνομα καὶ ἡ αὐθεντία) may not be humiliated."[4]

[1]St Basil, *On the Holy Spirit,* 29, ed. B. Pruche (SC, 17), Paris, 1947, p. 251; Engl. tr., Crestwood, NY, 1980, p. 110.

[2]G. Horner, *The Statutes of the Apostles, or Canones ecclesiastici,* London, 1904, p. 133.

[3]*In ep. B. Pauli commentarii,* ed. H.B. Swete, Cambridge, 1880-82, II, p. 124-5.

[4]Canon 6.

Clearly, the Church was rapidly forgetting its humble origins, and successors of the Galilean fishermen were developing more worldly concerns. Nevertheless, "village-bishops" (χωρεπίσκοποι) did not all disappear immediately, even if their powers rapidly diminished as they were gradually transformed into simple auxiliaries of the city-bishops.

St Basil (d. 379), in Caesarea-in-Cappadocia, still exercised primacy over fifty "rural bishops,"[5] even if the collection of rules which came to us as "canons of the council of Laodicea" had, at approximately the same time, prohibited their appointment.[6] Thus, whereas several "country-bishops" had attended the council of Nicaea (325) and signed the decree on their own right, they acted only as delegates of city-bishops at Chalcedon (451).[7] In this subordinate capacity, they are mentioned in Eastern and Western sources, as late as 787,[8] and the title *chorepiscopos* survived in some Eastern churches throughout the Middle Ages.

In the Greco-Roman world, the cities—whether they were large metropolises or small rural centers—carried a tradition of local self-government, embodied in a council (*curia*), made up of all property-owning citizens (*decuriones*), who assumed financial responsibilities for the city's welfare. However, as city councils grew in size, or became restricted to a hereditary oligarchy, city government was largely taken over by appointed imperial administrators, responsible to the provincial governor or the vicar of the diocese. Large cities, like Antioch, where there might have been as many as 1200 decurions,[9] also served as residence to high imperial officials,[10] which greatly overshadowed the officers of the curia. As a consequence, in the fourth and fifth

[5] St Gregory of Naz., *De vita sua*, PG 37, col. 1060 A.

[6] "One should not appoint bishops in villages and country-districts, but travelling inspectors (περιοδευτάς), and those already appointed should do nothing without the opinion of the city-bishop." (Canon 57)

[7] Cf. H. Gelzer, *Patrum Nicaenorum nomina*, Leipzig, 1898 and, more recently, E. Hönigmann "Une liste inédite des pères de Nicée," *Byzantion*, XX, 1950, pp. 63-71; for Chalcedon, see ACO II, 1, 1, p. 58, 60, 63, etc.

[8] II Nic., canon, 14; on the *chorepiscopoi*, cf. N. Afanassieff, *"Neudavshiisya tserkovniyi okrug,"* *Pravoslavnaya Mysl'*, IX, Paris, 1953, pp. 7-30 and A. Jones, *Roman Empire, II,* pp. 877-879.

[9] Libanius, *Or.* XLVIII, 3.

[10] The following were in residence at Antioch: the *comes Orientis* (in charge of the whole "diocese" of Orient), the consular of Syria, and the *magister militum per Orientem,* or military commander of the Roman troops in the eastern parts of the empire. Cf. especially, J.H.W.G. Liebeschuetz, *Antioch. City and Imperial Administration in the Later Roman Empire,* Oxford, 1972.

centuries, in spite of a general tendency towards urbanization, municipal autonomy declined. Its social role, however, was picked up by the Church. The appearance in practically every city of a Christian bishop and his clergy who were not imperial appointees, became a significant factor in the life of the Church, and also in society at large. Bishops began to represent city interests much more authoritatively than the old municipal *curia.*

Except in the case of the imperial capital, Constantinople, "it is remarkable how little the imperial government interfered in episcopal elections."[11] The norm, which was generally accepted in the fourth and fifth centuries and which was confirmed by the legislation of Justinian in 528,[12] was to have three candidates nominated by *the clergy and people* of the vacant see, for election and consecration by the metropolitan and the bishops of the province. A reverse procedure—nomination of three candidates by the bishops, from which the people would choose one—was also considered as acceptable.[13] However, while the concept of "people" could be clearly defined, in pre-Constantinian times, as long as Christian communities were small and generally composed of committed Christians, the situation in the large churches of imperial times was different: the "people of God" (λαὸς) became frequently undistinguishable from a "mob" (ὄχλος), and church rules began to prohibit "mob" participation in episcopal elections.[14] Henceforth, in practice, only the members of the city *curia* and other officials, or aristocrats, took part in such elections. Nevertheless, and in spite of practical limitations, an active lay participation was considered necessary and normal, albeit troublesome.

For instance, in Rome, a majority of clergy and laity, meeting at the Church of St Laurence elected Damasus to succeed the deceased pope Liberius (366 A.D.), but another election—that of Ursinus—took place at the Julian basilica (Santa Maria in Transtevere). The eventual result was a riot at the basilica of Liberius (Santa Maria Maggiore) which left one hundred and thirty-seven dead.[15] The issue was eventually solved through the intervention of emperor Gratian (375-383)

11Jones, *Roman Empire,* II, 919.

12CJ I, 3, 41, p. 2.

13Council of Arles (*ca.* 450), can. 54; cf. numerous examples of popular participation in episcopal elections, in Jones, *op. cit.,* III, p. 314, note 119.

14Laod., canon 13.

15Ammianus Marcellinus, *Res gestae,* XXVII, 3, 12-13, ed. J.C. Rolfe (Loeb Classical Library) III, p. 18-19.

in favor of Damascus. In the light of such events, one better understands the conciliar warnings against the power of "mobs!" Other examples—fortunately less bloody—of lay participation in episcopal elections are often found in the sources. Thus, in the case of Bassianus of Ephesus, his popular election had to be discussed at length at the council of Chalcedon (451), because none of the bishops, except one, Olympius of Theodosiopolis, accepted to attend his consecration.[16] Sometimes, as in the case of St Martin of Tours, in distant Gaul (372), the people elected a holy ascetic; subsequently, the bishops objected against his "despicable appearance," "dirty clothes" and "unkempt hair." They were forced—evidently by the people—to consecrate him anyway.[17] Popular acclamations could also be decisive in some cases, like that of St Ambrose of Milan, a yet unbaptized Roman aristocrat and governor of Emilia.[18] Such expressions of the will of the people may not have been as spontaneous as they appear in the lives of saints, but the fact that hagiographers point to them so frequently, clearly indicates that the procedure was seen as ecclesiologically and canonically normal.

Once elected, consecrated and enthroned, a bishop held his position for life, and transfers from one diocesce to another were formally forbidden by canons.[19] Even the great St Gregory the Theologian, was forced to resign the see of Constantinople (381) because he had been earlier consecrated bishop of Sasima. Exceptions to this rule were extremely rare. As a result, in each city, the bishop, practically unmovable, invested with judicial authority by imperial law (see *supra*, p. 14-5), controlling important financial means and administering a number of charitable institutions, often became, as the only locally-elected official, the very embodiment of urban self-government and identity. It was natural for him, as in the case of Flavian of Antioch—eloquently described by St John Chrysostom in his *Homilies on the Statues*—to intercede officially with the emperor (in this case Theodosius I) on behalf of the citizens, and against the exaction of local imperial administrators (387 A.D.). Similarly, certain archbishops of Alexandria, like Peter, Theophilus, or Cyril, naturally acted as spokesmen for their city, which was second in importance only to Rome and

[16]ACO, t. II, vol. II, part 3, p. 49 (408).

[17]Sulpicius Severus, *Vita Martini*, 9, ed. J. Fontaine, Paris, 1967 (SC, 133), p. 270-272.

[18]Paulinus, *Vita Ambrosii*, 6-7, ed. M. Pellegrino (Rome, 1961), pp. 58-60.

[19]Nicaea, canon 15; Antioch, canon 21.

Constantinople. These powerful archbishops even received the nickname of new "pharaohs."

Under the bishop's direct control stood the clergy, made up of priests, deacons and a number of lower officials in "minor" orders. Since "the great majority of the higher clergy, the urban deacons and priests, and the bishops, were drawn from the middle classes . . . and above all curiales,"[20] it was natural that as carriers of local urban traditions they would strengthen the concept of a local church. In Rome, the term *curia* was even retained to designate the bishop's administrative office. This permanence of the local clerical administration assured continuity in times of crisis. The unity of the Church depended upon formulas drawn by bishops' councils, and the emperors actively intervened not only in convoking them, but also in securing the enforcement of their decisions. This implied the removal of bishops belonging to the opposition. No one challenged such imperial powers—not even St Athanasius, sent into exile by Constantine and then by Constantius[21]—and even pope Leo considered the exile of heretics by the civil authority, as the emperor's sacred duty.[22] After Chalcedon (451), the Byzantine government extended the character and the scope of such interventions: by appointing Chalcedonian bishops, it acted in direct opposition to the clergy and laity of many Eastern sees, especially Alexandria. At the time of Justinian, this policy led in turn to the creation by James Bar'Addai of an illegal, "underground" Monophysite episcopate, whose incumbents were sometimes consecrated without appointment to a permanent urban see. These developments had serious consequences for the theology of the episcopate. Some bishops gradually detached themselves from concrete sacramental and pastoral functions in a local church. The episcopate itself was more often understood as an individual ministry, privilege, or "character," with which a person was invested by virtue of the "apostolic succession." In a different ecclesiological context, partially under the influence of Augustine's refutation of Donatism, a similar evolution occurred in the medieval Latin West.

In the major cities and in the provinces, the post-Constantinian

[20]Jones, *Roman Empire,* II, p. 923-924.

[21]See his recognition of this power, both when it was ("unjustly") exercised against himself (*Apologia ad Constantium,* 24-25, PG 25, 624-627), or ("justly") against Arians (*Ibid.,* 35, col. 641).

[22]"If my brother Anatolius (of Constantinople)," the pope writes to emperor Leo in 457, "is found to be remiss and too indulgent to restrain those men, be so good in

period was characterized by a growth in the number of clergy, by the new role of the Church as manager of numerous welfare and social institutions, and by increased ecclesiastical revenues.

Priests were normally entrusted with administration, teaching and preaching, as shown by the example of St John Chrysostom, who delivered most of his sermons while being a priest in Antioch (386-397). Deacons and deaconesses, besides such sacramental duties as bringing communion to the sick, were occupied with social work and administration. Sometimes they exercised great influence. St Leo, while still only a deacon in Rome, was influential enough to receive personal letters from the archbishop of Alexandria, Cyril; and, in 440, at the suggestion of the imperial court in Ravenna, was sent on a diplomatic mission to Gaul.

While it is difficult to draw a systematic picture of social and welfare institutions, which were under ecclestiatical jurisdiction,[23] their importance can be seen in the examples of the church of Alexandria, where the ecclesiastical payroll included 500 *parabalani,* or hospital attendants.[24] In Constantinople, 950 *decani* were in charge of assuring burials of needy citizens.[25] Hospitals, orphanages, alms houses and hostels were normally managed by priests or deacons. Special legal assistants (ἔκδικοι) were often also of clerical rank. A rapid growth in the number of clergy was, therefore, inevitable. In 537 the newly-rebuilt "Great Church" of the imperial capital of Constantinople was served by as many as 60 priests, 100 deacons, 90 subdeacons, 110 readers, 25 singers, 100 doorkeepers, and 40 deaconesses.[26] In the more modest Western imperial residence of Ravenna, there were still sixty clergy of all ranks,[27] and eighty in Apamea in Syria (in 451).[28]

In each church, finances were supposed to be managed by a priest-treasurer, carrying the title of *oeconomus* (οἰκονόμος), as required by the council of Chalcedon.[29] However, the bishops kept personal

virtue of your faith to administer to the church even the remedy of removing such men, not only from the clerical ranks, but from the territory of the city," *Ep.* 156 (97), ACO, II, vol. IV, p. 104 (tr. E. Hunt, New York, 1957, p. 247).

[23]On this, see the well-documented study of D.J. Constantelos, *Byzantine Philanthropy and Social Welfare,* New Brunswick, NJ, 1968, pp. 152-276.

[24]CT XVI,2,42-43, tr. cit., p. 448.

[25]CJ I,2,4.

[26]*Nov.* III,1, p. 21.

[27]Agnellus, *Liber Pontificalis eccl. Ravennatis,* 60, MGH, *Scr. rer. Longobardorum saec.* VI-IX, Hannover, 1878, p. 321.

[28]ACO III,103-106.

[29]Canon 26.

control of the revenues, and normally remained in charge of disbursements.

We have noted earlier that with the establishment of Christianity under Constantine, the wealth of the Church grew immensely; as a consequence, the management of ecclesiastical finances became more complicated. Systems varied from place to place. Ecclesiastical revenues grew not only because of the rapid increase of church membership—and therefore of donations—but also because of generous imperial gifts and endowments, particularly in the imperial capitals of Rome and Constantinople, and in pilgrimage centers, like Jerusalem. Bequests to the Church, or to monasteries, became an almost obligatory sign of Christian piety. Significantly, however, there was a widespread feeling that donations to the Church should always remain spontaneous. The code of Justinian warns against the practice by some clergy of exacting "first fruits," or otherwise taxing the faithful: the emperor commanded that every donation proceed from "free will" (αὐθαί-ρετος γνώμη).[30] The insistence on freedom was apparently viewed as a characteristic trait of the Christian religion itself, opposed, on this point, to Old Testament legalism. The practice of tithing (Num. 18:21-32) was never seen as a Christian obligation, at least in the East. In the West, it appears only in Merovingian Gaul in the late sixth century.

Since the clergy, and particularly the bishops, practically controlled church property, one of the major concerns of the conciliar and imperial legislations was to make sure that a clear distinction be drawn between the clergy's private belongings, and those of the Church. Bishops were warned against disposing of Church property in their own, or their relatives' interest, and were allowed to leave to their heirs only that which was acquired by them before their elevation to the episcopate: the rest was to be inherited by the Church.[31]

Clergy were, of course, supported from Church revenues, but this compensation took a variety of forms. From a letter of pope Gelasius (492-496), we learn that in Rome all liquid revenues were divided into four parts: one for the bishop, one for the clergy, one for maintenance of church buildings and one for the poor.[32] Different forms of distribution were used elsewhere. In the sixth century in Constan-

---

[30]CJ I,3,38.

[31]Apostolic canon 39; CJ I,3,41, etc.

[32]Gelasius, *Ep* 14, 27; ed. A. Thiel, Brunsfergae, 1867 (repr. Hildesheim, New York, 1974), p. 378.

tinople, the clergy of St Sophia received fixed salaries, rather than shares of the existing revenue.[33] Bishops in major cities were paid salaries much superior to those of professional men like doctors or teachers, and comparable to those of provincial governors. The bishop of Ravenna, the civil capital of Italy, was paid 40 lbs. in gold, *i.e.* as much as the Augustal prefect and *dux* of Egypt.[34] Lower clergy were compensated according to a descending scale. Although, in 452, Valentinian III prohibited clerics from practicing a trade to supplement their income,[35] there were, as late as the seventh century, examples of lower clerics forced to hold secular jobs.[36] Such cases were evidently due to necessity.

Under the new conditions of privilege and financial security for some only, various forms of bribery—or simony—crept into customary practice. There was fierce competition for ecclesiastical positions of wealth and influence. Both councils and emperors condemned such abuses, but, significantly, they were attempting only to limit them, without even pretending to suppress them altogether.[37] Reflecting the situation in Antioch and Constantinople at the beginning of the fifth century, the writings of St John Chrysostom (d. 404) contain an abundance of examples illustrating corruption among clergy and the difficulties which the author faced in his attempts at eradicating it. The shining examples of a few saintly and unmercenary bishops—St John himself, St Martin of Tours, St John the Merciful of Alexandria—must have been rare exceptions.

2. *Clergy: marriage or celibacy?*

Since the beginnings of Christianity, the functions of bishop and priest were bestowed upon celibate, or monogamous men (1 Tim 3:2; Tit 1:6). Unmarried women could accede to the order of deaconesses,

---

[33]Justinian, *Nov.* 3, 1 (A.D. 535), ed. cit., p. 20.

[34]Cf. figures in Jones, *Roman Empire*, II,906; III,308.

[35]CT, *Nov.* 35, 4, tr. C. Pharr, p. 546.

[36]Cf. two clerics, one a reader, one working as a cobbler in Alexandria, in the *Life of St John the Merciful*, ed. H. Delehaye, in *AB* XLV, 1927, 44 A; Engl. tr. in Dawes and N.H. Baynes, *Three Byzantine Saints* (Repr. Crestwood, NY, 1979), p. 253.

[37]In 451, any ordination performed for money is declared null by the Council of Chalcedon, can, 2, which also demands the deposition of the ordaining bishop. However, Justinian, in his *Novella* 123, 3 (A.D. 546) defines quite a scale of legal ordination fees to be paid by the candidates: 20 lb. gold to each bishop participating in the ordination of any of the five patriarchs, and less, in the case of other sees.

the functions of whom were primarily connected with the baptismal preparation of women. Deaconesses disappeared in the West by the sixth century, but survived in the East until the late Middle Ages. Their ordination was liturgically similar to that of the deacons.[38] Since all sacred functions were closed to women in pre-Christian Judaism, and since, by contrast, priestesses existed in most pagan cults of the Roman world, the discipline of the Church concerning men and women in the ministry must be considered as distinctively Christian. Socially, women did often exercise leadership (in Byzantium, they even reigned as empresses in their own name), and some, like Mary Magdalene and Helen, mother of Constantine, were liturgically venerated as "equal to the apostles." However, presidency at the eucharistic meal and the particular pastoral responsibility of the *episcope,* were associated with the "fatherhood" of God, and the ministry performed by Christ as the Bridegroom of the Church. They could be fulfilled only by men. Some sources suggest that women-presbyters (πρεσβύτιδες) were found in some churches, but they disappeared when presbyters, and not only bishops, assumed regular presidency at eucharistic celebrations.[39] There is no evidence that women ever presided over the eucharistic meal.

By the end of the seventh century, East and West were clearly set on two distinct solutions to the alternative between marriage or celibacy for clergy. The West opted for the rule of celibacy, although the observance of this rule did not become universal for several more centuries. The East, on the contrary, continued the New Testamental practice of admitting strictly monogamous candidates to the diaconate and the priesthood, but restricted episcopacy to men leading a celibate life. The Western practice is enshrined in a long series of papal decretals, while the discipline adopted in the East is sanctioned by the council *in Trullo,* or Quinisext (692), which the Byzantine Orthodox world viewed as carrying ecumenical authority.

Neither the Eastern nor the Western solution was achieved without debate. There were variations both in the actual practice and in the motivations put forward by proponents of the two disciplines.

[38]L. Bréhier, *Les Institutions de l'Empire byzantin,* Paris, 1949, pp. 514-515; S. Troitsky, *Zhenskoe tserkovnosluzhenie;* E. Theodorou, Ἡ "χειροτονία" ἤ "χειροθεσία" τῶν διακονισσῶν, Athens, 1954. Cf. the Byzantine rite for ordaining deaconesses in J. Goar, *Euchologion,* Venice, 1730, (repr. Graz, 1960), pp. 218-219.

[39]This may be the most likely meaning of canon 11 of the council of Laodicea (fourth century), περὶ τοῦ μὴ δεῖν τὰς λεγομένας πρεσβύτιδας, ἤτοι προκαθημένας ἐν τῇ ἐκκλησίᾳ καθίστασθαι (Rhalles-Potles, III, 181).

These motivations included varied attitudes toward sexuality, the survival among Christians of the notion of ritual purity, inherited from the Old Testament, and also material considerations, related particularly to inheritance laws, from which clergy children could profit. Strangely enough, the Pauline argument generally put forward in modern Roman Catholicism and justifying celibacy by the freedom it secures (cf. 1 Cor 7:33) for a full-time priestly ministry, is practically never used in documents of the early church.

The admission of married men to the episcopate and the presbyterate seems to have been general before the fourth century. Most authoritative sources, however—particularly Tertullian[40] and Origen[41]—give a strict interpretation to the Pauline precept that a bishop should be "the husband of one wife" (1 Tim. 3:2) and connect this precept directly to the presidency at the Eucharist: a remarried man cannot "preside," or "offer." But such ideas were not shared by all. Hippolytus of Rome, for example, complains that under his competitor, pope Callistus, men who successively married two, or three times were admitted to the episcopate.[42] Similarly, Theodore of Mopsuestia interprets 1 Tim 3:2, as forbidding simultaneous polygamy for bishops, but not excluding remarried widowers from the episcopate.[43] Theodoret of Cyrus belonged to the same liberal tradition,[44] and faced serious criticism for defending it. Indeed, other Antiochenes, like the great Chrysostom, and other ecclesiastical luminaries of the time disagreed with his interpretation of 1 Tim. Some adopted a totally negative attitude towards married clergy. St Epiphanius of Cyprus and St Cyril of Jerusalem preach total continence for all servitors of the altar.[45] Nevertheless, the easy-going tradition of Theodore of Mopsuestia and Theodoret remained the pattern in the Nestorian church of Persia, which admitted both married bishops and the remarriage of priests.[46]

Eventually, the various practices of the early Church gelled into the two canonical patterns which would distinguish the East and the West until the modern period.

40*Ad Uxorem* I, 7, CSEL, 70, p. 107.

41*Hom. on Luke,* 17, GCS 35, 120-121.

42*Refutation of heresies* 9, 12, 22, GCS 26, pp. 249-250.

43*Comm. on I Tim.,* ed. H.B. Swete, II, Cambridge, 1882, pp. 99-106.

44*Letter* 110, ed. Y. Azéma (SC, 111), Paris, 1965, pp. 40-42.

45Epiphanius, *Against heresies,* 59, 4, GCS 31, pp. 367-368; Cyril, *Catech* XII, 25, *PG* 35, col. 757A.

46Cf. J. Labourt, *Le Christianisme dans l'Empire perse sous la dynastie sassanide* (224-632), Paris, 1904, pp. 141-191.

In the East, the principle of married priesthood was sanctioned forever at the council of Gangra (*ca.* 340 A.D.): "If anyone shall maintain, concerning a married presbyter, that it is not lawful to partake of the oblation when he offers it, let him be anathema" (canon 4). Furthermore, the so-called "Apostolic Canons"—reflecting the discipline of the church of Antioch in the fourth century and formally endorsed as authoritative by the Byzantine church—proclaim: "Let not a bishop, presbyter, or deacon put away his wife under the pretense of religion; but if he put her away, let him be excommunicated" (canon 5). The same attitude appears in an account that at the council of Nicaea, the principle of married clergy was formally endorsed by the Fathers.[47] However, emperor Justinian (527-565) prohibited the elevation of married bishops having children or grandchildren (to prevent the latter from eventually inheriting church property), and formally restricted the episcopate to men unmarried, widowed, or separated from their wives.[48] This legislation, initially purely civil, received an ecclesiastical sanction at the Council *in Trullo* in 692 A.D. However, the Council does not mention children as an impediment to episcopal consecration of a formerly married man.[49] The obvious contradiction between these new provisions and Apostolic canon 5, is presented by Byzantine canonists as a matter of discipline.[50] Consequently, the spiritual and theological legitimacy of a married episcopate, practiced in the early church, remained unchallenged in principle, but forbidden in practice.

The endorsement of an unmarried episcopate by the council *in Trullo* was accompanied by a formal demand of strict monogamy for priests and deacons, and their wives. Not only was ordination restricted to candidates who married only once, with no possibility of remarrying in case of widowhood, but men married to widows, or divorcées, were also excluded from the priesthood, or the diaconate (canon 3). This rule remained permanent in the East. It reflected the views of early Christian writers, like Origen and Tertullian, and struck a compromise

[47]According to Socrates (*Hist. eccl.,* 1:11, PG 67, col. 101 C-102 B), a motion to impose celibacy on clergy was defeated at the council through the opposition of a great ascetic, St Paphnutius of Thebais. The episode, if legendary, reflects the beliefs of Socrates himself (early fifth century).

[48]CJ I,3,41,2-4; 47; *Nov.* VI, 1, p. 36.

[49]Canon 12 and 48 ("The wife of him who is advanced to the episcopal dignity, shall be separated from her husband by their mutual consent, and after his ordination and consecration to the episcopate she shall enter a monastery situated at a distance from the abode of the bishop and then let her enjoy the bishop's provision. And if she is deemed worthy, she might be made a deaconess.")

[50]Cf. especially Zonaras, *Commentary on Apost. canon 5,* Rhalles-Potles, II, 7.

between the liberalism of Theodore of Mopsuestia and the strict demand of celibacy preached by St Epiphanius and St Cyril of Jerusalem. What it did maintain was that clergy were to proclaim, not only in words, but also in deeds, the ideal form of Christian marriage —one husband and one wife, united forever in the image of Christ and the Church (Eph. 5). Departures from this ideal could be tolerated for the laity only.

In the West, the trend requiring clergy continence became very early the dominant teaching of the Church. As clearly shown, with remarkable consistency and continuity in all the sources,[51] this trend did not object in principle against the ordination of married men, but required that after ordination, they abstain from sexual relations. The motivations for this attitude were 1) a view of sex as a form of morally degrading animality, and 2) the permanence of the Old Testament idea of ritual impurity, caused by sexual intercourse (Lev 15:18). The first motivation, while it did not originate with St Augustine, found great reinforcement in his strong views on "concupiscence" as the channel of transmission of sin; the second, ritual argument was applied to the Christian Eucharist which, if celebrated daily, made sexual continence a permanent requirement for the one who performed the Offering.

Beginning with the council of Elvira (305 A.D.; canon 33), the two arguments will be invoked by popes Damasus (366-384), Siricius (384-399), Innocent I (401-417), Leo I (440-461)—who extends the demand of continence even to subdeacons—and Gregory the Great (590-604). The same arguments will be affirmed by Western councils (Rome, 386; Turin, 389; Carthage, 390 and 401; Toledo, 400 and 589; and several councils in Gaul), and adopted by authors like St Jerome, St Ambrose and St Isidore of Seville. The constant repetition of such injunctions clearly shows that the norm was often ignored. It gained a more universal acceptance in the West only after the eleventh century, particularly with the reformed papacy.

It should be noted that the ritual continence by married priests, deacons and subdeacons on the eve of a celebration of the Eucharist was also required in the East,[52] but, in the absence of a daily celebra-

---

[51]Cf. particularly, Roger Gryson, *Les origines du célibat ecclésiastique du premier au septième siècle*, Paris, 1970, pp. 127-201. The author makes extensive use of primary sources and of the previous secondary literature on the subject.

[52]Council *in Trullo*, canon 13.

tion, it did not imply perpetual abstention by priests from cohabitation with their wives. It does appear, however, that, as a general rule, the East understood celibacy and continence less as a preservation of ritual purity and more as an ascetical anticipation of the eschatological *parousia,* where there will be "neither male, nor female." The proper context for such asceticism was therefore seen in the monastic discipline.

3. *Regional primacies*

Neither the New Testament, nor the early Christian tradition and practice knew any formally defined organization of the Church above the level of the local eucharistic community. However, at all times, the faith of the Church presupposed a strong awareness of unity between the local churches. In apostolic times, this unity was expressed, for example, in the moral authority of the original community of Jerusalem, an authority sanctioned, in particular, through the special collection required by the apostle Paul from communities founded by him. In later times—as can be seen from the witness of Tertullian and St Irenaeus (second century)—the need for unity within a single universally-held "apostolic tradition" required constant contacts between the churches. Moreover, a gathering of several bishops was necessary for the ordination and installation of a new bishop in each church. Churches which were actually founded by apostles, (Ephesus, Smyrna, Antioch, Thessalonica and many more in the East; Rome alone in the West) enjoyed particular respect in their role of preserving the common "apostolic tradition."

With the establishment of Christianity under Constantine, the new and unavoidable relationships of the Church with the administrative units of the empire required better defined structures. As pertinently stated by A.H.M. Jones, "the constitution of the church . . . grew from bottom upwards, and it was only gradually that bishoprics were grouped in provinces, and provinces in larger units of church government. Its growth was irregular, depending on the varying success with which greater sees, by gradual encroachments, hardening into custom, established their ascendency over their lesser neighbors. The process was slow, extending over the fourth and fifth centuries, and until it was completed there was ample room for conflict between the rival great sees in the no man's lands between them . . ."[53] At no time, however, did anybody challenge the territorial principle, according to which there could be only one bishop and one church in each place[54]: indeed the principle reflected the very nature of ecclesiastical unity.

The initial "provincial" groupings were formally sanctioned by the council of Nicaea (325 A.D.). Within each province (Lat. *provincia;* Gr. ἐπαρχία), all the bishops were to meet twice a year as a council, or "synod" for the election of any new bishop, for acting as an ecclesiastical tribunal and for solving issues of common concern. All decisions were to be ratified by the Metropolitan, or bishop of the provincial capital, who thus held veto power over all decisions.[55] Disputes were supposed to be settled in this manner, so that the ecclesiastical provinces were independent in all administrative and disciplinary matters. The possibility of a recourse to the bishop of Rome, in case of a conflict between a bishop and his metropolitan, was established in principle by the council of Serdica (343), but the powers of Rome were limited to setting up a new tribunal composed of bishops coming from provinces located in the vicinity of the area where the conflict had occurred.

However, Nicaea itself recognized that in some areas "ancient customs" contradicted the newly established "provincial" system and gave special privileges to some major sees. Its canon 6 formally admitted that extraordinary "ancient customs" allowed the bishop of Alexandria to consecrate all the bishops of Egypt in the several "provinces" and Pentapolis, and the Roman pope to do the same in the so-called "suburbicarian" provinces of central and southern Italy, including Sicily but excluding Sardinia (where there was a metropolitan in Cagliari). The same canon 6 of Nicaea also recognized a less clearly defined "supra-provincial" authority of Antioch.[56] A similar regional primacy over Africa existed *de facto* in Carthage. On the other hand, the bishop of such imperial residences as Milan and, particularly,

---

[53]*Roman Empire,* II, p. 874.

[54]Cf. J. Meyendorff, "One Bishop in One City" in *Catholicity and the Church* (Crestwood, NY, 1983), pp. 111-220.

[55]Canons 4 and 5 of Nicaea. It is to be noted that a civil "province" was a relatively small administrative unit. There were more than twenty *provinciae* in continental Italy alone, and (in the fifth century) over one hundred and twenty provinces within the Empire as a whole.

[56]In 431, however, the archbishop of Antioch was rebuked in his attempt to assume the right of consecrating the metropolitan of Cyprus, although the island was part of the "diocese of Orient" within which Antioch exercised its primacy. This is the origin of the "autocephaly" of the small church of Cyprus.

Constantinople, extended a similar *de facto* authority very widely, much beyond a single province. St Ambrose of Milan consecrated a bishop in Sirmium, in the Illyricum (376) and St John Chrysostom effectively interfered in the affairs of the ancient church of Ephesus. In spite of such infringements, the Nicaean "provincial system" was generally adhered to in the East (but not in Egypt), and in Northern Italy. In Gaul, it was instituted only following the council of Turin (400). However, even in regions where the system was enforced, the metropolitans, while preserving the power to preside over provincial synods and to consecrate bishops, soon became themselves dependent upon major centers—the future "patriarchates." Such regional centralization—which in Egypt had prevented the creation of metropolitan districts altogether—grew very rapidly in the civil "dioceses" of Thrace, Asia and Pontus. Each "diocese" consisted of several "provinces," and was led by local primates, or "exarchs of dioceses" at least since 381 (cf. canon 2 of Constantinople; canons 9 and 17 of Chalcedon). The archbishop of the new imperial capital of Constantinople, after receiving "equal privileges" with Rome at the second ecumenical council (381), was granted the right to ordain the metropolitans in all three dioceses (Chalcedon, canon 28). At the council of Chalcedon (451), through the efforts of the shrewd archbishop Juvenal, Palestine was formally separated from the diocese of Orient, where Antioch held primacy, and Jerusalem was erected into an independent primacy.[57] In the Balkan peninsula, which was part of the Western Empire, Thessalonica, capital of the diocese of the Illyricum, was the seat of an archbishop to whom pope Siricius (384-399) granted the rights of a metropolitanate over the entire "diocese."[58] Also, Justinian (527-565), desiring to honor his modest birthplace in Macedonia, renamed it "Justiniana Prima" and established it as an archbishopric, with jurisdiction over the "diocese" of Dacia. The traditional Roman jurisdiction in the area was maintained with the new archbishop receiving the title of papal vicar.

The incumbents of the newly developed "diocesan" or supra-"diocesan" primates generally exercised their ecclesiastical government

[57]ACO II, vol. I, 3, p. 364-366.

[58]*Ep* 14, PL, 13, col. 1148 ff. In 421, emperor Theodosius II took the seemingly logical measure of transferring Thessalonica from the "old" to the "new" Rome, Constantinople. The edict was included in the code (CT XVI, 2, 45, tr. cit. p. 449). But papal protests obliged him to rescind the measure, so that the popes kept their jurisdiction over Thessalonica until the eighth century.

over the provincial "metropolitans" with the help of councils. Thus, in Rome, the council of "suburbicarian" bishops met frequently to discuss and issue the more solemn decisions of the popes, whereas a "standing synod" (σύνοδος ἐνδημοῦσα), composed of the often numerous metropolitans or bishops who happened to visit Constantinople at a given time, was set-up in the "new Rome."[59]

This gradual and very pragmatic trend towards grouping ecclesiastical provinces around major centers resulted, in the sixth century, in a structure with several centers enjoying various degrees of administrative powers over areas of various sizes.

In the East, these centers were:

—*Constantinople,* with jurisdiction over three dioceses: Thrace, Pontus, Asia;

—*Alexandria,* with strictly centralized powers over one diocese, Egypt (which included Libya);

—*Antioch,* a loose primacy over the diocese of the Orient, amputated of Palestine and Cyprus;

—*Jerusalem,* with primatial powers over three provinces in Palestine;

—*Thessalonica,* attached in 437 to the Eastern empire, but headed by a papal vicar with jurisdiction over the prefecture of Illyricum (*i.e.* contemporary Macedonia, Bulgaria and Greece);

—*Justiniana Prima,* leading the diocese of Dacia (detached from the Illyricum);

—*Cyprus,* a lonely survivor of the old provincial system, with a metropolitan independently presiding over the bishops of one province.

In the West, *the Roman bishop* directly consecrated all the "suburbicarian" bishops of Central and Southern Italy and the islands. Elsewhere in the West, his authority was of a moral nature and the "metropolitans" acted independently, although a growing tradition,

[59]Cf. J. Hajjar, *Le Synode permanent* (σύνοδος ἐνδημοῦσα) *dans l'église byzantine au XIe-siècle* (OCA, 164), Rome, 1962.

which we will examine below, demanded that disputed questions be deferred to Rome. Such deferring, however, was adamantly rejected by the bishops of Africa, grouped around their *de facto* primate in Carthage, and often challenged by some important sees, such as Ravenna —particularly enhanced by Justinian in 546—Arles, Milan and Aquilea.

The title of "patriarch" was not adopted immediately or uniformly to designate the supra-metropolitan primates. It was widely used in Rome at the time of St Leo (440-461) and seems to have been introduced in Constantinople under Acacius (472-488). In Alexandria and Antioch, the titles of "archbishop" or "exarch of diocese" were preferred over "patriarch" until the reign of Justinian (527-580).[60] In his legislation dealing with religion, the same emperor envisioned the universal Church as divided into five patriarchates—Rome, Constantinople, Alexandria, Antioch and Jerusalem.[61] Eventually, Byzantine texts would compare the five sees with the "five senses" of the empire. However, this system of "pentarchy" never really coincided with reality: not only were there within the Empire centers such as Carthage or Cyprus, which did not belong to any of the "five" patriarchates, but, precisely under Justinian, the anti-Chalcedonian schism deprived the Egyptian Christians of their normal status within the imperial church; moreover, in the next century, the Muslim conquest left imperial Christendom with only two real centers—Rome and Constantinople—headed by an "ecumenical pope" and an "ecumenical patriarch," respectively.[62]

Also excluded from Justinian's ideal scheme were the ancient churches of the East, located beyond the imperial borders, whose heads were generally adopting the title of *catholicos*. Some of them rejected the Orthodox faith of Ephesus and Chalcedon (the catholicos of Seleucia-Ctesiphon, with its daughter-church in India, was Nestorian; the Armenian catholicos was Monophysite), but the catholicos of Georgia eventually maintained the Chalcedonian faith. The existence of these ancient centers added to the *de facto* structural pluralism of the universal Church. The attempts of Justinian and of later Byzantine emperors to reduce it to a unified imperial model of "five patriarchs" never fully succeeded. Equally unsuccessful was the trend to

[60]G. Guademet, *op. cit.,* p. 394.
[61]Cf. *Nov* 109 (541), 131 (545) and 123, 3 (546); pp. 518, 655, 597.
[62]On the latter title, see below pp. 305-306.

view the universal Church as a single centralized body under the power of the bishop of Rome.

4. *The primacy of Rome by 451 A. D.*

The abundance of secondary literature—inevitably determined by confessional presuppositions, positive or negative—concerning the origins and growth of a "Petrine" primacy, makes it difficult to present, in a few pages, an objective view of Rome's exact role within the universal Church around the year 451. The conjecture that, from the very apostolic times, the position of the bishop of Rome among the other bishops was like that of Peter among the apostles; and that the *logia* of Jesus referring to Peter (Matt 16:18; Luke 22:32; John 21:15-19) were uniquely applicable to the bishop of Rome, or the opposite assumption—that the rise of the church of Rome was only due to its position in the imperial capital and was, therefore, of purely human origin—exercise an inevitable influence upon many authors' vision of historical reality. There is today, however, some agreement on one point: whether or not it was of divine origin, the Roman primacy, as it existed in the fifth century, was already the result of a development—a development which continued through the early Middle Ages to reach its apogee with the Gregorian reforms in the late eleventh century. It is, therefore, a matter of theological judgement whether this Western historical process—which was not really understood, or accepted in the East—was a legitimate one. The facts illustrating it can be recognized by historians on both sides of the confessional fence.

It is undeniable that, in the first half of the fifth century, the bishop of Rome enjoyed a strong *de facto* authority in helping to solve doctrinal and disciplinary disputes. This authority was recognized in some ways both in the East and in the West, but it had not formally been defined in any conciliar decree. Only the canons of the local council of Serdica (343), gave clerics dissatisfied with the disciplinary judgments of their own metropolitans, the right to request in Rome the establishment of a new tribunal of neighboring bishops. According to those canons, the role of Rome was therefore to assure correct procedures within existing structures of local churches, as defined in

Nicaea, and not to issue personal judgments.[63] The division of the empire into Eastern and Western parts after Constantine's death (337) contributed to the pope's prestige. Alone among the major leaders of the Church, he was out of direct reach of the powerful emperor of Constantinople, and the much weaker Western emperors were not really in a position to control him. In any case, in 476, the Western empire collapsed. It is therefore, primarily against imperial interventions in ecclesiastical affairs that Eastern bishops sought and cherished the support of the Roman bishops. That appeals to the pope were primarily caused by such political factors—and not necessarily by Roman prestige as such—is shown by the fact that letters were usually addressed not only to the Roman pope, but to several major bishops of the West. For instance, in 382, the Eastern bishops gathered in Constantinople wrote a collective letter "to the honored and revered brothers and concelebrants Damasus (of Rome), Ambrose (of Milan), Britto, Valerian, Acholius, Anemius, Basil, and the other holy bishops gathered in the great city of Rome," calling them to unity with the council of 381 and urging them to abandon their support to the small, "old Nicaean" church of Paulinus in Antioch.[64] The Easterners clearly did not consider Rome as the sole and ultimate criterion of communion, but appreciated the Roman pope's—and his colleagues'—eventual support in solving the ecclesiastical situation in the East. Similarly, St John Chrysostom, exiled in 404, appealed not only to pope Innocent, but also to Venerius of Milan and Chromatius of Aquileia.[65] In such appeals, the name of the Roman bishop always appears first, but this obvious sign of priority never excludes the authority of others.

Gradually, a certain divergency begins to appear on two points: the definition of the *origin* of Roman primacy and the manner in which it was to be *exercised*.

The earliest Christian tradition associated the origin and prestige of the Roman church with the preaching and martyrdom of the two apostles *Peter and Paul,* not exclusively with Peter.[66] Pilgrimages *ad limina apostolorum* (in the plural) contributed to this, and indicate that the authority of Rome was not derived from Christ's words to

[63]On this, see H. Hess, *The Canons of the Council of Serdica* A.D. 343, Oxford, 1958.

[64]Theodoret, *Hist.,* V, 9, 1-18, ed. Parmentier, p .289.

[65]Palladius, *Dialogue,* 2, PG 47, col. 12.

[66]On this important point, see the recent research by P. Grelot, "Pierre et Paul, fondateurs de la 'primauté' romaine," *Istina,* XXVII, 1982, n. 3, pp. 228-268.

Peter in an exclusive way. It is the doctrine of Cyprian of Carthage, who had singled out Peter as the model of the episcopal ministry, which probably helped create the notion that the bishop of Rome derives not only his episcopacy, but his primatial authority as well, from Peter alone, exclusively. In fact, however, Cyprian's view of Peter's "chair" (*cathedra Petri*) was that it belonged not only to the bishop of Rome but to every bishop within each community. Thus Cyprian used not the argument of Roman primacy but that of *his own* authority as "successor of Peter" in Carthage.[67] In any case, throughout the fourth century, several texts emanating from, or related to Rome (including the canons of Serdica), refer to a moral authority of the Roman bishop, emanating from his "proximity" to Peter: the bishop of Rome was a bishop among other bishops—and in that sense a successor of Peter—but the relics of Peter made the Roman episcopacy particularly "close" to Peter. It seems that the Eastern church was also ready to accept a moral primacy of Rome interpreted along these lines.

A clear divergence of opinion as to the implications of Roman authority appeared when, in the first years of his reign, emperor Theodosius I (379-395) presided over the liquidation of Arianism at the general council of the East—eventually to be recognized as the "second ecumenical" council—in Constantinople (381). Canon 3 of that council gave the bishop of Constantinople "an honorary seniority (πρεσβεῖα τιμῆς) after the bishop of Rome, because that city is the New Rome." The text could be easily interpreted as implying that the primacy of "old" Rome had become obsolete after the transfer of the imperial capital to Constantinople. The Western episcopate, led by pope Damasus, disagreed with the decisions and policies of the council, and refused to enter into communion with its leaders (which included the great Cappadocian Fathers). It is then that a famous papal text, known as the *Decretum Gelasianum,* solemnly affirmed that the Roman church was the head of all the churches by divine decree, on the basis of the words of Christ addressed to Peter.[68]

[67]This is particularly true for Cyprian's treatise *On the unity of the Catholic Church,* where Rome is not mentioned (cf. M. Bévenot, *The Tradition of Manuscripts of the "De unitate,"* Oxford, 1961; also M. Bévenot's comments on his translation of Cyprian's treatise in *Ancient Christian Writers,* 25, 1957). However, Cyprian does also recognize the church of Rome, as *ecclesia principalis unde unitas sacerdotalis exorta est,* the "most ancient" church, where Peter established the episcopate, which later spread to the entire West (*Ep* 59(55), 14).

[68]Text in E. Dobschütz, *Das Decretum Gelasianum,* Texte u. Untersuchungen, 38, 3, Leipzig, 1912. The attribution of this text, in some manuscripts to popes Gelasius (492-

Both sides were undoubtedly aware of the ancient tradition which recognized the bishop of Rome as the "first bishop," or "primate" of the universal episcopate. However, the council of Constantinople, by attributing the second rank to the bishop of the new imperial capital could also be understood as implying that the pope had been honored for no other reason than the political position of "older" Rome. This interpretation of canon 3 will be formally endorsed in 451 by the council of Chalcedon. It is precisely this view which was opposed by the *Decretum*. "The holy Roman church," is proclaimed, "was placed at the head of the other churches not by some council (as was now the case for Constantinople), but it received primacy through the words of our Lord and Savior: *Thou art Peter, and upon this rock I will build my church . . .*"

Both positions took into consideration the text of canon 6 of Nicaea (325), which endorsed "ancient customs" and recognized the special privileges and regional primacies of three cities: Alexandria, Rome and Antioch. However, in the East, these privileges were seen as the purely practical consequences of their being the three major cities of the empire,[69] so that the addition of a fourth "primate"—Constantinople—was seen as a natural consequence of socio-political change, emerging with the reign of Constantine. The *Decretum*, however, offers a different explanation: Alexandria was elevated because it was founded by a disciple of Peter, St Mark, and Antioch received a primacy because St Peter himself preached there (Gal. 2:11-17). This exclusively "apostolic" and "Petrine" criterion, was thus applied to all primacies and aimed at totally excluding the primacy of Constantinople, and also that of such centers as Milan, the new imperial residence in the West, whose bishop was acquiring a power similar to his colleague in Constantinople. It was a rather artificial device, and it provided no explanation for the generally recognized precedence of Alexandria (founded by Peter's disciple, Mark) over Antioch, where Peter's preaching was attested in Scripture, and for the absence of any claims to primacy in other Eastern "apostolic churches" (Ephesus, Corinth,

496), or Hormisdas (514-523), and also the very boldness of its claims, have led some scholars to ascribe it to a later date (P. Battifol, *Le Siège apostolique*, Paris, 1924, pp. 146-150; F. Dvornik, *The Idea of Apostolicity*, Washington, DC, 1958, pp. 56-88). However, a broader consensus (Turner, Chapman, Caspar, Kidd), in conformity with the oldest and best sources, attributes the kernel of the *Decretum* to Damasus (cf. also H. Jedin-J. Dolan, *History*, II, pp. 253-254).

[69]On this, see our study, "The Roman Primacy in canonical tradition up to the Council of Chalcedon," in *Orthodoxy and Catholicity*, New York, 1966, pp. 56-58.

etc.), even in Jerusalem itself! However, the idea enshrined in the *Decretum* would henceforth be consistently upheld in Rome and become a sort of *leit-motiv* in the Roman understanding of the universal Church structure.

Thus, a gradual polarization occurred between this Roman view of ecclesiastical authority, whose origin is seen exclusively in Christ's words addressed to Peter and which is inherited in a pre-eminent way by the Roman bishop as Peter's successor, and the one which Francis Dvornik calls "accommodation."[70] The ecclesiastical authority of some churches, including that of Rome, reflects historical realities, not a divine command. It is conditioned by the orthodox faith of the incumbent, and is controlled by the consensus of the whole Church. This concept does not deny the particular role of the apostle Peter and his martyrdom in Rome; but his ministry is seen, following Cyprian, as being fulfilled by each bishop in his community, not by the Roman bishop alone.[71]

This underlying difference in understanding the *origin* of the Roman primacy gradually influenced the manner in which the popes *exercised* their ministry and the reaction of the other churches to the growing self-assurance of "Peter's successors."

The "decretals" of popes Siricius (384-399) and Innocent I (407-417) expressed a trend which followed the model defined by Damasus. Writing to Himerius, bishop of Tarragona in Spain, in 384, Siricius expresses the conviction that "St Peter protects and watches over us"; he defines the Roman church as the "head of the body" to which Himerius belongs. His solutions of disciplinary problems raised by Himerius, are presented as final "decisions of the Apostolic see."[72] Similarly, in 416, writing to Decentius, bishop of Eugubium (Gubbio, in Central Italy), Innocent I defines that Roman customs as "handed down to the Roman church by the prince of the apostles, Peter, and

---

[70]See especially *Byzantium and Roman Primacy,* New York, 1966.

[71]This view was rather generally implied in the East, where Cyprian's writings were hardly known. St Gregory of Nyssa, for example, speaks of the powers of the keys (cf. Mat 16:19) transmitted by Peter to the bishops (*De castig.* PG 46, 312 C). In the West, the numerous references to Mat 16:18 in the writings of St Augustine, appear primarily in passages referring to the Donatists and defending the idea that the sacramental power of remitting sins belongs to the *Church* and is exercised by bishops. Augustine does not mention any connection between Mat 16:18 and Rome (see especially A.M. La Bonnardière "*Tu es Petrus.* La péricope Matthieu 16:13-23 dans l'oeuvre de St Augustin." *Irénikon,* XXXIV, 4, 1961, pp. 451-499.)

[72]*Ep* 1 (Jaffe, 255). PL 13, cols. 1132-1147.

here kept until this very day, are to be observed everywhere."[73] In the mind of the popes, the Petrine foundation clearly gives the Roman church a divinely established and, therefore, final authority in ecclesiastical affairs.

During the first half of the fifth century, there are, however, only isolated instances when the Roman bishops have the opportunity to exercise the authority which—as they believe—belongs to them by divine right. In practice they exercise direct canonical power in only ten provinces, which are subject, in civil matters to the prefect of Rome. In those provinces—Central and Southern Italy, Sicity, and Corsica—they elect and consecrate bishops and preside over synods.[74] In other parts of the Western empire, the Nicaean system of metropolitan provincial synods is accepted as a basic pattern of ecclesiastical polity. In Northern Italy, the major sees of Milan and Aquilea have no administrative dependence upon Rome. However, some more distant areas accept direct papal control. In Thessalonica, capital of the Illyricum and former imperial residence, bishop Acholius already in 381, establishes a permanent contact with his Roman colleague, Damasus, and acts as his representative or "vicar." In 385, pope Siricius gives Anisius of Thessalonica the right to confirm all the episcopal elections in Illyricum (probably also including Dacia).[75] Just as the bishop of Constantinople begins to exercise *de facto* authority in the dioceses of Asia Minor, the pope establishes a *de facto* "patriarchate" in the Balkan peninsula. But the head of this "patriarchate"—the bishop of Thessalonica—is subject to the pope. This delegation of powers to the bishop of Thessalonica—the foundation of what is generally referred to as a papal "vicariate" in the Illyricum—was confirmed by pope Innocent I in 412, and later by pope Boniface. In 437, in spite of the fact that the Illyricum is now attached to the Eastern empire, pope Sixtus III succeeds in maintaining his former rights in the region.[76]

It is possible that papal authority was accepted gladly by the bishops of the Illyricum precisely because Rome was, in fact, sufficiently

---

[73]*Ep* 34, 2 (Jaffe, 311), PL 20, col. 552 A.

[74]Cf. P. Gaudemet, *L'Eglise et l'Empire romain*, Paris, 1958, p. 445.

[75]*Ep* 4, (Jaffe, 259), PL 13, col. 1148-1155.

[76]*Ep* 9, 10, PL 50, cols. 612-624. On the origins of the vicariate, see P. Streichman, "Die Anfänge des Vikariats von Thessalonica," *Zeitschrift für Rechtsgeschichte, Kan. Abt.*, XII, 1922, pp. 330-384; see also S.L. Greenslade, "The Illyrian churches and the Vicariate of Thessalonica," JTS 46 (1945), 17-29.

distant and, therefore, less domineering than the neighboring growing power of Constantinople.

But contemporary attempts at expanding papal disciplinary authority in other areas of the West met with resistance. In Gaul, where the principle of primacy by provincial "metropolitans," as defined in Nicaea, was introduced only at the council of Turin (400), there occurred a Roman attempt to introduce greater centralization. In 417, pope Zosimus gave Patroclus, bishop of Arles (that city was the seat of the imperial prefect of the Gauls), the right to confirm episcopal elections in five provinces.[77] The move was fiercely resisted, especially by Proculus of Marseilles. We will see how it later backfired with St Hilary of Arles (429-449) standing up to the pope not only in the name of local "provincial" independence, but in the name of what eventually could have become a "patriarchate" of the Gauls in Arles.[78]

Finally, in Africa, where the moral and doctrinal authority of pope Innocent I—with explicit references to St Peter—was welcomed in 417 by St Augustine and other bishops (in reference to Pelagianism), the discplinary claims of Rome were passionately rebuked in 418. Examining the case of a presbyter Apiarius—deposed in Africa and received in Rome—the African bishops formally forbade "appeals beyond the sea" (*transmarinum judicium*).[79] Furthermore, writing to pope Celestine in 420, the Africans proclaimed what amounted to a formal denial of any "divine" privilege of Rome. "Who will believe," they stated, "that our God could inspire justice in the inquiries of one man only (*i.e.* the pope) and refuse it to innumerable bishops gathered in council?"[80]

If one were to summarize the position of the church of Rome in the Christian world by the middle of the fifth century, one would have to admit a clear reluctance—both in the East and in the West—to admit a direct connection between its unquestionable prestige, as the church founded by Peter and Paul in the imperial capital and as the *locus*

[77]*Ep* I,2, **PL** 20, col. 644 A.

[78]In addition to the abundant literature on the ecclesiastical affairs of Gaul in Western languages, see also the very well documented book of N. Malitsky, *Bor'ba gall'skoi tserkvi protiv pap za nezavisimost'. Opyt tserkovno-istoricheskogo issledovaniya iz IV-VI vv*, Moscow, 1903.

[79]African code, (= "canons of the council of Carthage"), 125. The African code was also included in the canonical *corpus* of the Byzantine Church.

[80]Letter *Optaremus*, Mansi, IV, col. 515-516. Cf. J.B. Brisson, *Autonomisme et christianisme dans l'Afrique romaine de Septime Sévère à l'invasion vandale*, Paris, 1958. See also G. Denzler, *Das Papsttum und der Amtszölibat. I. Die Zeit bis zur Reformation* (= *Päpste u. Papsttum, 5, 1*), Stuttgart, 1973.

of Peter—who was seen as model, or prototype of the episcopal ministry—and the formal exercise of doctrinal disciplinary authority over other churches. However, the bishops of Rome themselves—especially since Damasus—had no doubt that this connection existed, and they invoked it systematically, in their "decretals" and in the measures they took to build up a "patriarchal" jurisdiction in certain Western areas and a moral primacy universally. The powerful personality of pope Leo the Great, which we will discuss below, contributed much to the acceptance of an "apostolic" and "Petrine" papacy throught the West. In the East, resistance to such an interpretation of Roman primacy will be firm though not always consistent.

CHAPTER III

SPIRITUAL LIFE:
LITURGY, MONASTICISM, THE SAINTS

The transition of the Christian Church from the status of a persecuted minority to that of an official state religion was largely completed by 451 A.D. The change inevitably influenced all aspects of the Christian life, as it had influenced church organization. However, changes in the liturgy, in sacramental practice, in church architecture, in iconography—as well as the variations in religious and social consciousness, which these changes reflected—were largely spontaneous developments. Church legislation never pretended to codify the process completely, except in the field of penitential discipline.

In all major urban centers of the Empire, the patterns of Christian worship, replacing the old pagan cults, were now determined by the needs of crowds filling church-buildings, erected at lavish expense to accommodate thousands of worshippers. It was inevitable that, from the fourth to the sixth centuries, such city-churches would develop what scholars have called a "cathedral" rite,[1] which included features clearly distinct from the elements inherited from pre-Constantinian Christianity. In the same period, however, in the Egyptian, Palestinian or Syrian deserts, other thousands of Christians were establishing another pattern of worship: the monastic liturgical *ordo,* which then stood parallel to, and often in competition with, the "cathedral" rite. It also corresponded to a different type of spirituality and to the particular requirements of monastic communities.

In the major centers of Christianity, new liturgical traditions emerged. In the East, Antioch, Alexandria, and the pilgrimage-oriented

[1]Cf. A. Baumstark, *Liturgie comparée,* Chevetogne, 1953, p. 124.

communities of Palestine created distinct liturgical forms. In the West, the Roman church had its own changing tradition, somewhat different from the practices prevailing in Milan, in Gaul, and in Spain. However, it is not the variety of liturgical practices which is really remarkable, but rather the ongoing continuity with primitive Christianity, and the preservation of a basic unity, especially in the celebration of the central mysteries of Christianity: baptism and the eucharistic meal.

1. *The liturgical traditions: unity in diversity*

The early and widespread adoption of the Greek term "liturgy" (λειτουργία) to designate the corporate worship of the Christian communities is significant in itself. The existing secular meaning of the term referred to actions which involved the life of a community as a whole—e.g. a Greek city, or *polis*—actions which, therefore, were of interest to all its members and thus determined the responsible self-understanding of the group. A Christian "liturgy" could not, therefore, be reduced to either piety alone, or to the social aspects of community life. It involved life as such, and signified its continuity with the past, its present identity and its future destiny. Within a Christian context, this meant that the liturgy had to express the life of the Church, the apostolic tradition preserved by it and the eschatological expectation of the Second Coming of Christ. It is understandable, therefore, that the liturgical and sacramental nature of the Christian assembly determined the character and the functions of the various ministries, especially the episcopate (cf. *supra,* pp. 41-2).

This central and determining role of the liturgy was universal in the Christian Church before and after the establishment of Christianity under Constantine. The historical and comparative study of liturgical traditions, which followed the systematic publications of texts in the last century, contributed greatly to a better understanding of theology, ecclesiology and spirituality in the early Christian centuries.[2] Among Roman Catholic scholars, this interest in ancient liturgies arose, partly, as a reaction against the idea prevailing for centuries in the West, that the medieval Latin tradition of worship, as sanctioned by the Roman magisterium during the period of Counter-Reformation (sixteenth

---

[2]See especially, the work of scholars like Dom Guéranger, A. Dmitrievsky, J. A. Jungmann, J. M. Hanssens, S. Salaville, A. Raes, B. Botte, A. Baumstark, and others.

century), is the only legitimate form of worship in the Catholic Church. Rejecting this simplistic view, contemporary comparative study of the liturgy often tends to emphasize the *diversity* of traditions, insisting on the judicial independence of distinct "rites,"[3] an approach which would be anachronistic as far as the ancient church is concerned. In Antiquity and the early Middle Ages, local bishops, and particularly the heads of major religious centers, were each empowered to change local usages, but local traditions remained very open to the practices of sister-churches.

In fact, around 450 A.D., there was enough uniformity in the common liturgical tradition for clergy of all the major ecclesiastical centers—Rome, Constantinople, Alexandria, and Antioch—to celebrate the Eucharist together, as can be ascertained, for example, from the descriptions found in conciliar acts. Furthermore, such frequent contacts and concelebrations led to direct borrowings, or more subbtle cross-fertilizations. Thus, Constantinople adopted much of the tradition of Antioch, as did the Christian communities in East-Syria, which had been conquered by the Persians. Alexandria and Rome developed common features; and eventually, the Egyptian church also borrowed its eucharistic canons from Antioch. Eastern influences significantly modified the liturgy in Gaul, and finally, in the early Middle Ages, the liturgies of Rome and Constantinople acquired, in their respective spheres, the character of trans-clutural and, therefore, truly "catholic" vehicles of the common tradition. When controversies involved liturgical rites—as, for example, certain canons of the council *in Trullo* (692), criticizing some Roman or Armenian practices—the debate was not about diversity as such, but about the theology or discipline implied by each rite (*e.g.* the relation between fasting and the Eucharist).[4]

There were indeed divisive factors in the Church of the fifth century, but this divisiveness was linguistic and cultural—and, eventually, doctrinal—but not liturgical. Even after the Nestorian and the Monophysite schisms in the East, the dissidents fully maintained liturgical traditions constituted before the schism and preserved

[3]The official acknowledgement of the various "rites" by the Vatican authority implies a legalism, which was quite unknown in the early Church.

[4]Canon 52 of the council *in Trullo* forbids the celebration of the eucharistic liturgy during Lent—a prohibition which was ignored in the West—and criticized other practices, Latin and Armenian. Similarly, canons of African councils (393 and 397) warn against the adoption of trinitarian heresies, which might be contained in "foreign" eucharistic canons, but do not condemn either variety, or foreign influences *per se* (Mansi, III, 884, 895, 922).

them for centuries. However, the schism, and the later Muslim occupation, had a stifling effect on worship: change became suspect, and
external influences were frowned upon, so that "rites" were maintained
for their own sake, as the main expression of sectarian religious identity. This fixation of mutually independent "rites" is generally associated by historians of the liturgy with the sixth and seventh centuries.
The distinct and fixed "rites" constituted an important and unchangeable link with the apostolic and catholic past, but were hardly meant
to reflect unity and catholicity *in the present,* as was still clearly the
case earlier, within the flexible and living diversity, which still existed
in the fifth century.

The fundamental unity of the Christian faith was probably best
reflected in the liturgy of Christian initiation—baptism, anointment
and eucharistic communion—which was celebrated in a largely uniform
manner throughout the universal church. In the second half of the
fourth century this uniformity is attested by four preserved collections
of pre-baptismal instructions, which also describe the appropriate
liturgical acts. These are the *Catechetical Homilies* of four eminent
bishops living in opposite ends of the empire: Cyril of Jerusalem,
Theodore of Mopsuestia, John Chrysostom and Ambrose of Milan.
Differing only in detail (*e.g.* the number and significance of pre-
baptismal, or post-baptismal anointments), the rituals described by
these four authors include exorcisms and instructions, spread throughout the weeks of Lent, and culminating in the baptismal liturgy of the
paschal night. Inherited from the pre-Constantinian era, the liturgy of
initiation was basically maintained in the following centuries, in spite
of the fact that the character and conditions of the Christian mission
and the catechumenate were changing quite radically.

Although the texts frequently affirm that a three-year "catechumenate"—or period of instruction—was a condition for admission
to Christian baptism, it is obvious that when Christianity became a state
religion and former pagan millions sought membership in the Church,
this discipline could not be maintained, except in principle. On the
other hand, the existence of the catechumenate—i.e. that of a specific
category of prospective Christians—gave many a convenient reason for
postponing baptism (and the strict disciplinary, moral and sacramental
requirements presupposed by it) until adulthood or, very frequently,
until the last hours before death. Emperor Constantine himself and his
immediate successors followed that pattern, as well as many state

officials, a practice strongly criticized by St John Chrysostom.[5] Indeed, his predecessor Nectarius, in 381, but also the great St Ambrose of Milan in 373 (both former state functionaries) had to be baptized urgently just before being elevated to the episcopate, as they had been elected while still catechumens. This situation made it necessary for the Church to establish two categories of catechumens: the larger group postponed baptism indefinitely, but another category, known as "those preparing for illumination" (Gr. οἱ πρὸς τὸ ἅγιον φώτισμα εὐτρεπιζόμενοι; Lat. *competentes,* or *electi*), who had registered for baptism during the nearest Easter night, was required to follow a special course of instruction during lent, and special prayers were said publicly for them.[6]

In the fifth century, the urgings voiced by most Church leaders in the East and in the West, in favor of infant baptism,[7] tended to reduce the number of adult catechumens, but the liturgy of Christian initiation remained basically the same, as shaped by the requirements of the earlier period. No special form of infant baptism was ever devised. On the other hand, the massive collective baptisms performed in Germanic, Celtic, or Slavic lands made little use of the ancient institution of the catechumenate, rendering it largely nominal.

In the fifth century, the central mystery of the Church—the Eucharist—was based, in all the churches, on a largely similar scheme consisting of a "liturgy of the Word," or *synaxis,* centered upon the reading of Scripture and preaching, and the sacramental part, which included the eucharistic prayer itself, or *anaphora.* The latter was based on the *berakah*—the Jewish prayer used by Jesus himself at the Last Supper—but included the Christian elements of the New Covenant. Chanted or recited aloud by the chief celebrant, and addressed to God the Father, the eucharistic prayer followed an initial dialogue with the congregation and normally included five main parts: 1) an act of thanksgiving and glorification (Lat. *praefatio*) for the divine *oikonomia,* or plan of creation and salvation; 2) the *Sanctus,* which had the congregation join the angelic choirs in proclaming the "holiness" of God; 3) the *anamnesis,* or commemoration of the Cross and resurrection of Christ, including a solemn repetition of the "words of

---

[5]*Cat. hom. ad illum,* 1, 1. PG 49, col. 223.

[6]Such prayers are still part of the contemporary Byzantine liturgy of the Presanctified Gifts, to be said in the second half of Lent.

[7]Cf. Gregory Naz. and Chrysostom in the East and, of course, St Augustine in the West.

institution" ("This is my Body . . .," "This is my blood . . ."); 4) the
epiclesis or invocation of the Holy Spirit upon the assembled people
and the offering of bread and wine, which gave a fully trinitarian
dimension to the prayer; and 5) an *intercession* for the living and the
dead.

The exact wording of the *anaphoras* varied, but the variations
remained within the same basic structures. The order of the parts
could change (*e.g.* the intercession and the *epiclesis* could occur before
the *anamnesis*). Some churches gave greater development to some parts
or, as in the West, adopted a whole series of "prefaces," which varied
with the church calendar. The *epiclesis* was either "consecratory"—i.e.
it included a formal prayer asking the Father to send His Spirit to
"change" the bread and wine into the Body and Blood of Christ—or
it simply requested salvation for the recipients of the sacrament. The
absence of the *epiclesis* in the Roman liturgy gave pretext to bitter
controversy with the Greeks in the late Middle Ages.

Tracing such variations, historians of the liturgy generally assign
the role of a major center to the church of Antioch, which influenced
decisively the liturgical traditions of the other Eastern churches. Also
designated as "West Syrian," the Antiochian tradition used a number
of *anaphoras*. It adopted the so-called *Liturgy of St James* (perhaps
importing it from Jerusalem) and the *Anaphora of the Twelve
Apostles,* which certain Antiochene clerics (St John Chrysostom, Nestorius) had brought to the imperial city when they moved there before
431, and which served as a model for the short medieval Byzantine
anaphora, known as "Liturgy of St John Chrysostom." But Constantinople also preserved the *Liturgy of St Basil,* originating from Cappadocia. Distinct liturgical traditions existed also in East Syria. They were
preserved exclusively in Syriac, and are sometimes considered as most
archaic (the *Liturgy of Addai and Mari*). This tradition was maintained by the Nestorian church in Persia, and transmitted to its
daughter-church in India (Malabar). However, the Nestorians also
accepted some "West-Syrian," or Antiochian eucharistic canons, translated from the Greek. Alexandria maintained a local *anaphora,* known
as *Liturgy of St Mark* (also attributed by some manuscripts to St
Cyril), but the Egyptian church soon adopted a parallel use of the
Greek (Antiochian) liturgies of St Basil and St Gregory the Theologian.[8] These were passed on from Alexandria to the church of Ethiopia,

[8]In all Eastern traditions, the attribution of eucharistic prayers to individual apostles,

which added to its usage several local *anaphoras,* whose exact origins are sometimes difficult to ascertain.

In the midst of great cultural pluralism and in the absence of an administrative center which would regulate liturgical practice authoritatively, the unity in content and basic structure of the various eucharistic prayers can only be explained by the frequent contacts between the communities, by their sharing of a single theological inspiration, and their sense of belonging to the one catholic tradition of the Church.

In the West, there was less linguistic pluralism than in the East. The only challenge to the *Latin* expression of the Christian tradition came from the Goths, who used a Gothic Bible and the Gothic language in worship. Both were inherited from Ulfilas, who had been consecrated *Arian* bishop in Constantinople in 341, and thus became the father of Gothic Arianism. The "Gothic religion" was, for a time, passed on to the Gepids, the Vandals of Africa, the Alans, the Burgundians, the Suevi of Spain, and the Lombards of Italy. But the conversion of all these tribes to Catholic Christianity, in the sixth and seventh centuries, restricted their cultural originality, so that Latin became the only language of worship. But linguistic unity did not imply liturgical uniformity.

In the fifth century, two major liturgical traditions became dominant: the Roman, largely adopted also in Italy and in Africa, and the Gallican, with ramifications in Spain and the Celtic lands. While the Gallican tradition—perhaps as a reaction against Gothic Arianism—adopted many trinitarian features coming from the East, the Roman church tended to emphasize more exclusively the mediation of Christ, which explains the absence of an *epiclesis* in the Roman canon of the mass (although one existed at the time of Hippolytus in the third century).

The development of the Roman liturgy during our period is relatively well known. The so-called "Leonine," "Gelasian" and "Gregorian" *sacramentaries* are compilations of sacramental prayers attributed respectively to popes Leo I (440-61), Gelasius (492-96) and Gregory I (590-604). Being in fact of later origin, the "Gregorian" sacramentary, although undoubtedly associated with the liturgical activities of Gregory I, reflects later and more rigid forms, fixed at the time of pope Gregory II (715-31). They were preserved in the West practically

or saints, is conventional. However, there is reason to admit the direct authorship of St Basil for the Constantinopolitan liturgy, known under that name.

until the reforms of Vatican II. In addition, the so-called *Ordines Romani,* dating essentially from the seventh century, give detailed descriptions of the ceremonial, of the rubrics, processions, and other rituals performed in Rome.

Eventually, the practice of the Roman church was adopted throughout the Latin West. This liturgical centralization started as a free and organic process, in every way similar to the influence of the Constantinopolitan liturgy in the East. Before the eighth century, one knows of no attempts by Roman popes to impose liturgical uniformity, or even to give liturgical advice, except when requested by other Western bishops.

In the consciousness of fifth-century Christians, the Eucharist remained very much the central mystery of the faith and the criterion of membership in the Church. Communion of the laity at each celebration—except for those formally excommunicated—remained the general norm, as described and encouraged by St Basil.[9] But practices were changing, since St John Chrysostom is already forced to criticize those who abstain from communion, claiming "unworthiness."[10] Indeed, the great crowds which filled the huge basilicas of the post-Constantinian era inevitably acted more like spectators than participants. If catechumens typically left before the *anaphora,* the new and more lenient penitential discipline allowed for the emergence of the category of "hearers," who attended the eucharistic liturgy without sacramental participation.[11] These and other facts show that the Church itself became concerned with protecting the Mystery from a laity, whose membrship had ceased to be restricted to responsible, informed and committed Christians. Soon lay persons were not allowed any more (except for the emperor) to receive the Body of Christ in the hands, and drink from the Cup. In Constantinople, since the seventh century communion was given to the laity with a special spoon. In the West, eventually—and for the same reasons—communion began to be dis-

9"It is good and beneficial to communicate every day . . . I indeed communicate four times a week," *Letter* 93, ed. Deferrari, III, 145. Daily communion was also the norm among the monks in Egypt and, in the sixth century, in Palestine (cf. texts in A. J. Festugière, *Les Moines d'Orient,* Paris, 1961, III, 1, p. 89; IV, 1, pp. 59-62, 126, etc.)

10*Hom. in Eph* III, 4, PG 62, col. 20; cf. also Cyril of Alexandria, *Com. on John* IV, 2, PG 73, cols. 584-5.

11This category included for example the large number of people under temporary penitential excommunication, such as those engaged in a second or third marriage (see above pp. 9-11).

tributed under one species only. This is also the reason why—in the East particularly—the liturgical forms gradually came to be viewed as a system of symbols manifesting heavenly realities to a reverently watching assembly, including those who did not partake of the sacrament. This process occurred between the fifth and the seventh centuries. The writings attributed to St Dionysius the Areopagite, especially his *Ecclesiastical Hierarchy* (later fifth century), are the best witnesses of that development. Liturgical worship remained a corporate act, which was seen as including heavenly and earthly realities, but the act of partaking of the Body and Blood of Christ could now be interpreted as a matter of individual readiness, or choice.[12]

With the establishment of the celebration of Christmas in the fourth century, a yearly liturgical calendar was developed concurrently with the paschal cycle. It befitted the pastoral need to give Christian worship a more dramatic and spectacular character, able to secure the interest and participation of the large congregations in the major cities. With the confirmation by the council of Ephesus (431) of the title of *Theotokos,* or Mother of God, for the Virgin Mary, an added impulse was given to the development of a "Marian" cycle of feasts, with the West generally following Eastern initiative. This new insistence on the liturgical commemoration of individual biblical events— or, in the case of the Virgin, of events like her Nativity, or "Repose" (κοίμησις), which were not reported in canonical Scriptures—was now accompanied with the cult of saints, predominantly martyrs, but also, soon, holy monks, military saints, or other holy people. The commemorative, representative, or dramatic requirements of these new liturgical celebrations led in the West to the composition of special "prefaces" for the *anaphora* to be celebrated on each particular day, as found in the Roman *sacramentaries.* The East, on the contrary, kept a fixed and unchangeable eucharistic canon, but witnessed rich growth of hymnography. The "cathedral" rite of the major city churches, by adopting hymnography, became even more clearly distinct from the office cele-

---

[12]This does not mean, of course, that the post-medieval practice for laity to partake only once to four times a year came immediately into being. Regular participation in communion remained the norm both in the East and the West. In Rome, the paten, on which the eucharistic bread was placed for distribution to the people, was big enough to be carried by two clerics (*Ordo* I, 103, ed. M. Andrieu, "Les *ordines romani,*" *Spicilegium sacrum lovaniense,* 11, Louvain, 1931). This information can be compared with the evidence furnished by the enormous size of contemporary Byzantine liturgical vessels. (Cf. in particular K. Weitzman ed., *The Age of Spirituality. Late Antique and Early Christian Art, Third to Seventh Century.* Princeton University Press, 1979, pp. 592-619).

brated in the monastic communities, where recitation of psalms remained the almost exclusive form of corporate worship.[13]

In terms of hymnographic development, Syria's influence was as decisive as its role in modelling the eucharistic canons (see above, p. 72). Following a Syrian poetic tradition which goes back to the fourth century (especially St Ephrem), a great poet, Romanos the Melode, came to Constantinople from Antioch in the first half of the sixth century and became the famous author of *Kontakia,* long rhythmic poems, involving a cantor, whose recitation was accompanied by the congregation singing a refrain. The pattern was adopted from the responsorial or antiphonal recitation of psalms in the cathedral rites. Easy to memorize and didactic in content, the *Kontakia* of Romanos received great popularity and served as the nucleus for the late hymnographic developments in Byzantium. The latter in turn—thanks to the mediation of Byzantine settlements in Italy (6th-11th cc.)—influenced the Latin church as well. In general, however, the West was much more reluctant than the East to replace psalms, and other biblical texts, with newly composed hymns. In Spain, the first council of Braga (563) expressly forbade the use of hymns, so that the council of Toledo (633) had to justify the practice, which was becoming general, in spite of the Braga prohibition.

2. *Liturgy and art*

In the fifth century, the Christian Church was in a position to dominate cultural development within the empire, and its liturgy served as the main framework, within which musicians, architects, mosaicists, painters, and other categories of artists, exercised their talents, frequently with imperial patronage. It is precisely the liturgy which gave an inner spiritual coherence and theological meaning to the various forms of art: the *cult* was thus creating a *culture,* which will be that of the Christian Middle Ages, East and West, and which—as distinct from the secularized culture of modernity—viewed spirit and matter, beauty and wisdom, heaven and earth, as united in the resurrected and deified humanity of Jesus Christ, and manifested not only in Him as a historical person, but also in the Saints, in the sacramental nature of the Church

---

[13]In Byzantium, extensive use of hymnography in monasteries will come about only after the eighth century.

and in the entire creation, restored to its original purpose of reflecting the eternal Wisdom of God.

The emerging forms of Christian art re-present this spiritual and theological world view.

Music was one form of art which was essential to liturgical action, but it is also the aspect of early Christian culture about which we know the least. The earliest musical signs deciphered by modern scholars belong to the later medieval period. However, by using indirect evidence, musicologists have established the fact that Christian liturgical music was rooted primarily in the tradition of the Jewish synagogue, whereas hellenistic elements were adopted only gradually and in a subsidiary way.[14] This fact becomes fully understandable when one remembers that the Christian Church used the Jewish Psalter as its principal hymnbook, and that the Jewish *berakah* was the basis of the Christian eucharistic prayer. Since, in the ancient world, poetry and music were always transmitted together, it was natural that synagogal musical forms be adopted by Christians together with texts and other forms of worship. Furthermore, as we have mentioned in the preceding sub-chapter, the earliest forms of original Christian hymnography came from Syria, where the semitic Syro-Aramaic literary traditions were close to those of late Judaism.

In the Christian liturgy, East and West, only vocal and monophonic music was used until the end of the Middle Ages. Instrumental music was seen as inconsistent with the New Testament idea of the Church as Body of Christ, which offers to God not material, but living sacrifices, and, in the case of music, live human voices. Music was understood not as an end in itself, but as an expression of human togetherness in prayer and as a means of using liturgical texts more clearly and more meaningfully. In the East, the imperial capital of Constantinople integrated other existing musical traditions in a single prevailing "Byzantine" tradition. In the West, textual evidence points to the existence of old Frankish, Gallican, Mozarabic (Spain) and Ambrosian (Milan) traditions, which were superseded by the so-called Gregorian chant, associated with the name of pope Gregory I (590-604). Modern research has demonstrated more parallels than contrasts between the Byzantine and the Gregorian musical traditions. This

---

[14]The classic, though partly superseded study on the subject, is by E. A. Wellesz, *A History of Byzantine Music and Hymnography,* 2nd ed., Oxford, 1961, cf. also E. Werner, *The Sacred Bridge,* London-New York, 1959.

parallelism and common origin are further illustrated by the existence, both in the East and in the West, of a system of eight "tones," or *modes,* for the performance of hymns, proper to each liturgical time, or season.

The continuity between the Jewish and the Christian musical traditions has no parallel in the representative, or pictorial field. With important exceptions in the late period (notably the third-century synagogue of Dura-Europos, Syria, which presented a clear parallel with early Christian art), the Jewish faith adhered to the Old Testament prohibition of "graven images." Christianity, by contrast, was based on the doctrine of a God, who made himself visible and, therefore, representable in the Incarnation: "Who has seen Me, has seen the Father" (John 14:9). Within the Church, some "iconoclastic" trends seem to have existed from the beginning (and would eventually result in the iconoclastic movement of the eighth century), but, since Constantine and with widespread imperial patronage, images representing Christ, the Virgin Mary, martyrs and saints, as well as biblical scenes from the Old and New Testaments, sometimes used symbolically, appeared practically everywhere. By the middle of the fifth century, there were established patterns of representative Christian art, closely linked to the liturgy and to private piety as well.

There was no ambiguity among Christians as to the purpose of art: "There were no Christian images made for the sake of producing a pretty fresco or an appealing figurine or genre scene. Indeed, we know of no such art for art's sake."[15] But, at the same time, in order to meet the need for didactic representation, theological definition, or mystical contemplation, Christian artists used the forms available in the Greco-Roman society which surrounded them. Indeed, this society was not "iconoclastic," like the Judaic tradition, from which Christians had inherited their Scriptures and liturgy; on the contrary, it was "iconic" throughout, using images constantly, as means of communicating religious, or other ideas.

It is a fact, therefore, that "from its beginnings, Christian imagery found expression entirely, almost uniquely, in the general language of the visual arts and with the techniques of imagery commonly practiced within the Roman Empire."[16] But it is also obvious that, from the fifth

---

[15]André Grabar, *Christian Iconography. A Study of its Origins.* The A. W. Mellon Lectures in Fine Arts, 1961, Princeton, 1968, Introduction, p. XLIX.
[16]*Ibid.,* p. XLIII.

to the seventh centuries, the style and the character of Christian art gradually modified the traditions inherited from Antiquity to acquire a different and typically Christian identity. This process parallels the development of the theological language which also used Greek concepts and terms to designate a totally different, Christian content. This does not mean necessarily that, in the seventh century, art was "more Christian" than in the fifth, but that pagan Antiquity, to which the Christian message was originally addressed and into which it had to become "incarnate," had ceased to be a source of active inspiration: it was replaced by the Christian Middle Ages.

Of course, this "incarnation" of the Christian message into the artistic language of Antiquity was deliberately selective. Only those iconographic concepts, which were applicable to Christian topics, events, and ideas were integrated into Christian art. For example, the "triumphal" iconography, used to depict imperial victories, was used in the mosaic of the arch in the church of Santa Maria Maggiore in Rome (*ca.* 430), as well as on the famous eschatological, beardless image of Christ—Emmanuel in the apse of S. Vitale, in Ravenna (sixth c.), and on the apse-mosaic of the Transfiguration at the monastery on Mt. Sinai (sixth century). In all these and many similar cases, the artistic language of the pagan imperial cult was applied to the eschatological Christ, coming in power. And then too, the more spiritualized forms of late Hellenistic art, inspired by Neo-Platonism and applicable to the biblical idea of a transcendent 'God,' were also directly borrowed by Christian artists. This selectivity and, of course, the distinctly Christian subjects being represented, gradually disclosed essential differences between pagan and Christian art. This evolution shows that the Christian Church initially adopted an artistic language which contemporary society could understand but eventually, since its message was quite distinct from that of paganism, new Christian forms and methods of communications were brought into play.

The use of mosaic—an expensive and durable form of art, inherited from ancient Rome by the established imperial Church—has preserved exquisite monuments of Christian art from the fifth to the seventh centuries in churches of Rome, Ravenna, Thessalonica, Mt. Sinai, and elsewhere. But many portable objects of art—illustrated books, sculptures and icons—have also survived. It does appear that it is the fifth century—notably after the council of Ephesus (431), and other definitions which centered on the Incarnation—that saw the beginning of a really popular veneration of images of Christ, the Virgin and saints. The cult of an icon of the Virgin, known as *Hodegetria* ("The Leader-on-the-way") which was adopted as a palladium protecting Constantinople, originated during the reign of Theodosius II (408-450).

Imperial patronage bestowed upon the Church by Constantine and his successors resulted in extraordinary architectural programs in both the Old and the New Romes, in other major cities and at pilgrimage-centers like Bethlehem and Jerusalem. Extensive church building continued in the fifth and the sixth centuries.

Functionally, a Christian church building served as the general meeting place of a local congregation for the celebration of the Eucharist. This function was clearly distinct from that of a pagan temple, centered around the statue of a god, to which sacrifices were offered individually. This explains why the architectural models, used for Christian places of worship, were secular. The most widely used model was that of a *basilica,* used previously in building large meeting places, especially halls for imperial audiences, or court sessions. The basilica was a rectangular structure with a roof supported by ranks of columns leading to an apse, a semi-circular podium covered by a semi-dome. Sitting or standing in the apse, the presiding personage—the emperor, the judge, or, in a church, the bishop—dominated the assembly. The altar table was placed between him and the congregation.

In each city—big or small—a single main church served as the regular place for the celebration of the Eucharist by the local bishop. The other churches were generally located at the burial place of a saint, or a martyr, hence the designation of such churches as *martyria*.[17] But *martyria* were also built to commemorate the place of a miracle (e.g. Santa Maria Maggiore in Rome, built after 432), or to house important relics (church of the Holy Apostles, Constantinople, sixth century). In Rome, the main church, built by Constantine, was located near the Lateran palace, the residence of the bishop, whereas St Peter's, St Paul-outside-the-Walls, St Mary Major were the main *martyria*. In Antioch and Constantinople, the popular designation of the episcopal cathedral was "Great Church," because of its great size and beauty. The *Domus Aurea* ("golden house") or "Great Church" of Antioch was built by Constantine and Constantius. It was octagonal in shape and cov-

[17]Cf. A. Grabar, *Martyrium: Recherches sur le culte des reliques et l'art chrétien,* 2 vols., Paris, 1943-6.

ered with a hemispheric dome.[18] This model may have inspired the architects commissioned by Justinian to build a new cathedral for the imperial capital, to replace the old basilica dedicated to Christ, as "Wisdom of God" (*Sophia*), which had been burned down during the Nika rebellion (531). The new St Sophia, completed in 537, was an original architectural creation, where the structures of a longitudinal basilica and that of a centralized, domed building were combined. The "Great Church" of Constantinople became the wonder of the Christian world for centuries, and still stands today.

3. Development of monasticism.

In the fourth century, the monastic movement had arisen spontaneously, so that neither the leadership of the Church, nor the imperial administration was initially sure of its real place in the Church and in society. By the end of the century, however, wheat and chaff had been separated somehow. The extreme ascetics (Messalians, Euchites, Eustathians) who had condemned marriage as such, viewed sacraments as unnecessary and, in fact, had used the monastic vocation to create a separate church, were formally condemned at the councils of Gangra (*ca.* 340) and Side (*ca.* 390). But the authority and the example of the great Egyptian models of monastic life—St Anthony, the father of hermits, and St Pachomius, the creator of the *coenobium,* or community life—remained unassailable. The great St Athanasius himself had written the *Life of St Anthony.* St Basil—independently of Pachomius— had defined the spiritual principles of community life. The "sayings" of the Egyptian Fathers (cf. the collections knows as *Apophthegmata Patrum*) had become universally popular. Palladius of Hellenopolis had published his *Lausiac History* of monks. St Jerome and his disciple Rufinus had popularized the ideas of Palestinian and Egyptian monasticism in the Latin language. Similar hagiographical literature continued to appear in the fifth century, *e.g.* the *Philotheos Historia* on Syrian monasticism by Theodoret of Cyrus.

This extraordinary popularity of monastic literature and the large number of men and women who were following the monastic calling did not mean that all spiritual and doctrinal problems, connected with monastic life, had been solved. The "messalian" deviation of the

[18]Cf. G. Downey. *A History of Antioch in Syria,* Princeton, 1961, pp. 342-46.

monastic ideal had been eliminated in principle. But the ideas of Origen, based on Neo-Platonism and interpreting spirituality in terms of a return of the mind to a primeval state of contemplation, remained popular. They implied the pre-existence of souls and excluded the biblical doctrine of creation. The fact that they had been promoted by one of the intellectual leaders of Egyptian monasticism, Evagrius Ponticus (d. 399), provoked bitter conflict in Alexandria and in Constantinople in 400-404, involving St John Chrysostom himself.

Thus, by the time of the council of Chalcedon (451), monasticism had become a universally admired ideal and also an institution, acknowledged in its eremitic, coenobitic and several intermediary forms, by conciliar decrees and imperial legislation. Also, throughout the fifth, the sixth and the seventh centuries monks, whose numbers kept increasing prodigiously, would take an active part in doctrinal disputes, connected primarily with christology, but also with Origenism.

In Egypt, the coenobitic rule of St Pachomius continued to be followed not only at Tabennisi, in Upper Egypt, where it had been established by the founder, but also in the Eastern suburbs of Alexandria, within the Nile delta, where archbishop Theophilus built the monastery of *Metanoia* ("Penitence"), near Canopus (*ca.* 390). This monastery seems to have remained Chalcedonian during the fifth and sixth-century controversies. The so-called "White" and "Red" monasteries, across the Nile from Tabennisi, were purely Coptic communities. Their great leader Shenute of Atripe followed the Pachomian rule; he also imposed upon his monks a most rigorous asceticism, inspired by the eremitic tradition. Shenute became an impetuous supporter not only of St Cyril at Ephesus (431), but also of Dioscoros, at the "Robber council" of 449. Equally involved in the opposition against Chalcedon were the more than sixty monastic foundations in the desert to the south of Alexandria. These were following the anchoretic pattern, and included the ancient shrines of the founders of monasticism: Nitria, Cellia, Scete,[19] and others.

Following the Muslim conquest of Egypt in the seventh century, these monasteries survived in the fold of the Coptic church, which became monolithically opposed to Byzantine Chalcedonian orthodoxy. Some of these communities are experiencing a remarkable period of revival in our own time.

[19]The names of these early settlements were adopted universally as common designation: a "cell" (Gr. κελλίον), or skete (a hermit's dwelling).

In Syria and Mesopotamia, where most Christians spoke Syriac—a language, close to the Aramaic used in Palestine at the time of Christ—the roots of monasticism go deep into the extreme asceticism of the Encratite movement (second century) and, in the opinion of some scholars, directly into Manichean dualism.[20] Whether or not the connection was direct, it is certainly no accident that Mani himself (216-277) belonged in his youth to the Jewish-Christian community of the *baptistai* in Southern Babylonia under Persian rule. Radical ascetic trends existed within Jewish circles at the time of Christ. Both early Manicheism and the ideals of permanent celibacy, promoted very early among Syrian Christians, may have grown on the same receptive soil.[21]

Of course, the "great" tradition of the Christian Church rejected such extremism, especially at the council of Gangra (*ca.* 340). The council was held in Cappadocia, where the tradition of inordinate asceticism, coming from neighboring Syria and Mesopotamia, had inspired the "encratite," "messalian" and, later, "eustathian" sectarians. The canons of Gangra specifically condemned those who considered marriage as evil, and, in particular, rejected the married priesthood.[22] The same moderate and positive attitude towards marriage was expressed in the so-called *Syrian Didascalia,* a fourth-century disciplinary collection. However, the two great Syrian spiritual writers of the fourth century, Aphrahat and St Ephrem, while accepting the possibility of admitting married couples to baptism, still viewed sexual abstinence as normative after baptism for all committed members of the Church.[23] Obviously, the monastic ideal was considered as the only criterion of true Christianity, and the most popular model of the Christian life, for simple people as well as intellectuals. Theodoret mentions the existence of coenobitic communities of monks,[24] but, in his descriptions, he

[20]Cf. particularly A. Vööbus, *History of Asceticism in the Syrian Orient, I: The Origin of Asceticism: Early Monasticism in Persia,* Louvain, 1960 (= CSCO 184).

[21]Robert Murray, *Symbols of Church and Kingdom. A Study in early Syriac Tradition,* Cambridge, 1975, p. 17-18.

[22]On the somewhat ambivalent attitude of St Basil the Great towards the council of Gangra, and the history of monasticism in Eastern Asia Minor, see the works of J. Gribomont, now conveniently gathered in a single volume in *St Basile, Evangile et Eglise. Mélanges.* I, Bellefontaine, 1984. See also J. Meyendorff, "St Basil, Messalianism and Byzantine Christianity," SVQ, 24, 1980, pp. 219-234 (repr. in *The Byzantine Legacy in the Orthodox Church,* Crestwood, NY, 1982, pp. 197-215).

[23]See the texts in A. Vööbus, *Celibacy, a requirement for admission to baptism in the early Syrian Church,* Stockholm, 1951; cf. also his *History of Asceticism,* pp. 93-5, 175-8.

[24]See, for example, *Hist. philoth.* 27, PG 82, col. 1484 C.

dwells almost exclusively on hermits who practice the most severe forms of asceticism: some live without ever sleeping under a roof, without using fire or artificial light; some never eat or drink cooked food; some bind their feet, lock themselves in cages, wear chains and artificially maintain flesh wounds on their bodies. Theodoret also emphasizes the great diversity of such ascetical attitudes: the monk is always alone with God, and his efforts to reach Him are his own, unhampered by external rules, or disciplines.

Perhaps the most extraordinary form of Syrian asceticism is shown by the "Stylites" (from Gr. στύλος, "column"). The most famous among them was St Symeon who, with the permission of the abbot of his monastery near Antioch, lived for forty-seven years (412-459) in a little hut built on top of a column, or pillar, from where he preached to thousands coming to see him. Another younger "stylite," also named Symeon, followed his example for sixty-eight years.

During the christological disputes of the fifth and sixth centuries, a majority of Syrian monks followed the "Monophysite" opposition to the council of Chalcedon. The lives of these anti-Chalcedonian ascetics are described in detail by the famous historian John of Ephesus (d. *ca.* 595-6), who attributed the survival of the "true faith" in Syria to their zeal.[25] Indeed, their ascetic struggle against cosmic evil and the fallen flesh may have instinctively driven many monks to a christological position which stressed the Divinity of the Savior at the expense of His humanity. As a contrast, the Nestorian church, whose membership was of the same Syrian background but which followed the most sophisticated, hellenistic school of Theodore of Mopsuestia, adopted a more liberal policy in sexual morals, approving of married bishops and re-married priests, and, for a time at least, saw its monastic tradition deteriorating. However, not all Syrian monks were polarized between "Monophysite" and "Nestorian" attitudes. Some, like the great St Symeon the Stylite, as well as St Symeon "the Younger" (d. 596) were Orthodox Chalcedonians and their beliefs played a decisive role in maintaining the Chalcedonian faith in Western Syria and in Palestine.

Another aspect of Syrian monasticism, which should mitigate one's impression of its somewhat eccentric asceticism, is its missionary concern. The efforts of monks to convert pagans are noted by all sources, and the extraordinary expansion of Christianity beyond the

25Cf. his *Lives of Eastern Saints*, ed. and tr. E. W. Brooks, in *PO*, 17-19 (1923-5).

Eastern borders of the Empire is almost entirely the work of Syrians. It will be examined in the next chapter.

Palestinian monastic communities, although created in great numbers already in the fourth century, acquired great prominence and influence in the fifth and the sixth. Although influenced by both Syrian and Egyptian models, Palestine—a natural passageway between Syria and Egypt, and a great center of pilgrimages—developed a more international, more "catholic" and generally speaking, more harmonious vision of the monastic life, without abandoning anything of the ascetic ideal itself. In 429, St Euthymius (d. 473) founded his first *lavra* near Jerusalem. The term *lavra* designated a settlement of monks living in separate individual, or semi-individual cells, but recognizing a single abbot (or *archimandrite*) and gathering together on Saturdays, Sundays and feast days for the Eucharist. An East-Syrian himself, St Euthymius gathered Syrian, Cappadocian, Egyptian and even "Roman" monks within his community. One of his monks, a Cappadocian, was the great St Sabas (439-532), who eventually founded his own *lavra* in the Palestinian desert East of Jerusalem. His personal holiness, his sense of leadership and involvement in general church affairs made him one of the greatest monastic personalities of all times. His tenure was stormy, however, and included a bitter fight against a part of his community, who adopted the views of Origen and seceded to form a "New Lavra," near Bethlehem (508). In the person of St Theodosius (d. 529)—another Cappadocian—Palestinian monasticism also found a leader of strict community life: his *coenobium,* to the East of Bethlehem, was a model imitated by many. With the exception of a brief fall of St Theodosius into the Monophysite camp (from which he recovered), all the leaders of Palestinian monasticism were Orthodox Chalcedonians. In 516, during the anti-Chalcedonian reaction which marked the reign of emperor Anastasius, a crowd of ten thousand monks, led by Sabas and Theodosius, forced a vacillating patriarch John of Jerusalem, who had previously rejected Chalcedon, to reaffirm his faithfulness to the Council and anathematize Nestorius, Eutyches, Severus of Antioch and Soterichus of Caesarea-in-Cappadocia, as heretics.[26] The only major Palestinian monastic personality to adopt a consistently—and heroic—anti-Chalcedonian attitude is Peter the "Iber-

---

[26]Palestinian monasticism of that period is known to us through the remarkable *Lives* of St Sabas, St Euthymius, St Theodosius, and other personalities, composed by a contemporary, Cyril of Scythopolis. Cf. a French tr., and study of these *Lives* in A. J. Festugière, *Les Moines d'Orient,* Paris, 1961. Cf. also D. J. Chitty, *The Desert a City.*

ian" (or Georgian), a teacher of Severus of Antioch and the founder of a Georgian monastery in Jerusalem, before becoming bishop of Gaza (452).

In all parts of the Christian world, the monastic models of Egypt, Syria and Palestine found thousands of enthusiastic adepts. Following the multicultural traditions of the Palestinian *lavras,* the hermits living on the Sinai peninsula, eventually settled into a big monastery for which Justinian built a fortress and a remarkable basilica-shaped church, decorated with mosaics (556-7). The monastery, later dedicated to St Catherine, was built on the spot thought to be the place where God spoke to Moses in a burning bush. The library of the monastery—which still exists today, reflecting the international composition of the brotherhood—contains Greek, Latin, Syriac, Coptic, Armenian, Georgian and Slavic manuscripts, and its collection of icons is the most ancient and representative in the world. Towards the end of the sixth century, Sinai produced several eminent spiritual writers including John, author of the *Ladder of Paradise* and Anastasius, who later became patriarch of Antioch (559-70, 593-9). Medieval Byzantine hesychasm—the eremitic tradition of the Jesus prayer—is frequently associated with the Sinai tradition, although the term "hesychast" and the Evagrian concept of "pure prayer" were used universally to define eremitic monastic spirituality.

Gradually, the monastic movement established itself in cities as well. In 446, in Constantinople, the "archimandrite" Eutyches became the spokesman of Monophysitism. In 518, the abbots of sixty-seven monasteries of the capital signed a Chalcedonian *libellus,* demanded by pope Hormisdas. The city monasteries included the community of the so-called "Non-Sleepers" (*Akoimetai*), which had been established in Constantinople by a Syrian, Alexander, in 405. The "Non-Sleepers" became quite active and influential in the theological debates of the sixth century.

Most important historically, however, is the monastic expansion which spread from East to West. The steady contact between the various parts of Christian society within the Empire, made it inevitable that a movement as prominent as Eastern monasticism would find adepts in Latin speaking regions. St Jerome, and the community of learned and pious women which he directed in Rome and Bethlehem,

An Introduction to the Study of Egyptian and Palestinian Monasticism under the Christian Empire, London, 1966, repr. Crestwood, NY, n.d.

popularized Eastern monastic ideals. Eminent bishops, like St Ambrose of Milan, St Augustine of Hippo, St Paulinus of Nola supported both these ideals themselves and the groups of Christians who began to practice them spontaneously. In Gaul, St Martin, before being elected bishop of Tours (*ca.* 371), was the leader of a hermitage and as a bishop continued to be an example of asceticism, He inspired the development of monasticism, especially in the south of Gaul. It is there that St Honoratus established the famous monastery of Lérins (*ca.* 405-410). Bishops, like St Hilary of Arles and St Exuperius of Toulouse actively supported monastic communities. But the movement also encountered opposition, not only among pagans, but also in some Christian circles, including bishops. This opposition seems to have been stronger in Latin speaking countries, but it existed also in the East.[27] Around 386, the bishop of Avila in Spain, Priscillian, was beheaded in Trier, residence of the ursurper emperor Maximus, after having been condemned as a heretic by councils in Zaragoza and Bordeaux. The exact content of his teachings is difficult to ascertain today (they probably contained Gnostic and Manichean elements), but "Priscillianism" was closely associated with ascetic practices. After Priscillian's condemnation, such practices continued to be viewed with suspicion by the Spanish councils until the seventh century.

In order to gain full acceptance, as in the East, Latin monasticism needed an advocate who could express Eastern ascetic and spiritual ideals in their authentic Christian content, without the eccentricity of a St Jerome, and free from Manichean associations. Such an articulate advocate came in the person of St Cassian.

Born in a Romanized family in the Balkans (contemporary Dobrudsha), he joined monastic communities first near Bethlehem, then for ten years, at Scete in Egypt. Eventually he lived as a deacon in the entourage of St John Chrysostom in Constantinople, and was involved in ecclesiastical affairs. Emigrating to the West, he knew St Leo of Rome personally. He also became the founder of the monastery of St Victor in Marseille (which had a convent of nuns as

[27]St Jerome published special tracts against two Christian laymen, Helvidius and Jovinianus, and a priest, Vigilantius, who had attacked monastic asceticism. St John Chrysostom mentions cases when monks were hissed at in the streets of Antioch. In Constantinople, there was also opposition by bishops like Gregory of Nazianzus, Chrysostom and Flavian against the troublesome and extremist attitudes adopted by some monks (see especially G. Dagron, "Les moines et la ville," *Travaux et Mémoires,* 4 (1970), pp. 229-276.

a dependence). There, in 424-8, he wrote in Latin his two famous works on the monastic life, the *Institutes* and the *Conferences*. Describing in detail the principles of the coenobitic rule of Pachomius and the Evagrian ideals of the eremitic, contemplative life (which Cassian considers as superior to coenobitism), he attributes the founding of the monastic ideal not to the Egyptian Fathers, but to the apostles themselves. Thus, Cassian brought from the East the idea that monasticism is, in fact, identical with the Christian life itself, or rather that it is its most perfect and complete expression.[28] In writing about the spiritual life, Cassian followed the thought of Eastern Fathers, taking for granted the notion of "synergy," *i.e.* that Christian life requires cooperation between divine grace and human freedom. This concept clashed with the thought of St Augustine about "prevenient grace" and predestination. The polemics which developed around the issue before the death of Augustine (430) and of Cassian (*ca.* 433) were inconclusive. However, the later dominance of Augustinian thought in the West caused the name of Cassian to be found on a list of heretics, contained in an anonymous sixth century text misattributed to pope Gelasius (492-6). In it Cassian was associated with so-called "semi-Pelagianism." However, the local church of Marseille continued to venerate him as a saint, as the Orthodox Church still does today.

This unfortunate controversy had little effect on the decisive influence exercised by the writings of St John Cassian upon the most eminent leaders of monasticism in the West, including St Caesarius of Arles in particular. This is also the case of St Benedict, whose remarkable personality and achievements were made known through the *Dialogues* of pope Gregory the Great (590-604).

Born in Nursia, Benedict (*ca.* 480-*ca.* 547) started his monastic career as a hermit in Subiaco, south of Rome. Later he became the abbot of the famous monastery of Montecassino, where he wrote his *Rule,* borrowing generously from earlier sources, such as St Augustine, St Cassian, St Basil, and other Eastern models, available through Jerome's and Rufinus' translations.[29] Faithful to the spirit of his

[28]A. de Vogüé, "Monachisme et église dans la pensée de Cassien," in *Théologie de la vie monastique*, Paris, 1961, pp. 213-240, cf. also O. Chadwick, *John Cassian,* 2nd ed., Cambridge, 1968.

[29]Another anonymous monastic rule, known as the *Regula Magistri* ("Rule of the Master") appeared almost at the same time as the *Rule* attributed personally to St Benedict. It is more directly influenced by Cassian. Scholars are still unsure as to the exact relationship of the two rules and as to the personal role of St Benedict in their composition.

predecessors, St Benedict adds his own sense of order and of strict coenobitism, such as the requirement of "stability." A monk was required to stay for life in the community where he was tonsured (the Easterners were more inclined to travel and change).

The *Rule* of St Benedict, attractive through its christocentricism, its clarity and its faithfulness to tradition, tended to replace earlier Western monastic rules, including those brought to France by the Irish monk, St Columban (c. 543-615), the founder of the abbey of Luxeuil, in the Vosges, which became the mother-house of more than 100 other French monasteries. In Spain, as the anti-ascetic trend which followed the condemnation of Priscillianism began to wane, Eastern monastic influences reappeared again. St Martin of Braga came from Palestine around 550 and established the monastery of Dumio. St Isidore of Seville (d. 636) became the author of a *Rule of Monks*, based on the Rules of Pachomius, Cassian, Caesarius of Arles, and Benedict. This development was understandably encouraged by the conversion of the Visigothic king Reccared from Arianism in 589.

Fully dependent upon the monastic ideology of the East, the various Western monastic movements were in general less inclined to ascetic extremism than their Eastern counterparts. The genius of the various Western Fathers consisted in their ability to adopt the Eastern tradition to the climatic and cultural conditions of the "barbarian" West. One of the traits of Western monasticism (which it actually shares with Syrian monks) is its involvement in missionary activity throughout "barbarian" Europe (see below, pp. 314-21). Until the second millenium, the freshness, the variety and spiritual freedom of early monasticism were fully maintained, both in spirit and in forms, especially through the coexistence of both coenobitism and eremitism— the Eastern "hesychasm"—as the two models of monastic life. The appearance of the *Rule* of St Benedict did not imply the creation of a Benedictine "order."[30] The monasteries adopting the Rule, which was generally used in combination with local tradition, remained independent communities, as was the case with the Eastern monasteries.

The quite spontaneous emergence of monasticism in the fourth century, first in the East, then in the West, and the involvement of monks in church activities and doctrinal controversies had naturally raised the issue of relationship with the established structure of the

[30]The term "Benedictines" itself was not used before the fifteenth century when the entire Western monastic system came to be understood in terms of centralized "orders."

Church. Originally a lay movement, monasticism naturally depended upon the sacramental ministry of the bishops (except when it began to deny its necessity, falling into "messalianism"). Eventually, however, the abbots received ordination themselves, and the problem of episcopal power over them arose inevitably. The issue was solved by the canons of the council of Chalcedon (451) in favor of a local episcopal jurisdiction over the monasteries. The system was further confirmed and codified in great detail in the civil legislation of emperor Justinian (527-565), which was accepted in the West not only in connection with the Byzantine reconquest of Italy, Africa and Spain, but also through the policy of pope Gregory the Great (590-604) and the legislation of local Western councils. However, the issue was debated in Africa. The council of Carthage (525) formally reserved for monasteries the right to elect their abbots and limited episcopal power to the right of ordaining monastic clerics. In fact, in this respect, practices varied, but within the limits of the ecclesiological principle that a local bishop has pastoral competence upon monasteries within his diocese. The principle was not challenged, except in the specific case of Celtic monasticism (see below, pp. 141-2). In the West, the system of local episcopal jurisdiction began to change in the high medieval period when the necessity grew to protect monastic life from excessive control by lay patrons. Arising together with papal centralization, monastic "orders" exempt from episcopal authority, were meant to protect the monks from this secular dependence. In the East, the old regime (with only some exceptions, such as the *stavro-peghion,* or dependence of a monastery directly upon a patriarch) tended to prevail, and monasteries remained canonically parts of the local dioceses.

4. Saints, relics and holy places

The development of monastic asceticism and spirituality would not have been so universal and so vigorous in the Christian Church, had it not responded to an existing spiritual quest and to the way the Christian revelation itself was understood.

In Late Antiquity—as distinct from our own secularized society—emperors, philosophers and simple folk alike shared a consciousness that "the Supernatural was constantly available to men."[31] Everyone accepted the idea that a person could manifest divine reality to others either by special divine election, or by virtue of a position he or she occupied, or through personal merits. In pagan society, Neo-Platonism developed its own type of "holy man," in which a "saint" was not always clearly distinguishable from a "sorcerer." And of course, there was also the "divinity," or "holiness" of the emperors . . .

The Old Testament revelation, on the other hand, affirmed that God *alone* is "holy"; the biblical "holy men"—especially the prophets— were His spokesmen, but they did not possess any holiness of their own.

Against this background, the Christian Gospel affirmed that the Holy One Himself had assumed humanity, making His personal holi- ness—not an abstract heavenly "Supernatural"—accessible to humans. There were obvious analogies with Hellenistic and Platonic idea of holiness, but also radical differences: Christ, the personal incarnate Logos, was the only Mediator between God and man (cf. I Tim 2:5), and holiness was always an *eschatological gift.* When the divine presence manifested itself in a human person, it was always by anticipa- tion of the future universal Kingdom of Christ, and therefore, it concerned the Church as a whole, and could be acquired only within its sacramental reality. Also, Christian holiness—*i.e.* "life in Christ" and participation in His divinity—was conditioned by a personal, ascetic effort of purification. It was not a pagan, magical mastery of the Super- natural, but God's response to a human free quest and an effort of love. The Greek Fathers spoke of "cooperation" (συνεργία, cf. I Cor 3:9) between divine grace and human freedom in attaining holiness (or *theosis,* "deification"). This concept which was generally accepted in Eastern monasticism, inspired the early Western monks as well, especially through the work of St Cassian.[32] This is why, through- out the early medieval period, both in the East and in the West, Christian spiritual consciousness recognized itself in the Saints—both during their lifetime and after their death—as the witnesses *par excellence* to Christian truth. Their authority did not really compete

---

[31]Peter Brown, *The Making of Late Antiquity,* Cambridge, Mass., 1978, p. 99; cf. also, by the same author, "The Rise and Function of the Holy Man in Late Antiquity," *Journal of Religious Studies,* 61 (1971), pp. 80-101.

[32]The exaggerated fear of Pelagianism (a doctrine which attributed the attainment of holiness to human effort alone), stemmed from the Augustinian doctrine of grace. It was not yet dominant in the West in the period under discussion.

with the sacramental structures, which was the basis for episcopal and conciliar ministry and responsibility, but it served as a powerful corrective to institutionalization and legalism, which became a real spiritual danger in the "imperial" church.[33] The roles played by St Symeon the Stylite, or by St Sabas of Palestine, in maintaining Chalcedonian orthodoxy, or, in the way of contrast, by Shenute, in promoting anti-Chalcedonian opposition in Egypt, are striking examples of the role of the "saint" in doctrinal controversies. But saints were able to play such a role because the masses of Christians discerned the anticipation of the Kingdom more vividly in them than in many bishops, and certainly better than in imperial power. However, asceticism was by itself no guarantee of orthodoxy. Occasionally, the spiritual teaching of certain ascetics made their contemporaries (and even later generations) forget about some doctrinal ambiguity, even straight heresy of an asetic. Thus the writings of Evagrius, of the anonymous author of the *Areopagitica* (a Monophysite, most likely), of St Isaac of Nineveh (a Nestorian bishop) or—in the West—St Cassian, remained among the classics of Christian spirituality, despite the formal condemnations aimed at such authors.

The veneration of the Saints, begun during their lifetime, continued after their death. Since, originally, martyrdom—or "witnessing" (μαρτυρία) to Christ's resurrection through death for Him—was seen as *the* perfect expression of Christian "holiness," the veneration began immediately upon the death of a saint.[34] This became also the case with holy monks, whose ascetic renunciation of the world was seen as a voluntary martyrdom,[35] and included all other forms of Christian holiness.

Until the second millenium of Christian history, the Church knew no established procedure of "canonization." The veneration of a martyr, or a saint arose spontaneously, in the place where he had lived and died. It was based simply on the conviction of those who knew him or, as began to happen later, of those who witnessed the miracles or signs performed through his mediation, that he, or she was indeed a

---

[33]Cf. my discussion of this aspect of early church polity in reference to the doctrine of St Basil of Caesarea ("St Basil, the Church and Charismatic Leadership" in J. Meyendorff, *The Byzantine Legacy in the Orthodox Church,"* Crestwood, NY, 1982, pp. 197-215; repr. from SVQ, 24, 1980, pp. 219-234).

[34]Cf. the case of St Polycarp of Smyrna, *Martyrdom of Polycarp.* 18, ed. and tr. E. Goodspeed, New York, 1950, p. 254.

[35]Cf. L. Bouyer, *The Spirituality of the New Testament and the Fathers,* New York, 1960, pp. 305-306.

participant of the Kingdom. The local bishop—or, in a monastery, the abbot—would then annually preside over a *synaxis,* or eucharistic celebration, on the day of his death and, if possible, on the very spot of his burial.[36] In all the major cities—and elsewhere—special churches, or *martyria,* were built on the tombs of particularly venerated saints. In Byzantium, beginning with the sixth century, special hymns were composed to glorify certain specific saints on the day of their commemoration. Each church developed its own martyrology (Gr. *synaxarion*) or list of locally venerated saints with basic information about their persons. The saints admitted in the lists of Rome and Constantinople were eventually venerated everywhere in the West and in the East, respectivly. Following the council of Ephesus (431), which confirmed the title of *Theotokos* ("Bearer of God") to be used for the Virgin Mary, the developing veneration required the building of *Martyria* (*e.g.* St Mary Major on the Esquiline in Rome) associated with signs, miracles or objects connected with her person.

The custom of an annual celebration of the Eucharist on the tomb of martyrs reflected the concreteness of the Christian faith in the resurrection. Gradually, the Eucharist itself began to be so closely associated—in popular piety—with a martyr's remains, that churches which were not located on martyr's tombs desired to acquire their own *reliquia* to be placed below the altar table. Thus began a totally new form of the veneration of relics. Roman law, confirmed by Christian emperors,[37] affirmed the absolute inviolability of graves, so that exceptions, allowing fro transfers of relics, required high-level administrative decisions. No wonder that such exceptions seem to have begun in Constantinople, an imperial capital devoid of local saints, where the exception gradually became the rule. Transfer of relics into one of the city churches generally coincided with the Saint's inclusion into the martyrology of the capital, so that such a "transfer" became the origin and the equivalent of a "canonization." This was, for example, the significance of the return of the body of St John Chrysostom to Constantinople in 438. Eventually, the toleration of transfers led to the practice of parceling out the relics to satisfy a wider demand. This custom was enhanced by the availability of other "relics," which were gathered in great numbers, throughout the fifth and the sixth centuries.

---

[36]On this, see the classic studies of H. Delehaye, especially *Sanctus, Essai sur le culte des saints dans l'Antiquité,* Brussels, 1927, pp. 162-189, and P. Brown, *The Cult of the Saints. Its Rise and Function in Late Antiquity,* Chicago, 1981.

[37]CT IX,17,1, tr. cit., p. 239.

Thus, the imperial palace and the churches of Constantinople included relics of Christ's Passion, pieces of the "True Cross," the Veil of the Virgin, the rod of Moses, the right hand of St Stephen brought in by empress Pulcheria in 428, etc.[38] However, there were also pilgrimages not only to Jerusalem, Bethlehem and other shrines in the Holy Land, but also to places, where eminent saints were buried (St Thomas in Edessa, St John and the "Seven Sleepers" in Ephesus, St Symeon the Stylite near Antioch, St Demetrius in Thessalonica, etc.). Thus, the ancient tradition of venerating the tomb itself was not entirely superseded by the widespread practice of transfers.

In the West, no center of pilgrimage could compete with the tombs of St Peter and St Paul in Rome. Typically, the popes remained opposed longer than anyone to having the tombs of the martyrs opened and their relics parcelled out. It appears that no Roman relics were unearthed before the siege of Rome by Wittiges in 537, when some bodies of saints, buried in suburban areas, were carried within the city walls to save them from profanation by the Goths. But it is not before the eighth century that the Eastern practice of morcelling and distributing relics was admitted on a grand scale, and even then, the official motivation was their safety from barbarian pillaging.[39]

The veneration of the Saints themselves, of their portraits (or "icons") and of their earthly remains reflected an essential aspect of the Christian faith, sharply distinct from Platonizing hellenism. It flourished in spite of obvious abuses and superstitions, the impossibility to authenticate relics in the midst of so many transfers, and the historical unreliability of many hagiographical legends. In the Incarnation, God assumed human life in its fullness, and the discovery of the divine presence involved the body, as well as the soul. Since God Himself had suffered in His assumed human body, the human forms and bodies of His witnesses had to be seen as sharing in the glory of His resurrection.

---

[38]See particularly J. Ebersolt, *Sanctuaires de Byzance, Recherches sur les anciens trésors des églises de Constantinople,* Paris, 1921; on the "True Cross," see A. Frolow, *La relique de la vraie croix,* Paris, 1961.

[39]H. Delehaye, *ibid.,* pp. 196-199.

CHAPTER IV

CULTURAL VARIETY AND MISSIONARY EXPANSION IN THE EAST

Around 451, the "Eastern part" of the Roman Empire (*pars Orientis*)— roughly corresponding to the territories administered by the praetorian prefect of the East—included the Eastern half of the Balkan peninsula (Mesia, Thrace), Asia Minor, Syria, Palestine, Egypt and Lybia. As Germanic barbarians occupied most of the West, the emperor residing in Constantinople also assumed direct control of the Illyricum—the Western half of the Balkan peninsula, including Greece—which had been previously under the jurisdiction of the emperor of the West.

Although Latin remained the official language of the courts and the administration until at least the sixth century, Greek was used in the churches and by the intellectual circles in major urban centers. However, except in Greece and Western Asia Minor, the vast majority of the population spoke neither Latin, nor Greek. The largest and the most influential ethnic groups within the Eastern part of the empire were the Syrians, the Armenians, the Arabs and the Egyptian Copts. This cultural and linguistic pluralism within the imperial borders helped the Christian Church to expand further eastwards, beyond imperial territories. Numerous Syrians and Armenians lived in Persian dominated areas and were in constant touch with compatriots within Roman borders. In India, Christian communities traditionally associated with the preaching of St Thomas, existed at least since the second century. In the Caucasus, Armenians and Georgians had been converted to Christianity since the fourth century, and so had the Ethiopians on

95

the Eastern horn of Africa. On the upper Nile, Christian missionaries were active among the Nubians, and other peoples of the region. All these nations read Scripture and worshipped in their own languages, often developing indigenous liturgies and forms of piety.

1. *The Syriac tradition*

There is every reason to believe that the roots of Syriac Christianity are to be found in Judaeo-Christian groups of the subapostolic period. Being very close to Aramaic, the Syriac language was not very different from the dialect spoken by Jesus himself. Scholars do not exclude the reality of some historical nucleus in the famous account of the so-called *Doctrine of Addai* (fifth century), which reports that Christ sent Addai (or Thaddeus), one of the seventy apostles, to convert King Abgar in Edessa, capital of the Osroene in Mesopotamia. This mission would have marked the beginning of Christianity among the Syrians. However, other indications point to Adiabene, a region to the East of the Tigris river, within the borders of the Persian empire, as the area where Jews first translated the Bible into Syriac (the so-called *Peshitta*) for new converts to Judaism, and which might have also been the birth-place of Syriac Christianity.[1]

In the fourth and fifth centuries, Syriac speaking Christians were in the majority throughout the Roman diocese of the Orient. They also existed in great numbers in Mesopotamia. They provided a natural channel for further expansion of Christianity. Their history was determined by the constant wars and political competition between the two world empires of Christian Byzantium and Zoroastrian Persia. Caught in the middle of the struggle and constantly faced with urgent religious and political options, the leaders of the Church were primarily concerned with sheer survival. Thus, from 340 to 383 the Christians of Persia were violently persecuted, so that the Roman empire appeared to be their only hope. Many Christians, including St Ephrem the Syrian and his school, found refuge within the Roman borders in Edessa. During a more favorable period in the relations between the

---

[1]Cf. the very complete survey of the evidence and of secondary literature in Robert Murray, *Symbols of Church and Kingdom, A Study in early Syriac Tradition*, Cambridge, 1975, pp. 1-38. For a succinct history of Syrian Christians, see W. Stewart McCullough, *A Short History of Syrian Christianity to the Rise of Islam*, Chico, CA., 1982; cf. also N. V. Pigulevskaya, *Kul'tura siriitsev v srednie veka*, Moscow, 1979.

two empires—the reigns of the Roman emperors Theodosius I (379-395), Arcadius (395-408) and Theodosius II (408-450)—the Church in Persia, headed by the bishop of Seleucia (who carried the title of *catholicos*), reorganized itself, being in full communion with rest of Christendom. It is then that Syriac Christianity had probably the best chance of becoming a real nerve-center of Christianity in the region and the workshop of its missionary expansion towards the East. The Syrian bishop Marutha of Maipherkat travelled repeatedly (in 399, then in 409) between Persia and Constantinople, and personally influenced the Persian King Yazdegerd in favor of Christianity. Presided by the catholicos Isaac, the council of Seleucia (410), not only accepted the creed of Nicaea, but also adopted a discipline and an ecclesiastical organization similar to that prevailing in the Roman empire and sanctioned by the Nicaean canons.

This peaceful period was interrupted by new persecutions under the son of Yazdegerd, Bahram V, and by a new war between the empires (421-422). Even if freedom of conscience for Christians was soon regained, the Persian church decided to protect itself against future accusations of pro-Byzantine sympathies. In 424, the council of Markabta proclaimed total doctrinal and disciplinary independence from the "western fathers." The decision did not change anything radically since the Christians of Persia were never really "dependent" on the West, but it reflected the need for self-defense and created a situation conducive to separatism.

The title of "catholicos" assumed by the bishop of Seleucia-Ktesiphon did not originally exclude some spiritual dependence upon Antioch—the traditional center of Syrian Christianity—but tended to reflect total administrative self-rule more and more. Eventually, the catholicos became the natural head of Nestorian Christendom of the East.

Extreme asceticism and the general attitude towards marriage which we described in the preceding chapter, remained the most controversial features of Syrian Christianity. In later times they led to disciplinary divergences within its several divided segments. But the main and the richest contributions of Syria to the Christian tradition lies elsewhere— in its exegetical, liturgical, spiritual and poetic legacies. Preserved by the Syrians themselves through centuries of isolated existence, this Syrian inheritance was transmitted westwards, primarily through the cosmopolitan centers of Edessa and Antioch.

In the middle of the fifth century, Syriac Christians lived on both sides of the constantly changing borders between the Roman and the Persian empires. Syrian Christianity represented a world by itself, culturally quite distinct from the civilization, which, within the borders of the Roman *oikoumene,* was gradually building up a synthesis between Christianity and hellenism. Spiritual leaders like Aphrahat (*ca.* 270-345), and St Ephrem (*ca.* 306-373) knew no Greek. The bishops of the great imperial city of Antioch were all Greek-speaking, but Syriac was spoken by the majority of the population.[2] There existed a strong tradition of Christian learning, which owed nothing to the Greek or Latin West, but which stood in the direct tradition of the Jewish synagogal schools. One such Christian school existed—at least since the early fourth century—in Nisibis. St Ephrem was one of its teachers until 363, when, fearing persecutions fater the capture of Nisibis by the Persians, he moved to Edessa. This "pro-Roman" move coincided with St Ephrem's support of the Nicaean Orthodox faith and his establishing links with the Cappadocian Fathers. In Edessa, he opened another school, which acquired great prestige and influence. Like its Jewish models, the school originally constituted a disciplined—in fact monastic—liturgical community and the teaching was primarily based on memorization and recitation of Scriptural texts.[3] In Edessa, however, it was inevitably drawn into the intellectual movement of the Greek Christian world—particularly Antioch—and adopted the exegetical methods of the Greek West-Syrian "Interpreters," Diodore of Tarsus and Theodore of Mopsuestia, whose writings were translated into Syriac. At the same time, the school of Edessa continued to attract numerous students from beyond the Persian border. In the fifth century many alumni of Edessa—Barsauma of Nisibis, Rabbula of Edessa, Philoxenos of Mabbugh, Acacius of Beit Araniaye, and others —would become the leaders of Syrian Christianity. The activity of the school of Edessa between 363 and 457 carried a tremendous potential for cross-fertilization between the Greek and Syrian worlds, and could have played a decisive role in preserving the unity of these traditions.

Unfortunately, the school was drawn into christological debates in such a way that its unifying role ended dramatically. Unable—or unwilling—to understand the terminological sophistication introduced

[2]Cf. G. Downey, *A History of Antioch in Syria from Seleucus to the Arab Conquest,* Princeton, N.J., 1961, p. 534.

[3]Cf. A. Vööbus, *History of the School of Nisibis,* Louvain, 1965.

in the christological debates by Greek theology, especially by the Chalcedonian definition of 451, the leaders and the students of the school of Edessa were polarized between the two extreme positions: Nestorianism and Monophysitism.

In 435, following the condemnation of Nestorius (431) and the emigration of Nestorians to Persia, Bishop Rabbula of Edessa took a strongly Cyrillian stand and opposed the Nestorian teaching of Theodore of Mopsuestia, which had been previously accepted at the school. Ibas, his successor on the episcopal see, adopted the opposite view. Faithful to Theodore of Mopsuestia, he established contacts with Nestorian emigrés in Persia. Another follower of Theodore, Narsai, headed the school since 437, and had to suffer greatly during the monophysite reaction led by Dioscoros of Alexandria in 449. In spite of the rehabilitation of Ibas at Chalcedon (451)—a controversial step which would create problems later—most of the faculty and students headed by Narsai emigrated back to Nisibis, under Persian rule (457), where they became supporters of Nestorianism. Those of the faculty and alumni who remained on Roman territory generally stood for Monophysitism during the anti-Chalcedonian reaction under emperors Zeno (479-91) and Anastasius (491-518). Weakened by christological divisions and deprived of its former prestige, the school of Edessa was formally closed by Zeno in 489.

The christological disputes of the fifth century—which will be discussed at greater length below—contributed to further isolate Syriac Christianity from the mainstream of Christian thought in the following centuries. Its traditions of exegesis and spirituality, which went back to the very origins of Christianity, were preserved, but only selectively, particularly in the liturgical and hymnographic patterns maintained at Antioch. For example, without the poetic legacy of Syrian hymnography, the sixth-century *kontakia* of the Antiochian deacon, Romanos the Melode, would not have been written. However, the emergence, in the Greek-speaking world, of a theology using concepts and developing terminological systems, had little effect on Syrian thought. St Ephrem's legacy was one of poetry, reflecting the Christian mystery with great beauty and depth, but using few philosophical concepts and limited to a biblical imagery almost exclusively. Although Syriac Christianity produced several eminent theologians, who argued passionately either for the Nestorian, or the Monophysite causes, it seems that the christological debates had little practical influence on the spirituality and piety inherited from ancient times by the masses.

Used by many Christian communities living under different political systems and belonging to doctrinally opposite camps, the Syriac language was never monopolized by a single ethnic group, or nation, as was the case of other Middle-Eastern languages. In all its branches, Syrian Christianity remained aware of the universality of the Gospel and this awareness outlived the christological schisms. Its missionary enthusiasm and effectiveness were quite remarkable.

The austere ascetics of the Syrian desert actively preached to the pagans of the neighborhood of Antioch, Edessa and Emesa.[4] St Symeon the Stylite was instrumental in the conversion of Arab tribes, establishing an Arab Christianity, which, in the case of the Christian Kingdom of the Ghassanids, became quite influential in the sixth century. It penetrated the Southern Arabian region (Najran) and survived Islam. St John Chrysostom was already aware of this missionary vocation of Syrian monks and corresponded on the matter with a community of Zeugma, on the Euphrates.[5] Also in Mesopotamia, St Alexander, founder of the monastery of the "Non-Sleepers" (*Akoimetai*), was a missionary, before moving to Constantinople where he died (430), having introduced the "Non-Sleeping" rule in a new community there. Christian bishoprics were established as far as the Persian Gulf, at Rewardashir and on the islands of Bahrein: they were represented at the council of Seleucia in 410.

The missionary activity of Syrian Christians, frequently monks, also included traveling to foreign countries for the sake of the Gospel. Although the early history of Christianity in India, Armenia, Georgia and Ethiopia is clouded by legendary accounts, there is no doubt that, in these four countries, the Syrians contributed decisively to the establishment of the Church. As we will see later, the Nestorian Church of Persia would continue this missionary movement throughout Asia until the late Middle Ages.

---

[4]Cf. Anatoly, *Istorichesky ocherk siriiskogo monashestva do poloviny VI-go veka,* Kiev, 1911, pp. 155, 172-5. O. Hendricks, "L'activité apostolique des premiers moines syriens," *Proche-Orient Chrétien* 8 (1958), pp. 4-25.

[5]*Letters,* 49, 53-54, 123, 126 (PG 52, cols. 635, 639-9, 676-8, 685-7).

2.   *Christianity in the Asian subcontinent*

In his famous *Christian Topography,* composed in 520-522, the Alexandrian traveller Cosmas Indicopleustes signals the existence of a large, international and Greek-speaking Christian community on the island of Socotra in the Indian Ocean, off the Arabian and African coasts. He also describes a "Persian" church on Ceylon (Sri Lanka), and a bishopric in "Kalliana," or Quilon in Southern India.[6] The first two of these indications may refer to merchant settlements. According to Cosmas, the clergy of both Socotra and Ceylon were ordained "in Persia," *i.e.* by the (Nestorian) catholicos of Seleucia-Ctesiphon. In the case of the Christians of India, however, he seems to refer to an ancient commuity with roots possibly going back to apostolic times.

Indeed, a tradition found in the Syriac apocryphal *Acts of Judas Thomas,* written in Mesopotamia in the third century, affirms the apostolic origin of Indian Christianity. Although the Syriac original of the *Acts,* identifies the apostle, who went to India, as St Jude, a local tradition alive to this day follows the Greek version in calling him Thomas. Another tradition, recorded by Eusebius, points at Bartholomew as the first missionary to India.[7] Although most of these legends are historically unreliable by themselves, their number and consistent indications that Christianity existed in India since pre-Constantinian times, are quite impressive. Furthermore, recent research points to actual Jewish settlements in India at the time of Christ, which make the information about apostolic presence there even more plausible.

It is difficult to ascertain further what proportion of Christians in India, in the fourth and fifth centuries, was autochthonous. Some were certainly recent foreign refugees. It is known, for instance, that, during the persecution of Christianity in Persia by Shapur II (309-79), many Christians left the country and took refuge, either on Roman territory (cf. St Ephrem, supra, p. 98), or in India.

In any case, the existence of the Church there remained continuous throughout the early medieval period. The language of worship and

[6]Ed. W. Wolska-Conus (SC, 197, Paris, 1973), p. 65 (PG 88, cols. 169 AB).

[7]There is an abundant literature on the sources of the Thomas legend; for a general discussion of the issue see L. W. Brown, *The Indian Christians of St Thomas,* Cambridge, 1956 (repr., 1982), pp. 43-64. Furthermore, the tomb of St Thomas, venerated even today in Mailapur, may go back to 50-100 AD (Cf. G. Schurzhammer, "New light about the tomb of Mailapur," OCA, 186, Rome, 1970, pp. 99-101).

literature was predominantly Syriac, and the Nestorian catholicos of Seleucia-Ktesiphon was the canonical source of episcopal ordinations until the Portuguese conquest in the sixteenth century.

3. *Armenia and Georgia*

Although clouded in legends and described in sources revised by later editors, the establishment of Christianity in the regions of the Caucasus, in the kingdoms of Armenia and Georgia, was one of the important developments in the history of the Church in the early fourth century. Following their conversion, the histories of these two small neighboring Christian nations are, for a time, practically inseparable. However, speaking two very different languages, they eventually followed different ecclesiastical and cultural paths. Both produced original and creative Christian literatures which incorporated early Christian documents, so that, today the knowledge of both the Armenian and the Georgian languages is indispensible for access to many early Christian historical data. Their later history was often tragic, not only because of the aggressiveness of neighboring empires—the Roman, the Persian, the Arabic, the Turkish and the Russian—but also because of their mutual distrust and competition.

The nation, known to the Greeks as "Armenian," but designating itself as "Haikh" (and its country as "Hayastan"), speaks a language of Western Indo-European origin, which makes historians believe that Armenians, until sometime before 1000 B.C., lived in the Northern Balkans. Then, they migrated to the region known as "Little Caucasus," to the South of the Great Caucasian range, and to large sections of Eastern Anatolia. Their northern neighbors, who since the Crusades are known as "Georgians" (from the Persian *gorji*) describe themselves as *Kartveli*, although in Greek (and Byzantine) terminology they used to be called "Iberians" ("Ι6ηροι, from an old Iranian name of the country). Their language belongs to the local "Caucasian" group, and has a pre-Christian literary history going back at least to the fifth century B.C. There are several related dialects of Georgian: Mingrelian, Laz, Svan, and others. The traditional borders of Georgia include the Southern slopes of the Great Caucasian range from the coast of the Black Sea to the lower basin of the Kura river.

In the early fourth century, both countries were ruled by local princely families. Sovereignty over them constantly passed from Rome to Persia, and back to Rome. Christianity was eventually adopted by the ruling monarchs of both countries, making it a state religion at once, inevitably having to face Persian displeasure.

In both countries, Christian missions were active before the official princely conversion. The Syriac character of basic Christian terms in the Armenian language points to the Syrian origin of the first Christians.[8] Greek words used in Svanetia (Western Georgia) indicate the existence of early Greek missions there, which might have also been active among the Lazes, the Georgian tribes on the Black Sea coast. This western region of Georgia remained under Greek ecclesiastical rule from the time of Justinian until the eleventh century.[9] However, the two events, which entered the consciousness of both nations as symbols of their true spiritual birth are respectively connected with two saints: St Gregory of Armenia and St Nino of Georgia.

During a bloody feud between pro-Roman and pro-Persian nobles, which took place in Armenia in the second half of the third century, a Parthian prince murdered the Armenian King Khosrov. Gregory, the murderer's son, escaped to Caesarea-in-Cappadocia on Roman territory; baptized a Christian, he returned to Armenia, suffered persecution by King Trdat, son of Khosrov, but, eventually converted the king, his former persecutor, to Christianity. Around the year 314, Gregory was consecrated bishop of Ashtishat, a city to the West of Lake Van in Anatolia, by St Leontius of Caesarea and became the first head of an organized church in Armenia. The title of "catholicos" is applied to him by later sources although it does not seem that the title was used officially before the fifth century to designate heads of the Armenian and Georgian churches. The missionary effect of Trdat's conversion and of St Gregory's consecration concerned all the peoples of the region: Christian priests were sent to other neighboring nations —the Abkhazians and Aghouans (or "Albanians"), so that the new church, which used Greek and Syriac in worship, was not limited to the Armenian nation alone. This explains why St Gregory the Illuminator is highly venerated throughout the medieval period, not only by

[8]Cf. R. W. Thomson, *Agathangelos: History of the Armenians,* Albany, N.Y., 1976, p. IX, XCVI. The legends about a mission of the apostles Thaddeus and Bartholomew to both Georgia and Armenia perhaps point to the same Syrian origins of early Christianity in the Caucasus.

[9]Cf. P. Peeters, "Les débuts du Christianisme en Géorgie d'après les sources hagiographiques," *AB* 50 (1932), pp. 13-18.

Armenians but also by the Byzantines and the Georgians.[10]

After the death of St Gregory the Illuminator, the leadership of the church became a hereditary function in his family. His son, Rstakes (or Artakes) was ordained bishop by his father and was present at the council of Nicaea, 325. His grand-son, Gregory, became the first bishop of the Aghouans. However, a rival house, that of Albianos, occasionally succeeded in gaining church leadership in the same hereditary fashion, but only for brief periods. There is every reason to believe that the church was dependent on Caesarea, until bishop Nerses, "the Great," was poisoned by King Bab (373 or 374). The archbishop of Caesarea, St Basil the Great, protested and declared that no further consecrations would take place. The king then organized the church independently under a primate consecrated locally (but still chosen among the descendents of Gregory).[11] It is possible that there was some dependence upon the Syrian catholicosate of Ktesiphon. Under the last "Gregorid" catholicos Isaac (390-439), another decisive event took place in the history of Armenia. A remarkable scholar, St Mesrop (or Mashtots), invented an Armenian alphabet and presided over the translation of Scripture into Armenian, ending the period of dependence upon either Greek or Syriac worship and literature.

The restoration of Persian rule over most of Armenia, the violent persecutions of Christians by the Persian king Yezdegerd II (439-457) and an Armenian anti-Persian rebellion, which Byzantine emperor Marcian refused to support, widened the gulf between Armenian Christians and the rest of the Christian world. The isolated Armenian church found itself in a situation similar to that of Syrian Christianity. The ties with the West—ineffective as they were politically after the show of indifference by emperor Marcian—compromised the Armenians in the eyes of the Persians. Thus, the Armenian catholicosate, which now possessed administrative independence from Caesarea and a cultural identity different from that of the Syrian Nestorian catholicos of Seleucia-Ktesiphon—who claimed jurisdiction over the Armenians but

[10]For a critical examination of the highly controversial information given by one major source—the *History* of "Agathangelos" (late fifth century), see R. W. Thomson, *op. cit.*, who gives an English translation of the *History*. See also N. Ya. Marr, "Kreshchenie Armyan, Gruzin, Abkhazov i Alanov sv. Grigoriem" (The baptism of the Armenians, Georgians, Abkhazians and Alans by St Gregory) in *Imp. Arkheologicheskoe Obshchestvo, Zap., Vost. Otdelenie*, XVI, St. Petersburg, 1904-05, pp. 63-211.

[11]On these events, see N. G. Garsoian "Politique ou orthodoxie? L'Arménie au quatrième siècle," *Revue des études arméniennes*, n.s.4. (1976), pp. 297-320.

against whose pernicious "heretical" influence they had been warned by Proclus of Constantinople (433)—first ignored, then rejected the council of Chalcedon (451). It is also at that time that the civil and religious capital of the country was moved from Ashtishat to Dvin. One should note, however, that the schism between the Armenian catholicosate and the imperial Orthodox Church was not final in the fifth century. Numerous attempts at union took place. The existence of several Armenian Chalcedonian dioceses and a large population of Chalcedonian Armenians within the Byzantine empire allowed them to play a leading role in medieval Byzantine society (see below, Chapter VIII).

The conversion of Eastern Georgia, or Iberia—with its capital in Mtskheta—occurred around 330 A.D. a few years after the establishment of Christianity in Armenia by St Gregory. There was obviously some connection between the two events, since we know of the penetration of clergy, ordained by Gregory, among Western Georgians. The legendary accounts frequently confuse facts pertaining to the two stories.

A Christian slave woman, named Nino, attracted the Georgians' attention to her religion by performing healings in the name of Christ—including that of the East Georgian King Mirian's wife. Eventually, the king himself was saved by praying to Christ, was converted, and, following St Nino's instructions, contacted emperor Constantine, requesting him to send Christian clergy and baptize the country.[12]

As in the case of the Armenians, the existence of Christian communities in several parts of Georgia before 330 provided a basis for legendary accounts of apostolic preaching by St Andrew or St Bartholomew. Georgians liked to emphasize this direct connection of their faith with Jerusalem. This concern was also embodied in the hagiographic account of St Nino converting not only King Mirian, but also the Jews of Mtskheta and obtaining from them an extraordinary relic, the Tunic of Christ, which had been miraculously entrusted to their care after the crucifixion on Golgotha. The Tunic was henceforth venerated throughout the Middle Ages at the great

---

[12]This account is found in the *Ecclesiastical History* of Rufinus (I,10) composed around 403 A.D. Most historians accept the basic historicity of the account. In later centuries, the activities of St Nino were surrounded with legendary embellishments (cf. the texts translated in English in D. M. Lang, *Lives and Legends of the Georgian Saints*, second edition, revised, Crestwood, NY, 1976, pp. 13-39).

patriarchal cathedral of Mtskheta.[13] This veneration was accompanied by a strong Georgian tradition of pilgrimages to Jerusalem and other forms of contact with the Holy Land.

It is impossible to prove or disprove the legendary accounts concerning the origins of the Tunic venerated in Mtskheta. The spread of Christianity in the Jewish diaspora, and the very early connections of this diaspora with Syriac Christianity are acknowledged facts, which could very well have occurred in the Caucasian regions also. The Georgian church deeply venerates the "Syrian Fathers"—including especially St David of Garesja—who, in the fifth and sixth centuries established monasticism in Georgia, while also introducing learning and theology. Syrian monks undoubtedly brought with them many legendary or semi-legendary accounts on the origins of Christianity, which were then adopted by the Georgians.

Whether or not direct connections occurred between king Mirian and Constantine, or between St Nino and Jewish Christians, it is difficult to deny that, institutionally, the East-Georgian Church was associated, at least until the late fifth century, with the ecclesiastical center established by St Gregory in Ashtishat and Dvin. That center, although belonging to the Armenian Kingdom, was not, at that time, an exclusively Armenian catholicosate, but a regional primacy using Greek and Syriac in worship. Even as the national Armenian identity was developing under Catholicos Isaac (390-439), St Mesrop, the translator of the Armenian Bible, also made translations into Georgian.[14] There was nothing unnatural, therefore, in the ecclesiastical unity between Dvin and Mtskheta.

It does appear that the situation changed following the joint Armenian and Georgian rebellion against the Persians in 482-84, which was supported by the Byzantine emperor Zeno. Whereas the Armenian leader Vahan eventually reached a settlement with the Persians, king Vakhtang I of Georgia adopted a more definitely pro-Roman orientation and, through Constantinople, arranged (*ca.* 486-88) for the consecration of a separate catholicos in Mtskehta. The new catholicos, was consecrated by the patriarch of Antioch, Peter the Fuller, together with twelve other bishops.[15] This is the traditional date of the estab-

---

[13]This tradition is in competition with two Western versions which have the Tunic venerated in Trier, Germany, and in Argenteuil, France.
[14]F. Tournebize, *Histoire politique et religieuse de l'Arménie*, I, Paris, n.d., p. 78.
[15]Cf. C. Toumanoff, "Caucasia and Byzantium," *Traditio* 27 (1971), pp. 167-69;

lishment of Georgian "autocephaly," although this term should not be used anachronistically in the modern sense of a totally independent national church. The event primarily marked a new cultural and moral dependence of the Georgian catholicosate upon the patriarchate of Antioch and implied, until the eleventh century, the acceptance in Georgia of Antiochian liturgical usages.[16] The first catholicoi were Greeks or Syrians, the first known Georgian incumbent being Sabbas I (523-52). Actually, there are sources indicating that the patriarchate of Antioch re-asserted at least twice the existence of an independent Georgian church (in the eighth and the eleventh centuries[17]). These restatements indicate the continuation of some spiritual dependence of Georgia upon Antioch throughout the centuries, as well as its *defacto* independent existence.

Naturally, the establishment of a catholicosate in Mtskheta weakened the authority of the catholicos of Dvin, but the two churches remained for a time in doctrinal unity. Indeed, under emperor Zeno, the empire lived under the regime of the *Henotikon,* which implied *de facto* renunciation to Chalcedon. Peter the Fuller was an anti-Chalcedonian, and so was undoubtedly the formal position of the new catholicos of Mtskheta. In 505-6, at the synod of Dvin, Armenian and Georgian bishops formally accepted the *Henotikon* and, at least implicitly, rejected Chalcedon.[18] Thus the orthodoxy of the Georgian

M. Tarchnisvili, "Die Entstehung und Entwicklung der Kirchlichen Autokephalie Georgiens," *Kyrios* 5 (1940/41), pp. 177-93 (= *Le Muséon,* 73, 1960, pp. 107-126).

[16]Cf. Wachtang Z. Djobadze, *Materials for Study of Georgian Monasteries in the Western Environs of Antioch-on-the-Orontes,* Louvain, 1976, pp. 63-85.

[17]An Arabic source of the eleventh century mentions that the patriarch of Antioch Theophilactos (745-751), formally granted to the Georgian catholicos the right to consecrate his bishops; also, at that time, the patriarch of Jerusalem Sergius allowed the Georgians to consecrate chrism. These actions seem to imply that the Georgians were previously in some canonical dependence upon Antioch and received their chrism from Jerusalem (on these episodes see N. Ya. Marr, "Istorichesky ocherk gruzinskoy tserkvi s drevneishikh vremen," *Tserkovnye Vedomosti,* St. Petersburg, 1907, Prilozhenie No. 5 (*Predsobornoe Soveshchanie*) pp. 126, 130). In the eleventh century, the reconquest of Armenia and parts of Georgia by Byzantine emperor Basil II raised the issue of the canonical status of Georgian dioceses under Byzantine occupation. This provoked a new statement by the patriarch of Antioch, Peter III (1052-56) on Georgian autocephaly granted by Antioch. This statement is not preserved in its original text, but is quoted by the renowned canonist Balsamon (another patriarch of Antioch, but titular, twelfth century) PG 137, col; 320; Eng. tr., *SVQ,* 15, 1971, No. 2, p. 35) Historians are divided as to the chronological implications of Balsamon's statement, and whether the words "patriarch Peter and his synod" refer to Peter the Fuller (fifth century), or Peter III (eleventh century).

[18]Cf. below, Chapter VIII p. 282. Some later sources speak also of a council held in Vagharshapat in 491. Vagharshapat is the ancient name of Echmiadzin, which, in

church can be considered as doubtful in the last years of the fifth century.[19] It was fully clarified at the beginning of the seventh. The Byzantine emperor Maurice (582-602), having established peace, and even an alliance with Persian king Chosroes II, obtained for his Georgian protegé, king Guaram—the builder of the famous Sion cathedral in Tbilisi—the possibility to head an independent buffer state between Rome and Persia. It is then that Kirion (or Kvirion), who had served as secretary of the Armenian catholicos Moses II and had been ordained a priest by him, assumed the catholicosate of Mtskheta (590-604). Having studied in Nicopolis, on Byzantine territory, he must have been tri-lingual in Greek, Armenian and Georgian. Armenian sources accuse him of having ordained a "Nestorian" (*i.e.* Chalcedonian orthodox) bishop in Sis and of promoting worship in the Georgian language. By 600-601, supported also by the Aghouans (Albanians), he formally broke with the catholicosate of Dvin, declaring himself Chalcedonian orthodox.[20]

The option taken by Kirion can be better understood in the context of the conditions which existed within the Armenian catholicosate itself. In 574, Armenian catholicos John II had escaped Persian repressions and gone to Constantinople, where he accepted the council of Chalcedon before his death (594). Under emperor Maurice, a successor—Chalcedonian catholicos John III—had been elected in Roman occupied Armenia and resided in Avan (across the river Azat from Persian-held Dvin). In the last years of the sixth century, there were therefore two Armenian catholicoi, so that by accepting Chalcedonian orthodoxy, the catholicos of Mtskheta did not break with all Armenians, but only with the stubbornly anti-Chalcedonian catholicoi of Dvin, Moses and Abra-

accordance with a legenday vision of a mystical temple by St Gregory the Illuminator, became the holy place of the Armenian Church.

[19]Here again there is some controversy. Apologists of Georgian independence and unwavering orthodoxy maintain that the non-Armenian bishops present in Vagharshapat in 491 or Dvin in 505-6, came from Aghouania (or "Albania") near the Caspian sea, and not from Mtskheta (see P. Goubert, "Evolution politique et religieuse de la Géorgie à la fin du VIe siècle," *Mémorial Louis Petit*, Bucharest, 1948, p. 119). For the opposite, and more probable view, see N. Ca, Marr, *Ibid.*, p. 116; and Toumanoff, *op. cit.*, p. 138. On the origin of the "Albanians," see C. F. J. Dowsett, *The History of the Caucasian Albanians by Movses Dasxuzanci*, London, 1961. The official adherence of the Georgians to Monophysitism in the sixth century is confirmed by the famous monophysite activities of Peter the Iberian, bishop of Gaza in Palestine, whom the Georgian Church, in spite of its eventual acceptance of Chalcedonian Orthodoxy, venerates as a great ascetic saint (see D. L. Lang, *op. cit.*, p. 57-80).

[20]On these events see P. Goubert, *op. cit.*, pp. 120-5; C. Toumanoff, *op. cit.*, pp. 152-3, 174-84.

ham, who enjoyed Persian patronage. In the correspondence exchanged between Mtskheta and Dvin in 601-608, the Armenian side invokes the unity of the (Persian!) empire,[21] whereas Kirion stresses "the true [orthodox Chalcedonian] faith held in Jerusalem." Kirion also establishes contacts with ecclesiastical personalities in the West, including pope Gregory the Great.

In 607-8, after the murder of Maurice by Phocas, war resumes between Persians and Romans. Soon Chosroes II overruns the whole of Armenia. The Chalcedonian orthodox Armenian catholicos John III is taken prisoner and dies in captivity, while those members of his flock who intended to keep the Chalcedonian faith flee either to Byzantium or to Georgia. It is then that the final break takes place between Dvin and Mtskheta, with catholicos Abraham of Dvin anathematizing Kirion, the Georgians, the Aghouans (Albanians) and those who sided with them (Third council of Dvin, 608-09).

Although the sources describing these events are rather scarce and generally quite partial to one side or the other, it is clear that the actions of Kirion did not simply consist in asserting Georgian ecclesiastical independence; they are also to be understood within the context of the possibilities, cherished during the hopeful reign of Byzantine emperor Maurice, for a reunion of all the Christians of the area inside Chalcedonian orthodoxy. A large Armenian Chalcedonian population continued to exist in Byzantine Asia Minor and several Armenian Chalcedonian dioceses remained canonically dependent on the Georgian catholicosate of Mtskheta[22] until the eleventh century. The Turkish conquest of Asia Minor, following the battle of Mantzikiert (1071), by making impossible the patronage of the Chalcedonian Armenians by Byzantium, inevitably played an important role in finalizing the existence of separate Armenian and Georgian churches, as two clearly distinct national and religious groups.

---

[21]On the control exercised by Persian kings upon all the religious bodies of their empire, particularly the Armenian church, see N. Gersoyan, "Secular Jurisdiction over the Armenian Church (IVth-VIIth centuries)," in *Harvard Ukrainian Studies,* VII, 1983 (Essays presented to Ihor Sevcenko), pp. 220-250.

[22]On this see, N. Ca. Marr, "Arkaum, mongol'skoe nazvanie khristian, v svyazi s voprosom ob Armyanakh khalkedonitakh," *Imp. artheologicheskoe obshchestvo, Zap.-Vost. otdelenie,* XVI, St. Petersburg, 1904-5, pp. XXXVI-XXXIX; cf. also, for the later period. V. A. Arutyunova-Fidanyan, *Armyane-Khalkidonity na vostochnykh granitsakh vizantiiskoy imperii (XIV),* Erevan, 1980.

4. Arab Christians

Without ever being organized into a single religious group, christianized Arab tribes and regional kingdoms had existed since the fourth century in Syria, in the Roman province of Arabia (whose territory corresponds to the contemporary kingdom of Jordan), and beyond the Roman borders, in the Persian empire and in the Southern parts of the Arabian peninsula. The ecclesiastical, cultural and political importance of these communities, particularly in Syria, was substantial.[23] It is there, before Islam, that the classical Arabic language was first spoken and written (with an alphabet of twenty-two letters derived from the Syriac). The New Testament was translated into Arabic. It is for these educated Christian Arabs of Syria that the Quran was put into writing, rather than for the unlettered Bedouins of the Arabian peninsula, who were the first followers of Muhammad. Soon after the Prophet's death, Syria became the center of the khalifate.[24] Eventually, the virulent proselytism of Islam in the seventh century swept the Middle East and monopolized the mainstream of Arab civilization. If that extraordinary Islamic phenomenon had not occurred, Christian Arabs would probably have occupied a leading position among the cultural families of Eastern Christianity.

Historical and hagiographic sources of the fourth and fifth centuries contain several stories dealing with the conversion of nomadic tribes. The converts are generally designated as "Saracens," and live in the Syrian, Palestinian or Sinaitic deserts. Rufinus reports that around 374, a "Saracen" queen, named Mawuia (or Maria) was converted, and that a neighboring ascetic named Moses, was installed as bishop in her "kingdom." More precise information is given by Cyril of Scythopolis in his *Life* of St Euthymius the Great concerning the Saracen sheik Aspebet, who, after his conversion, was consecrated in 427, as "bishop of the *parembolaï*" ("camps") by Juvenal of Jerusalem and was present at the council of Ephesus (431).[25] Another bishop of

[23]On the well-documented presence of important Arab Christian groups within the Roman empire since the fourth century, see Irfan Shahid, *Byzantium and the Arabs in the Fourth Century*, Washington, D.C., 1984.

[24]F. Nau, *Les Arabes chrétiens de Mésopotamie et Syrie du VIIe et VIIIe siècles*, Paris, 1933, pp. 5, 96.

[25]Cf. A. J. Festugière, *Les moines d'Orient. I. Culture ou sainteté. Introduction au monachisme oriental*, Paris, 1961, pp. 87-95.

parembolai in Phoenicia, Eustathius, was present at Chalcedon.[26] Christian Arab chieftains were eventually able to constitute kingdoms independent of both the Romans and the Persians and became involved in political confrontations and wars between the two empires. Thus, Christianity penetrated in the distant kingdom of the Lakhmids, centered on the city of Hirah, on the lower Euphrates. Hosea, bishop of Hirah, was present at the council of Seleucia in 410. Another king, al-Noman (d. 418), was converted under the influence of St Symeon the Stylite, whose missionary activity among Arab tribesmen around Antioch, including pilgrims from Hirah, has been noted earlier. The church of Hirah remained in the orbit of the catholicosate of Seleucia-Ktesiphon and followed it into Nestorianism. Besides Hirah, several other dioceses with an Arab Christian population, existed in the orbit of the same catholicosate within the borders of Persia.

In order to counteract the influence of the king of Hirah—a vassal of Persia and a Nestorian—among the Arabs, emperor Justinian gave his support to the Ghassanid tribe, which populated the regions of Palmyra, Damascus and Hawran. The Ghassanid chief al-Harit (in Greek, Arethas) received the imperial title of *patricius* and his troops, as allied (*foederati*) of the Romans, triumphed over king al-Mundhir of Hira in 554.[27] Al-Harit himself and most of his subjects were under the direct influence of Syriac monophysite Christianity. As we will see below, their political and military usefulness to the empire was instrumental in assuring the restoration, under al-Harit's sponsorship, of a monophysite ("Jacobite") hierarchy in Syria.

Christianity also penetrated early in what was known in the classical sources as *Arabia felix* ("blessed Arabia"), the only fertile portion of the Arabian peninsula, near the Southern exit from the Red Sea, and corresponding today to the territory of Yemen. The area was the site of an ancient civilization, the kingdom of Saba (or Sheba), whose famous queen had visited Solomon in Jerusalem (I Kings 10:1-13). An early Christian mission, presumably Arian and headed by a bishop, the Indian Theophilus, had converted the local king and built three churches (ca. 356).[28] Between *ca.* 378 and 525, the area was occupied by the independent state of Himyar. In the following decades,[29] Syriac influence was strong in the region, espe-

---

[26]Cf. S. Vailhé, "Notes de géographie ecclésiastique," EO IV, 1900, pp. 11-15.

[27]Cf. H. Charles, *Le Christianisme des Arabes nomades sur le limes et dans le désert syro-mésopotamien aux alentours de l'Hégire*, Paris, 1936, p. 55-64.

[28]Philostorgius, PG 65, col. 482-486.

cially in the city of Najran. A local businessman, Hannan, was converted to Nestorianism during a trip to Hirah. It is probable, however, that the Christian community of Najran eventually adopted Monophysitism. Perhaps in opposition to the expansionist tendencies of both the Roman empire and the neighboring Ethiopian kingdom of Aksum, king Abukarib of Himyar (ca. 440) adopted Judaism. His successor, Dhu-Nuwas entered history, as a bloody persecutor of the Christians of Najran.[30] A massacre of Christians, perpetrated *ca.* 524, brought about the wrath of emperor Justin I, who encouraged his ally, the Ethiopian king Ella-Asbeha (Elesboas, Elesthaios) of Aksum, to invade the country, kill Dhu-Nuwas, and annex Himyar (525).

The later history of Christianity in the region is obscure. There is evidence of resistance against Ethiopian occupation, of divisions between the various sects of Monophysitism (Julianists, Phantasiasts) and lingering Nestorianism. Local initiative aiming at safeguarding the community against foreign interventions resulted, after a refusal to accept a Chalcedonian orthodox bishop from Constantinople, in the consecration of a bishop by Himyarite *priests*(!). This tragic history ended in the seventh century with the advent of Islam.

The solid foundations of Arabic Christianity, laid before the seventh century, explain the survival of Arab-speaking Christian communities, belonging to all three main branches of Eastern Christianity, and divided on christological grounds: Chalcedonian orthodoxy, Monophysitism and Nestorianism. The Arabic Christian literature of the following centuries,[31] both translated and original, shows the vitality of these communities. The Arabic language became the necessary vehicle of Christian thought and communication within the new society dominated by the Qurran, and was widely used by all Christians, including those who had preserved Syriac or Greek in their liturgy.

[29]Cf. especially J. Ryckmans, "Le Christianisme en Arabie du sud préislamique" in *L'Oriente cristiano nella storia della civiltà,* Rome, 1964, pp. 413-453; J. S. Trimingham, *Christianity among the Arabs in pre-Islamic times,* London, 1979; I. Shahid, "Pre-Islamic Arabia," in *Cambridge History of Islam,* I, 1970, pp. 3-29.

[30]For a full analysis of hagiographic sources see I. Shahid, *The Martyrs of Najran,* Brussels, 1971.

[31]Cf. G. Graf, *Geschichte der christlichen arabischen Literatur,* 2 vols., Rome, 1944-47.

5. *Egypt, Ethiopia and Nubia*

In the fourth and fifth centuries the great Egyptian city of Alexandria remained a major metropolis, largely Greek-speaking, economically and politically integrated into the Roman imperial system and rivaling Rome and Constantinople in population.[32] As a big seaport, with commercial contacts throughout the Mediterranean world— and particularly the function of shipping Egyptian wheat to the old and the new imperial capitals—Alexandria had a population of very mixed backgrounds, which developed a rather justified reputation of easily harboring corruption and engaging in violence. Also, since before the Christian era, it was a center of Hellenic learning and intellectual pursuits. It had a large Jewish community and was the birthplace of the Greek translation of the Bible (the "Septuagint"). With the advent of Christianity which was adopted not only by the urban proletariate, but by intellectuals like Clement and Origen, it became a hot-bed of theological thought and the location of a famous Christian catechetical school.

The church of Alexandria claimed to have been founded by the Evangelist Mark, and was proud to show numerous locations where the Holy Family itself was supposed to have stayed after its flight to Egypt (Mt 2:15-20). However, such references to holy origins were easily matched elsewhere in the East, and in themselves could not justify the role played by the bishops of Alexandria in the history of the early Church. This role was created by the importance of the city, which was, before the advent of Constantinople, unquestionably the second metropolitan center of the empire after Rome; by the personal influence and universal prestige acquired by bishops like Athanasius, Theophilus, or Cyril; by the immense wealth of the Egyptian church; and by the intellectual and scientific resources available in the city. These resources were especially useful for the computation of the Easter date which became a privilege of the bishops of Alexandria and gave them an opportunity for writing annual encyclical letters to the world episcopate. Another significant trait of Egyptian Christianity was the

---

[32]The most comprehensive account of social and religious life in Egypt during this period is still to be found in J. Maspéro, *Histoire des patriarches d'Alexandrie depuis la mort de l'empereur Anastase jusqu'à la réconciliation des églises jacobites (518-616)*, Paris, 1923, especially pp. 23-64. Cf. also E. R. Hardy, *Christian Egypt: Church and People (Christianity and Nationalism in the Patriarchate of Alexandria)*, Oxford, 1952.

almost exclusive power which the incumbents to the see of Alexandria exercised over all the Egyptian bishops. This power, which excluded the presence in Egypt of regional "metropolitans," was formally endorsed at the council of Nicaea (canon 6)—as an exception to the system of provincial metropolitans existing elsewhere—and extended to Lybia and Pentapolis. It resulted in the fact that the Egyptian bishops, numbering close to a hundred, were all ordained by the patriarch of Alexandria, depended on his leadership and expertise in practically every way, and uniformly followed him in his theological or ecclesiastical options.

This overwhelming power expressed itself in the title of "pope" which originally was frequently used to designate all bishops, especially in the West (papa—"father"), but eventually became the privileged title of the bishops of Rome and Alexandria. At the end of the Arian controversies, however, the power of the Eastern—Alexandrian— "pope" was directly challenged by an upstart: the bishop of Constantinople, the "new Rome," to whom the council of Constantinople (381) had given "privileges" equal to that of the "old" Rome, placing him distinctly above Alexandria (canon 3). The Egyptian primate had no part in this decision, and formally rejected it. Neither Timothy of Alexandria (381-385), nor his successors, Theophilus (385-412), Cyril (412-444) or Dioscoros (444-451) acknowledged the legitimacy of that council, which would eventually be recognized as "second ecumenical" by the Chalcedonian orthodox Church.[33] The Alexandrians consistently denied the newly established authority of Constantinople, which directly challenged Alexandrian leadership in the East. The entire episode of the condemnation of St John Chrysostom by Theophilus has no other meaning. The Alexandrian archbishops gladly accepted the title of "ecumenical archbishop" (οἰκουμενικὸς ἀρχιεπίσκοπος), used by their supporters.[34]

The competition between Alexandria and Constantinople in the late fourth and the fifth centuries clearly shows that the goal of the Egyptians was not simply to preserve the autonomy of a "national" Egyptian church, but rather to maintain their own authority *within* the imperial church, or *oikoumene*—an authority, which, in their

---

[33]In 449, Dioscoros specifically refers to the council of Ephesus (431) as "second," associating it with Nicaea (Mansi, VI, cols. 625 D, 644 A).

[34]Cf. Olympus, bishop of Evaza at the "Robber council" of Ephesus (449), Mansi, VI, 855 B.

opinion, was earned by the heroic struggle of St Athanasius against the Arians and of St Cyril against Nestorius, justified by the cultural legacy of Alexandria, and confirmed by the unswerving orthodoxy of the Alexandrian church, in the midst of a general apostasy to Arianism in the fourth century, and the easy acceptance of Nestorianism in Constantinople in the fifth century. Although the Alexandrian archbishops may have thought that the mere location of their church, away from the imperial residences, gave them greater freedom of action and doctrinal security, they never objected in principle against the accepted role of the emperor in church affairs. Both Cyril and Dioscoros solicited and gladly welcomed imperial help against their adversaries. Similarly, after 451, the Egyptian leaders of Monophysitism did the same, whenever they were given the possibility of influencing the court. This "ecumenical" vision and ambitions of the Alexandrian bishops, however, were not really understood by the Egyptian masses, which followed them not because they shared their theological views, but because the "pope" had become a symbol of Egyptian identity, trampled down and despised by foreigners. When forced to choose between their pope and the emperor, the simple Egyptian folk never hesitated, and supported the new "pharaoh," (as the Alexandrian bishop was called by his enemies). The archbishop's moral prestige only grew stronger when he was threatened with physical violence.

The archbishop of Alexandria and his court spoke Greek, and his involvement in the theological debates of the day was also expressed almost exclusively in that language. But the population of the country beyond the limits of the big city knew no Greek. For the Egyptian—or "Coptic"—peasants of the Nile valley, Alexandria, a city created by Greeks and the capital of Hellenism, was not really a part of Egypt: one would "leave Alexandria" to "go to Egypt."[35] The Coptic language spoken exclusively throughout Egypt was based on ancient Egyptian, but used the Greek alphabet, supplemented with seven signs taken from the "demotic" form of ancient Egyptian. Many religious terms, connected with Christianity, were also borrowed from the Greek.

Spoken by the peasant population, Coptic was likewise the language of the monks, whose numbers and world fame gave Egyptian Christianity its peculiar character. Although little original theological literature appeared among the Copts, such treasures of ascetic spiritual-

[35]*Life of St Daniel of Skete,* in *Revue de l'Orient Chrétien,* 5, 1900, p. 72.

ity as the *Letters* of St Anthony, the *Rule* of St Pachomius, the *Sayings* of the Desert Fathers were written in Coptic. Basic texts of the Greek and Syriac Fathers were soon translated, as well as some writings produced by Gnostic and Manichean communities. The great Shenute (or Shenuda), abbot of the White Monastery near Atripe, in Upper Egypt (*ca.* 348-466) showed a real mastery of the Coptic language in his treatises and sermons. Thus, the real strength of Egyptian Christianity did not lie in its relatively meager intellectual achievements, but in the spiritual strength and the number of its monastic communities. Under Shenute, at the White Monastery, there were 2,200 monks and 1,800 nuns. The Pachomian monks, at the time of the founder, were more than 3,000 and their number increased substantially later. When, in the fifth century, Palladius was writing his *Lausiac History,* the town of Oxyrhynchos was populated by more monks than lay people, and the bishop, in his pastoral visits in the neighborhood, could visit as many as 20,000 nuns.[36]

In the Greek-speaking Christian world, Egyptian monasticism was universally admired, but intellectuals, and even educated ecclesiastics, tended to look down upon the average, illiterate Coptic Christian. In the seventh century, St Anastasius the Sinaite, after explaining the trinitarian and christological problems in terms of nature and *hypostasis,* notes that such distinctions are inaccessible to "Egyptian minds" (οἱ αἰγυπτιάζοντες τὸν νοῦν). The same author mentions Coptic as a "simple language" (ἰδιωτικὴ διάλεκτος) of the crowds.[37] Justified, or not, such snobbery could only lead to a defensive reaction of the Copts, who liked to refer to the antiquity of their civilization, to the ascetic achievements of their saints, and, last but not least, to the *de facto* power and influence of their country and its patriarch. These are the elements which contributed to the gradual strengthening of Egyptian nationalism—a natural reaction of a monolithic and numerous population ruled by a foreign power.

Already in the fourth century, St Athanasius, persecuted by the Arian emperor Constantius, and whose concerns and commitments were still quite removed from any nationalism, found refuge and support among Coptic monks. The reliance of Theophilus and St Cyril upon the same support was just as deliberate and as effective. Crowds of monks were ready to respond whenever the patriarch needed them

---

[36]Cf. figures and sources in J. Maspéro, *ibid.,* p. 55.
[37]*Hodegos* (PG 89, col. 257), and 10 (*ibid.,* col. 161 A).

to act as a pressure group at church councils (431 and 449), or to destroy pagan temples and Jewish synagogues in Alexandria, or demonstrate against the Roman prefect. The same monks would refuse to accept the condemnation of their patriarch Dioscoros at Chalcedon (451), and would henceforth, by overwhelming majority, oppose the Chalcedonian patriarchs imposed on Egypt by imperial power.

The central and authoritative position of Alexandria and the vitality of Egyptian Christianity were expressed in missionary expansion, not quite as active, but somewhat similar to that which originated in Syria. Quite naturally, this expansion took place primarily on the African continent, and concerned the eastern "horn" of Africa and, later, the region of the Upper Nile. It was generally coordinated with Byzantine imperial policies in these regions, and illustrated the uninterrupted connection of the Egyptian church with Byzantium, even after Chalcedon.

The kingdom of Axum, in what will later be known as Ethiopia (or Abyssinia), has a history going back to at least ten centuries before the Christian era. Its territory occasionally extended beyond the Red sea upon the Yemen, or the Arabian peninsula. This is the partial explanation of the legend according to which the queen of Sheba (or Saba in Southern Arabia) was actually an Ethiopian sovereign. According to the legend, her famous visit to king Solomon (I Kings 10:1-13), resulted in the birth of a son, king Menelik I, who eventually brought the Ark of the Covenant from Jerusalem to Axum, as a gift of his father, Solomon. The meaning of this legend, which originated in the Middle Ages, was to give a glorified justification not only to the traditional titles of the Ethiopian negus ("Lion of Juda"), but also to the many Judaic features of Ethiopian Christianity (dietary laws, ritual circumcision, Sabbath, etc.), whose origins are obscure. These Judaizing elements were most probably either imported from Yemen, or at least strengthened by Yemenite influence, at the time of Ethiopian occupation after 525.[38]

Historically reliable information places the origin of Christianity in the kingdom of Axum in the middle of the fourth century.[39]

---

[38]See above, p. 112. The theory according to which these elements of Judaism go back to an hypothetical Judeo-Christian upbringing of St Frumentios, are too far-fetched; cf. the exposition of that theory in E. Isaac, "An obscure component in Ethiopian Church history. An examination of various theories pertaining to the problem of the origin and nature of Ethiopian Christianity," *Le Muséon*, 85, 1-2, 1972, p. 225-258.

[39]The episode related in Acts 8:26-39 about the "Ethiopian" eunuch, in the service

According to Rufinus, whose story is repeated by the church historians of the fifth century (Socrates, Sozomen, Theodoret), two Syrian young men from Tyre, Frumentius and Aedesius, shipwrecked in the Red Sea, found refuge in Ethiopioa and became the tutors of Aeizanes (Ezana), the young crown prince of the Axumite court. Under their influence, once he had assumed the throne, Aeizanes made Christianity the official religion of his realm. His former tutors returned to the Roman empire. Aedesius became a priest in his native Tyre, whereas Frumentius travelled to Alexandria, met St Athanasius the Great, reported to him about his missionary success, and was consecrated bishop for the Ethiopians under the name of Abba Salama ("father of peace"). This story—which is somewhat analogous to the spontaneous establishment of Christianity by lay missionaries in Ireland, Armenia and Georgia—is further confirmed by an indisputable source, St Athanasius himself. In his *Apology to Constantius,* he gives the text of a letter addressed around 356 by that Arian emperor to king Aeizanes, demanding that Frumentius, consecrated by the "criminal" Athanasius, be sent back for indoctrination to George, the Arian archbishop of Alexandria.[40] This competition between Arianism and Orthodoxy in the region is shown also in the mission of the Arian bishop Theophilus to Himyar (358), which was then Axumite territory.[41]

The historical consecration of St Frumentius by the archbishop of Alexandria served for centuries as a symbol of the relationships between Christian Egypt and Christian Ethiopia, but it does not seem that the canonical dependence of Ethiopia upon the Coptic monophysite patriarch of Alexandria was formally established before the tenth century. Information is quite scarce as to the history of Christianity in Ethiopia in the years following the conversion of king Aeizanes, but the available sources point to mainly Syrian and Greek influences upon the new church. Ethiopian tradition recounts the coming, at the end of the fifth century, of nine saints, who translated the New Testament into Geez,

of Queen Candace, baptized by the apostle Philip, does not necessarily refer to an Axumite. Any dark-skinned person was designated as "Ethiopian" and "Candace" was not a proper name, but the title of the queens of Meroe in Nubia.

[40]*Apol. ad Constantium,* 29-31, ed. J. M. Szymusiak (SC, 56), Paris, 1958, pp. 121-126.

[41]Cf. above, p. 111.. Since Rufinus, in his account of the story of Frumentios, speaks of "India," and not of Ethiopia, an attempt has been recently made to deny altogether his mission to Axum (F. Altheim and R. Stiehl, *Christentum am Roten Meer* I (Berlin, 1971), pp. 393-483. However, the letter of Constantius to Aeizanes seems to be a rather uncontrovertible proof of the traditional version of Frumentios' mission.

the ancient Ethiopian language, and founded nine monasteries, which became the craddle of a flourishing Ethiopian monasticism. The group was headed by Apa Michael Aragawi, the founder of the monastery of Debre Dauro, near Axum. The ancient Ethiopian biblical text points to a Syriac (and not Greek Alexandrian) original and the names of the newly-founded monasteries recall the location of Syrian monastic centers. It is therefore likely that the "nine saints" were Syrian monks, who performed a task of evangelization quite comparable to the Syrian missions in the Caucasus, in Persia and in India.

Other information points to links between Ethiopia and the Byzantine empire. During the reigns of Justin I (518-527) and Justinian I (527-565), the kingdom of Axum was a close ally and a commercial partner of the empire, which explains its armed intervention into Southern Arabia, sponsored and supported from Constantinople.[42] The conquest of Egypt by the Muslims in the seventh century created a serious obstacle to further links between Alexandria and Axum. For centuries, Ethiopia would remain as an isolated Christian enclave in East Africa. Seeking friendly support, it consolidated its ties with its Coptic brothers down the Nile, and eventually (by the tenth century) accepted overwhelming control by its original mother-church of Egypt. This administrative tie would be severed only in the twentieth century.

One of the obstacles in the relationships between Egypt and Ethiopia was the control of Nubia (present-day Eastern Sudan) by several pagan tribes. The establishment of Christianity in those regions which had been, since Antiquity, under the cultural and religious influence of Egypt, with an active civilization centered in Meroe, was effected through direct Byzantine imperial intervention in the sixth century.[43]

The temple of Isis, on the island of Philae, marked the border between Egypt and Nubia. Christianity had penetrated the area and a bishop of Philae, Theodore, was appointed in 526. He may have been instrumental in converting the neighboring king of the Novadae. However, Philae still remained a center of pagan worship for the troublesome tribes of Blemmyes (a general term which designated

[42]Cf. *supra*, p. 112.
[43]The important study by A. Rozov on Christian Nubia remains a fundamental resource on the subject (A. Rozov, *"Khristionskaya Nubia,"* in *Trudy Kievskoi Dukhovnoi Akademii*, 1889-1890 (and separately).

peoples reluctant to accept Roman rule in the area). The Blemmyes made frequent raids not only on Egypt and Ethiopia, but even on the monastic settlements located at Raithu on the Sinai peninsula, where they massacred the residents.[44] In 535, the imperial general Nerses put an end to the worship of Isis at Philae. The temples were converted into churches and the statue of the goddess brought to Constantinople. Furthermore, upon imperial urgings, Silko, the king of the Novadae inflicted a decisive defeat on the Blemmyes. Although the imperial government seems to have made an effort to establish Chalcedonian orthodoxy in the area, the first bishop, Theodore, had been appointed by the monophysite "pope" of Alexandria, Timothy III. Timothy's successor Theodosius—the real inspirer of the monophysite survival during the reigns of Justinian and Justin II—who was living under surveillance at Constantinople, succeeded in appointing Longinus, as bishop of the Novadae in 566. Thus, Nubia followed Egypt into the monophysite camp. It remained a Christian country until the late Middle Ages.

Following the example of the Nubian tribes, several other Christian centers appeared among the nomadic populations of the Sahara, almost to the Atlantic ocean, as is shown by archeological remains, liturgical books (in Greek and Nubian) and remnants of a Christian vocabulary in the language of the local Tuaregs. The total victory of Islam throughout the Sahara may have occurred only as late as the fifteenth century.[45]

6. Indigenous Christian churches and the imperial center of Byzantium

The preceding summary description of the missionary expansion of Christianity in the East is by no means complete. Goths and Huns in Europe, numerous minor ethnic groups in the Caucasus, the inhabitants of small islands of the Persian Gulf and the Indian Ocean, as

[44]The massacre is commemorated in the Byzantine calendar on Dec. 18. To avoid further incursions, Justinian built the famous fortified monastery of Sinai, with a church dedicated to the Theotokos, on the legendary spot where Moses saw the Burning Bush (cf. R. Devreesse "Le Christianisme dans la péninsule sinaïtique des origines a l'arrivée des Musulmans," Revue Biblique 49 (1940), pp. 205-223).

[45]W. H. C. Frend, "Nubia as an outpost of Byzantine cultural influence" Byzantinoslavica, 29 (1968), pp. 319-326; cf. also Th. Papadopoullos, Africanobyzantina. Byzantine influences on Negro-Sudanese cultures, Athens 1966 (= Πραγματεῖαι τῆς Ἀκαδημίας Ἀθηνῶν, 27).

well as African tribes were also reached by the preaching of the Christian Gospel in the fourth, fifth and sixth centuries. Information about these events is often semi-legendary, and many facts are still to be discovered, especially in hagiographic materials, although the main historical patterns are clearly visible.

In many cases, direct or indirect imperial support originated the missions. But more often than not the establishment of new churches was initiated spontaneously by the witness of lay men and women without any organized or professional missionary organization, or planning.[46] Spontaneity is the common trait in the histories of the aristocrat St Gregory the Illuminator, of Armenia; of the slave-girl St Nino of Georgia; of the two ship-wrecked young men Frumentius and Aedesius of Ethiopia; and of the Syrian merchants who brought Christianity to India. Many other similar cases may have remained unrecorded forever. The recorded cases were shrouded in legends, but, characteristically, the legends themselves tend to emphasize, rather than obscure, the free and spontaneous character of the conversions. Popular tradition describes miraculous events, supporting the missions, but little man-made organization. This is the way people wanted to remember their acceptance of the new faith.

The witness of the monks was another powerful means of Christian expansion. Within the borders of the empire, St Symeon the Stylite won the admiration of Arab tribesmen, as did St Euthymius in Palestine, and the ascetic Shenute in Upper Egypt and Nubia, drawing entire peoples to Christianity. But monks were also engaged in the tasks of teaching, evangelization and translation, which strengthened the faith in the converted nations. These tasks had, of course, to be performed both within and outside the imperial borders, and Syrian monks— although they belonged to the most ascetic and "detached" of all the Christian monastic traditions—set the greatest example of missionary zeal, comparable in every way to the achievements of their brothers of the Latin West, with their reputation of activism and more moderate asceticism. From Georgia to Ethiopia, and from Mestopotamia to India, it is the educational work of the Syrian monks which laid the foundations for local cultures, and gave the newly baptized catechumens direct access to Scriptures and Christian learning.

[46]Cf. I. Engelhardt, *Mission und Politik in Byzanz, Ein Beitrag zur Strukturanalyse byzantinischer Mission zur Zeit Justins und Justinians.* (Miscellanea Byzantina Monocensia, Heft 19), München, 1974.

It is worth noting that monks, as well as the initial spontaneous witnesses to Christianity, were laymen. Most of the accounts describe the intervention of bishops and clergy, not as the beginning of the mission, but as the necessary consequence of its success. In some cases, it was the original lay missionary who eventually obtained ordination to the episcopate (St Gregory of Armenia, St Frumentius of Ethiopia); in others, the local newly converted leaders requested foreign bishops from a respectable Christian authority (emperor Constantine himself for the Georgians, Alexandria for the Nubians, Seleucia-Ktesiphon for the Indians). It does appear, therefore, that, following the original Christian understanding of ministries, bishops and priests were identified with sacramental and teaching functions, within an already established local church, whereas the immediate missionary and apostolic responsibilities were rather attributed to the laity. In a particular sense, such lay prerogatives belonged to the Christian emperor, "equal to the apostles."

Later legendary accounts reflect the natural desire to "authenticate" local traditions of Christianity by associating local churches with the preaching of the apostles themselves. Such claims existed in the Caucasus, in India and in Africa—but are obviously unverifiable, with the Syriac tradition alone having possible direct Judeo-Christian roots.

All these various factors, which contributed to the spreading of the Christian faith in the East, illustrate two important aspects of Eastern Christianity: its rapid indigenization and its variety. Rarely was it promoted by cultural imperialists, striving (as would so often occur in later centuries) to integrate newly converted peoples into their own civilization. The possibility, and even the necessity, of translating Scriptures from Greek, or Syriac, into the native tongues was never questioned, but only sometimes delayed for a few decades in the absence of competent translators. In India, where the use of Syriac continued for centuries, the situation may have been determined by the fact that the community itself was largely composed of Syriac speaking emigrants from Persia. Only later, did Christian communities of the Middle East, ghettoized in a Zoroastrian or Muslim environment, became defensive and frozen in their pasts, clinging to their ancient languages and, therefore, by necessity, loosing their original missionary spirit and sense of responsibility.

The rapid indigenization of the Christian Church implied a variety of linguistic usages and practices. However, it would be highly anachronistic to identify this organic diversification, so characteristic of the fourth, fifth and sixth centuries, with ecclesiastical nationalism, as it appeared later. In every instance, conversion to Christianity implied a cultural revolution, the rejection of deeply rooted traditional pagan ethics and traditions. Until the sixth century, paganism remained strong in the most conservative—and therefore potentially "nationalistic"— groups of society: the aristocracy and the peasantry. This was true of both Greek-speaking and Latin-speaking citizens of the empire, as well as in Egypt, where many temples of the ancient Egyptian gods had to be destroyed in the first decades of the fifth century in Alexandria, though others survived much longer among the peasant population further up the Nile. The conversion of rulers in distant countries like Armenia, Georgia and Ethiopia was followed in each case by conservative pagan attempts to restore the ancient ways, and provoked Christian martyrdom. Everywhere, therefore, Christianity appeared as a novelty, implying a break with ancestral customs, the acceptance of foreign religious guidance and the risk of antagonizing powerful rulers, especially the Persian kings. In most cases, however, conversion was linked to the possibility of entering the orbit of the Christian Roman empire and receiving its support.

There is no doubt that all the ecclesiastical centers of the Christian East, both within and outside of the imperial borders, possessed a definite understanding of Christian universalism. Their missionary zeal was the best proof of it. Christ was always seen as the Savior of the entire world, not as a local or tribal deity. As members of the Church, all nations were united in faith and accepted the same episcopal structure. The necessity to obtain episcopal ordination served as a powerful link with important centers: Alexandria, Antioch, Caesarea-in-Cappadocia (for the Armenians), Seleucia-Ctesiphon (for India and Arabia). These centers were conceived as united with each other in a common confession of faith, which was best expressed in the creed of Nicaea. Later disputes were generally interpreted as debates on the true meaning of that original and truly universal confession.

Starting with the reign of Theodosius I and the council of Constantinople of 381, the relationship between the major ecclesiastical centers began to be defined more precisely, following the imperial administrative system. The council disavowed the interventions of the archbishop of Alexandria in the affairs of Antioch and Constantinople, declared that the competence of Eastern primates be limited by the territory of the civil "diocese" in which they were located (canon 2) and, last but not least, granted the see of Constantinople, the "New Rome," an honorary primacy "after the bishop of Rome," but above Alexandria.

The real importance of these decisions—which would eventually contribute to the Egyptian revolt against the imperial system—is that the emperor and his administration were formally recognized as the main agents of universal Christian unity. In fact, of course, the emperors had been acting in this capacity since Constantine, but the scandals of the Arian controversies, in which the authority of Constantine and his successors was morally compromised, required somewhat of a new beginning. Upon assuming the throne, Theodosius restored Nicaean orthodoxy and the Church again placed its trust in the empire, with the somewhat idealistic hope that it would fulfiill its unifying role faithfully.

In the East, Alexandria never explicitly recognized the decisions of 381, but there was no opposition in principle to the new imperial regime. There was actually no center of universal unity competing with the empire. The bishop of the "old Rome" was himself seen as part of the imperial system, rather than as an independent "apostolic" authority, and his competence was essentially limited to the West. In the East—not by virtue of any divine election, but because of the centrality of the imperial capital and the availability of imperial help and powerful cooperation—the archbishop of the "New Rome" assumed a *de facto* leadership. Thus, in 435, it was Proclus of Constantinople who was consulted by the catholicos Isaac of Armenia on christological matters and, in response, issued his *Tome to the Armenians*, which, characteristically he forwarded not only to those who requested his opinion, but to all the bishops of the East demanding that they too condemn the controversial excerpts from Theodore of Mopsuestia, which had been debated in Armenia. Similarly, Proclus, following the example of his predecessor John Chrysostom, intervened in many Eastern provinces, which were not normally in his jurisdiction, including particularly eastern Asia Minor. This leadership of Constantinople, exercised sometimes by powerful patriarchs, but, even more often, directly by the emperor, responded to an obvious need for coordination and unity—the same need which, in the West, called for the development of the Roman papacy.

Ecclesiologically, the Eastern system remained based on the idea that each local church, once established in the fulness of sacramental reality and guaranteed by the episcopate, was the same One Church which had existed since Pentecost, and that its unity with other churches was based on sharing the same faith and on the identity of spiritual gifts received by all. Cooperation and coordination between the churches were supposed to express this basic unity, but the practical modalities of this coordination were optional and changing. The unifying role was easily attributed to the emperor, provided that he was orthodox and therefore well-disposed to the Church. Whenever he betrayed the orthodox faith, his prerogative and authority disappeared: he became a "tyrant" (τύραννος, literally "usurper"), and his orders were to be resisted.

This role ascribed to the imperial system was recognized by Christians beyond the borders of the empire. Significantly—as we have just seen in the case of the Armenians and the *Tome of Proclus*—the theological leadership of bishops and theologians, mostly Greeks and citizens of the empire, was not challenged as such. The various christological schisms originated with ideas and formulas devised by Greeks within the empire, which were then accepted and followed by the various indigenous communities. As these formulas were sometimes contradictory, and as the empire committed itself to different ones at different times, schisms eventually became permanent. The system, therefore, disclosed its major disadvantages, as the Empire showed itself unable to fulfill its unifying role consistently.

As a major political and military power, the Roman empire was feared and hated by its political competitors, so that the Persians, and later the Muslim Arabs, deliberately protected and encouraged Christians to defect from that religious unity which was sponsored by Constantinople. The power of the empire was also dreaded by some because, as any authoritarian state, it used force to impose the solutions which it considered proper at a given time, violently persecuting the dissidents. Such a treatment inflicted upon Egypt, a country with strong ethnic identity, favored a separatism, which did not exist earlier. Thus, the military and political nature of the empire proved to be not only unifying, but also divisive. Eastern Christendom never accepted the emperor's infallibility ("caesaro-papism") and, actually, learned by experience how to resist the arbitrary actions of the State, but this experience was acquired at a very high price, of which the lasting schisms of the fifth and sixth centuries were the heaviest.

This negative record of the Christian imperial system should not, however, make us adopt unreservedly a totally black picture of the Byzantine legacy within Christendom. The acceptance of Christianity by society at large, led by Orthodox emperors, allowed for the development of a Christian culture, which was truly universal in scope. It was not a "national" Greek culture, although it expressed itself primarily in the Greek language. Armenians, Syrians and Egyptians not only contributed to it on the cultural and intellectual levels, but were welcomed, until the High Middle Ages, into high administrative positions of both the empire and the Church. The liturgy, the art and the theology which were produced in Constantinople, always represented a synthesis of various elements coming from different Christian traditions. Even the ecclesiastical unionism, practiced by Zeno, Justinian, Maurice and Heraclius—clumsy as it was, because of the political and violent means used by these emperors—was motivated by Christian universalism, of which, in the East, they considered themselves as responsible and legitimate custodians.

CHAPTER V

THE WEST IN THE FIFTH CENTURY: CHRISTIANITAS AND ROMANITAS

The fifth century marked the collapse of the imperial system in Italy, Germany, Britain, Gaul, Spain and Northern Africa, but not of the imperial "idea," or the Graeco-Roman civilization. Roman administration was replaced by Ostrogothic rule in Italy and Visigothic dominion in Gaul and Spain. Franks and Burgundians established themselves in countries to the North and East of the Loire river, while Vandals conquered Africa. As we have seen earlier, the invasions—especially the sack of Rome by Alaric in 410—terrified contemporaries, but the Germanic barbarians had neither the strength, nor the desire to destroy the age-long culture which was dominant in the conquered areas. Their numbers were relatively small, and, in most cases, they gladly accepted the legal status of *foederati,* which implied the fiction that they were not conquerors, but "guests" or allies ("federated") of the Romans. Indeed, they nominally recognized the authority of the emperor, who had lived in Ravenna since 401-402. The deposition in 476 of Romulus Augustulus—the last Western emperor—by Odoacer was not seen as the end of the empire (it produced much less impression on contemporaries than the sack of Rome by Alaric in 410), for a fully legitimate Roman emperor still resided in distant, but how prestigious, New Rome—Constantinople.

The practice prevailed to grant the imperial title of patrician to the *de facto* Barbarian rulers. The Ostrogothic ruler Ricimer, who had enthroned and deposed several puppet-emperors residing in Ravenna since 456, had received such a title. After 476, Odoacer had the Roman

Senate humbly solicit the same title for him from emperor Zeno. The request, in his case, was turned down, but his enemy and successor, Theodoric (493-526) was made *magister utriusque militiae et patricius,* and also used the titles of *princeps* and *rex* ("king"). This recognition of the permanence and legitimacy of the Roman empire, now centered in Constantinople, by the Barbarian rulers of the West will constitute an essential feature of both political and ecclesiastical developments in the following centuries, until the independent assumption of the imperial title by Charlemagne in 800.

Historians argue the question of the impact of the Barbarian presence upon social and economic structures of the disintegrating empire. The latest scholarly consensus tends to emphasize that there was no massive expropriation of Roman property, at least in Italy and Gaul, and that, in general, the Barbarians—prior to their cultural incorporation into the Roman society—were living on imperial territory as a foreign army, enjoying legally the country's "hospitality."[1] This initial separatedness between Romans and Barbarians expressed itself also in law and religion.

While the Roman—or Gallo-Roman—majority preserved Roman law, as it was codified in the Theodosian (or later Justinianic) codes, and expanded in the *novellae* of the Eastern emperors, the Germanic peoples were carrying their own tribal legal traditions, which were not yet integrated into national territorial laws. Furthermore, and most importantly—as we have seen earlier—the Goths, though Christian, did not belong to Nicaean orthodoxy, but to Arianism. They used their own Bible, translated into Gothic, and their own liturgical tradition. Since, however, their leaders generally sought incorporation into Roman culture, the forthcoming centuries would witness the simultaneous and gradual disappearance of Arianism, of Germanic laws, and of the Gothic language and liturgy. The major agent of this development would be the Church, centered around the Roman bishop. It would give birth to Latin medieval Christendom.

Remaining in Rome,—the "eternal city" now deserted by the emperors—the Roman popes became, in the West, the symbol of *Romanitas.* They were in constant touch with Constantinople, and acted as transmitters of imperial laws and decrees. However, they generally refused to act simply as imperial agents, especially since the support

---

[1]Cf. a review of sources and secondary literature in W. Goffart, *Barbarians and Romans, A.D. 418-584. The Techniques of Accommodation,* Princeton, 1980, pp. 206-230.

given by the Eastern *basileis* to Arianism, then to Monophysitism, demanded that they occasionally stand up to Constantinople. They could do so, they thought, because their prestige in Christendom was not due to imperial administrative decisions only, but to the fact that they occupied the chair of St Peter. Within the political void created by the barbarian invasion, in the eyes of Western Christendom, the popes were therefore identified both as successors of St Peter and as substitutes for the emperor. Being themselves convinced that they were performing an essentially apostolic mission towards the Western Barbarians, while also standing up, whenever necessary, against imperial abuse and heresy coming from the East, they boldly began to describe their own function in the universal Church as one of *government*. The term, which under popes Leo and Gelasius had entered the papal vocabulary to designate their authority, was not only *primatus* (which traditionally was used only for spiritual "primacy"), but also *principatus,* heretofore designating the *emperor's power.* Pushed by circumstances, the Roman bishops now understood their role as heads of a "body" (*corpus*) of Christians. But this "body" was not simply a spiritual and sacramental entity in the Pauline sense, but a concrete, legally definable organism, endangered by the Arian barbarians and by imperial doctrinal vagaries. This development which was provoked by historical circumstances, involved subtle shifts in the fields of ecclesiology and eschatology. The popes were not always equally affirmative in proclaiming their authority. There was resistance to their claims, both in the East and in the West. But the remarkable missionary, moral and doctrinal achievements of the Roman see obtained universal, and well-deserved respect. The real and very serious problems, connected with the confusion between "primacy" and "principality," between sacramental episcopal ministry and political power, between missionary expansion and Latin cultural integration will appear only later, and will have serious consequences, especially in the relations between Rome and the East.

1. On the Danube and beyond

Since Arianism had become the official confession of most Christian Germanic rulers of Central Europe, the interrelation between the Barbarians and the Church was practically limited to areas south of the old Roman Danubian frontier. However, some significant presence of catholic Christianity remained alive in borderlands, where Barbarian culture was dominant.[2] Thus, the episcopal see of Tomi, at the mouth of the Danube, was celebrated by the activities of St Theotimus, a friend of St John Chrysostom. In the first half of the fifth century, St Nicetas of Remesiana (modern Nis in Yugoslavia) was an impressive personality and a Latin literary figure of some stature. In addition to composing six books of *Instructions* to candidates for baptism, Nicetas wrote liturgical hymns (including perhaps the famous "Pseudo-Ambrosian" *Te Deum laudamus*). His legacy contributed to the perpetuation of a Christianity of Latin expression in the Balkan peninsula, of which the contemporary Romanians are the most prominent witnesses.

Further to the Northwest, in what had been the Roman province of *Noricum Ripense* (South of Vienna), the imposing personality of a lay monk, St Severinus (d. 482), founder of monastic communities and arbiter of disputes, gained universal respect and provoked conversions of Arians to orthodoxy.

The survival of such active communities and the continuous presence of competent leadership illustrate the vigor of the catholic orthodox tradition in areas ruled by Arian Goths and points to its eventual triumph over Arianism.

2.   *Christian Gaul: ecclesiological issues and debates on Augustinism*

Of the countries occupied by Germanic tribes in the fifth century, Gaul had—aside from Italy—the oldest tradition of Christianity, going back at least to the second century (St Irenaeus of Lyon), and a relatively solid ecclesiastical organization. Since the council of Turin (400 A.D.), the latter followed, in principle, the "provincial" organization defined at Nicaea. During the reign of emperor Valentinian III (423-455), the able Roman general Aetius succeeded in maintaining Roman rule in large sections of the country. Also, he secured a sense of solidarity between the Germanic chiefs and the local Gallo-Roman population against a common enemy, Attila's Huns. Indeed, Attila was prevented from taking Paris—a miracle attributed to the intercession of a holy woman, St Geneviève—and was defeated by Aetius near Troyes (451).

[2]On this, see especially J. Zeiller, *Les origines chrétiennes dans les provinces danubiennes de l'empire romain,* Paris, 1918.

The saintly catholic bishops Anianus of Orléans (St Aignan) and Lupus of Troyes (St Loup) were credited by the population for saving their cities from the Huns.

However, after the death of both Aetius (454) and Valentinian III (455), Roman rule collapsed. By the end of the century, the Visigoths, with their capital in Toulouse, had occupied the whole country south of the Loire. The Burgundians were solidly established in the Rhône valley. Both Visigoths and Burgundians were Arian. The Northeastern part of the country was still the territory of the pagan Franks.

The Arian, or pagan rulers of Gaul remained respectful of Roman traditions and tolerant of the catholic church. In 450, there were 116 or 117 episcopal sees,[3] grouped in seventeen provinces in accordance with the canons of Nicaea. Applied rather loosely in the Northern and Western parts of Gaul, the Nicaean system was enforced more strictly in the Southeast, where the Roman traditions were strongest. Around the bishop of Arles—the residence, since around 400, of the powerful imperial prefect of the Gauls[4]—the process leading to the creation of a "patriarchate" seemed to be in the making and implicitly serious ecclesiological problems were raised. In the absence of imperial decrees or conciliar provisions—which normally directed the development of ecclesiastical organization in the East—it was pope Zosimus in 417 who entrusted Bishop Patroclus of Arles with the "supra-metropolitan" rights—similar to those of an Eastern "patriarch"—of consecrating bishops in five provinces (cf. above p. 65). As in other cases of emerging primacies, the powers of Arles were challenged by the bishops of the area (Proclus of Marseilles, Hilary of Narbonne, Simplicius of Vienna) who sought to preserve their autonomy, and by the already established primacy of Rome.[5] The popes of the first half of the fifth century attempted to restrict the powers of Arles, which Zosimus had defined, until they faced, in the person of St Hilary of Arles (430-449), a primate resolute enough to fight for his authority.

An ascetic and former abbot of Lérins, Hilary imposed himself as

---

[3]Cf. E. G. Griffe, *La Gaule chrétienne à l'époque romaine*. II. *L'Eglise des Gaules au Ve siècle*. 2nd ed., Paris, 1966, p. 125; cf. also pp. 236-309.

[4]On the eve of the Barbarian invasions, the "prefecture" of the Gauls included the civil "dioceses" of Gaul, Spain and Britain.

[5]Similarly, almost at the same time, the emerging centralization of power in Asia Minor in the hands of the bishop of Constantinople was opposed "from below" by the bishops of Ephesus, and resented by the traditional Eastern authority of Alexandria.

a real head of the church in the whole of Gaul. He presided over councils of bishops in Riez (429), Orange (441) and Vaison (442). In Besançon—beyond the borders of the recognized jurisdiction of Arles—he deposed the local bishop Celidonius, who had been married to a widow and was accused of having, before his episcopacy, as a civil magistrate, pronounced death sentences (444). However, Celidonius appealed to Rome and was received in communion by pope Leo. Hilary immediately came to Rome to protest against the Roman intervention in the affairs of Gaul. He was rebuked and imprisoned on Leo's orders. Eventually, the pope, with imperial concurrence, deprived the bishop of Arles of his primatial privileges. Emperor Valentinian III himself affirmed the powers of Rome over Gaul (445). Attempts at reconciliation between the pope and St Hilary did not seem to have been fully conclusive until the latter's death in 449, probably still out of communion with Leo.[6]

Under Hilary's successor Ravennius, the see of Arles made attempts to restore its primacy—which had been transferred to Vienna by pope Leo—and was supported by the episcopate of Gaul. Eventually, in 514, with St Caesarius as bishop, the authority of Arles took the form of a papal vicariate, established by pope Symmachus, somewhat similar to the vicariate of Thessalonica.[7] This victory of papal authority in Gaul illustrates the fact that, in the West, civil and cultural *Romanitas* was generally seen as inseparable from the apostolic Petrine interpretation of the papacy. However, as the case of Arles shows, the imposition of Rome's power did not go unchallenged, on the part of those who held other views on the right of local bishops and provincial primacies.

Throughout the fifth century, catholic Christianity in Gaul showed remarkable vitality—spiritual, organizational and missionary. Not only through political circumstances, but also thanks to the spiritual prestige and pastoral skills of such bishops as St Hilary and St Caesarius of Arles, St Avitus of Vienna and St Germanus of Auxerre, Arianism lost much ground and Gaul became, at the end of the fifth century, almost uniformly orthodox.

[6]On the conflict see especially the *Life* of St Hilary (text in PL 50) and the *Letters* of St Leo. Canonically, the appeal of Celidonius to Rome could be justified by the canons of Serdica (343), but the attitude of Hilary seems to indicate that those canons were not received in Gaul.

[7]The title of vicar implied not so much an administrative dependence upon Rome, as an exemption from judicial responsibility to the regional episcopate. Cf. P. Lapin "Sud'by sobornago printsipa v zapadnom patriarkhate" (= The fate of the conciliar

The most decisive event, in this respect, occurred in 498 or 499, when the young pagan king of the Franks, Clovis, was baptized not into Arianism, but into catholic Christianity in Reims, by the local bishop Remigius (St Remi), together with three thousand of his warriors. Having married a catholic Christian, Queen Clotilda, in 493, Clovis had successfully invoked "her God" before a victory over the Alamanni. This played a decisive role in his conversion. As a Christian he entered into close contacts and correspondence with the catholic bishops, especially St Avitus of Vienna. With their sympathy and encouragement, he destroyed the rule of the Arian Visigoths in Southern Gaul (507-511), extending the borders of his kingdom to the Pyrenees. The Burgundians, who had helped Clovis in his war against the Visigoths, soon rejected Arianism, only to be incorporated themselves into the Frankish kingdom (536). The victories of Clovis were greeted by Gallo-Roman bishops as triumphs of the Church itself, and emperor Anastasius of Constantinople granted him the title of consul.

The new presige of the Franks and the close collaboration of Clovis with the bishops allowed him to hold a first council of his realm in Orléans in 511. The agenda, approved by the king, included a reorganization of the church within the *Regnum Francorum*. Although sanctioning the victory of Catholic—and Roman—orthodoxy over Arianism, the council *de facto* acted as the assembly of a national church, with the king playing the role previously reserved to the emperor or his commissioners. Henceforth, the Frankish church, though formally very respectful of the bishop of Rome, would develop in total administrative independence, and exercise an increasing influence not only in Germanic lands, but also in Italy.

Although the church in Gaul under Roman rule, never developed a really original theological tradition comparable to the African (Tertullian, Cyprian, Augustine), it produced several well-educated ecclesiastical writers and poets. These included Sidonis Apollinaris, a former pretorian prefect and prefect of Rome, who became bishop of Clermont (d. 479), and St Avitus of Vienna (d. 519). Most of them fared well under Visigothic kings who were culturally committed to Roman traditions in spite of their Arianism, so that some historians believe that a survival of the Gothic rule would have been more favorable to an

principle in the Western patriarchate), *Pravoslavnyi Sobesednik*, Kazan, 1909, 2, Sept. pp. 349-84; Nov. pp. 613-34.

organic development of Christian civilization in Gaul than the Frank-ish conquest.[8] It is true that the Franks were seen by many as the hope of orthodoxy, following the period of anti-Catholic persecutions by the Arian Visigothic King Euric (466-484), but such anti-catholic policies were rather exceptional on the part of the Visigoths, whereas the Frankish rule, though welcomed by St Avitus, proved in the long run to be something of a cultural regression.

In the history of theological thought and spirituality, the most significant events in the history of Christian Gaul were connected with the monastery founded by St Honorat on the island of Lérins, near Marseille. Inspired by the ascetic ideas brought from the East by St Cassian (see above, Chapter III), the community of Lérins trained a whole generation of monks, of whom several were elected to the episcopate. Churchmen coming from Lérins were different from the scholarly, aristocratic types, represented by Sidonis Apollinaris or St Avitus. Rather indifferent to secular culture, they were inspired by monastic asceticism, and also social activism, which made them popular with the masses and respected by the Barbarian rulers. The group in-cluded Ruricius of Narbonne, Venerius of Marseille, Lupus of Troyes, Eucher of Lyon, Valerian of Cimiez, Faustus of Riez and, last but not least, the great metropolitans of Arles, St Hilary and St Caesarius. Several of them became directly involved in a debate, which will influence crucial later developments in Western Christendom, and which was centered on the doctrine of St Augustine on "prevenient grace" and predestination.

It is not easy to define accurately the various positions of the protagonists in a debate which started before the death of St Augustine (430) and St John Cassian (433), and continued in Southern Gaul for several decades. In many Western circles the towering and truly unique legacy of St Augustine defied competition and criticism. His writings were treated as the tool *par excellence* for the understanding of Scripture, and as a unique source of theological thinking. Few minds were able to grasp the nuances, and contradictions, of Augus-tinian thought, or to engage in a constructive criticism of the more radical positions of Augustinism. The Roman pope Celestine himself, in an epistle to the bishops of Gaul, praised the doctrines of Augustine.[9]

---

[8]See, for example, G. de Plinval in A. Fliche et V. Martin, eds. *Histoire de l'Eglise. 4. De la mort de Théodose à l'élection de Grégoire le Grand,* Paris, 1948, p. 410.

[9]*Ep* 21, PL 50, col. 530.

As a result of this Roman endorsement, opposition to Augustinism, promoted in Lérins, acquired the additional flavor of local Gallic autonomy.

Through Cassian, the monks of Lérins had adopted the Eastern ideals of ascetical effort, as condition for the acquisition of divine grace. In his polemics against Pelagius, however, St Augustine had affirmed the ultimate sovereignty of God, whose grace *alone* could save man from sin: the error of Pelagius consisted precisely in attributing salvation to human merits, not to divine grace. Against objections coming already in his lifetime from Marseille, Augustine—informed about the existence of those critics by his friend and disciple, Prosper of Aquitaine (*ca.* 390-*ca.* 463), another Gallic monk, who eventually became secretary of pope Leo I—hardened his positions, by affirming that grace is necessary not only for the *process* of salvation, but that it alone can *initiate* faith in man, and that, consequently, only the *elect* who received it "preveniently" are saved, so that, outside of those few privileged souls, human nature goes to perdition, having no legitimate claim to divine mercy. Not only does salvation require a "prevenient" grace, but even "perseverance" in virtue must be attributed only to grace, not to human effort.[10]

Such views, promoted much more consistently by some disciples of Augustine, than by Augustine himself, created problems for the entire Eastern tradition, which—perhaps failing to resolve the issue rationally—supported a common sense attitude: divine grace and human freedom are both necessary at all stages of the spiritual life for communion with God and salvation. In the East, the just people of the Old Testament—kings, prophets, ancestors of Christ—although not yet reached by the grace of baptism, were venerated liturgically as saints, so that the Church clearly acknowledged their human achievements. And, of course, the entire monastic tradition respected the individual just who not only through grace, but also through their ascetic exploits, had acquired "boldness" before God.

So John Cassian was the one who objected to the substance of Augustine's arguments without naming him directly. But soon another monk of Lérins, Vincent—a brother of St Lupus, bishop of Troyes—also launched an implicit attack on Augustinism on different grounds. Rightly seeing in Augustinism a particular and highly individual inter-

---

[10]Cf. particularly Augustine's *De praedestinatione sanctorum* and *De dono perseverantiae.*

pretation of the Christian message, he invoked against it the tradition of the universal Church. In his famous *Commonitorium,* he objected against the monopoly of Augustinian thought, which seemed to overwhelm contemporaries. Only that doctrine is binding, he wrote, which is held "everywhere, always and by all" (*quod semper, quod ubique, quod ab omnibus creditum est*).[11] To the exegetical authority of Augustine, for example, he opposes that of Origen. To the argument that Augustine "developed" dogma, he objects that any change of formulation "must truly be a development, and not a transformation of the faith. Understanding, knowledge, and wisdom must grow and develop . . . in the same dogma, the same sense, the same meaning," and always follow the criteria of universality, antiquity and consensus. Clearly inspired by the views of tradition expressed, in the second century, by Tertullian and Irenaeus of Lyons, Vincent of Lérins deliberately argues in a circular manner: truth is that which is universally accepted, and universal Christian communion requires truth. He denounces any monopolization of tradition, and appeals to the mystery of the Holy Spirit preserving the Church on the right path. In his case, the "monks of Marseille" manifest a sense of catholicity and concern for universal unity, which can be explained only by the Eastern connections established by Cassian. Of course, they also clearly reject Pelagianism as such, and avoid any frontal attack on St Augustine himself.

The direct argument against predestination and the idea that human nature is totally depraved outside of baptism is continued by Faustus, abbot of Lérins for thiry years (433-462), then bishop of Riez (462-485). Rejecting Pelagianism, he nevertheless—very much in the Eastern spirit—invokes "the race of Abel," the just men and women of the old dispensation, in whom the image of God remained indestructible and who used their freedom—even before the coming of grace with Christ—to choose between sin and righteousness.[12]

Soon the "monks of Marseille" faced a strong Augustinian reaction, which found unexpected allies in the East. In his desire to defend the natural "goodness" of human nature against Augustinian pessimism, Faustus had used expressions emphasizing the integrity of the human nature in Christ and His authentically human characteristics and activity. In a somewhat superficial analysis, these expressions could

---

[11]Ed R. S. Moxon, *Commonitorium,* 2, Cambridge, 1915, p. 10; Engl. tr. by R. E. Morris, New York, 1949 (Fathers of the Church, 7), p. 270.
[12]Cf. for instance, in *De gratia* II, 8, CSEL, 21, p. 76.

easily serve to establish a parallelism between the main intuition of Pelagianism (the autonomy of the *humanum*) and the strictly "diphysite" thought of Theodore of Mopsuestia and Nestorius. This superficial parallelism—which failed to account for the Eastern patristic concept of "synergy," or "cooperation" between grace and freedom, one which allowed for both the integrity of human nature and the absoluteness of grace—was picked up in Constantinople (mainly for political reasons) by the Scythian monks (headed by John Maxentius).[13] Concerned about eradicating Nestorianism and promoting the Cyrillian "theopaschite" formulas—"the Son of God suffered in the flesh"—they sought the support of the Roman Church, whose prestige was restored in Byzantium under emperor Justin I (518-527). Approaching pope Hormisdas, through the intermediary of Possessor, an African bishop in exile in Constantinople, and later travelling to Rome themselves, the Scythian monks dispensed much energy to associate—in the minds of churchmen East and West—Nestorius with Pelagius, and Cyril with Augustine.[14] In the light of this association, they, in fact, demanded the condemnation of Faustus of Riez as an enemy of both Cyril and Augustine, the two great theological luminaries of the universal Church.

As pope Hormisdas showed reticence, the Scythian monks called for the support of several African bishops, exiled in Sardinia by the Vandals, but always ready to stand up for their great theologian, St Augustine. One of them, Fulgentius, the bishop of Ruspe, produced a monumental refutation of Faustus, in the name of the most extreme Augustinian positions on the radical corruption of fallen human nature and the total impotence of free will, without grace, to achieve any goodness pleasing to God.[15]

The activity of the Scythian monks and the writings of Fulgentius —although they failed temporarily to sway the Roman Church in favor

---

[13]On the Scythian monks and their involvement in christological debates, see below, Chapter VI, pp. 218-9). Originally from "Scythia," *i.e.* the region of the lower Danube, subject to the bishop of Tomi, they spoke both Latin and Greek and, therefore, were probably more aware of the Western debates on Augustinism than most Eastern theologians.

[14]On this episode see the very pertinent account of Duchesne, *L'Eglise* pp. 54-63.

[15]The writings of Fulgentius have recently been published by J. Fraipont, in *Corpus Christianorum* 91 and 91a (Turnhout, 1968). See also G. G. Lapeyre, *Fulgence de Ruspe* (Paris, 1929). Although Fulgentius came out as an ally of the Cyrillian "Scythian" monks, his christology lacks the Cyrillian dimension of "deification" which itself presupposed "synergy" between human and divine activity. This illustrates again the unfortunate superficiality of the entire debate on Augustinism in the fifth-sixth centuries.

of the "theopaschite" formula—made it impossible for the episcopate of Gaul to remain silent on the issue of Augustinism.

The see of Arles was then occupied by a former monk of Lérins, St Caesarius (503-542). Having fully restored relations with Rome and having been invested since 514 with the title of papal vicar over Gaul and Spain, he also succeeded in establishing regular collaboration with the Gothic kings Alaric II of Toulouse (whose power would eventually be suppressed by the Franks) and, especially, Theodoric (508-526). While residing in Ravenna and controlling Rome, the latter also kept Gothic power over Southern Gaul. Under such favorable conditions, Caesarius acquired great renown as a pastor and preacher. At the Council of Agde (506) he introduced a series of disciplinary reforms in the spirit of *Romanitas,* which affirmed the independence of bishops from local civil and judicial authority, proclaimed the inalienability of ecclesiastical properties, imposed discipline on clergy (including priestly celibacy), and established sacramental requirements for laity (regular communion, marriage requirements, etc.).

Neither St Caesarius himself, nor the Roman bishops of the time were theologically equipped to solve the riddle of the debates on grace and free-will, initiated by the polemics between Cassian and Augustine. But the authority of the latter was so much revered in the West and so often promoted in papal letters, that the issue could not be simply ignored. An inconclusive council was held in Valence (528), where Augustinism was criticised. However, the thought of St Augustine was formally endorsed in the canons of the council of Orange (529). They were signed by Caesarius and only twelve other bishops: the others either avoided involvement or belonged to the anti-Augustinian opposition, supporting the Lérins tradition.

Canons 1-8 of Orange affirm the Augustinian doctrine of original sin, *i.e.* that the hereditary descendants of Adam have their freedom "vitiated" and need grace even to obtain the "beginning of faith" (*initium fidei*), or the desire to be saved. By itself, fallen nature is not capable of any good work deserving salvation. Canons 9-25 contain a compendium of quotations from St Augustine, but also present an attempt to moderate extreme Augustinism. The Augustinian texts affirming predestination in an explicit manner, or denying any human role in "perseverance" for good, are significantly omitted.

The personal influence of St Caesarius—who would not forget

his training at Lérins—is generally credited for this relative moderation of the council of Orange. Neither Cassian, nor Faustus, nor any of their writings were condemned explicitly. The writings of St Cassian, although they were now often labelled as "semi-Pelagian," continued to be used not only by St Caesarius himself, in drafting his famous monastic Rule (*Regula sanctarum virginum*), but especially by St Benedict of Nursia and his successors.[16] Included among the saints in the East, Cassian would also enjoy local veneration as a saint by the local church of Marseille. A contemporary anonymous catalogue of heretics—among whom his name was included—and which was spuriously attributed to pope Gelasius,[17] did not succeed in obliterating his prestige completely.

It remains, however, that—in spite of its moderation—the council of Orange, whose decrees received the approval of pope Boniface II,[18] confirmed the eminence of St Augustine to the West, thereby disarming his critics. Later, the decrees will be used to bring about many theological impasses and tragic disputes. In retrospect, it would seem that the authority of St Augustine himself would have been better served had it not become so absolute, so exclusive in the West, and had the second-rate theologians, who were his disciples in the fifth and sixth centuries, been more attentive to the truly catholic and cautious legacy of the monks of Lérins and their references to the faith of the Church held "by all, everywhere, at all times," a faith which could never be exhausted by a single local interpretation, however prestigious and respectable, like that of Augustinism.

3. The British Isles: St Patrick; the Irish monks

Like Gaul, with which it entertained constant relations, Celtic Britain, in the fourth century, included a Christian minority and became closely integrated in a Christian Roman world. Bishops from the island participated in most councils related to the Arian disputes. Pelagius, whose doctrines caused so much concern to St Augustine, was a Britton. The existence of episcopal sees in *Eboracum* (York), *Londinum* (London) and *Colonia Lindiensium* (Lincoln) is well attested in the sources.

---

[16]Cf. O. Chadwick, *John Cassian,* Cambridge, 1968, pp. 152-53.
[17]Cf. *supra,* p. 88.
[18]PL, 65, col. 31-34.

Better attested still is the missionary activity of St Ninian, who, between 397 and 401, built the first Christian church in Scotland.

After 407, Barbarian invasions on the continent forced Roman troups to leave Britain. By 441-2, the island itself was invaded by pagan tribes from Northern Germany, the Saxons and the Angles. The local Celts, many of them Christian, found refuge in what is today Cornwall, Wales and French Brittany. The Church on the troubled island continued to be the object of pastoral solicitude both from Rome and from the episcopate in Gaul. As directed by pope Celestine, St Germanus of Auxerre made two trips to Britain (429-31 and 446-7). According to Prosper of Aquitania (Aquitaine), his primary goal was to combat heretical Pelagianism, but missionary and pastoral concerns also motivated the trips.

There are also legendary accounts about the spread of Christianity in Scotland. One of such legends reports that, in the fourth century a Greek monk, St Regulus (St Rule), brought relics of St Andrew, the Apostle, converted the king and built a church. This legend which is the origin of the modern city of St Andrews is connected with the tradition that St Andrew preached in Scythia—*i.e.* modern Russia— and the idea that Scythians and Scotts are ethnically related. The Vikings, who were roaming in the early Middle Ages between Kiev, Novgorod and Northern Europe may have contributed to the spread of St Andrew's legend.

Almost simultaneously (432), some sources indicate that pope Celestine sent a bishop, Palladius, to Ireland (*Ivernia, Hibernia*), which was populated by the still pagan *Scotti*.[19] However, the real credit for the evangelization of Ireland belongs to a remarkable— originally lay—missionary, St Patrick. (His full name was Magonus Sucatus Patricius.)

Born in a Romanized family of Christian Brittons,[20] he was kidnapped at the age of sixteen by "Scottish" raiders and spent six years as a slave in Ireland. Having escaped his captors and returned home, he was called in a vision—as he himself relates in his *Confession* —to return to Ireland as a missionary. Before doing so he travelled "to Gaul and Italy," although the exact chronology and details of the

---

[19]Some historians (cf. L. Duchesne, *Histoire ancienne de l'Eglise,* Paris, 1929, p. 618) doubt the historicity of the mission of Palladius, which is attested by Prosper of Aquitaine, but ignored by Irish sources.

[20]On the circumstances, many quite obscure, of the life of St Patrick, see R.P.C. Hanson, *Saint Patrick,* Oxford, 1968.

travel are obscure,[21] but most traditions point to some experience acquired by St Patrick at the monastic communities in Southern Gaul (Lérins) and his consecration as a bishop by St Germanus of Auxerre.

Once in Ireland, as a missionary bishop, *ca.* 432, his activity was centered in the Northern part of the island, around Armagh. There is little evidence of any coordination with the mission of Palladius, which was probably located in Cellfine in the South. The date of Patrick's death is uncertain (probably *ca.* 460). His writings—the *Confession*, the *Letter to Coroticus*—reflect his long and hard work as a dedicated apostle, totally unselfish, who succeeded single-handedly, against very serious odds, in baptizing thousands and in establishing the clerical structure of a new church.

It does seem probable that the organization of the Irish church by St Patrick (and, perhaps, Palladius) was in every way similar to the universal diocesan pattern, which existed elsewhere both in Britain and on the continent. However, the gradual de-Romanization of the British Isles, caused by the Anglo-Saxon invasions, caused the development among Celtic Christians, in Wales, Brittany and, especially Ireland, of a peculiar *monastic* domination of ecclesiastical structures. Whereas in the Greco-Roman world, the episcopate was essentially shaped by the existence of cities which controlled the surrounding countryside, the small tribal kingdoms of the Celts, the Irish and the Picts were more easily christianized and pastorally led by monastic communities, whose ascetic ideals seemed particularly appealing. Although the exact reasons and the details of the process are little known, the results, in the fifth and sixth century, were a fascinating phenomenon not only in the British Isles, but elsewhere in "barbarian" Western Europe, where Irish monks would later extend their missionary activities.

The available information is connected with monastic personalities, frequently closely related to local tribal leaders, like Illtud, abbot of the monastic island of Calday, and such communities at St David's in Wales, St Samson's of Dol in Brittany. The lives of abbots like St Finian, St Brandon and in the sixth century St Columba of Iona in Scotland, and the other St Columba (or Columban), who came from the monastery of Bangor and started the immigration of Irish monks to the continent, are equally fascinating. They inform us that monastic communities monopolized ecclesiastical leadership, so that parish

[21]According to Hanson, *op. cit.,* p. 188, the trip is legendary.

clergy and diocesan structure practically disappeared. The see of Armagh itself, created by St Patrick, reorganized itself on a monastic basis.

Several of the abbots had received an episcopal consecration, but, in other cases, the sacramental episcopate was bestowed upon a monk of the community, while the abbot kept administrative control over both the monastery, the daughter houses and the surrounding area. It does seem certain that, in some cases, abbots acted as bishops (and even ordained clerics) without having received the episcopate themselves.

In the fifth and sixth centuries, the Celtic church led a somewhat marginal existence, beyond the mainstream of Christendom. The judgment that "the British isle fell back to barbarism"[22] might be a little too harsh, but there is no doubt that the fate of the Celtic church, which today would be referred as "indigenization"—*i.e.* an adaptation of church life to local conditions—developped at some expense of universal consciousness. The Celtic church had really become indigenous, and this created ecclesiological and canonical problems. The issue of the true nature of the episcopate was certainly one of these, as were the particular methods of evangelization by travelling monks celebrating the Eucharist in private homes with the laity assuming certain sacramental functions,[23] or the refusal of Celtic clergy to integrate themselves into the normal canonical order, wherever one was in fact established, as in Britanny.[24] But the missionary zeal of the Irish monks and their achievements were remarkable. This success was perhaps due to the authentic spiritual tradition—similar in its rigor and its sense of independence to that of Syrian monasticism—which they generally maintained. Certain communities counted hundreds, sometimes thousands of monks. Ascetic practices included hundreds of daily prostrations, long hours of prayer with extended hands and prolonged immersion in cold water, even in the winter, to master fleshly temptations. Of course, the monasteries, in a country practically deprived of literacy, were also the only centers where books were kept and Latin language used, establishing conditions for perpetuating Christian culture.

[22]L. Duchesne, *Ibid.,* p. 624.
[23]Cf. the criticism of such practices by three bishops from Gaul, cf. J. Friedrich in *München, Akademie der Wiss, Sitzungsberichte,* 1895.
[24]The authority of the metropolitan of Tours over Brittany was challenged for centuries by Celtic clergy.

The reestablishment of generally accepted patterns of ecclesiastical polity in Britain will have to await the conversion of the Anglo-Saxons under the auspices of pope Gregory the Great in the early seventh century.

4. *Spain: Arians and Orthodox*

The Christian faith established itself in Roman Spain early and solidly. In the early fourth century, Bishop Ossius of Cordoba was the main ecclesiastical advisor of emperor Constantine and played a decisive role at the council of Nicaea. While standing unanimously behind Nicaean Orthodoxy, the Spanish episcopate had been touched and divided by Priscillianism (see above, p. 87)—a sect connected with both Gnosticism and monastic asceticism, and some debates connected with it continued as late as 563 (council of Braga).

However, as in other countries of Western Europe, a real disruption occurred in the fifth century with the barbarian invasions. Pagan Suevi, Arian Vandals, Alans and Visigoths installed themselves in the country, with only occasional attempts by imperial authorities to reassert administrative control. It is true that by 429, the Alans and Vandals left for Africa. But the ensuing war between the Suevi and the Visigothic king Theodoric II ended with a Visigothic victory and the massive conversion of the Suevi to Arianism (466). Under the fiercely Arian king Euric (466-484), who resided in Toulouse, the catholic church in Spain went through a difficult period, which was fortunately followed by the more tolerant reign of the Ostrogothic king Theodoric who, residing in Ravenna, dominated vast territories in Italy, Southern France and Spain. Several councils of the Spanish episcopate restored order and discipline in the Church, and reestablished contact with the Roman pope, whose see was also under the sway of Theodoric.

The situation improved even more when Chararic, king of the Suevi, impressed by miracles occurring at the tomb of St Martin of Tours, was converted to orthodoxy (*ca.* 550-55). This conversion was strengthened by the arrival of a monk from Pannonia, Martin, who established a monastic community in Dumio and, soon, was consecrated metropolitan of Braga (561-580). Bringing with him the spirit of Eastern monasticism, St Martin of Braga was also instrumental in encouraging competent anti-Arian theological literature, which gradually manifested the intellectual superiority of the catholic clergy over the Arians, and facilitated the romanization of the Gothic nobility. John of Biclar, a young Visigoth, even went to study in Constantinople.[25]

This trend toward romanization was rendered easy, among the Visigoths, by similar processes occurring in Gaul, and by the skillful and competent activities of St Leander, bishop of Seville, who succeeded in converting Hermenegild, the son of king Leovigild (568-586) to catholic orthodoxy. A war resulted between father and son, which ended with the capture of Seville, where Hermenegild resided, by Leovigild (584) and the execution of Hermenegild (585).[26] Leander himself had taken refuge in Constantinople (579-582), where he secured the support of emperor Tiberius II and obtained the personal friendship of St Gregory the Great, who was then a papal representative in the imperial capital.

King Leovigild did not limit himself to the persecution of Catholics. His reign was also marked by attempts to update the "Gothic religion," to make it more acceptable as a common Christian confession in Spain, to abolish the practice of rebaptizing catholic converts to Arianism, to use theological formulae more acceptable to orthodox piety, and to integrate Gothic and Roman legal systems. However, these attempts came too late. After his death, his second son and successor Recared (586-601) presided over the solemn conversion of the Visigothic nation to orthodox catholicism at the council of Toledo (589). As is well-known, this council—in circumstances still quite obscure—seems to have introduced a usage of the creed with the addition of the word *Filioque* (*a Patre Filioque procedit*—"The Holy Spirit which proceeds from the Father *and the Son*"). The intention was clearly to emphasize the divinity of the Son against Arianism, and the influence of the works of St Augustine on the Trinity facilitated the addition. It is very doubtful, however, that anyone in Toledo was aware of possible objections. Such ignorance is astonishing, particularly on the part of a St Leander, who during his recent sojourn in Constantinople should have been aware of the original text of the creed and of the importance attributed in Byzantium to doctrinal texts formally

[25]On this, see J. Fontaine, "Conversion et culture chez les Visigoths d'Espagne," in *La Conversione al Cristianesimo*, Spoleto, 1967, pp. 96-108.

[26]Modern historians (cf. J. Fontaine, *ibid.*, p. 115) emphasize the political aspects of the story. In his *Dialogues*, St Gregory the Great, however, presents Hermenegild as a martyr of the faith.

approved by ecumenical councils, and used throughout the universal church.

The addition to the creed—so casually and almost inadvertently made in a country which was then rather peripheral in the Christian world—would eventually be adopted in the Frankish kingdom and, in the eighth century, used by Charlemagne in his challenge to Byzantium.

5. *Africa: Arian persecutions*

The five Roman provinces of North Africa—except for the Western-most province of Mauritania Tingitana (contemporary Northern Morocco) which belonged to the prefecture of Gaul—constituted a separate diocese of Africa, a part of the prefecture of Italy. It covered the territories of contemporary Tunisia, Algeria and Lybia. By the beginning of the fifth century, Christianization had been largely completed, and the African church (centered around Carthage) could boast of a genuine local theological tradition with authors like Tertullian and Cyprian. Of course, until his death in 430, it was also dominated by the great figure of St Augustine, bishop of Hippo, in the province of Numidia. The African church had known internal crises, and a substantial proportion of its Christian population still belonged to the Donatist schism. However, and quite suddenly, both Catholics and Donatists were faced with a totally unexepected and fierce external menace: the occupation of the country by the militantly-Arian Vandal kings.

Germanic in origin, like the other barbarian tribes who had entered Western Europe, the Vandals had received Christianity from the Goths in its Arian form, but, unlike the Goths who were generally quite tolerant of the catholic populations controlled by them, they turned out as violent persecutors of Nicaean orthodoxy.[27]

Approximately 80,000 Vandal tribesmen, led by king Gaiseric (428-477), leaving Spain, where they had sojourned for a while, rapidly

---

[27]Our information about the Vandals in Africa comes largely from an eyewitness of the later period of their rule (he writes around 480), Victor of Vita, author of a *Historia persecutionis Africanae provinciae,* ed. M. Petschenig in CSEL 7, Vienna, 1881. Efforts by some historians to discredit the accuracy of Victor's descriptions are not fully convincing. The real horror of the persecutions are corroborated by other writers, including Fulgentius of Ruspe and Ferrandus, as well as by archeological evidence.

conquered Roman Africa in 432-439. In 435, the imperial government of Ravenna thought it inevitable to recognize them as *foederati,* which made their presence on Roman territory formally legal, like that of other barbarians. Parts of Numidia and the two provinces of Mauritania remained in Roman hands only until 455, when the Vandals finally took control of all Africa. Lacking any real power over the invaders, the emperors could only occasionally intervene on behalf of the catholic clergy and population; since the very beginning of Vandal rule, when they refused to join the Vandal Arian church, headed by its own "patriarch," they were violently persecuted. Conversion to Arianism implied new baptism, and imperial Roman laws which deprived heretics of civil rights were applied to the Orthodox. The threat became more immediate when Gaiseric, during a raid on Italy, succeeded to hold Rome itself for two weeks (June 445), to take the dowager empress Eudoxia and her two daughters prisoner and to marry his son Huneric to one of them, dreaming of restoring an Arian Roman empire, at least in the West.

His treatment of the catholic church in Africa was exceedingly brutal. The capture of Carthage in 439 was accompanied by massacres. The bishop Quodvultdeus was banished with many of the clergy, and the primatial see of Africa remained vacant until 454. After a brief tenure by Deogratias, another vacancy lasted until 481. During that period, of the 164 communities in proconsular Africa—i.e. the small territory surrounding Carthage—only three were occupied by catholic bishops.[28] There were hundreds of executions, thousands of deportations and, understandably, quite a number of defections to Arianism.

Perhaps, the culmination of the conflict occurred in the last year of the reign of king Hunneric (477-484). By the king's order, a debate on the faith took place in Carthage with the Arians, at which all the catholic bishops were convoked. Four hundred and sixty-six came.[29] The assembly was presided by the king and the Vandal patriarch Cyrila. The catholic bishops succeeded in reading a written profession of orthodox faith, but were declared to be losers. Following the debate—which was supposed to have given a "last chance" to the orthodox cause—the catholic church was formally outlawed. All

[28]Victor of Vita, *Historia* 1, 29, ed. cit., p. 13.
[29]Cf. the list in *Notitia provinciarum et civitatum Africae,* in CSEL, 7, p. 117-134. Africa was known to have kept the ancient practice of considering the bishop as the only normal celebrant of the Eucharist. As a result, each community, or "parish" was headed by a bishop, hence the existence of a very numerous episcopate.

churches were either closed or transferred to Arians, new ordinations were forbidden, as well as all other public celebrations. Liturgical books were destroyed. Many bishops, who refused to apostasize were tortured, some exiled to Corsica, others reduced to slave labor. Some mitigation of the terror occurred under king Gunthamund (484-496), but persecution was resumed by Thrasamund (496-523).

During the latter's reign, the Vandal leadership seems to have become worried by the activities of orthodox exiles, who, for under-standable reasons, were giving them a bad press. The king decided to make an attempt at reconciliation. The intellectual leadership in the exiled community belonged to Fulgentius, bishop of Ruspe, whose radical Augustinian writings, directed against the monks of Lérins, were mentioned earlier. In 515-517, Fulgentius was allowed to return to Carthage to engage in debates with Arians and to publish refutations of Arian beliefs. Nevertheless, the reconciliation attempt ended in failure. Fulgentius, however, acquired the reputation of an honest and fearless defender of orthodoxy, a reputation which added to his prestige as spokesman for Augustinism.

A radical change occurred under Hilderic (523-530)—a son of Eudoxia, daughter of Valentinian III—who took decisive steps in the direction of integrating the Vandal Kingdom into the Empire. All the anti-catholic decrees were abolished, and the church was allowed to organize itself. In 525, a "general" council of sixty orthodox bishops—the small number of participants can only be explained by years of terror—was held in Carthage. Unfortunately, these peaceful policies—probably coordinated with Constantinople—did not last. In 530, Gelimer, a grandson of Gaiseric, led an anti-Roman rebellion, pro-claimed himself king and had Hilderic imprisoned. By this time, how-ever, the empire, whose leadership had just been assumed by Justinian I (527-565) possessed both the means and the energy to react. It did so in a spectacular manner. A Roman expedition led by Belisarius and supported by the local population, destroyed the Vandal kingdom in a six month campaign (533-34). Captive Gelimer was led through the streets of Constantinople, a prisoner; and the male Vandal population was either massacred or sold into slavery. All the previous rights of the catholic Church, as state religion of the Empire, were restored in Byzantine Africa, and all dissident or heretical assemblies—including Arians and Donatists—were placed under ban.

6. St Leo the Great and the self-conscious papacy

We have discussed earlier the position of the Roman church within the Christian universe by the middle of the fifth century (Chapter II). With St Leo the Great (448-461), the view which the popes held of their own mission finds a spokesman capable of giving it moral prestige, administrative skill and theological articulation. Leo's predecessors asserted their authority only when circumstances allowed, but the new pope was able consciously to promote and express papal authority with eloquence, spiritual assurance and a systematic use of the Petrine "primacy texts."

Born in Tuscany, in the last years of the fourth century, Leo entered the orders of the Roman church, as a minor cleric, at a very early age, perhaps already under pope Zosimus (417-418). Under Celestine I (422-32), he was ordained a deacon and assumed the role of theological advisor to the Roman bishop. It is he who engineered the active participation of the Roman Church in the christological debates of 428-431. Acting on behalf of the pope, he solicited the right person—St John Cassian, an Easterner and a friend of Chrysostom, now residing in the West—to write a treatise on christology, which would allow Latin churchmen to find the right side in the debate between St Cyril of Alexandria and Nestorius.[30] While John Cassian was —as we have seen earlier—a critic of extreme Augustinism, St Leo, like most Latin theologians, revered the memory of Augustine. It might have appeared to him therefore that St Cyril, with his insistence on the divine Logos, as the only personal subject of Christ and the only "actor" of salvation, was closer to Augustine than was Nestorius. A personal understanding was established between Cyril and Leo. The powerful Alexandrian archbishop corresponded with the Roman deacon,[31] and pope Celestine gave Cyril the right to act "in his place" at the council of Ephesus (431). Grateful for this support, Cyril arranged (without debate) a condemnation of Pelagius at Ephesus (431), following Rome's example. This cooperation between Rome and Alexandria could not have occurred without Leo's active participation and advice.

Symptomatically, Leo's concerns and connections were, even then,

---

[30]Cf. the treatise De incarnatione by Cassian in PL 50, cols. 9-272.
[31]Cf. Cyril, Epist. 56, PG 77, col. 320.

not only theological and ecclesiastical. Being still only a Roman deacon, he was also a trusted consultant of the imperial court of Valentinian III, residing in Ravenna. In the spring of 440, he was dispatched to Gaul on a purely political mission of reconciliation on the occasion of a conflict between the Roman generals Aetius and Albinus. It is during this mission that pope Xystus died and Leo was hurriedly recalled to Rome to be elected and consecrated bishop (September 29, 440).

In order to grasp Leo's own understanding of his role as Roman pope, one has to remember that, like most of his contemporaries in the East and the West,[32] he believed in the providential nature of the Roman empire, as instrument of Christian unity and mission. Actually, he only repeated an idea dear to Eusebius, to John Chrysostom, to Gregory of Nazianzen, or to Prudentius when he exclaimed in one of his sermons:

> That the consequences of this unspeakable generosity (brought by the Incarnation) might be made known throughout the whole world, divine providence fashioned the Roman Empire; the growth of which was extended to boundaries so wide that all races everywhere became next-door neighbors. For it was particularly germane to the divine scheme that many kingdoms should be bound together under a single government, and the world-wide preaching should have a swift means of access to all people, over whom the rule of a single state held sway.[33]

It was quite natural for him, therefore, to act and to be seen as a guardian of the *Romanitas*, not only in such assignments as the mission to Gaul, mentioned above, but also in the more celebrated meeting with Attila in 452, when, as a member, together with two senators, of an imperial delegation, he succeeded in preventing the invasion of Italy by the Huns; or when, in 455, he negotiated, with partial success only, the sparing of Rome's population and treasures by the invading Vandals, led by Gaiseric.

When one carefully analyzes Leo's statements about the establishment of the Roman church by St Peter, one discovers that, even there, the idea of the providential empire is not forgotten. Indeed, in his

---

[32]Cf. references above, pp. 28-38.
[33]*Sermon* 82,2, PL 54, col. 423.

view, as the apostles, following Pentecost, went to preach the Gospel in various countries, "the most blessed Peter, prince of the apostolic order, was destined for the capital of the Roman empire, so that the light of truth might be spread more efficiently from the very head to the whole body of the world."[34] It is not only that Peter gives Rome its prestige, but the spiritual dimension, expressed by Peter, was itself manifested precisely in Rome because of its being the imperial capital.

But, of course, Leo's thought did not stop there. As a pastor, a keen observer and a participant in the tragic events of his time, he witnessed the disintegration of the political *Romanitas*. He was fully aware that, although the Roman empire had been invested with a providential mission to direct the corporate unity of all Christians, this function could now be only partially fulfilled by the eastern emperor of Constantinople. The true center of eternal unity had to remain, and indeed, remained, as a "rock," embodied in the ministry of the "heir" of St Peter in Rome. To the legitimate emperor in the East, Leo always pays the usual respects; he recognizes his role in summoning councils and, even, uses for him such rhetorical epithets as were also used, even more generously, by the Greeks. Thus, addressing Theodosius II, he exclaims: "There is in you not only a royal, but also a priestly mind."[35] However, in Leo's perspective, the disintegration of the empire and the transfer of the imperial residence from Rome to Constantinople—or, in the case of the West, to Ravenna—only served to unveil another, and higher aspect of the divine plan: the recognition of Rome as the seat of St Peter's vicar.[36] Indeed, while emperors might abandon their capital and empires themselves disappear, "there abides that which the Truth itself has ordained, and so blessed Peter, in retaining the rock-like strength which he received, *does not abandon the government of the Church* committed to him."[37]

We have seen already that the authority of the Roman bishop, as successor of Peter, had been affirmed earlier, especially by popes like Damasus and Siricius; in the case of St Leo, however, the idea is proclaimed with much greater solemnity, eloquence and consistency by a pope whose moral character and devotion to the Church were

---

[34]*Ibid.*, 3, col. 424; the concept of "head of the world" (*caput mundi* or *caput orbis*) designating Rome is a standard Roman expression, often used by St Leo.

[35]*Ep* 24 (*Ep 2* in ACO, t. II, vol. 4, p. 2).

[36]"Through the blessed Peter's holy see, thou (O Rome) didst attain a wider sway by the worship of God than by earthly rule." *Sermon* 82,1, PL 54, 423 A.

[37]*Sermon* 3.3, PL 54, vol. 146B.

universally admired. Furthermore, when compared to his predecessors, Leo can be seen as introducing two subtle, but quite important, shifts in the ecclesiastical self-understanding of the church of Rome.

The first is closely linked with Roman legal principles. Leo's vision of the Church is that of a universal body (*corpus*), which "is not merely a pneumatic or sacramental or spiritual body, but also an organic, concrete and earthly society."[38] The Roman concept of a universal *corpus*, ruled by an emperor or "prince" (*princeps*), is identified, in Leo's thought, with the "body of Christ" (*corpus Christi*) of the New Testament writings. Of course, Christ himself is head of the body, but since He also made Peter "prince of the whole Church" (*quem totius ecclesiae principem fecit*),[39] "principality" within the body belongs also to Peter and his successors. In early Latin Christian terminology, the term *principalitas* had already been used to describe the role of the Roman Church.[40] It is therefore the use of another term—*principatus*—by St Leo, which constitutes a deliberate shift in favor of a legal title which so far had been an exclusive monopoly of the emperor.[41] Leo does not hesitate: the apostle Peter "received the *principatus* from the Lord,"[42] which was the same as to say that Peter and, by implication, his successor, or heir, occupies, within the "body" of the Church the position which is, in secular society, attributed to the emperor. "In the whole world, Peter alone is chosen . . ., so that, even if there are many priests and shepherds in the people of God, Peter may properly rule (*proprie regat Petrus*) over those whom Christ *also* rules in an eminent way."[43]

The second shift in Leo's thought is closely associated with his

[38]Walter Ullmann, *The Growth of Papal Government in the Middle Ages. A Study of the Ideological Relation of Clerical to lay Power,* London, 1955, p. 3; cf. also, by the same author "Leo I and the theme of Roman Primacy," JTS 11 (1960), pp. 25-51.

[39]*Sermon* 4,4, PL 54, col. 152A.

[40]Cf. the famous passage of St Irenaeus (*Adv. Haer.* III,3,2) which, being a translation of the Greek, may simply mean "antiquity" (*principium*—ἀρχή; *principalitas* —ἀρχαιότης). In any case, it hardly implies powers of jurisdiction.

[41]No wonder that the imperial chancery, even at the court of Ravenna which was very favorable to pope Leo, avoided using the term *principatus* in addressing the pope (cf. Ullmann, *Ibid.*)

[42]*A domino acceperit principatum, Ep* 9, *praef.,* PL 54, col. 625A; the term *principatus,* had already been appropriated to the Roman Church by Boniface I in 422 (Cf. PL 20, col. 778), but this was an exceptional usage.

[43]*Sermon* 4,2, PL 54, col. 149-150; there are many parallel texts in Leo's letters and sermons. He even used to speak of "fullness of power" (*plenitudo potestatis*) of the pope (Ep 14,1 PL 54, col. 671), a key expression in the late medieval definitions of papal power; cf. T. Jalland, *The Life and Times of St Leo the Great,* London, 1941, pp. 64-85.

concept of the *corpus*. It concerns the relationship between Peter and the episcopate as a whole, based on the scriptural evidence of a pre-eminence of the "first" apostle Peter among the Twelve. This pre-eminence was not really a controversial point. Not only Leo, but indeed all the patristic authors of the East and the West recognized it.[44] What really represents an issue is an eventual *succession* of Peter. It cannot be solved on any Scriptural evidence, but essentially depends on ecclesiological presuppositions. For St Leo, as for all other Christian authors, the position occupied by Peter was of course based on his con-fession of Christ as Son of God (Mat 16:16), *i.e.* the faith of the Church.[45] But how and by whom is the faith of Peter maintained in the Church *after* Peter? St Leo had, of course, been an assiduous reader of the one Latin author—St Cyprian of Carthage—who coined the concept of the "chair of Peter (*cathedra Petri*), as the center and criterion of church unity. However, for Cyprian, the "chair of Peter" was a sacramental concept, necessarily present *in each local church*: Peter was the example and model of each local bishop, who, within his community, presides over the Eucharist and possesses "the power of the keys" to remit sins. And since the model is unique, unique also is the episcopate (*episcopatus unus est*) shared, in equal fullness (*in solidum*) by all bishops. St Leo is aware of this connection, established by Cyprian, between Peter and *all* the bishops. Indeed all of them are "partners of his office" (*consortes honoris sui*), but—and here is the subtle shift—the bishop of Rome alone truly occupies the see of Peter (*Petri sedes*).[46] Consequently—the logic is inevitable—the power of local bishops is not only dependent upon the person of Peter, but also upon the person of his "heir," whose responsibility is universal. "For although every shepherd presides over his own flock with a particular responsibility . . .," proclaims St Leo, "we have a duty which is shared with them all; in fact the function of each one is a part of our work; so that when men resort to the see of the blessed apostle Peter from all quarters of the whole world, and seek from our bounty his love of the whole Church entrusted to him by the Lord, the greater our duty to everyone, the heavier we feel the burden which rests on our shoulders."[47]

[44]Cf. my review of such texts among Greek authors in J. Meyendorff *et al., The Primacy of Peter in the Orthodox Church*, London, 1963 (article "St Peter in Byzantine theology").

[45]The centrality of the faith in Leo's ecclesiology is well emphasized in the classical book by P. Batiffol, *Le siège apostolique* (359-451), Paris, 1924, pp. 420-423.

[46]Cf. *Sermon* 2,2, PL 54, col. 144A.

[47]*Sermon* 5,2, PL 54, col. 153CD.

Indeed, if the *corpus Christi* is not realized fully in the sacramental, pneumatic reality of the local eucharistic gathering, but is identified, as it certainly was by St Leo, with the empirical organization of the world Church, it implies the existence of a single head invested with a "principate," or monarchical power. In the light of his vision of the *corpus* of Christians, "the horizontal theory of Cyprian belongs to the realm of speculation; it neither corresponded to the facts nor to the exigencies of government."[48] The "chair of Peter" was in Rome alone!

This monarchical vision of the universal church—as monarchical as the Roman empire, whose unifying function it assumed—has led many to interpret St Leo's thought as anticipating, in every way, the theory of papal infallibility and universal jurisdiction as it was defined by the First Vatican council (1870).[49] In reality, there was some mystical, unreal quality about St Leo's claims: neither in the West, nor in the East, had the Roman bishop in fact ever exercised the powers which were implied by the logic of Leo's thought. Perhaps, as Louis Duchesne remarks, if the Western empire had lasted longer, with all emperors as open to papal influence as was Valentinian III, more ecclesiastical centralization would have been achieved in Latin Christendom. But, in Leo's time, the principles of ecclesiastical coordination beyond the level of the diocese, remained quite vague.[50] In a sense, the East was even more ready to recognize some Rome-centered unity, but not with the same "apostolic" dimension. Pope Leo himself seemed to be aware of the distance which separated his "Petrine" scheme from the practice of the church in his time, a practice which remained based on regional, or universal consensus of the episcopate, as witness of a common tradition, rather than on compliance with a single "Petrine" center. Karl F. Morrison is, therefore, right in speaking of a peculiar "Janus complex" which characterized the activities of the popes of the fifth century, not excluding Leo: there was a very slow shift from the old notion of a *continuum* of tradition, expressed by consensus, to a new "Roman" notion of the Truth being defined by discretion of the "center" (imperial, or papal). Pope Leo, in his personal public state-

---

[48]Ullman, *op. cit.,* p. 7.

[49]Cf. B.J. Kidd, *The Roman Primacy to A.D. 461,* London, 1936, p. 153; also the Orthodox bishop F(eodor), "Iz istorii papstva. Znachenie papy L'va velikogo v razvitii idei papstva," *Bogoslovsky Vestnik,* 1912, II, pp. 477-510.

[50]"Le groupement de l'épiscopat, le régime des conciles, les rapports avec le Saint-Siège, tout cela était, en Occident, fort peu défini" (L. Duchesne, *Histoire ancienne de l'Eglise,* III, Paris, 1929, p. 676; cf. also p. 679).

ments, tried to emphasize the discretion side of the Janus, but settled with Tradition, wherever he had no practical choice.[51] However, his inner conviction, enshrined in his writings, will be fully understood and used in later times, when the concept of papal authority will develop sufficiently and acquire, in the West, the prestige and the means to match theory with practice.

The "Janus complex" can be illustrated by the facts of Leo's long tenure as bishop of Rome. His correspondence and activities show an extraordinary sense of pastoral responsibility and concern for detail, as well as theological competence, but no direct attempts at imposing papal power in areas where no precedent for it existed.

In Rome itself, he devoted considerable energy in fighting Manichean sectarians, many of whom were refugees from Vandal persecutions in Africa. He established a church investigation of their activities and obtained a formal decree of Valentinian III making Manicheism illegal and its adepts formally deprived of civil and property rights. T. Jalland may not be quite correct in calling this "the first known example of a partnership between Church and State in carrying out a policy of religious persecution,"[52] for the earlier measures of a Theodosius I against heretics condemned by councils were certainly also condoned by the Church, but the episode is clearly a good illustration of Leo's understanding of the Empire's role in sustaining the Church by legal and administrative means.

Beyond Rome, the reign of Leo did not coincide with any particular reinforcement of ecclesiastical centralization in the West. In Italy and the surrounding islands—which formed the territory where the bishop of Rome exercised the rights of a metropolitan—the bishops were encouraged to attend annual synods in Rome, in accordance with the canons of Nicaea. In Leo's days, the annual synod was held on the anniversary of Leo's consecration (September 29).[53] The occasion gave the pope regular opportunity to define his understanding of the "Petrine office"—in a solemn sermon addressed every year to the bishops. However, even if Leo frequently gave detailed pastoral advice to his Italian colleagues, he did not interfere in episcopal elections, but only presided over the sacramental consecration which sanctioned them. In Spain and Africa held by barbarians, his contacts with the local

---

[51]K.F. Morrison, *Tradition and Authority in the Western Church, 300-1140*, Princeton, 1969, pp. 77-94.

[52]*The Life and Times of St Leo the Great*, London, 1941, p. 49.

[53]Cf. for example, Leo's letter to the bishops of Sicily, *Ep* 16, 7 PL 54, col. 702 BC.

bishops were only episodic without any administrative implications. In Gaul, as we have seen earlier,[54] St Hilary of Arles rejected the claim of the pope to receive appeals against the judgment of local synods. This challenge to Roman authority could be overcome by Leo only with the help of an imperial decree of Valentinian III. As noted by Louis Duchesne,[55] the Western Church never met, as such, in a general council, which means that there existed no reality corresponding to a single "Western patriarchate," but only the potential for the establishment of separate patriarchates in Arles, Carthage, and Thessalonica. However, there was a sense of universal moral and doctrinal authority located in the church of Rome In his writings and activities, Leo contributed much to the growth of this latter perception, which also existed in the East.

The involvement of the Roman church in the christological debates in the East is essentially of St Leo's making, first as theological advisor of Celestine I and then as pope. It was an extraordinary and really unprecedented involvement, which will be mentioned again in the next chapter. It illustrates not only the personality of St Leo, but also the same "Janus complex," which characterized his way of asserting his authority in the Church.

Solicited first by the archimandrite Eutyches, whom he congratulated for his anti-Nestorian zeal (448), then by Flavian of Constantinople, Leo had been invited by emperor Theodosius II to attend an ecumenical council in Ephesus (449). As he did often in his correspondence with Western bishops, he reacted by expressing his opinion clearly and at sufficient length, but without taking the time to inform himself, with real thoroughness, of the circumstances, the vocabulary and the problematics involved in the debate. He held, undoubtedly, the conviction that Peter indeed spoke through him. His famous letter—or *Tome*—to Flavian of Constantinople did not prevent Monophysitism from triumphing as the "Robber council" in Ephesus. But two years later, it marked a high point in the Eastern recognition of Roman authority during the council of Chalcedon (451). Leo did not participate personally in the council, but his legates at Chalcedon carried with them another remarkable letter addressed to the assembled fathers and expressing the pope's wish that "the rights and honor of the most blessed apostle Peter be preserved"; that, not being able to come

[54]Cf. supra, pp. 131-2.
[55]*Op. cit.*, p. 673.

himself, the pope be allowed "to preside" (προεδρεύειν) at the council in the persons of his legates; and that no debate about the faith be actually held, since "the orthodox and pure confession on the mystery of the Incarnation has been already manifested, in the fullest and clearest way, in his letter to bishop Flavian of blessed memory."[56]

No wonder that his legates were not allowed to read this unrealistic and embarrassing letter before the end of the sixteenth session, at a time when acrimonious debates on the issue had already taken place! Obviously, no one in the East considered that a papal *fiat* was sufficient to have an issue closed. Furthermore, the debate showed clearly that the *Tome* of Leo to Flavian was accepted *on merits*, and not because it was issued by the pope. Upon the presentation of the text, in Greek translation, during the second session, part of the assembly greeted the reading with approval ("Peter has spoken thus through Leo!" they shouted),[57] but the bishops from the Illyricum and Palestine fiercely objected against passages which they considered as incompatible with the teachings of St Cyril of Alexandria. It took several days of commission work, under the presidence of Anatolius of Constantinople, to convince them that Leo was not opposing Cyril. The episode clearly shows that it was Cyril, not Leo, who was considered at Chalcedon as the ultimate criterion of christological orthodoxy. Leo's views were under suspicion of Nestorianism as late as the fifth session, when the same Illyrians, still rejecting those who departed from Cyrillian terminology, shouted: "The opponents are Nestorians, let them go to Rome!"[58] The final formula approved by the council was anything but a simple acceptance of Leo's text. It was a compromise, which could be imposed on the Fathers when they were convinced that Leo and Cyril expressed the same truth, only using different expressions.

Even more symptomatic is the acceptance by the Council of the famous canon 28, whose importance in the history of Eastern ecclesial structures will be discussed below.[59] The text makes two major points. First—reflecting the desire of the government of emperor Marcian and

[56]ACO II, 2, vol. 1, part 3, pp. (444) 85; the text of the letter in *Epist. Coll.* M, ACO II, 1, 1, pp. 31-32.

[57]*Ibid.*, II, 2, vol. 1, 2, pp. (277)81 (The episode appears as a part of the third session in the Greek acts). The acclamation "Peter has spoken thus through Leo," often quoted as a triumph of Roman authority, seems to have actually been a defensive reaction against objections by the Illyrians.

[58]*Ibid.*, p. (321)125.

[59]Pp. 179-83.

his wife Pulcheria to associate Rome and Constantinople, as the two "imperial" centers of the Church against the pretensions of Alexandria—the text confirms the decision of 381 to give the ecclesiastical "New Rome" the second place of honor after the "Old Rome." It then goes further than the council of 381, by explicitely interpreting the primacy of both Romes in purely empirical or political terms, as determined by "the presence of the emperor and the Senate." The second point consists in formally establishing a "patriarchate" of Constantinople (whose position, so far, had been purely honorary), and giving its bishop the right to consecrate the metropolitans in three imperial dioceses: Thrace, Pontus and Asia. The second point was of a purely practical and administrative nature, but the first consisted in a formal denial of the very basis of Leo's ecclesiology: the primacy of Rome was of a political nature, established "by the Fathers," and not a divine institution, or "chair of Peter."

The reaction of the papal legates to the adoption of this text, as well as the letters written on the subject by pope Leo himself after the council, are a good illustration of the "Janus" quality of Rome's attitude on the issue of its primacy. The only ground used by the legates and the pope to justify their objections—which they voiced with great force—is that canon 28, by setting up a Constantinopolitan "patriarchate" and by assigning it the second place after the "Old Rome," was infringing upon the letter of canon 6 of Nicaea, which had mentioned only three "primacies": Rome, Alexandria and Antioch. In their protest, the legates invoked papal instructions ("You are not to allow any addition to the decision of the fathers of Nicaea"), and, after the council, the pope himself wrote to emperor Marcian: "The privileges of the churches established by the canons of the holy fathers and prescribed by the decrees of the council of Nicaea cannot be set aside." In his letter to empress Pulcheria, he is more blunt: "Resolutions of bishops which are repugnant to the rules of the holy canons laid down at Nicaea, by the authority of the blessed Peter the Apostle, . . . we annul and cancel" (*cassamus*). Finally, to Anatolius, he writes: "The Nicene council has been endowed by God with so high a privilege, that ecclesiastical decisions . . . inconsistent with its decrees, are altogether false and devoid of authority."[60]

[60]All these texts are to be found in ACO. For a very accurate description of Chalcedon's procedures and a translation of all relevant texts, consult F. X. Murphy, *Peter speaks through Leo. The Council of Chalcedon, A.D. 451*, Washington, D.C. 1952.

Clearly, the pope was fully aware of the incompatibility between the text of canon 28 and his own understanding of the position of Rome in the universal Church, but he also knew that his claims in this regard would simply not be understood in Constantinople, if he expressed them as he usually did in addressing Western bishops. This is the reason for his relatively moderate stand, and his appealing to Nicaea only. In doing so, he stood on common ground with the East, by relying on the old concept of episcopal consensus: to be binding and recognized, the rights of churches must be defined by conciliar decrees. Meanwhile, his own concept of "apostolic primacies" was also implicitly safe. As we have seen earlier canon 6 of Nicaea was—quite unrealistically—interpreted in Rome as supposedly recognizing the primacies of Rome, Alexandria and Antioch as, all three, "Petrine" sees.[61]

There is no doubt therefore, that the personal, almost mystical conviction of being, as bishop of Rome and heir of Peter, responsible for the doctrinal and disciplinary welfare of the universal church, never left pope Leo. But equally clear is the fact that this Roman claim was not fully understood by others, and virtually inapplicable in the historical circumstances of the fifth century. To that situation, St Leo adapted himself as he could, losing neither his personal dignity, nor the authentic concern for orthodoxy and unity, which character-ized his remarkable personality, as a bishop of the Church.

7.   *Leo's successors and the Laurentian schism*

Since the removal of the permanent imperial residence to Ravenna, the bishop of Rome was unquestionably the major personality of the ancient capital. In 476, when the empire disappeared altogether, his position underwent no major change. The Gothic rulers, who were in effective control of Italy, were not only tolerant of the catholic Church, but also interested in using it as a diplomatic link with the empire in Constantinople.

[61]This moderation, or inconsistency of St Leo in his arguments against canon 28 led Martin Jugie to believe that the pope did not see any negation of the "Petrine" Roman primacy in the text (*Le Schisme byzantin*, Paris, 1941, p. 16-17). However, it is unlikely that the pope was as naive as Jugie supposes. His belief in the apostolicity of sees and the lack of such apostolicity in the case of Constantinople, which makes that church ineligible for primacy, is clearly expressed in his letters to Marcian and Anatolius (Cf. the comments of E. Herman, "Chalkedon und die Ausgestaltung des Konstantino-politanischen Primats" in *Chalkedon*, II, pp. 465-6.)

Residing at the palace of the Lateran, with the neighboring "Golden basilica" (*basilica aurea*) as his cathedral, the pope directly administered the three other large *martyria,* also built in basilican form —St. Peter's on the Vatican, St Paul's on the *via Ostia* and the *basilica Liberiana,* begun under pope Liberius on the Esquiline, rebuilt by Xystus III, and dedicated to the Virgin, in commemoration of the Council of Ephesus (431)—as well as twenty-eight urban *tituli,* or parish churches. Although many of the buildings were rebuilt or re-modelled during the Renaissance, a surprisingly large number of these churches preserve their essential fifth-century appearance even today.

Traditionally, the election of a new pope followed the same procedure as that of any other bishop with the participation of the clergy and selected laity of the city. The episcopal consecration was then performed by neighboring bishops (*episcopi suburbicarii*). The political and social role played by the Roman pope implied that the elections were supervised and approved by the Gothic kings. The first papal election to be held following the formal disappearance of the Western empire (476) took place in 483, following the death of pope Simplicius. The electoral assembly of clergy and senators, presided by the pretorian prefect Caccina Basilius, on behalf of king Odoacer, performed the election of pope Felix III. Similar procedures were followed for the election of popes Gelasius (492-6) and Anastasius II (496-8). But in 498, a crisis occurred. The local Roman clerical party supported the election of Symmachus, whereas the aristocratic senatorial group was for Laurence (498-506). It was king Theodoric who was the real and sole arbiter of the struggle. The relative benevolence of the Gothic kings guaranteed a great measure of order and continuity, so that, as under Roman rule, their choice fell often on the closest friends of preceding popes (Leo was Celestine's deacon and advisor; Hilary occupied a similar position under Leo, and Gelasius had been the main advisor of Felix).

In order to understand the full dimensions of the Roman crisis of 498, which inaugurated the "Laurentian schism," reference should be made to Eastern ecclesiastical affairs, which will be discussed further in the next chapter.

The single most important issue which preoccupied the immediate successors of St Leo was the policy of Eastern emperors towards the opponents of the council of Chalcedon and their attempts to settle the issue through compromise. Unable to perceive the subtleties of

Greek christological terminology, and understandably distrustful of Byzantine imperial politics, the popes stood for the authority of the *Tome* of Leo and, together with most Latin churchmen familiar with the vocabulary of Tertullian, Augustine and Leo, feared the slightest departure from the letter of the Chalcedonian definition. Meanwhile, in the East, emperor Zeno thought that he had found a way to calm the anti-Chalcedonian opposition, by issuing a document known as the *Henotikon* (482). It contained an uncontroversial condemnation of both Nestorius and Eutyches and a forceful endorsement of St Cyril's *Anathematisms*. It also claimed to reject all heretics who taught wrongly "in Chalcedon or any synod whatever."[62] This last ambiguous reference was intended to please the Monophysites without offering a formal disavowal of the Chalcedonian faith. On the basis of the *Henotikon,* and under imperial pressure, the Chalcedonian patriarchs of Constantinople and Jerusalem entered in communion with the monophysite archbishops of Alexandria and Antioch.

A strong protest of the Roman pope Felix III against this ambiguous deal resulted in a schism between Rome and the patriarch of Constantinople, Acacius, presumed drafter of the *Henotikon,* but a Chalcedonian by conviction.[63] Political circumstances were making this Roman stand possible. The Gothic domination of Italy was giving the Roman church full independence from direct imperial pressure and some leverage in dealing with Constantinople. Indeed, the imperial government was counting on the pope to maintain its interests in the West and, on the other hand, could not ignore the prestige of the successors of St Leo. As a result, the attitude of the popes carried weight.

The architect of the papal policies in what is usually called the "Acacian schism" was Gelasius, a member of pope Felix III's clergy, and eventually a pope himself (492-96). In spite of his brief pontificate, he showed himself, in the pastoral, administrative and ideological fields, as a personality almost as influential as Leo. Although the so-called *Decretum Gelasianum* was not written by him,[64] his letters

---

[62]There is an annotated translation of the *Henotikon* in CN III, p. 924-927.

[63]A total rejection of Chalcedon was as unacceptable to Constantinople as it was to Rome, especially because the canonical rights of Constantinople now depended upon canon 28.

[64]Cf. *supra,* p. 61-62; on the role of Gelasius at the papal court of his predecessors Simplicius and Felix III, see H. Koch, *"Gelasius im Kirchenpolitischen Dienst seiner Vorgänger,"* München, 1935 and W. Ullmann, *Gelasius I,* (492-496). *Das Papsttum an der Wende der Spätantike zum Mittelalter* (= *Päpste und Papsttum,* 18), Stuttgart, 1981.

to emperors Zeno and Anastasius, protesting their attempts at imposing imperial power on the Church, are manifestations of papal independence and served as powerful precedents for the medieval struggle between Church and State in the West. Recognizing the divine origin of the *imperium,* Gelasius affirms nevertheless that the emperor does not possess the power to define Christian principles governing Christian society: the power to do so belongs to the "priesthood," and particularly to the pope, as successor of Peter.[65] In a famous letter to emperor Anastasius I, Gelasius wrote: "There are essentially two powers governing the world: the sacred authority of the pontiffs and the power of the kings. Of these two powers, the priests carry a weight that is all the more heavy in that, at the divine last judgment, they will have to render an account for the kings themselves."[66] Consequently, "Christian emperors must submit their actions to the bishops."[67]

These texts of Gelasius not only became classical references of papal self-consciousness in the West, but also established the Roman church as an ultimate recourse for those who, in the East, would have to fight heretical emperors in the seventh and eighth centuries. It remains, nevertheless, that even those historians who, otherwise, admire the uncompromising firmness of pope Gelasius, must recognize that "he defended his view vis-à-vis Constantinople with a roughness that was bound to make the opponent obdurate rather than flexible."[68] After the death of Acacius and the brief patriarchate of Fravitas (489-90), patriarch Euphemius (490-95) of Constantinople broke fellowship with the monophysite patriarch Peter Mongus of Alexandria, adopting a clearly Chalcedonian stand. He approached Rome, seeking restoration of communion and papal support, since he found himself in conflict with emperor Anastasius who still supported the *Henotikon.* But Gelasius, in a blunt and ironical letter to Euphemius, demanded that the name of Acacius be striken from liturgical commemorations in Constantinople,[69] a condition which the Easterners were unwilling

[65]Cf. particularly W. Ullman, *The Growth of Papal Government in the Middle Ages,* London, 1955, pp. 14-31.

[66]*Ep* 8, PL 59, 42A.

[67]Letter of Felix III to Acacius (most probably written by Gelasius), *Ep* 1, PL 58, col. 894-6; on the role of Gelasius in writing the letters of Felix, see H. Koch, "Gelasius im Kirchenpolitischen Dienst seiner Vorgänger Simplicius und Felix III," *München, Bayer. Akad. der Wiss., Sitzungsberichte, Phil. Hist. Abt.,* 1933, vol. 6. It should be noted, however, that Gelasius never claimed political supremacy over emperors and never considered exscommunicating Zeno (Richards, *Popes,* pp. 21-24.)

[68]Jedin-Dolan, *History,* II, New York, 1980, p. 618.

[69]*Ep* 11, PL 59, col. 13-19.

to meet, since Acacius—though tactically at fault—had never been formally condemned for heresy, but only unilaterally deposed by Rome.

Thus, behind the dispute surrounding the name of the deceased Acacius, stood the ecclesiological issue of the Roman claim to be recognized as the sole criterion of ecclesial communion. Although the "Acacian" schism would eventually be resolved and communion restored, the ecclesiological issue—as in the case of canon 28 of Chalcedon —would remain. Patriarchs Euphemius (490-495) and his successor Macedonius (495-511) are, even today, considered as schismatics by Rome, but in Constantinople, they would not only remain in the diptychs (or liturgical commemorations), but even entered into the catalogue of holy confessors, because both were deposed by Anastasius I for their defense of Chalcedon. In the name of papal claims, the Roman church tragically neglected the true defenders of Orthodoxy in the East.

But it soon appeared how controversial those claims were not only in the East, but also in the West. After the death of Gelasius, his successor, pope Anastasius II (496-498), began making concessions in order to restore relations with Constantinople. This led a number of Roman clergy to break fellowship with the new pope, because he had "communicated with a deacon of Thessalonica, Photinus by name, who was of the party of Acacius . . . without consulting the priests or the bishops or the clergy of all the catholic Church."[70] This episode, while showing the anti-Byzantine feelings of many among the Roman clergy, also indicates that such feelings did not necessarily imply an unconditional acceptance of papal authority! This would be illustrated much more clearly during the so-called "Laurentian" Schism.

In November 498, following the death of pope Anastasius II, as the deacon Symmachus was elected pope at the Lateran, the priest of Santa Prassede, Laurence was acclaimed as pope at the basilica of St Mary. The Roman clergy were split evenly between the two candidates, whereas the majority of the Senate and the aristocracy, where loyalty to Constantinople was stronger, supported Laurence. Symmachus was backed by local Roman popular forces. Also, Laurence and his party were favoring the pro-Byzantine policy of pope Anastasius. Both candidates were summoned to Ravenna, where the Arian Gothic king Theodoric gave support to Symmachus, whose election was recognized as canonical at a council in Rome on March 1, 499. His competitor

[70]*LP*, p. 258 (tr. p. 114).

Laurence renounced his claim to the papacy. However, this was only the beginning of troubles. An active opposition to Symmachus remained. The bishops themselves called on the Gothic king to intervene directly. Theodoric, reluctantly accepting the role of arbiter, visited Rome in 500, where he was solemnly met by Symmachus, and convoked a new council of bishops in 501. Symmachus was accused by his enemies of immoral conduct and the two parties clashed on the issue of the date of Easter. The Eastern church was following the Alexandrian computation, the date of Easter being set on the Sunday following the Jewish Passover moon (14 Nisan), which itself followed the vernal equinox. The Roman church, meanwhile, kept an unadjusted date of the equinox, according to the old Julian calendar (March 25, rather than the correct date of March 21) and postponed the date of Easter, if Nisan 14 fell on a Saturday. As a result, Rome and the East sometimes celebrated Easter on different days.[71] St Leo the Great, for the sake of unity, had decided in 444 and 455 to follow the Alexandrian rule, but Symmachus, to please local feelings, followed the "old" Roman calendar in 501. Summoned again by an angered Theodoric, he locked himself at St Peter's, while Peter of Altinum, a *locum tenens* appointed by Theodoric, occupied all the other churches of Rome and presided over the celebration of Easter in 502 according to the Eastern practice. In the midst of popular violence, Symmachus had to accept conciliar judgment (502). Soon Laurence returned to Rome. There was an abundance of polemical literature and much more violence. Each party accused the other of moral and canonical crimes. Part of this literature is contained in the so-called "Symmachian forgeries" which invoked fictional precedents to promote the principle that "the first see shall not be judged by anyone" (*prima sedes a nemine judicatur*), and that the conciliar actions judging Symmachus were invalid.[72] It is only in the fall of 506 that King Theodoric was persuaded to give again his all-out support to Symmachus who had been exonerated by the council in 502. But the sequels of the schism were liquidated only with the election of pope Hormisdas (514-523).

Of course, the schism created great embarrassment for the Roman church and provoked apologetic arguments, which included not only the *Forgeries* mentioned above, but also a treatise by the Milanese deacon Ennodius aimed at proving that popes can be judged by God

---

[71]See the detailed description of the issue in Duchesne, *L'Eglise*, pp. 138-9.

[72]The text of the forgeries in L. Duchesne, *LP*, In tr. pp. CXXXIII ff.

alone, but not by other bishops.[73] With the rise of the papacy, these arguments will often be used and quoted, but in the first years of the sixth century, they were hardly convincing. In fact, the unity between Rome and Constantinople and, indeed, the prestige of Rome were eventually restored not by apologetic arguments, but only by the armies and policies of emperor Justinian I. By reconquering Italy, Justinian reestablished the old idea of *Romanitas* which integrated the Roman church again into the Byzantine political system.

What still remained, however, was the almost mystical conviction of the Roman bishops that somehow the spiritual and doctrinal responsibilities for the universal Church belonged to them. That mystical conviction continued to clash, not only with the unifying and controling function claimed by the Byzantine emperors, but also with the more subtle consciousness of local churches (and, indeed, of the ecumenical councils meeting in the East) that the most authentic sign of ecclesial truth was not to be found in Rome alone, but resided rather in episcopal consensus. Both the "Acacian" and the "Laurentian" schisms had illustrated and confirmed the existence of a tension between the papacy on the one side, and the ecclesiological consciousness of many on the other, not only in the East, but also in several Western areas of the former Roman Christian world.

[73]Text in PL 63, col. 167-208. The most complete recent analysis of the events and issues of the "Laurentian," or the "Symmachan" schism is by Richards, *Popes*, pp. 69-99.

CHAPTER VI

THE COUNCIL OF CHALCEDON
AND ITS AFTERMATH

The council of Ephesus (431) had marked the irretrievable defeat of Nestorianism in the East, and the triumph of the christology expressed by St Cyril of Alexandria and based upon the concept that there was only one *subject* or "hypostasis" of Jesus Christ. This subject was the pre-existing Logos, the second Person of the Trinity. The unity of subject implied the "divine Motherhood" of Mary, the Virgin (she was indeed the "Mother of God," and *Theotokos,* "God's Bearer"), and "theopaschism" (no one else but the Son of God Himself suffered on the cross in His fleshly nature). This christology of Cyril was actually in full conformity with the faith of Nicaea. Indeed, the Nicaean creed literally affirmed that same unity of subject. It was the Son of God, "consubstantial with the Father" who "was incarnate of the Holy Spirit and the Virgin Mary . . . was crucified under Pontius Pilate, suffered and was buried." The same person, or subject was proclaimed to be both Son of God and son of Mary—a kerygmatic affirmation implying that, in order to save His creation, the Creator assumes in full the fallen, mortal conditions of humanity, makes it "His own" even in death, in order to have it participate in His own eternity through the resurrection.

However, St Cyril had imposed his views in Ephesus with some brutality. He had obtained the full support of pope Celestine of Rome, who had received the right advice from his deacon Leo, a correspondent of Cyril, but Cyril himself was not able to use a consistent terminology. For instance, the terms "nature" (φύσις) and *hypostasis* he used

165

interchangeably, and spoke both of the "one incarnate *hypostasis*," and the "one incarnate *nature*" of the Logos. The theologians of Antioch, where Nestorius had also been trained, were accustomed to a more rational and intellectually disciplined approach to biblical exegesis and christological issues. They lacked the kerygmatic spirit of St Cyril, but their logical concern for the preservation of Christ's authentic *humanity* was legitimate. Of course, Cyril himself was always ready to reject Apollinarianism (*i.e.* the idea that Christ possessed a human body, but lacked the spiritual and intellectual dimensions of humanity, which in Him were replaced by divinity), and clearly affirmed his belief in the full humanity of Jesus (especially in his *Letters to Succensus*), but he was sometimes contradictory in his use of theological vocabulary. Fortunately, no christological terminology as such, except for the confirmation of the title *Theotokos* for the Virgin, was endorsed at Ephesus. This allowed an understanding between St Cyril and the Antiochenes, which was sealed by a famous letter of Cyril to John of Antioch in 433.

This agreement with Cyril did not mean that all problems had been solved in depth. Indeed, on the one hand, the christology which made Nestorianism possible, and which had been taught by the great luminaries of the school of Antioch, Diodore of Tarsus and Theodore of Mopsuestia, did not disappear in Antioch. Theodoret remained faithful to it, and an eminent professor of the school of Edessa, Ibas, who eventually became bishop of that city, wrote to "Maris," a Nestorian of Persia—perhaps the catholicos Dadiso of Seleucia-Ctesiphon (the word "Mar" means "Lord" in Syriac)—praising the authority of the great exegete, Theodore of Mopsuestia.

On the other hand, after the death of Cyril (444), some of his radical and generally unenlightened disciples began to speak of Christ as if His humanity, united "naturally" with divinity, was immediately and totally "deified" from the time of His conception by Mary, so that it could not be described any more as being identical or "consubstantial" with *our* humanity. Eutyches, an archimandrite of Constantinople, was particularly vocal on this point and became the founder of the heresy known as "monophysitism." His group adopted a "fundamentalist" attitude regarding Nicaea. The Nicaean creed, they said, proclaimed Christ to be "consubstantial with the Father," but did not include the formula: "consubstantial with us." Thus the Eutychians would not allow any doctrinal formulation beyond the Nicaean.

Eutyches was condemned by a local synod, presided over by Flavian of Constantinople (448). However—and quite unfortunately—Dioscoros of Alexandria, deacon and successor of Cyril, stood up in his defense. Obtaining imperial support, he presided over a second council at Ephesus, also known as "Robber council" (449), at which he rehabilitated Eutyches, deposed Flavian of Constantinople, Domnus of Antioch, Theodoret of Cyrus and others, refused to read Pope Leo's *Letter to Flavian,* which opposed Eutychianism, and established a sort of Alexandrian dictatorship over the entire East. The papal legate, Hilary, left the assembly in protest. This extraordinary "overkill" of real, or imaginary "Nestorians" by Dioscoros, whose personal christological convictions were not really different from Cyril's, made it necessary to clarify issues, reexamine terminologies and reestablish a catholic consensus. Furthermore, following the accidental death of emperor Theodosius II (July 28, 450), his sister Pulcheria took power in Constantinople. Reserving her virginity, she entered a formal marriage of convenience with the elderly senator Marcian, who was proclaimed emperor (August 24). The new government moved decidedly towards the convocation of a new, and truly representative ecumenical council.

1. *The Council of Chalcedon: the doctrinal accomplishment*

The history of the debates at Chalcedon has been written many times and needs no detailed repetition. Convoked originally to meet on September 1 in Nicaea in order to affirm a symbolic continuity with the First council, the assembly was transferred by Marcian to the Constantinopolitan suburb of Chalcedon, where imperial presence and supervision were easier. Attendance was much larger than at any council so far: over five hundred bishops, including the occupants of the four major Eastern sees—Constantinople, Alexandria, Antioch and Jerusalem.[1] Pope Leo who, after the Robber council of 449, had threatened, with the help of the Western emperor Valentinian III, now temporarily residing again in Rome, to hold a council in the West, accepted to be represented by legates. As we have seen in the preceding chapter, he also posed surprisingly sharp conditions for his participa-

---

[1] Cf. E. Hönigmann, "The original lists of the members of the council of Nicaea, the Robber-synod and the council of Chalcedon," *Byzantion* XVI, 1, 1944, pp. 22-80.

tion: that the legates be admitted to chair the meetings and that his *Tome to Flavian* be recognized as a final statement of christological faith. Rome's support was considered so important that the first condition was granted, but only in a formal way. The papal legate Paschasinus, bishop of Lilybaeum in Sicily, occupied the first seat and became the ecclesiastical president of the council. The papal letter to Flavian, however, was examined only on its own merits, and checked against the uncontested authority of Cyril. In actual fact, the proceedings were led, not by the legates, but by eighteen lay imperial commissioners, including such high officials as the *magister militum* Anatolius, the praetorian prefect of the East Palladius, and the *praefectus urbis* Tatian.

This close involvement of the imperial court—dominated by empress Pulcheria, rather than Marcian—implies in fact that the council followed formal procedures, closely inspired by the rules of the Roman judiciary. Such formality was something of a novelty in the history of ecumenical councils. It did not exist at either Nicaea (325) or Constantinople (381): these two councils even left no formal minutes. The first council of Ephesus (431)—not to speak of the Robber council (449)—was entirely under the arbitrary command of the bishop of Alexandria, with no real opposition allowed. At Chalcedon, on the contrary, the various points of view were heard; minutes of the Robber council were read; commissions met to discuss controversial issues; draft resolutions were presented and some rejected. No such orderly procedures existed when, as in Ephesus, the imperial commissioners were instructed to let the bishops alone debate ecclesiastical matters. Unfortunately, neither the large attendance, nor the relative freedom of the debates assured the council of Chalcedon of swift acceptance by all. On the contrary, its definition provoked lasting opposition and led to further christological controversy.

The work of the council continued for over three weeks between October 8 and 31, 451. Seventeen plenary sessions were held at the church of St Euphemia, a locally-venerated martyr.[2]

In many ways, the general direction of the assembly became

---

[2]The voluminous minutes of the council of Chalcedon represent a major source of information about the Church in the fifth century, especially since they include the *Acts* of the council of Constantinople, which condemned Eutyches (448) and those of the Robber council (449). The complete text appears in the old conciliar collections published by Harduin and Mansi as well as in the critical edition by E. Schwartz (quoted here as ACO). A detailed analysis of the *Acts* is found in F. X. Murphy, *Peter speaks through Leo*, Washington, D.C., 1952. Cf. also several important passages translated in CN, 774-811.

apparent at the first session, when the council debated the personal status of Dioscoros of Alexandria and of the main spokesman of the "Eastern" or Antiochene group, Theodoret of Cyrus. The papal legates demanded the exclusion of Dioscoros, because he had insulted pope Leo, while the Egyptians and their allies violently protested the presence of Theodoret, who had criticized St Cyril. The imperial commissioners refused both requests. The solution adopted was to have both Dioscoros and Theodoret sit in the middle of the church, as defendants, with full rights of speech. This was reasonable not only for the sake of fairness, but also in terms of the general aims of Marcian's and Pulcheria's policies: to reestablish a consensus within the imperial church, which would be centered around the two imperial capitals of Rome and Constantinople. Following the solution of this procedural issue, the session was occupied, almost entirely, by the long reading of the minutes of the council of Constantinople which had condemned Eutyches (448) and of the Robber council (449). The reading was constantly interrupted with passionate outcries by the various factions of bishops. Former members of the Robber council, who signed the condemnation of Flavian and, implicitly, insulted Leo by refusing to read his letter, tried to justify themselves by either accusing Dioscoros of blackmail and violence, or more honestly, by asking the council's forgiveness. Among them, the most compromised was probably Juvenal of Jerusalem, who had been, with Dioscoros, a co-chairman of the Robber council. At Chalcedon—quite unconvincingly—he pleaded ignorance[3] and, in a spectacular gesture, rose from the seat he occupied next to the friends of Dioscoros and sat with the Antiochenes and the Constantinopolitans. Dioscoros, meanwhile, adopted a reserved and dignified attitude, showing understandable irony towards the bishops who supported him in 449, and were now joining his accusers. But he faced difficulty in justifying his attitude of 449 and, especially, the rehabilitation of Eutyches. He expressed quite clearly his own doctrinal position, which will remain that of most Eastern opponents of Chalcedon: Christ was fully God and fully man, and therefore "of two natures," but, after the union, it was not possible to speak of these "two natures," as distinctly subsisting, because their *union* into one being was a perfect union. Of course, he would not admit the use of the Greek word *physis* ("nature") for any meaning

---

[3]At Ephesus in 449, he had called Eutyches "very orthodox" (ὀρθοδοξότατον) ACO II, 1, 1, p. 182.

other than "concrete reality." Furthermore, as he and his supporters pointed out, St Cyril used the expression "*one nature* incarnate of God the Word," and never plainly spoke of two natures after the union. It is on the basis of this Cyrillian fundamentalism that Dioscoros considered the condemnation of Flavian in 449 to be justified: Flavian and Eusebius of Dorylaeum, the official accuser of Eutyches in 448, had spoken of "two natures after the Incarnation," and were therefore *de facto* "Nestorians." At Chalcedon, however, there was now a majority to affirm that Dioscoros was wrong in seeing a contradiction between Cyril and Flavian.

The imperial commissioners, in a concluding statement, affirmed their conviction that the condemnation of Flavian was unjust and that therefore those who condone it—*i.e.* the leaders of the Robber council: Dioscoros, Juvenal (his reversal did not help yet!), Thalassius of Caesarea, and others—ought to be deposed. However, the commissioners also declared that such action, demanding a cool head and free consultation, must be postponed to a later session. The closing of the meeting was marked by the singing of the hymn: "Holy God! Holy mighty! Holy and immortal, have mercy on us." It is the first recorded instance of the use of that hymn, which will become so popular, but also controversial, in later centuries.

Realizing that there was no real chance for his position to prevail at the council, Dioscoros of Alexandria failed to attend the other sessions. His deposition took place *in absentia* at the third session, but only after three successive summonses were delivered to him in person. Furthermore, and very significantly, the deposition mentions only disciplinary and canonical transgressions, not heresy. The official notice sent to him said: "Know you that because you despised the canons and disobeyed the present holy and ecumenical council, without taking account of other misdeeds of which you are guilty, since you have not consented, having been invited three times by the present holy and great council according to the canons, to give answer to the accusations brought against you, you are deposed from episcopacy and removed from all ecclesiastical rank, by this holy and ecumenical council, on this day, October 13."[4] The purely disciplinary, and not

---

[4]ACO II, 1, 3, pp. 41 (237)-42(238). Although this official notice is, undoubtedly, to be considered as the authentic conciliar decision concerning Dioscoros, the assembly also gave its approval to a statement by the legate Paschasinus signifying the deposition in "papal" terms: "The most holy archbishop Leo, through us (the legates) and the present holy synod, together with Peter the apostle, who is the rock of the catholic

doctrinal, character of the deposition will be duly noted by Anatolios of Constantinople (who knew Dioscoros well, having been his delegate —*apocrisiarios*—in the capital) at a crucial moment of the debate during the fifth session. In fact, his intervention was intended to maintain that, even if Dioscoros accused Flavian of heresy for confessing "two natures after the union," his own "Cyrillian" terminology was not necessarily heretical.[5] This makes it clear that the council of Chalcedon did at no time depart from its Cyrillian stand, which it wanted to affirm at all costs, even against the trend represented by the Roman legates. Of all the participants of the Robber council, Dioscoros alone was deposed. It is true that all of them—including Juvenal of Jerusalem— not only apologized, but also signed Dioscoros' deposition.

Faithfulness to Cyril was emphasized with equal clarity during the third and the fifth sessions, when the issue of a new doctrinal statement came to the floor. The need for a statement was raised by the imperial commissioners at the beginning of the second session, and was met with initial, nearly general opposition. Indeed, the papal legates had been instructed by pope Leo to maintain at the council that the papal *Letter to Flavian* was a sufficient expression of orthodoxy, and that no further debate was needed—only a formal acceptance of "Peter's faith." Actually, reluctance to produce definitions of faith was a general trend. The Eastern bishops themselves—including Dioscoros and his followers—liked to proclaim that the Nicaean creed was a perfectly sufficient statement of orthodoxy. In any case, neither Ephesus I (431), nor Ephesus II (the Robber council, 449) had produced statements of faith, but had only condemned the real, or supposed Nestorians in the name of the Nicaean faith.[6] Furthermore, Ephesus I had approved a resolution (later listed as "canon 7") forbidding "to present, to compose, or to write any formula of faith, other than the one which had been defined by the holy fathers gathered at Nicaea with the Holy Spirit."[7] This resolution was constantly

Church and the foundation of the orthodox faith, has deprived him of episcopacy and of every sacerdotal dignity," *ibid.*, p. 29(225). Another example of the ambiguities marking the position of the legates at the council!

[5]*Ibid.*, p. 124 (320).

[6]Writing to Acacius of Berea concerning Ephesus, St Cyril himself proclaims: "We were in council for the one true faith, confirming what has been defined about it by the holy fathers of Nicaea, crowning unanimously this great and holy council, because it has promulgated an exact definition." (ACO I, 1, 7, p. 142).

[7]ACO I, 1, 7, pp. 105-6. The text is also known as "canon 7" of Ephesus. The resolution was taken in connection with the prohibition of a local usage in Philadelphia, attributed to Theodore of Mopsuestia, which had Nestorian overtones. (Cf. P. Th.

referred to by the Alexandrians, who had not yet acknowledged either the council of Constantinople (381), or the creed attributed to it, which was indeed already an expansion of the creed of Nicaea. The church of Alexandria defined Orthodoxy as strict adherence to Nicaea alone, rejecting the council of 381 and the creed attributed to it. The council of Chalcedon is the first instance at which this attribution was made,[8] with the implication that the Ephesian resolution was only an *ad hoc* statement without relevance for the issue at stake at Chalcedon.[9]

The commissioners' request for a statement was very much in line with the empire's attitude towards ecumenical councils: the emperor gathered such assemblies with the express goal of obtaining clear guidelines in its policy of securing the unity of the Church. A simple reference to the authority of Nicaea was clearly insufficient in 451 to secure such clarity, since all the opposing parties referred to it and claimed that *their* respective statements were faithful to it. The logical tactic, for the commissioners, was therefore to have these various documents—all supposed to reflect the "ancient faith"—to be read, so that the bishops themselves could acknowledge the need to settle existing contradictions.

The readings included the two creeds of Nicaea and Constantinople, the first two *Letters* of St Cyril to Nestorius, the *Letter* of Cyril to John of Antioch signifying their reconciliation (433), and the *Tome* of Leo to Flavian. While the two creeds and the Cyrillian *Letters* were unanimously acclaimed by the bishops, the bishops of Illyricum (though technically submitted to the papal vicar in Thessalonica) and Palestine objected against some expressions of Leo's *Tome,* which they found in contradiction with the faith of St Cyril. This was, indeed, the real issue: it confirmed the necessity, voiced by the commissioners, to elaborate a new statement, acceptable both to Rome and to the Cyrillian majority of the council.

The *Tome* of pope Leo had been written by a person little versed

Camelot, *Ephèse et Chalcédoine*, Paris, 1961, p. 57). There are doubts as to whether an actual vote was taken on this resolution, which does not appear in all manuscripts of the *Acts* of Ephesus (cf. Bolotov, *Lektsii,* pp. 216-299).

[8]Cf. J.N.D. Kelly, *Early Christian Creeds,* London, 1950, pp. 296-301.

[9]One should note, however, that during the medieval period, the purported canon 7 of Ephesus was often understood as applicable to the creed of Nicaea-Constantinople, and invoked by the Orthodox against the *Filioque* interpolation. The argument however, is irrelevent, since the council of Ephesus meant "Nicaea" only, not Nicaea-Constantinople, and since the council of Constantinople, by expanding the creed of Nicaea, implicitly rejected the idea that nothing ever could be added to the original Nicaean text.

in the details of the christological controversy in the East, but it is a most impressive, harmonious, logical construction, which avoids the kerygmatic style of Cyril, as well as the errors of Nestorius. There is no evidence that the pope knew Greek, but he had studied the issues, by reading Tertullian and Augustine as well as the treaty *On the Incarnation* specially commissioned from St John Cassian. From Latin theology, he had acquired a vision of salvation, which insisted more on the ideas of mediation and reconciliation—i.e. the restoration of correct and originally-created harmonious relationships between the Creator and the creatures—rather than on the notion of deification, or *theosis,* so dear to the Greek Fathers. It was natural for him, therefore, to describe Christ as possessing two natures, or substances (*substantiae*); although he did not fully realize that the Latin *substantia* was naturally transcribed into Greek as *hypostasis,* which gave a dangerously Nestorian-sounding ring to his theology. He also emphasized an important common sense truth that the two natures of Christ necessarily kept their characteristics after the union (*agit utraque forma quod proprium est*)—since Christ never ceased to be both God and man, not in the abstract, but in concrete reality—and he added a concept important for the East: that the respective operations of divinity and humanity were active "in communion with each other" (*cum alterius communione*). Indeed, it is the concept of "communion" of divinity and humanity in Christ which was the basis of the doctrine of *theosis.* Finally, Leo, undoubtedly knowing what was really essential to Cyrillian theology and specifically opposing the "Nestorianizing" Antiochene theology, affirms "theopaschism": "One can say," he writes, "that the Son of God was crucified and buried, because one understands that there is a unity of person in both natures." It is true, however, that the normal Greek translation of *persona* being *prosopon,* his conception of Christ's personal unity could be understood to be only "prosopic" (as in Antioch), and not "hypostatic," or "natural" (as in Cyril).[10]

The turmoil provoked by objections to the text of Leo, and also by the fear of some that the whole of Cyrillian theology would be abandoned,[11] was so great that the comissioners had to use their

[10]For a more thorough discussion of these problems of terminology, Meyendorff, *Christ, passim.*

[11]Dioscoros, Juvenal, Thalassius of Caesarea, and other former leaders of the Robber council were absent, because they had been indicted at the previous session. The Illyrians insistently demanded that for the sake of Church unity, they be pardoned and readmitted

authority to close the session after having arranged for Anatolius of Constantinople—an avowed Cyrillian, a former friend of Dioscoros, but also a skilled ecclesiastical diplomat—to meet with the opposition and alleviate their doubts. Atticus of Nicopolis in Epirus—one of the objectors—demanded specifically that the *third* letter of Cyril, which contained the *Twelve Anathemas* and which had not been read at the plenary session, also be considered in the process of examining the orthodoxy of Leo.[12] Actually, the debates of the third session resulted in an inquiry into Leo's orthodoxy, judged on Cyrillian presuppositions.

It is at the beginning of the fourth session of the council that the *Tome* of Leo was finally declared to be above all suspicion of heresy. After a face-saving declaration by the legate Paschasinus ("The venerable Leo, archbishop of all the churches (!) has given us an exposé of the true faith . . . It is this faith which the council professes . . . without modifying, deleting or adding a single note"), the bishops declared one by one that Leo was in agreement with Nicaea, Constantinople Ephesus, *and Cyril.* The bishops of the Illyricum also signed the *Tome,* declaring that after the sessions with Anatolius, they were now able to do so, having been fully convinced of the orthodoxy of archbishop Leo, since "the legates have clarified for us, that which seemed contradictory in (Leo's) expressions." A similar declaration was made by the bishops of Palestine.[13] Although this session was formally in agreement with the instructions given by Leo to his legates—the *Tome* was accepted, as a statement of orthodox faith—it also looked as if Leo had been judged and acquitted with the christology of Cyril as a criterion of orthodoxy.

The same session was marked by the formal admission of Juvenal of Jerusalem, and the other former friends of Dioscoros, to the council's full membership. Of course, they too now subscribed to the *Tome* of Leo, and the conciliar fathers praised the restored unity of the Church. But, in fact, the future would not be as rosy as hoped. Indeed,

to the debates on Leo's *Tome.* This actually took place—except for Dioscoros—at the following session (Cf. ACO II, 1, 2, p. 82-83 (278-279)).

[12]There is little doubt that the letter was indeed brought to discussion in the group chaired by Anatolius, and there is no reason to believe that its reading was consciously avoided at Chalcedon, as some historians think (Cf. L. Duchesne, *Histoire,* III, p. 435; V. V. Bolotov, *Lektsii,* pp. 283-9; A. V. Kartashev, *Vselenskie Sobory,* Paris, 1963, p. 405, etc). These historians approach the entire christological debate on the premises of Cyril's *de facto* monophysitism, and of Antiochian (and *de facto* Nestorius') orthodoxy. However, a more balanced point of view tends to prevail today (Cf. P. Th. Camelot, *op. cit.,* p. 127; J. Meyendorff, *Christ, passim*).

[13]ACO II, 1, 2, pp. 102-3 (298-9).

the attempts made by the council fathers and the commissioners to obtain doctrinal compliance from a group of leading monks, including the famous Barsauma of Syria, were unsuccessful. These eminent ascetics who also had been active at the Robber council of 449, were brought before the assembly, but showed themselves less flexible than the bishops. They refused to anathematize not only Dioscoros, but even Eutyches, and thus became the real leaders of the anti-Chalcedonian opposition in the decades to come.

The attitude of the monks, their claim to be the only legitimate followers of St Cyril and their reluctance to reject Eutyches, showed clearly that the preservation of orthodox christology—including the legacy of Cyril—demanded a doctrinal clarification. The commissioners' insistence on a statement was not challenged anymore at the fifth session of the council. This session, held on October 22, had only a select attendance: the commissioners, the papal legates, the primates of the major sees (Constantinople, Antioch, Jerusalem) and fifty-two other bishops. The meeting looked more like a steering committee than a plenary session. A draft statement, probably authored by Anatolius of Constantinople, was placed on the floor. The text does not appear in the minutes, but, from the heated discussion that followed,[14] it is obvious that it contained the designation of Mary as *Theotokos*—a crucial anti-Nestorian statement confirming the decisions of Ephesus I—and that it defined the being of Jesus Christ as a union *of two natures,* using a strictly Cyrillian language. The adoption of such a text would have probably satisfied Dioscoros, and avoided the schism. Its pronounced "Cyrillian" character brought about a brief objection by John of Germaniceia, a friend of Nestorius and Theodoret, who apparently was opposed to the inclusion of the term *Theotokos.* His lonely voice was submerged by shouts: "Let Mary be designated as Theotokos in writing!" Much more serious was the formal and forceful protest of the Roman legates: "If the terms do not agree with the letter of the apostolic and most-blessed man, Leo the archbishop, let us have a copy, and we will return (to Rome), so that the council may meet there." As we remember, the official position of the Roman church was that all issues had already been settled in the *Tome* of Leo, and that, in fact, no further statement was necessary. Since a statement was demanded by the commissioners, it had, at least, to be in full conformity with the *Tome.* The embarrassed imperial

[14]ACO II, 1, 2, pp. 123-130 (319-326).

commissioners, whose major role was to secure the unity of the "two Romes," proposed that a new commission be formed of representatives of all parties in order to revise the draft. There was wild protest by the bishops against such a procedure. The majority was satisfied with the existing version. An appeal to the emperor by the commissioners and a direct order of Marcian were finally able to convince the assembly to establish the commission, and proceed with a new draft.

This episode is interpreted by historians in various ways, depending upon their presuppositions. The apologists of papal primacy see a direct victory of Roman authority. The Non-Chalcedonian Easterners, past and present, lament what they consider as a tragic capitulation before the pope and the emperor. Historians sympathetic to the Antiochian and Western christologies voice dismay at the "blindness" of the Greek episcopate, unable to comprehend the obvious heresy of Dioscoros, and praise the firmness of the legates.[15] None of the participants, however, saw the event in such simplified terms. In fact, the bishops had all subscribed to the *Tome* of Leo at the previous session. In their minds, this was a perfectly sufficient expression of their condemnation of Eutyches and their acceptance of the two natures formula, which was so forcefully promoted by Leo. When directly confronted by the commissioners—"whom do you follow, Leo, or Dioscoros?"—they answered without hesitancy: "We believe like Leo."[16] The reason why they were still reluctant to say "in two natures," rather than "of two natures," in the statement, was that they foresaw the dangerous consequences of totally rejecting the terminology used by Cyril. For them, as for the fathers of the Fifth Council which was to meet a century later when it would be too late to heal the schism, neither the terminology of Cyril ("of two natures"), nor that of Leo ("two natures" after the union) merited an independent and self-sufficient status: each served only for rejecting an erroneous doctrine, i.e. Nestorianism and Eutychianism, respectively.

Be it as it may, the commission met and produced the famous statement of Chalcedon, a careful compromise attempting to satisfy the Cyrillians (use of the terms *Theotokos* and "union in one hypostasis") as well as the Roman legates (affirmation of Christ "known in two natures . . . with the particularities of each nature being preserved")

---

[15]Cf., for example, A. V. Kartashev, who is particularly indignant at the statement by Anatolius that Dioscoros was not condemned "for his faith" (*op. cit.,* p. 404).

[16]ACO, ibid., p. 125(321).

and wisely confessing the mystery of the Incarnation by using the four negative adverbs ("unconfusedly, unchangeably, indivisibly, inseparably").

The status of the definition, or *horos* (ὅρος) was never intended to be that of a new creed. The use of the term "creed of Chalcedon" in contemporary manuals[17] is misleading. The text was not intended for liturgical, sacramental, or "symbolic" use, but was conceived only as a statement excluding both the Nestorian and the Eutychian heresies. In the preamble, it defines this negative "antirrhetic" intention of its drafters very clearly. The full text of the two creeds—Nicaea and Constantinople—is included in the definition, which then proclaims that these creeds were "sufficient" for the knowledge of truth. Only then, after this conservative and defensive affirmation does it recall Nestorianism, Eutychianism, and the letters by Cyril and Leo—both mentioned by name—written "for the establishment of the true faith." This mention of Cyril and Leo reflects once more the council's conviction that orthodoxy is expressed by them both, and not by either one of them in isolation.[18] The statement was not meant to replace either the *Letters* of Cyril, or the *Tome* of Leo, as expression of the true faith, but to find a christological terminology which would be faithful to both. It is, therefore, quite inaccurate to say that Chalcedon "disavowed" Cyril, as many historians unfortunately affirm even today, for then it could, as well, be seen as a disavowal of Leo (in its affirmation of a *hypostatic* union). The paragraph of the statement which had been so heatedly debated at the fifth session is as follows:

> Wherefore, following the holy fathers, we all with one voice teach that our Lord Jesus Christ is one and the same Son, the same perfect in divinity and the same perfect in humanity, truly God and truly man, the same consistent of a reasonable soul and body, consubstantial with the Father according to his divinity and the same consubstantial with us according to his humanity, similar to us in all things except sin; begotten of the Father before the ages according to his divinity, but the same begotten, in these last days, for us and for our salvation, from Mary the Virgin and Theotokos,

[17]Including the *History of the Church,* edited by H. Jedin and T. Dolan (New York, 1980).

[18]In this sense, the publication of the definition goes against the wishes of the legates who had insisted so much on making Leo the sole criterion of orthodoxy.

according to his humanity; one and the same Christ, Son, Lord, Only-Begotten, acknowledged in two natures (ἐν δύο φύσεσιν), without confusion, without change, without division, without separation; the difference of his natures never being abolished because of their union, but rather the characteristic property of each nature being preserved and concurring into one person and one hypostasis, (εἰς ἓν πρόσωπον καὶ μίαν ὑπόστασιν συντρεχούσης), not as if He was parted or divided into two persons, but one and the same Son, Only-Begotten, God, the Word, Jesus Christ; even as the prophets from ancient times spoke of Him, and as Jesus Christ Himself instructed us, and as the creed of the fathers handed down to us.

The statement was signed by 454 bishops at the sixth session, October 25, in the presence of emperor Marcian himself, who addressed the assembly first in Latin, then in Greek, and was acclaimed as "new Constantine," and his wife, Pulcheria, as "new Helen."

Also significant for future history were the actions taken at the ninth and tenth sessions (October 26-27): the rehabilitations of two eminent bishops who had been condemned by the Robber council, Theodoret of Cyrus and Ibas of Edessa. Theodoret had criticized Ephesus I and Cyril in his writings, while Ibas had written a letter to Maris the Persian, accusing Cyril of Apollinarism. Both rehabilitations were acted upon only after Theodoret and Ibas had formally anathematized Nestorius. Theodoret's initial reluctance to do so provoked the indignation of the bishops, but he was acclaimed as orthodox as soon as he finally said: "Anathema to Nestorius!" In fact, Theodoret was a learned and moderate man, an architect of the reconciliation between Cyril and John of Antioch in 433. He obviously hoped that unity could be restored without anathemas against former friends. But his rehabilitation and that of Ibas, which meant that the Council accepted in communion two eminent and articulate former critics of Cyril, will be used by Cyrillian "fundamentalists"—who will be known as "monophysites"—in their denigration of the entire accomplishment of Chalcedon.

2. The Council of Chalcedon: ecclesiastical order

By its location in a suburb of the capital, by the direction given to it by the imperial commissioners throughout the proceedings, by the role played by Anatolius, the bishop of Constantinople, in drafting the final statement, and even by the recognition granted to the pope's primacy (in spite of all the references to St Peter, the "old Rome's" prestige was always understood in the East in its imperial context), the council of Chalcedon was an "imperial" council, and its most concrete historical result, in terms of ecclesiastical order, was the formal sanction given to the position of the church of Constantinople.

Of course, not all of the administrative decisions taken during the last—seventh to seventeenth—sessions of the council were directly connected with the church of the capital. For instance, on October 26, at the eighth session, a final settlement was confirmed concerning the respective jurisdictions of Antioch and Jerusalem. Maximus of Antioch proposed, and Juvenal of Jerusalem accepted, that the three provinces of Palestine, which belonged to the imperial "diocese of the East"— the traditional ecclesiastical territory of Antioch—be submitted to the jurisdiction of Jerusalem. However, the two Phoenicias (contemporary Lebanon) and Arabia (Jordan's East bank), on which Juvenal of Jerusalem also laid claim, had to remain under Antioch. So ended, with a compromise, a long and undignified struggle by Juvenal for ecclesiastical power, which for a time, he hoped to exercise even over Antioch itself.[19] As a result, the church of Jerusalem would eventually obtain its fifth place among the great "patriarchates," although at Nicaea (canon 7), it was only mentioned as the see of Aelia, submitted to the metropolitan of Caesarea-in-Palestine.

The other disciplinary issues, involving the sees of Ephesus and Nicomedia, were directly related to the areas, where, since the late fourth century, the bishop of Constantinople exercised a *de facto*

---

[19]Already in 430, pope Leo and Cyril of Alexandria complained to each other of his intrigues. In 431, however, his support of Cyril against John of Antioch allowed him to seize *de facto* the two Phoenicias and Arabia, and to demand the "obedience" of John (ACO I, 1, 3, p. 18-19). Supported by empress Eudocia, wife of Theodosius II (she lived in Jerusalem in 441-60), he became one of the leaders of the Robber council in 449, only to "repent" at Chalcedon. On Juvenal, see the very complete article by E. Hönigmann, "Juvenal of Jerusalem," *DOP* 5 (1950), pp. 211-279. The fact that Juvenal is still counted among the Saints is presumably due to his firm stand against the monophysite monks in Palestine after 451.

authority, often resented by local bishops. One only has to remember the intervention of St John Chrysostom in the affairs of the church of Ephesus, which became a major factor in his deposition. In 451, the issue was a conflict of two candidates to the see of Ephesus, Bassianus and Stephen. The council decided that both should retire, and rejected the claims of Constantinopolitan representatives, who wanted to have a new bishop ordained in Constantinople: "Let the canons be obeyed," they shouted, and gave the clergy and people of Ephesus the right to elect their bishop. But significantly, the imperial commissioners had the final decision tabled until further examination of the issue[20] (which will result in the famous 28th canon). Another conflict opposed the bishop of Nicomedia, metropolitan of the province of Bithynia, to his colleague of Nicaea, who claimed metropolitan rights in Bithynia on the basis of the prestige of his city, seat of the first ecumenical council. Here again, the rights of Nicomedia were recognized in principle, but the archdeacon Aetios of Constantinople requested that "no prejudice should be exercised against the holy see of Constantinople," and the commissioners decided that "this is a matter to be taken up by the council in its proper order."[21] It is obvious that a draft of the 28th canon establishing the power of Constantinople over the area was already in preparation, and that the initiative for it was coming from the imperial throne itself.

Similarly, the twenty-seven disciplinary canons, which appear in the minutes as a result of the seventh session of the Council, include the granting to the bishop of Constantinople of the right to receive appeals from clergy unhappy with the judgment of their metropolitans (canons 9 and 17). It is not yet a very firm right, and seems to concern only the three dioceses of Thrace, Pontus and Asia: the appellants still have a choice between an appeal to the "exarch of the diocese"—i.e. the bishop of the principal diocesan city, seat of the imperial prefect—or the bishop of the capital. Canon 28 clarifies the situation in the three dioceses by establishing a firm Constantinopolitan jurisdiction. The right of appeal, defined in canons 9 and 17 will then have to be interpreted as applying not only to the above three dioceses (where "exarchs" were now suppressed) but everywhere, as a right of Constantinople to hear appeals against the judgment of other patriarchs (sometimes referred to as "exarchs").

[20]ACO II, 1, 3, p. 53(412).
[21]ACO II, 1, 3, p. 62(421).

It is impossible to know whether the text of Canon 28, with its broad implications, existed already in the form of a full draft before the council met, or whether the text was improvised on the basis of the events which took place during the sessions. There is no doubt, however, that Marcian and Pulcheria had definitely decided to put an end to the *de facto* power of the bishop of Alexandria. For decades, the latter was able to impose his will upon the universal church, without paying any attention to the honorary position acquired by Constantinople in 381 ("equal privileges with the ancient Rome," Constantinople, canon 3). Indeed, Alexandria did not recognize the council of Constantinople at all, and the imperial system implied by it. Neither was that council, until 451, formally acknowledged in Rome. But at Chalcedon, the creed of Nicaea-Constantinople was officially confirmed with Roman approval, and Eusebius of Dorylaeum testified that, when he had been in Rome in 449-50, he had read canon 3 of Constantinople to pope Leo personally and that he had received it.[22] It is possible, therefore, that the authorities of Constantinople were genuinely surprised by the stern Roman opposition to their plan at establishing imperial order in the Church, based upon the authority of the "two Romes."

On October 30, the text of the new canon was placed on the agenda, but the legates refused to attend the meeting, saying that they had no mandate for such matters. The commissioners allowed the meeting to proceed without their presence, on the premise that the matter was an "obvious one" (φανερά τινα), and concerned only with the three dioceses of Thrace, Pontus and Asia.[23] The text was voted upon and signed. But the legates must have been quite vocal in their protests, because, on the next day, a full session took place to examine the matter, with the commissioners, the legates and 214 bishops or proxies present. The text presented to the assembly, as already approved, was as follows:

"Following the judgment of the holy fathers in all things, and acknowledging the canon of the one hundred and fifty God-loving bishops, who met in Constantinople,

[22]ACO II, 1, 3, p. 97(456). However, pope Leo, in his letter to Anatolius of 452, emphatically declares that no canonical authority can supersede Nicaea and that, therefore, canon 3 of Constantinople has no validity for him (*Ep* 106,4, PL 54, col. 1005 BC).

[23]This is the way the matter is recounted by archdeacon Aetios of Constantinople on October 31, ACO III, 1, 3, p. 88(447).

the Queen-city, the New Rome, under the former emperor, the great Theodosius of pious memory, which has just been read, we also determine and decree the same things with regard to the privileges (πρεσβεῖα) of the most holy church of the above-mentioned Constantinople, the New Rome. For to the throne of the older Rome (τῆς πρεσβυτέρας Ρώμης) the fathers gave the privileges with good reason, because it is [24] the imperial city. Moved by the same considerations, the one-hundred and fifty bishops gave the same privileges (τὰ ἴσα πρεσβεῖα) to the most holy throne of New Rome, judging with good reason that the city honored by the presence of the emperor and the senate and enjoying equal (civil) privileges with the older imperial Rome, should also be magnified, as she is, in matters ecclesiastical, holding the second place after her.

(We also decree) that the metropolitans—and only the metropolitans—of the dioceses of Pontus, Asia and Thrace, as well as the bishops of the aforementioned dioceses who are in barbarian lands,[25] be ordained by the aforementioned most holy throne of the most holy church of Constantinople. This implies that each metropolitan of the aforementioned dioceses, together with the bishops of his province, should ordain the bishops of that province, as it is specified in the canons, however, as was just said, the metropolitans of the aforementioned dioceses should be ordained by the archbishop of Constantinople, after the holding (locally) of the usual unanimous elections, whose results are to be referred to him."[26]

[24]The text does not deny that the "older" Rome is still the capital of the "Roman" empire. In 451, it was still the resident of Valentinian III.

[25]This particular clause of the text has been (and, still is) a matter of heated discussion, because it serves as a basis for the contemporary claim of the church of Constantinople to exercise jurisdiction over all orthodox Christians living beyond the borders of the established boundaries of the autocephalous churches existing today. Such a claim has little connection to the literal meaning of the canon, which concerns "barbarian" lands, where no Roman "provinces" existed and, therefore, no metropolitans. The establishment of an ecclesiastical hierarchy in such lands followed "custom" (Council of Constantinople, 381, canon 2), and some of the bishops in barbarian lands were ordained by metropolitans of Pontus, Asia, or Thrace. It is those bishops exclusively who were now to enter the more centralized "imperial" system, endorsed by canon 28, and be ordained by Constantinople.

[26]ACO III, 1, 3, p. 88-9(447-8). Since the adoption of this important statement was a special action of the Council, it was not originally designated as the "28th canon,"

The text was giving a clear solution to the various conflicts which were discussed earlier. The jurisdiction of Constantinople would not consist anymore in honorary privileges, or in *de facto* authority. Without using the title yet, the archbishop of the capital had become a "patriarch," invested with a limited, but clear right of ordination in three dioceses, just like his colleagues of Alexandria, Antioch and Rome, who were mentioned in canon 6 of Nicaea as also enjoying "privileges." The ancient and prestigious primacy of Ephesus disappeared, as also the position of "exarch." Furthermore, and quite significantly, the canon endorsed the principle of a purely political rationale for the existence of primacies: the older Rome itself, it proclaimed, was granted privileges "by the fathers" because it was the imperial capital, not because it was founded by St Peter. Logically, therefore, the new capital, although it had no "apostolic" foundation, was entitled to the same status. We have discussed the Roman reaction in the preceding chapter. Let us simply remember here that the legates and, later, St Leo himself, based their objections exclusively on the rather artificial argument—which, on the level of doctrine has been invoked by the Eutychians—that the decisions of Nicaea could neither be modified, nor added to: Nicaea spoke of only three "privileged" churches(Alexandria, Antioch, Rome). Of course, St Leo understood all three as "Petrine" sees, but in the discussion on canon 28, he did not invoke the issue of apostolicity, which he knew the Easterners would simply not understand and which was not formally evoked in Nicaea.

At Chalcedon, the legates tried to have the bishops polled and voice complaints about possible pressures exercised upon them to force their vote. The poll gave no results: all the bishops declared that they were freely accepting Constantinople's new power. This unanimity, however, is somewhat surprising after the resistance which the bishop of the capital had faced not only during the preceding decades, but even at the previous sessions of the Council. The commissioners bluntly declared the issue closed—"All was confirmed by the council," they said—explicitly denying any papal right of veto.

This bluntness of the commissioners contrasts with the highly diplomatic letter sent by the council to pope Leo, asking him to

although it appears under this label in later Byzantine collections and commentaries (Cf. E. Schwartz, "Der Sechste Nicaenische Kanon auf der Synode von Chalkedon," in *Berlin, Akad. der Wiss., Sitzungsberichte,* 1930, p. 612).

accept canon 28. Following the pope's silence, new and equally diplomatic letters of Marcian and Anatolius were sent to the Roman pontiff. Indeed, the empire and the church of Constantinople needed Western support to maintain the new and more structured ecclesiastical system established by Chalcedon and which was to be challenged by so many in the East. It might have been to everybody's advantage—since the principle of Roman primacy was not denied by canon 28—if Leo had accepted the partnership of Constantinople, as "second" Rome,[27] and if Leo and Anatolius had been given full opportunity to cooperate in a common defense of Chalcedon against its detractors. But Leo remained adamant in principle, invoking the absoluteness and permanence of three primacies only, as defined in Nicaea. In practice, he could do nothing to suppress the new role of Constantinople. Without ever formally accepting canon 28, he reconciled himself personally with Anatolius, who had written a soothing and ambiguous letter about his own supposed uninvolvement in the drafting of the text. The latter was not listed among the conciliar "canons," but, was included in the minutes as a special statement. Its text was omitted in canonical listings which followed the council. But it appeared in the *Syntagma in fourteen titles* (sixth century), in all later Byzantine collections, and even in some sixth century copies of the oldest Latin canonical collection, the *Prisca.*[28]

The main body of the canonical legislation approved at Chalcedon —*i.e.* the twenty-seven canons—were aimed mostly at strengthening the moral and disciplinary power of the local bishops upon their clergy. There is no doubt that the stormy conflicts of 429-451 had created anarchy in many regions, and that the bishops who have been convinced to support the conciliar decrees needed a legislation which would be endorsed and supported by the empire to reassert their control over their flocks. However, this legislation, since is was based on the traditional ecclesiastical principles which recognized no formal

[27]One of the papal legates—and their translator—Julian of Kos, suggested to the pope to do just that. Cf. the analysis of the correspondence between Constantinople and Rome on this issue in P. Batiffol, *Le siège apostolique* (359-451), Paris, 1924, pp. 567-581; E. Herman, "Chalkedon und die Ausgestaltung des Konstantinopolitanischen Primats," in *Chalkedon,* II, pp. 459-90 and J. Meyendorff, *Orthodoxy and Catholicity,* New York, 1966, pp. 68-74.

[28]V. V. Beneshevich, *Kamonichesky Sbornik v XIV titulov,* St Petersburg, 1903, p. 155; cf. also F. Dvornik, "The see of Constantinople in the first Latin collections of canon law," *Zbornik Radova Vizantoloshkog Instituta,* VIII, 1 (Mélanges Ostrogorsky), Belgrade, 1963, pp. 97-101.

power *over* the local church, (except in the act of consecration of new bishops) represented a certain guarantee against further development of "patriarchal" centralization. The legislation was directed against ordinations "at large," without attachment of new clerics to a concrete community (canon 6), against arbitrary transfers or travels of clergy without the permission of their bishops (canons 5, 10, 11, 13, 20, 23), against appeals by clergy to civil courts in conflicts between themselves, liable to the episcopal courts (canons 9, 21), against clerical involvement in private business, or assumption of civil functions (canons 3, 7), against ordinations for money (canon 2), against marriages between lower clerics and heretics (canon 14), or the ordination of deaconesses before the age of forty (canon 15). In financial affairs, the discretionary power of the bishops and clergy was limited by the requirement that every church appoint a financial officer, or *oikonomos,* responsible for property, and specifically the bishop's property after his death (canons 22, 25, 26).

The most far-reaching measure, however, was concerned with the monastic movement. Canon 4 placed monks and monasteries under the bishop's control. It is significant that the measure was proposed by emperor Marcian himself, reflecting the state's concern with the massive and anarchical development of monasticism. In doctrinal disputes, the monks often assumed the role of watchdogs, or *vigilantes.* First and foremost in the minds of the fathers of Chalcedon themselves, was the brutal behavior of Syrian and Egyptian monks during the Robber council of 449 in Ephesus. Canon 4 said in part:

"Those who truly and honestly have entered monastic life deserve appropriate honor. However, since some, using the appearance of monasticism, disturb the affairs of both the Church and the State, moving throughout the city in a disorderly fashion (ἀδιαφόρως) and managing to establish monasteries independently, it appeared good (to us) that absolutely no one should be allowed to build or establish a monastery, or a house of prayer, without the approval of the bishop of the city, and that, whether in a city, or in the country, the monks be submitted to the bishop, and so practice quietude (ἡσυχίαν) and limit themselves to a life of fasting and prayer, staying at the places where they originally renounced the world (ἐν οἷς τόποις ἀπετάξαντο), avoiding every involvement or participation in either ecclesiastical, or worldly affairs, and never leaving their own monastery, except for an urgent need, by permission of the bishop of the city . . ."

The text sanctions measures taken at Chalcedon concerning a particular group of monks. The proceedings against them began with a procedure of identification, during which the status of several of the accused could not be established, whether they were priests, monks, or archimandrites, or vagabonds "living in tombs."[29] The famous Syrian ascetic Barsauma was accused of "killing the blessed Flavian" and the bishops complained that "he brought against us the whole of Syria." Obviously, Eutychianism was associated in the minds of many with the uncontrolled and anti-episcopal activity of unknown fanatics and self-proclaimed monks, described by Theodoret of Cyrus in his famous dialogue *The Beggar* ('Ερανιστής). Of course, the bishops did not identify monasticism as such with Eutychianism, but they tended to be weary of a lay movement which escaped the direct control of a hierarchy closely connected with imperial authorities. It is also true that many monks were more attracted by the God-centered, kerygmatic and formally conservative christology of Cyril, than by the more intellectual defense of the "two natures" by the theologically educated bishops of Antioch, Constantinople or Rome. Other Eastern ascetics actually tended to emphasize personal human effort in spirituality, rather than "grace" and "deification," sympathizing with Pelagianism and Nestorianism, rather than St Cyril. In Egypt, the great Pachomian monastery of Canopus opposed Dioscoros, who in Alexandria represented episcopal power and control, and sided with Chalcedon.[30]

Be it as it may, canon 4 of Chalcedon established an important institutional pattern. Henceforth, in the East, monastic communities would always remain canonically under the jurisdiction of the local bishops, and no religious orders "exempt" from episcopal jurisdiction would ever be created.[31] Ecclesiologically, the measure was justified:

[29]ACO II, 1, 2, pp. 114-121(310-17); on the whole attitude of the council towards monasticism, see L. Ueding, "Die Kanones von Chalkedon in ihrer Bedeutung für Mönchtum und Klerus," in *Chalkedon,* II, pp. 569-676.

[30]Cf. the discussion of the role of monasticism in the controversies of the fifth century, in Frend, *The Rise,* pp. 89-92.

[31]Exceptions were, in late Byzantium, the few so-called "stavropeghial" monasteries, which depended on the patriarch of Constantinople. But their establishment was due to

there existed a real danger for monasticism to develop outside of the sacramental structure of the Church. However, if the council of Chalcedon meant to quench the sense of spiritual independence and prophetic ministry which existed among the monastics, it certainly failed. Within the orthodox Chalcedonian church of Byzantinum, the monastic communities continued to represent a powerful spiritual force which, by its very existence, challenged the often more flexible and politically oriented mentality of the episcopate.

3. *The opposition to the Council in the East*

At Chalcedon, "the Fathers, following the express desire of the emperor, had promulgated a new definition of the faith, for which they felt no real necessity and whose language was inconsistent with their habitual (theological) language."[32] They were not partisans of Eutyches, and most of them had been shocked by the brutal behavior of Dioscoros, but for them, the authority of St Cyril was paramount. That of St Leo was acceptable too, but only as an antidote to Eutychianism, and so was the conciliar statement itself. Few of them were articulate theologians, so that, in the years which immediately followed the council, the only authoritative spokesman for Chalcedon in the East happened to be Theodoret of Cyrus, but his authority, in spite of his rehabilitation in 451, was marred by his earlier polemics against Cyril. And, in actual fact, Theodoret never really understood Cyril's christology. His writings continued to reflect the basic approach of Theodore of Mopsuestia, an attitude—so he thought—Chalcedon had legitimized.[33] The absence, in the Chalcedonian camp, of authoritative theological figures, able to defend the real spirit and intent of the council, i.e. the conviction that Leo, in essence, "spoke like Cyril" and that the reaffirmation of the full humanity of Christ after the union was not a contradiction, but a balanced reaffirmation of Cyrillian christology, had tragic consequences in the face of the spontaneous popular revolt provoked by the deposition of the Alexandrian pope, Dioscoros.

economic reasons primarily, and seldom pursued any particular missionary or educational goals, as the Western religious orders.

[32]Gustave Bardy in A. Fliche and V. Martin, eds., *Histoire de l'Eglise*, IV, Paris, 1948, p. 272.

[33]Cf. on this point, my discussion of Theodoret in *Christ*, pp. 31-33. The most authoritative study on Theodoret is still that of N. Glubokovsky, *Blazhenny Theodorit*, 2 vols. (Moscow, 1890).

The faith of the council was now declared obligatory to all. A decree of emperors Valentinian and Marcian, published on January 27, 452 declared that "none, either clergyman or governmental official, or of any other condition, henceforth should try to treat publicly about the Christian faith" . . . or "to dispute publicly matters once decided and rightly disposed" by the council. Contraveners, whether clerical or lay, were to be removed from office.[34]

Chronologically, the first direct and massive challenge to the council occurred in Palestine. Crowds of monks led by the abbot Theodosius (not to be confused with St Theodosius the Cenobite) and supported by empress Eudocia, widow of Theodosius II—who, while residing in Jerusalem, opposed the religious policies of her husband's successor Marcian—rebelled against Juvenal of Jerusalem. Upon his return from Chalcedon, the latter was prevented from assuming his see. Another Chalcedonian leader, Severian of Scythopolis was murdered. The opposition to Chalcedon initially included respectable monastic figures—St Gerasimus, St Gerontius, former confidant of St Melania the Younger. Only later would they change their attitude. In 451, the only really staunch supporter of Chalcedon was the great St Euthymius in his *lavra*. As Juvenal escaped to Constantinople, Theodosius was consecrated bishop in his stead, together with several other Monophysites. These included the famous Peter the Iberian, who was made bishop of Maiuma.[35] Eventually, Juvenal was restored to his see, but only through the intervention of Roman troops and bloody clashes with crowds of monks. Fortunately, in the following decades, Chalcedonian orthodoxy was promoted in Palestine not only by force, but also, quite successfully, by great monastic leaders, especially St Euthymius and St Sabbas.

In Egypt, Marcian's firm policy allowed for the election of a Chalcedonian archbishop, Proterius, to replace the deposed and exiled Dioscoros. Proterius had been a priest under Dioscoros and was, therefore, a firm Cyrillian. For a moment, pope Leo even suspected his orthodoxy. However, his acceptance of the council made him unacceptable to the majority of Egyptian Christians. Dioscoros had died

[34]English text of the decree in CN, II, pp. 804-5; another similar decree of March 13 by Marcian, *ibid.*, pp. 808-810.

[35]Being the founder of the Georgian monastery at Jerusalem and a renowned ascetic, Peter is venerated as a Saint by his native church of Georgia, now a staunchly Chalcedonian Orthodox Church. Cf. the *Life of Peter,* translated from the Georgian in D. M. Lang, *Lives and Legends of the Georgian Saints,* 2nd ed., Crestwood, NY, 1976, pp. 57-80.

in exile in 454, and the Monophysites, who did not recognize Proterius, considered the Alexandrian see as vacant. When emperor Marcian also died (457), a popular rebellion broke out leading to the murder of Proterius on Holy Thursday during his celebration of the eucharist. In the main church of Alexandria, the Kaisareion, now occupied by the Monophysites, two anti-Chalcedonian bishops, Eusebius of Peluse and Peter of Maiuma (we have already met the latter in Palestine) consecrated a new archbishop, Timothy. Being tall and thin in stature, he received the surname of the Cat (Αἴλουρος, *Aelurus*). Other Monophysite bishops were ordained throughout Egypt.

The new emperor, Leo I (457-474) was thus faced with an all-out challenge to his authority in Egypt. Not a theologian himself, he was the first Roman emperor to be crowned in an ecclesiastical ceremony by the archbishop. He also received firmly Chalcedonian advice from Anatolius of Constantinople, and after the latter's death (458), from his successor, Gennadius. On the other hand, pope Leo was urging him to take measures against Timothy. Like Rome, the church of Constantinople was now firmly committed to Chalcedon, not only theologically, but also institutionally: the Chalcedonian canons affirmed its jurisdictional powers and its honorary precedence over Alexandria. However, emperor Leo wanted to avoid an immediate use of force in Egypt to install a Chalcedonian archbishop, as Marcian did in Jerusalem. For a moment, he even envisaged holding a new council.[36] Instead, he took the rather unusual step of polling the entire episcopate of the empire, asking opinions concerning the legitimacy of Timothy's consecration and the validity of the council of Chalcedon. Significantly, the emperor also approached St Symeon the Stylite, and other respected representatives of Syrian monasticism, on the same issue. There could be no clearer recognition of the fact that, even after the publication of canon 4 of Chalcedon, the moral authority of eminent monks, parallel to that of the bishops, had remained great.[37] Almost unanimously the responses went against Timothy and in favor of Chalcedon. The Alexandrian pope was approached personally and called upon

---

[36]Pope Leo expresses his fear that at such an assembly the Chalcedonian definition would be questioned and a policy of theological compromise be initiated; cf. *Ep* 162, dated March 21, 458, PL 54, col. 1144 BC (cf. also *Ep* 161 to the clergy of Constantinople).

[37]The text of the letter of Leo to Anatolius of Constantinople, copies of which were distributed to other bishops, as well as the response of St Symeon, transmitted through the bishop of Antioch, are found in Evagrius, *Hist. eccl.* II, 9, ed. J. Bidez and L. Parmentier, reprt. Amsterdam, 1964, pp. 59-61.

to follow the majority of the episcopate, but he remained adamant in his rejection of Chalcedon. He was then arrested, in the midst of open popular insurrection. Roman troops put down the opposition at the cost of 10,000 victims. Timothy was exiled first to Gangra, then to Cherson in the Crimea.

His successor, another Timothy, called Salofaciol ("White Turban"), was elected and installed under the protection of imperial troops. Personally moderate and charitable—qualities which were sometimes recognized even by the Monophysites—he made "ecumenical" attempts at reconciliation, and went to the point of restoring the name of Dioscoros in the diptychs.[38] But the vast majority of Egyptian Christians, after what they considered the humiliation of their church at Chalcedon and the bloody repressions suffered from imperial troops, would have nothing to do with Timothy II, calling him despicably the "emperor's man," (βασιλικὸν)[39] or, in Semitic tongues, a "Melkite."

Emperor Leo's skillful handling of the bishops and his energetic use of force in Egypt maintained a semblance of unity in the East until the emperor's death in 474. However, this unity did not reflect a general and organic "reception" of the council of Chalcedon by either its supporters, or its opponents.

Throughout the entire second half of the fifth century, no real substantive theological debate on the meaning of the Chalcedonian definition took place, but much political infighting and sloganeering. As a result, the Chalcedonian statement of faith was gradually taken out of its proper context and used either to justify the survival of the old Antiochene christology, as if the decisive challenge by St Cyril had not shown its shortcomings and dangers, or to prove that Cyrillian theology had been abandoned. As we have seen in our discussion of the Acts of the Council, neither of these superficial interpretations is correct.

The predominance of Antiochene christology among the apologists of the council is obvious, first in their interpretation of the statement which proclaims that the characteristics of the two natures are "concurring in one person (πρόσωπον) and one hypostasis," and, second, in their aversion to "theopaschite" formulae. The two points are, of course, related. Since Diodore of Tarsus and Theodore of Mopsuestia,

---

[38]Zacharias, Hist. eccl. IV, 10 (Ed. and tr. E. W. Brooks, CSCO, Script. syri, III, 6).
[39]Evagrius, op. cit., II, 11, p. 63.

the Antiochenes had insisted upon the *concrete* integrity of both divinity and humanity in Christ, and designated them as "natures" which could not be confused, or even be seen in true "communion" with each other. Their relationship was seen as a "contact" (συνάφεια), whereas the oneness of Christ was expressed by the term "one *prosopon*," a weak term meaning "person," but also "mask" or "impersonation," or "role." For Theodoret and many other Chalcedonians, the expression "concurring in one *prosopon* and one *hypostasis*" implied a new and weakened use of the term *hypostasis*, as *synonymous with prosopon*. Taken by itself, the expression perhaps made such an interpretation possible. However, the entire context, which included not only the numerous formal declarations of "Cyrillism" by the fathers, but also the use of the term *Theotokos* in the definition, implied in fact that the word *hypostasis* designated the pre-existing *hypostasis* of the Logos, One of the Holy Trinity. The "Antiochene" interpretation of the statement appears not only in the writings of Theodoret, especially in his *Haereticarum fabularum compendium,* published in 453, and his letter to the Nestorian John of Aegaea, but also in what we know of the positions of Gennadius, archbishop of Constantinople (458-471), of his successor Macedonius (495-511), of the Acoemetae ("Non-Sleeping") monks, also in Constantinople, and other Chalcedonian churchmen of the period.[40] The common position of these apologists of the council was their avoidance of the notion of "hypostatic" union and its implications. They were of course not formally Nestorian and always defended themselves from teaching the doctrine of "two sons"—the pre-existing Son of God being distinct from the "son of Mary," born in history—but, in fact, just as their Antiochene teachers Diodore of Tarsus and Theodore of Mopsuestia, they were consistently reluctant to admit a real *unity of subject* in Christ. This was particularly evident whenever they touched upon Christ's passion. When asked the question directly—"*Who* suffered on the cross?"—they would answer: "the flesh of Christ," His "humanity," His "human nature," or "the things human" (τὰ ἀνθρώπεια), i.e. impersonal entities. Indeed, they would not admit the existence in Christ of a second person—this would be straight Nestorianism—but were unable to concede that, since only *somebody* (not "something") can really *suffer,* St Cyril

---

[40]For a more detailed review of this Antiochene diphysitism after Chalcedon, see my book *Christ*, pp. 31-37; cf. also, P.T.R. Gray, *The Defense of Chalcedon in the East (451-553),* Leiden, 1976, pp. 80-89.

was right, in the famous twelfth *Anathematism* of his third letter to Nestorius, in saying: God the Word "suffered in the flesh" (ἔπαθεν σαρκί).

It is this systematic reluctance by many Chalcedonians to accept "theopaschism"—which christologically was as essential as the admission that Mary was the "Mother of God," not of another, human person—which gave ammunition to the council's opponents.

It is true, of course, that most Monophysite polemicists were stubborn and grossly unfair. They were right in rejecting the Antiochene identification of the term *hypostasis* with *prosopon,* but wrong in not admitting that *hypostasis* could be distinguished from *physis,* and in believing that this distinction was contrary to St Cyril's thought. To remain faithful to Cyril, Dioscoros, at Chalcedon, rejected the formula "unity *in two natures*"; but this formula was really saying only that Christ was effectively both God and man after the union. Cyril himself had written: "The flesh remains flesh: it is not divine nature, though it be God's flesh: and similarly the Word is not flesh, although on account of His economy, He made flesh His own."[41] Cyril even had asked: "How could we not accept that two natures exist inseparably after the union?"[42] Cyril never formally distinguished "nature" from *hypostasis,* but then he used "nature" in two different senses: for him, Christ was "one nature incarnate," but in this "natural union," there were two "existing" natures! Was not Chalcedon right then to introduce a terminological clarification? The anti-Chalcedonians were also unfair to pope Leo, whom they considered as the real villain at Chalcedon. Indeed, Leo's *Tome,* for all its Western vocabulary, specifically included the "theopaschite" language, implying in Christ the single, divine Person of the Son of God, *subject* of His human experience and activity. The council was right in calling Leo a "Cyrillian." In a letter to emperor Leo brought to Constantinople by papal legates in 458, the pope even accepted fully Cyrillian terminology, to the point of avoiding the expression "in two natures."[43]

However stubborn and unfair, the "Monophysites" remained "strict Cyrillians."[44] It is their Cyrillian "fundamentalism" which

[41]*Ep 45 ad Succensum,* PG 87, col. 232.

[42]*Ep 46,* ibid., col. 244.

[43]*Ep 165,* PL 54, cols. 1155-1190; Leo specifically admits the orthodoxy of Cyril's formula "one nature incarnate of God the Word," as distinct from the Eutychian "one nature of God incarnate." If "incarnate' (fem. σεσαρκωμένη) qualifies "nature," and not "Word," it implies the existence of "the flesh after the union."

[44]This is admitted today by all historians of the period. The authoritative study on

prevented them from accepting the Chalcedonian statement. It must be recognized, however, that the writings and activities of the "Antiochene Chalcedonians" made it more difficult for the followers of Dioscoros and Timothy Aelurus to believe the assurances, so specifically voiced at Chalcedon, that the *Tome* of Leo and the final statement were to be read and understood only in the light of Cyril's christology, of Cyril's soteriology and Cyril's fundamental belief that union with divinity does not obliterate humanity, but makes it truly itself, in conformity with God's original creation. The lack of an articulate Chalcedonian theology, coupled with the brutality of imperial interventions, made the Chalcedonian definition into a symbol and a slogan. Both sides filled it with that content which suited their own emotional, political and, later, cultural tendencies, or interests. In reality, like all doctrinal definitions, the Chalcedonian statement did not only solve some problems: it also created new ones. Like all formulae using human language, it was incomplete, especially in its failure to affirm, with sufficient and convincing clarity, and not only by implication, that the term *hypostasis* designated the pre-existing hypostasis of the Second Person of the Trinity.

The situation required great minds, capable of solving problems in the manner in which the great Cappadocian fathers—St Basil, St Gregory of Nazianzus—had in the late fourth century solved the dilemma between the strict adepts of the Nicaean theology of Athanasius, and the *bona fide* critics of the *homoousios*, for whom the term implied modalism. The council of Chalcedon had attempted precisely a similar clarifying settlement, by using a language which would allay fears of Apollinarism and Eutychianism, existing in some minds, as well as fears of Nestorianism existing in others. But the success of this orthodox settlement needed pastoral tolerance, intellectual honesty and authentic desire for unity in truth. Instead, there was, on one side, christological ambiguity and imperial power-politics, and on the other, blind conservatism, brutal demagoguery and, later, the defense of ethnic particularism against imperial centralization.

During the reigns of Zeno (474-491) and Anastasius (491-518) there were also major attempts to impose unity by force through the

---

the issue is that of J. Lebon, *Le monophysisme sévérien. Etude historique, littéraire et théologique sur la résistance monophysite au concile de Chalcédoine jusqu'à la constitution de l'église jacobite,* Louvain, 1909.

avoidance of issues. This is the meaning of the publication, by emperor Zeno, of his famous *Henotikon.*

4. *Patriarch Acacius, the Henotikon and East-West conflict*

Already during the reign of emperor Leo I, it was becoming increasingly clear that in Egypt and Syria, the anti-Chalcedonian wave was mounting. Pope Leo had died in 461. Practically alone among the major personalities of the time, he had become aware, especially in his conciliatory letters to the emperor in 458, that Chalcedonian firmness required—and actually implied—faithfulness to the soteriological dimension of St Cyril's christology. The monumental figure of the great pope would be missed in the following decades. In Antioch, internal struggles in the church were provoking frequent changes on the episcopal throne. Short terms by Maximus, Basil, and Acacius, were followed by that of Martyrius. The latter was challenged by Peter the Fuller, a brilliant man and a Monophysite, who succeeded three successive times in having Martyrius expelled and in taking his place, only to be expelled himself in favor of imperial appointees: John Codonatus, Stephen—who was killed by a Monophysite mob—and finally Calendio (481). The christological tradition of the old Antiochian school was overwhelmed by Monophysite pressure. It was further weakened when, following the death of bishop Ibas (457), the school of Edessa—the nerve-center of Syrian theology and culture— emigrated to Nisibis, on Persian territory. The new school of Nisibis contributed greatly to the intellectual development and missionary expansion of Nestorian christianity, under the "great metropolitan" or "catholic bishop" residing in Seleucia-Ctesiphon. In Edessa, what had remained of the old school was closed by Zeno (489). In Egypt meanwhile, Timothy II Salofaciol held his position only under the protection of imperial troops.

The years following the death of emperor Leo I (474) were marked by a struggle for power between the late emperor's son-in-law, Zeno who first assumed the throne, and his brother-in-law, Basiliscus who overturned Zeno in January 475, only to be exiled by a returning Zeno in September 476. This dynastic instability manifested even more obviously the threat posed by the christological disputes to the unity of the empire.

Indeed, at this stage of the crisis, none of the competing groups deliberately challenged the role of the empire in maintaining Christian unity. The time at which Monophysitism would become a symbol of ethnic, or cultural self-affirmation by Syrians, Egyptian Copts, or Armenians had not yet come.[45] Of course, a degree of cultural separatism existed in Egypt since the beginning of the Roman conquest, and the Christian archbishops—as well as the monastic masses—used it in their interests, but all the major figures of the Egyptian church, including St Cyril, Dioscoros and Timothy Aelurus, were ready to accept and profit from the imperial system whenever the latter's policies coincided with theirs. Furthermore, most of the major personalities of the Monophysite camp including not only Eutyches himself, but also Dioscoros, Timothy, Peter the Fuller, Peter Mongos and, later, the great Severus of Antioch, were Greeks by language and culture.

There was, therefore, a chance for the empire to restore unity in the manner in which unity had been restored by Theodosius I following the Arian struggles. Perhaps, this would have been possible had imperial policies been guided by appropriate theological advice, as happened under Theodosius I (with the role played by the Cappadocian fathers), or later under Justinian (when the emperor was a theologian himself, but it was too late to heal the schism). In any case, if a chance of reconciliation existed, it was not taken. Blunt power was used instead for the sake of either the wrong options, or a policy of doctrinal compromise with the effect of deepening and widening the schisms. The emperors of that period initiated a new method of exercising their power in church affairs: the publication of doctrinal statements claiming to reflect a consensus, but in fact imposing imperial policy by force. It should be noted that such edicts were not supposed to be viewed as doctrinal definitions competing with creeds or conciliar statements. They usually took the forms of an imperial letter to a particular church. Formally, the emperors did not pretend to define doctrine, but only to give authoritative interpretations of the established teachings given by preceding councils. However, the distinction was rather theoretical, and the attempts were clearly "caesaro-papistic." It is

[45]A. H. M. Jones, the well-known historian of Late Antiquity, is the author of an important article, ("Were Ancient Heresies National or Social Movements in Disguise?" JTS, new series, 10, 1959, pp. 280-298) in which he challenges the view of many nineteenth century and modern historians who interpreted the rise of Monophysitism as a "national" movement. Unquestionably true after the seventh century, this view is unjustifiable in the fifth.

noteworthy that none of these edicts—whether they were published by orthodox, or heretical emperors[46]—was accepted by the Church as being in itself an authoritative expression of orthodox teaching.

The usurper Basiliscus, in order to establish his rule after his overthrow of the still formally Chalcedonian Zeno, decided to win the support of the Monophysites. His *Encyclical* was a letter addressed to the exiled Alexandrian archbishop Timothy Aelurus, whose stand the new emperor intended to vindicate. In the name of "unity," the "good order of the churches" and "world peace," Basiliscus declared that the true faith had been sufficiently well expressed in Nicaea and Ephesus I, that the *Tome* of Leo and "the things transacted in Chalcedon" were an "innovation," and that whoever would attempt to "advance" the faith of Chalcedon would be subject to exile, confiscation of property and extreme penalties."[47] Timothy Aelurus left his exile in the Crimea, was solemnly received at Constantinople, proceeded to Ephesus, where he presided over a council of bishops of the Asian diocese and solemnly cancelled canon 28 of Chalcedon, which had given the archbishop of Constantinople the right to consecrate the bishops of Ephesus. In Alexandria, where he returned immediately, his triumph was so complete, that he could even afford to be generous and provide a pension for Timothy Salofaciol. The latter peacefully retired to the Chalcedonian monastery of Canopus. The body of Dioscoros was returned to Alexandria and venerated as the relics of a confessor. In Antioch, Peter the Fuller was restored as archbishop and in Jerusalem archbishop Anastasius, successor of Juvenal, signed the *Encyclical*.

This incredible turn of events showed that the entire episcopate of the East was practically made up of either straight opponents of Chalcedon, or at least, of people called the "Hesitants" (Διακρινόμενοι),[48] who could easily approve Chalcedon under Leo and reject it under Basiliscus. But resistance came—and strongly—from the two "Romes." In a manner rather unusual for an archbishop of the capital, Acacius of Constantinople (471-89) refused to obey the em-

---

[46]The list of such edicts includes the *Encyclical* (475) and the *Anti-encyclical* (476) of Basiliscus, the *Henotikon* of Zeno (482), Justinian's decree about the Three Chapters (ca. 543), the *Program* of Justin II (571), the *Ekthesis* of Heraclius (638) and the *Typos* of Constans II (648).

[47]Text in Evagrius, *Eccl. Hist.*, III, 4, ed. cit., pp. 101-4; English translation in CN III, pp. 915-917.

[48]Cf. the article of G. Bareille, "Diacrinomènes," in Vacant-Mangenot, *Dictionnaire de théologie catholique VII*, cols. 732-3; cf. also W. H. C. Frend, *op. cit.*, p. 144.

peror and to welcome Timothy the Cat during his passage in the city. He also called for, and received, the help of a glorified ascetic, St Daniel the Stylite, who came down from his column, threatened Basiliscus with eternal punishment and called him a "second Diocletian."[49] Together with St Daniel, the patriarch held processions in the city and preached directly against Basiliscus. Finally, he wrote to pope Simplicius, who replied, praising his stand.

Whether or not this union of the two Romes had an independent effect, or whether it was a calculated move, anticipating the fall of Basiliscus, it frightened the emperor, who soon—and shamefully—published an *Anti-encyclical* formally cancelling the *Encyclical,* and specifically declared that "Acacius, the most pious and most holy patriarch and archbishop, should be restored in his rights to make ordinations in areas previously assigned to the throne of this glorious imperial city."[50] But his days were numbered. Zeno reentered the capital in September 476 and took drastic measures against the Monophysites: Peter the Fuller of Antioch, Paul of Ephesus (who had supported Timothy) and Timothy Aelurus himself were all deposed and exiled, although the latter died soon after receiving the imperial notification without having to leave Alexandria (July 31, 477). Immediately after his death, Monophysite bishops, evading imperial surveillance, consecrated Peter Mongos, a convinced anti-Chalcedonian as archbishop. Peter went into hiding, while Timothy Salofaciol recovered his throne. Of course the church of Egypt remained irremediably split, with the great majority supporting Peter.

The new imperial government, solidly installed in Constantinople, inevitably sought ways to stabilize the ecclesiastical situation. It had taken stern measures against the Monophysites, but knew that this would not suffice in the long run. Actually, none of the major sees was really at peace.[51] Calendio of Antioch, ordained by Acacius, was not even able to assume his throne. Martyrios of Jerusalem—successor of Anastasius who had signed the *Encyclical*—published an ambiguous circular letter which proclaimed only three councils (Nicaea, Constantinople, Ephesus I) as canonical. But it is certainly Alexandria which

---

[49]*Vita Danielis 44,73,* ed. P. Peeters, *AB* 32, 1913, pp. 121-214; English translation in E. Dawes and N. H. Baynes, *Three Byzantine Saints,* Oxford, 1948 (reprt. Crestwood, NY, 1977), p. 52.

[50]Text in Evagrius, *Eccl. Hist.,* III, 7, ed. cit., p. 107; English translation, CN, III, p. 918.

[51]A good description of the situation in Frend, *The Rise,* pp. 174-7.

caused the greatest concern. Following the death of Timothy Salofaciol (February 481), it became apparent that peace could not be reached unless Peter Mongos was recognized as archbishop. The majority would not accept any other candidate, and especially not John Talaia, a Chalcedonian priest and monk from Canopus, who was consecrated bishop by the Chalcedonian minority, following Salofaciol's death, in expectation of imperial recognition and support. The weakness of Talaia was compounded by the fact that he had made the wrong connections in Byzantium and was not a friend of Patriarch Acacius. His election was not recognized because Zeno and Acacius preferred a "deal" with Mongos. Talaia had to escape to Rome.

In general histories of the period, it is still current to present patriarch Acacius, as a crypto-Monophysite,[52] because he was labelled such by the popes during the later conflict with Rome. In fact, there is no reason to believe that his truly courageous opposition to Basiliscus, his stern condemnations in letters to Pope Simplicius of both Peter the Fuller and Peter Mongos[53] were insincere. Being a typical Byzantine prelate, he was fully aware that his position required not only firmness whenever real victory could be expected (as in the case of his struggle with Basiliscus), but also flexibility, when the interests of the empire directed it. Thus he managed the "deal" with Peter Mongos, leaving the direct responsibility to the emperor and, presumably, hoping that the Chalcedonian faith would nevertheless remain safe.

Thus, a letter of Zeno, dated 28 July 482 and known as the *Henotikon,* was addressed to the church of Alexandria. No bishop was designated by name. The emperor expressed concern for unity and solemnly proclaimed that the empire and "all the churches" accepted no other faith than the one expressed in the baptismal creed approved in Nicaea and in Constantinople, and that the council of Ephesus condemned Nestorius on the basis of this creed. However, the emperor immediately added an anathema against Eutyches without specifying which council proclaimed it, announced the acceptance of the *Twelve Chapters* of Cyril (i.e. his third letter to Nestorius) and published a confession of christological faith, which studiously avoided the use of the controversial terms "nature,'" *hypostasis* and *prosopon.* In

---

[52]Cf., for instance G. Bardy, in A. Fliche and V. Martin, *Histoire de l'Eglise,* IV, Paris, 1948, p. 290; for a contrary view, H. G. Beck in Jedin Dolan, *History* II, p. 425.
[53]Cf. *Collectio Avellana,* ed. O. Guenther, CSEL 35, 1, 66-67; and E. Schwartz, "Publizistische Sammlungen zum acacianischen Schisma," *Bayerische Akad. des Wiss., Abhandlungen,* Phil. hist. Abt. n.s., 10, 4 (1934), pp. 4-5.

content, however, the confession carefully maintained not only the Cyrillian affirmation of the oneness of Christ, including theopaschism ("we say that the miracles and the passion are of the One"—ἑνὸς εἶναι φαμέν) and condemned the doctrine of the "two sons," but also affirmed the point, important for the Chalcedonians and rejected by the Eutychians, that Christ is "consubstantial to us, according to his humanity." However, the point made by St Leo and the Chalcedonian definition that both the divinity and the humanity of Christ "preserved their characteristics" in the union, was omitted.

Technically uncontroversial, this first and main part of the *Henotikon* does, nevertheless, contain inner contradictions: if the Nicaean-Constantinopolitan creed is the only acceptable statement of faith, why is Eutyches, who accepted it, anathematized? And how to justify the doctrine of "double consubstantiality," which is not contained in the Nicaean creed?

Still more problems are found in the last paragraph of the document. It affirms that "neither the churches, nor Our Majesty accept any other creed (σύμβολον), or definition of faith (ὅρου πίστεως)" —an allusion which could be referred to the Chalcedonian statement, usually defined as ὅρος. The document then makes a curious, defensive statement, as if rejecting in advance the accusation of caesaropapism: "We have written those things not innovating in the faith, but for the sake of your information." Then comes a really crucial sentence: "Anyone who thought or thinks otherwise, either now or at any other time, *either in Chalcedon or at any other council*, we anathematize, particularly the aforementioned Nestorius and Eutyches, and those who think like they do."[54]

Both in form and in content, the *Henotikon* was an attempt to raise the debate to the level of christological concepts and away from the dead ends of terminology. If it had no other implications and if it had succeeded, the christological controversies could have subsided on the basis of a general return to the situation which followed the reconciliation between St Cyril and John of Antioch in 433. But the text itself made such a return impossible by mentioning, on the one hand, the condemnation of Eutyches, which occurred at Chalcedon, and, at the same time, by referring to Chalcedon in a definitely pejorative context.

[54]Evagrius, *Eccl. Hist.* III, 14, ed. cit., pp. 111-4, English translation in CN III, pp. 925-7. Recourse to the original Greek is important for an understanding of the many nuances of this highly ambiguous diplomatic document.

Nevertheless, in terms of inter-church relations in the East, some immediate results were obtained. All the major sees of the East entered into communion with each other again. Peter Mongos was recognized as archbishop of Alexandria and Acacius of Constantinople formally communicated with him. Since the official position of the church of Constantinople was, of course, Chalcedonian, Peter had to write to Acacius: "Leading us all, you have united the holy Church of God, having convinced us with compelling proofs, that the most holy and ecumenical council held in Chalcedon did nothing contrary (to Nicaea), and that it agreed with and confirmed the decisions of the Nicaean fathers."[55] This formal recognition of Chalcedon by a leader of the opposition was quite an event which seemed to justify the policy of Acacius. However, Mongos was soon faced in Egypt with monastic rebellions, which condemned him for being in communion with Chalcedonians. Some formally seceded from their archbishop (the so-called *Aposkhistai*, or *Akephaloi*, "Headless"). As a result, the archbishop anathematized Chalcedon and the *Tome* of Leo.[56] Understandably, both among Chalcedonians and Monophysites, he received the reputation of an unstable hypocrite.

In Antioch, the strictly Chalcedonian archbishop Calendio rejected the *Henotikon*, but was soon compromised in a political plot aiming at the overthrow of Zeno, and was exiled (484). The see was recovered by Peter the Fuller, who, not only recognized the *Henotikon*, but made himself its active promoter, introducing in particular, the liturgical usage of the interpolated Trisagion: "Holy God, Holy mighty, Holy immortal, who was crucified for us, have mercy on us." His goal was, of course, to proclaim "theopaschism," in a christological, Cyrillian sense. Unfortunately—and unnecessarily—the promotion of the hymn by Peter the Fuller and the stringent opposition to it in Chalcedonian circles both contributed to making it into a Monophysitic slogan.

Even in Palestine, where Chalcedon had strong monastic support, the *Henotikon* was accepted by Martyrios of Jerusalem, and prominent

---

[55]Text in Evagrius, *op. cit.*, III, 17, ed. cit., p. 115. There is also a collection of spurious letters, supposedly exchanged by Peter and Acacius, which presents Acacius as an opponent of Chalcedon, an obvious impossibility (cf. V. Grunnel, *Les régestes du patriarcat de Constantinople*, I, Paris, 1932, p. 156-9, 161, 164, 167.)

[56]Zacharias, *Hist. eccl.* VII, 1 (Ed. and tr. E. W. Brooks, CSCO, *Script. syri*, III, 6).

Chalcedonians welcomed the unification of the Church.[57]

The situation created by the *Henotikon,* as it is described by the historian Evagrius[58]—"in those days, the council of Chalcedon was neither openly proclaimed in the most holy churches, nor was it rejected by all; each bishop acted according to his conviction"—could continue only if it reflected a real agreement on the substance of christology and on a consistent interpretation of Church tradition. But this was obviously not the case. The régime of the *Henotikon,* maintained by emperors Zeno (474-491) and Anastasius (491-518), saw the gradual rise of a Monophysitism, which rejected ambiguities and insisted upon a formal and clear rejection of the council. For several decades the church of Constantinople, under Acacius and his successors, was practically the only Eastern center resisting that trend. Paradoxically, therefore, the bishops of the capital, the natural supporters of imperial policies, stood alone in opposing them. Their natural allies in the fight for Chalcedon would normally be the Roman popes. However, relations between the two Romes were fatally disrupted by the personal case of Acacius.

The case, as it was seen from Rome, has been already discussed in the preceding chapter. Since 476, the old imperial capital was under Ostrogothic rule, and the popes could freely face up to the power of the emperors of Constantinople.

It is at the beginning of the reign of pope Felix III (483-492), that Roman legates arrived in Constantinople to demand justice for John Talaia, the unhappy Chalcedonian competitor of Peter Mongos for the throne of Alexandria, and to support the cause of Chalcedonian orthodoxy, which, as the pope was informed by the *Akoimetai* ("Non-Sleeping") monks of Constantinople, was in jeopardy because of Acacius. Nevertheless the policy of the *Henotikon* was explained to them by the patriarch. They were impressed by his obviously Chalcedonian convictions and informed of the weaknesses of Talaia's claims. They also must have been cajoled by gifts and duly impressed by the prestige of the "New Rome." As a result, they solemnly concelebrated the liturgy with Acacius. Of course, this action was interpreted by all as the acceptance of the *Henotikon* by Rome.

Upon their return, however, pope Felix, and a council of seventy-

---

[57]Cf. John of Scythopolis, *Life of St Euthymius,* in A. J. Festugière, *Les Moines d'Orient,* II, Paris, 1961, pp. 121-2.
[58]*Hist. eccl.,* III, 30, ed. cit., p. 126.

seven bishops, disavowed them and deposed Acacius because of his recognition of Peter Mongos, who "had been ordained by heretics."[59]

The strong stand of Felix III against the ambiguities of the *Henotikon* certainly contributed to the cause of Chalcedonian orthodoxy, but the demands of his successors, especially Gelasius, that the patriarchs of Constantinople, Euphemius (490-5) and Macedonius (495-511), who formally broke with the Monophysite archbishops of Alexandria[60] and strongly fought for Chalcedon, also exclude Acacius from the diptychs, *exclusively* on the basis of his deposition by Rome, were highly unrealistic and anticipated the future schism between East and West.[61] Indeed, as seen by the Orthodox of the East, Acacius could not be held formally responsible for a document issued by the emperor, and his communion with Peter Mongos could not be held against him because it resulted from the latter's formal recognition of Chalcedon. Acacius could be considered guilty of tactical mistakes, but not of heresy.

5. The rise of Monophysitism under Anastasius

Assuming the imperial throne by marrying Zeno's widow, Ariadne,[62] Anastasius I (491-518) was an elderly, pious, but also quite competent and energetic ruler. Necessarily concerned with the widespread opposition to the council of Chalcedon, he remained faithful to the principles of the *Henotikon*, but pushed its interpretation even further in the anti-Chalcedonian sense. In Egypt, he fully condoned the occupation of the Alexandrian archbishopric by a succession of men who, unlike the ambiguous Peter Mongos, explicitly rejected the council: Athanasius II, John II Hemula, John III of Nikiu, Dioscoros II and Timothy IV.

However, the régime initiated by the *Henotikon* excluded a total triumph of Monophysitism and allowed for strong Chalcedonianism

[59]Evagrius, *op. cit.*, III, 21, ed. cit., p. 119; the sentence of the council in E. Schwartz, *Publizistische Sammlungen*, pp. 6-7.

[60]For Euphemius, see Theophanes, *Chronographia*, ed. de Boor, p. 135; on the fight of Macedonius against the Monophysites, especially Philoxenos of Mabbug, see A. de Halleux, *Philoxène de Mabbug*, Louvain, 1963.

[61]On the circumstances of the conflict, see above, pp. 60-4.

[62]On the exceptional role played by empresses like Eudocia, Pulcheria and Ariadne in solving dynastic, political and religious problems see K. G. Holum, *Theodosian Empresses. Women and Imperial Dominion in Late Antiquity*, Berkeley, 1982.

not only to maintain itself, but even to achieve dominance in several major sees of Eastern Christendom. As we have seen earlier, this "Chalcedonism," out of reaction against the Monophysites, would sometimes be taking the form of a revival of "Antiochene" christological language. This seems to have been the case with the Chalcedonian party in Constantinople, which included archbishops Euphemius (490-5) and Macedonius (495-511). Thus, the great theologians who —in the Monophysite camp—understood their struggle as a defense of St Cyril, could argue more convincingly that Chalcedon equalled a restoration of Nestorianism. These Monophysite theologians received wider audience at the court of Anastasius I, especially towards the end of his reign.

Besides Constantinople, the sees of Jerusalem (patriarch Elias, 493-516) and Antioch (Flavian II, 498-512) were occupied by Chalcedonians, but were facing strong and sometimes violent opposition.

In the anti-Chalcedonian camp, intellectual leadership was assumed by two men: Philoxenos—or Xenaia—bishop of Mabbug, and the great theologian, a convert from paganism, Severus. A Syrian without knowledge of Greek, Philoxenos had been consecrated bishop by Peter the Fuller and became the author of numerous writings against the council. In 506-7, he led a strong campaign demanding from his patriarch, Flavian of Antioch, a formal anathematization of Chalcedon. Unsuccessful in his attempt, he sent his confession of faith to the emperor and claimed imperial support, which he easily obtained, and was invited to the capital. However, the imperial decision was challenged by archbishop Macedonius, who refused communion to Philoxenos. The latter returned to Syria to continue his fight against Flavian who was eventually forced to a partial retreat: he declared that he accepted the condemnation of Nestorius and Eutyches, but not the Chalcedonian definition. This compromise did not help him much. In spite of staunch resistance by the Chalcedonians at the council of Sidon (512), the Monophysites eventually forced his deposition and exile. Severus became the new patriarch: he accepted the *Henotikon* (as most Chalcedonians were doing also), but also anathematized Nestorius, Eutyches, the *Tome* of Leo, and the council of Chalcedon.[63]

Born in Sozopolis in Pisidia and having received an excellent education in the fields of rhetoric, Greek, philosophy and law, Severus was baptized a Christian in 488. Attracted by the monastic ideal, he was

[63]Cf. his enthronement address, preserved in Syriac, and published in PO II, p. 322.

initiated to ascetism in Maiuma, the seat of Peter the Iberian. Theologically brilliant, able to exercise moderation, and even to criticize the "contentiousness" of Diocoros, but also uncompromisingly faithful to positions he considered to be true, he became the main spokesman for a christology, which claimed to be the only legitimate expression of Cyrillian orthodoxy. The success of his career was undoubtedly due to his impressive personality, but it would have been impossible without the emperor's patronage. He sojourned in Constantinople itself for three years (508-511), challenging the orthodox archbishop Macedonius, promoting the singing of the interpolated "theopaschite" Trisagion ("Holy God, Holy mighty, Holy immortal, who was crucified for us, have mercy on us."), and intelligently criticizing the limitations of the Chalcedonian definition and the weaknesses of its defenders.[64] Finally, on August 6, 511, Macedonius was deposed, exiled and replaced by Timothy (511-18). The new patriarch showed more lenience towards the Monophysites, without, however, entirely abandoning the basic Chalcedonian stand of the church of Constantinople.

Indeed, the council had partisans at the imperial court itself, including empress Ariadne. Following the introduction of the interpolated *Trisagion* at St Sophia in 512, riots took place, statues of Anastasius were overthrown and violence erupted against the Monophysites. The crisis was finally overcome through a courageous gesture of the old emperor. Showing his personal commitment to anti-Chalcedonianism, he appeared before the crowds at the hippodrome dressed in mourning clothes, without his imperial crown, and offered to resign the throne. His personal popularity, pious reputation and obvious sincerity won the day. He stayed on and was even able to quench the rebellion of Vitalian (513-515) who had espoused the Chalcedonian cause.

At Jerusalem, the Monophysite sweep was also strong, but ultimately unsuccessful. Patriarch Elias had refused to recognize the election of Severus in 512. He faced the opposition of Monophysite monks, supported by Olympius, governor of Palestine (*dux Palestinae*), who acted on instructions from Constantinople. The patriarch was finally deposed in 516. His deacon John was elected to succeed him and

---

[64]It is then that Anastasius published a text, which is referred to as a *Typos* and which may have been drafted by Severus. It anathematizes Chalcedon. It does not seem, however, to have ever received the status of an official imperial edict (cf. Ch. Moeller, "Un fragment du Type de l'empereur Anastase I," in *Studia Patristica* III (= TU 78), Berlin, 1951, pp. 240-7.)

expected to anathematize Chalcedon. However, on the day of his enthronement at which the emperor's nephew, Hypatius, and a great crowd were to witness his compliance with imperial demands, two leaders of Palestinian monasticism—St Sabbas and St Theodosius—standing on the ambo, and supported—according to accounts—by 10,000 monks, demanded, on the contrary, that he accept Chalcedon. After hours of chaotic disturbance the moral authority of the monks prevailed: John anathematized not the council, but Nestorius, Eutyches *and Severus*, accepting four ecumenical councils "as the four Gospels."[65]

These events clearly showed the failure of the *Henotikon*. The Roman popes may have been wrong in viewing it as a capitulation of the Chalcedonians—in fact, the example of the bishops of Constantinople and the events of Jerusalem proved the contrary—, but the situation also showed that no meeting of minds had occurred and that the issue required not only a formal peace, imposed from above, but also a theological solution.

The tragedy was compounded by the continuation of the schism between the Eastern defenders of Chalcedon and the church of Rome. As we have seen earlier, the popes, especially Gelasius, continued to demand not only the recognition of Chalcedon, but also that the name of patriarch Acacius be stricken from the diptychs of the church of Constantinople. During the reign of Anastasius, negotiations on this subject continued between the Roman bishops and the court of Constantinople. Indeed, the popes, while they refused communion to the bishops of the Eastern capital, did not consider the emperor as being excommunicated. While reproaching him for his meddling in church affairs by supporting the *Henotikon,* they continued to see in him the head of the *Romanitas.* The negotiations relative to Acacius were also closely connected with the request made by the Ostrogothic rulers of Italy, especially Theodoric, to be recognized by Constantinople, as imperial representatives in the West. Of course, such a recognition was also in the interests of the papacy.[66] However, following the intransigence of pope Gelasius (492-6) and the unfulfilled readiness of his successor Anastasius II (496-8) to compromise, the church of Rome was torn apart by the Laurentian Schism, with the Symmachian party favoring the tradition of Gelasius and the pretender Laurence rely-

[65]This famous scene is described in the *Life of St Sabbas* by John of Scythopolis, one of the major historical sources for the religious history of the period (Cf. A. J. Festugière, *Les Moines d'Orient,* II, Paris, 1961, pp. 78-80).

[66]Cf. on this connection, Richards, *Popes,* p. 62-68.

ing on "the Byzantine connection." The pro-Byzantine "Laurentians" were primarily representing the aristocratic, senatorial class, accustomed and loyal to Roman imperial policies and, therefore, showing understanding for the *Henotikon,* whereas the "Symmachians," appropriately called "young Turks" by a recent historian[67] were the architects of a more self-sufficient papacy, which saw its survival on an uncompromising application of the Petrine principle.

The year 518 saw the disappearance of several protagonists of the drama: Timothy of Constantinople, the exiled orthodox patriarchs Elias of Jerusalem and Flavian of Antioch. Emperor Anastasius himself also died that year, at the age of eighty-seven. A reconciliation had occurred earlier in Rome between "Symmachians" and "Laurentians," as a moderate "Symmachian," Hormisdas, was elected pope in 514. Union soon followed between Constantinople and Rome, with an apparent Roman and Chalcedonian triumph. In spite of appearances, however, the church of Constantinople never adopted the Roman point of view on Acacius (his successors Euphemius and Macedonius, excommunicated by the popes, were to be venerated as saints in the East). The union itself was engineered and imposed by a man with long-range vision and plans, Flavius Petrus Sabbatius Justinianus. This vision was one of an empire uniting again East and West, with the Roman pope rejoining the imperial system, and a theological solution being sought to the conflict between the defenders and the opponents of the council of Chalcedon in the East. All this meant abandonment of the *Henotikon.* But the religious policies of Zeno and Anastasius will still, in later centuries, be seen in a different light whether they will be viewed from the West, or the East. The West always tended to view these policies as a sheer betrayal of Chalcedon. In the East, however, the schism between those who rejected and those who accepted the council, was not yet seen as a final break. Those who had accepted the *Henotikon,* and interpreted it in a Chalcedonian sense, were not seen as heretics deserving *damnatio memoriae.* Not only Euphemius and Macedonius of Constantinople, but also Flavian of Antioch and Elias of Jerusalem preserved a saintly reputation, in spite of their acceptance of the *Henotikon.* And indeed, their merit in maintaining the Chalcedonian faith is as great as that of the more uncompromising bishops of Rome.

[67]*Ibid.,* p. 99.

CHAPTER VII

THE AGE OF JUSTINIAN

The imperial vision of Justinian became apparent already when he acted as the main advisor of his uncle, emperor Justin I (518-527). The latter had given him several ranking court titles and eventually made him co-emperor, on April 1, 527. The death of Justin, which followed soon, marked the beginning of the long reign of Justinian alone (527-565). Already under Justin, the religious policy of the empire had changed radically in favor of Chalcedon. The emperor, an elderly general, had been a commander of the palace guard under Anastasius. The fact that a Chalcedonian could have occupied such a responsible position illustrates that Anastasius, while personally favoring Monophysitism, was quite tolerant of the Chalcedonians, provided they respected the limits set in the *Henotikon.* Justinian's policy would be less tolerant towards dissenters and more energetically inclined towards imposing religious conformity throughout the empire. Several successive tactics would be used to obtain the needed results.

The political and religious ideology which inspired Justinian have been often described by historians. Its basic principles go back to the time of Theodosius I and have been discussed above (Chapter I). The only difference was that social development under Justinian had reached a stage which had prepared it for a monolithically Christian regime, so that the emperor could use the means at his disposal more thoroughly and more consistently in order to turn ideological principles into reality. These principles included first, Roman universalism, which led Justinian to military reconquest of the Western provinces lost to the barbarians. Indeed, he would not be content with the nominal recognition of Roman supremacy by the barbarian rulers.

Actually, he always shared with his uncle Justin a certain Western orientation in his conception of the empire, and tended to sacrifice the interests of the East in favor of achieving and maintaining his Western reconquests. Also, any concept of religious pluralism was foreign to the mind of Justinian. For him, the empire was a single God-established administrative structure, headed by the emperor, and accepting the truth of a single Christian orthodoxy, defined by ecumenical councils. Although Justinian possessed authentic and personal competence in the field of theology, he did not pretend that his role, as emperor, was to be the source of Christian orthodoxy. Of course, like all his predecessors, he used the unchallenged privilege of convening ecumenical councils and directing their procedures, but he always accepted the principle that it was the bishops' role to issue the doctrinal decrees themselves. In practice, however, since the existing decrees were interpreted differently by the various groups, he attempted—as Zeno and Anastasius had done in the case of the *Henotikon*—to issue his own interpretations, which, in his mind, were supposed to reflect the true mind of the Church and help to assure the good order of the empire.

In Justinian's view, the issue was not—as it is for us—in defining relations between "Church" and "State," as two distinct social structures. For Justinian, in terms of geographical extension, general goals and membership, the two coincided. God's will was to unite the "inhabited earth" (*oikoumene*) under Himself, as Creator and Savior. The Christian Roman emperor was entrusted with this task and in this sense he was accomplishing on earth the ministry of Christ Himself. The Church, however, was to realize sacramentally that which was implied by the Christian faith. The people of God were therefore to be led by two distinct hierarchies: the one, responsible for external order, welfare, security and administration, and the other leading the people of God into the sacramental anticipation of the Kingdom of God. Their competences were, therefore, distinct, but inseparable. Their activities and practical responsibilities necessarily overlapped. The bishops presided over the Eucharist and taught the faith, but the emperor alone could provide them with the means of getting together, of enjoying enough "good order" to be able to exercise their ministry properly, of making common decisions truly effective and applicable to all.

The most famous text issued by Justinian on this subject is his *Novella 6*, a "new" law, to be added to the *Code,* and addressed in

Emperor Constantine (324-337)—Roman
forum—4th century
*(Photo: Deutschen Archaologischen
Institut, Rome)*

Constantinople—The Walls, built by Theodosius II
(Photo: Dumbarton Oaks)

Emperor Anastasius (491-518) Golden coin.
Dumbarton Oaks, Washington, D.C.
(Photo: Dumbarton Oaks)

Emperor Marcian (450-457)—Constantinople.
Now in Barletta, Italy
*(Photo: Deutschen Archaologischen Institut,
Rome)*

Antioch—The Walls, rebuilt by Justinian—6th century
Engraving: Witt. Bartlett (London, 1837)
(Photo: Dumbarton Oaks)

A Christian bishop and his clergy—Maximianus of
Ravenna Mosaic—St Vitale—6th century
(Photo: Deutschen Archaologischen Institut, Rome)

Basilica of Santa Sabina, Rome—
5th century—The altar and the apse
(Photo: Thomas Matthews)

Basilica of Santa Sabina, Rome—
5th century—Interior
(Photo: Thomas Matthews)

Basilica of St John the Baptist—Monastery of Studios, Constantinople—5th century.
View from the East.
(*Photo: Thomas Matthews*)

The "Riha Paten," Constantinople, reign of Justin II
(565-578), Dumbarton Oaks Collection, Washington, D.C.
(*Photo: Dumbarton Oaks*)

The interior of a church in the fifth century: apse, bishop's place and the ambo in the center. Mtskheta, Georgia. Djvari church of the cross.
(Photo: Edition Leipzig)

A monastery in the Egyptian desert—St Anthony's. Contemporary view.
(Photo: Dumbarton Oaks)

Egyptian monastery—St Anthony's. Contemporary view.
(Photo: Dumbarton Oaks)

Monastic development: remains
of St Symeon's column, a
center of pilgrimage.
Kalat Sem'an near Antioch—
6th century
(Photo: Thomas Matthews)

Around St Symeon's column: a major community in Syria
(Photo: Thomas Matthews)

Justinian's building "The Great Church," St Sophia, Constantinople—6th century
(Photo: Dumbarton Oaks)

St Sophia: the narthex
(Photo: Dumbarton Oaks)

St Sophia: the "royal doors" from the narthex into the nave
(Photo: Dumbarton Oaks)

St Sophia: Interior view
(Photo: Dumbarton Oaks)

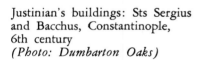

Justinian's buildings: Sts Sergius
and Bacchus, Constantinople,
6th century
(Photo: Dumbarton Oaks)

Sts Sergius and Bacchus: interior
(Photo: Dumbarton Oaks)

Emperor Justinian—St Vitale, Ravenna, 6th century
(Photo: Deutschen Archaologischen Institut, Rome)

Empress Theodora—St Vitale, Ravenna, 6th century
(Photo: Deutschen Archaologischen Institut, Rome)

Emperor Heraclius (610-641)—Golden coin. Dumbarton
Oaks Collection, Washington, D.C.
(Photo: Dumbarton Oaks)

Pope Honorius (625-633) [figure to the left] Contemporary portrait.
Church of St Agnese, Rome, 7th century
(Photo: Deutschen Archaologischen Institut, Rome)

Iona today
(Photo: Diane Clark)

Christian expansion: Celtic cross, Iona
(Photo: Diane Clark)

Christian expansion: Bana, Georgia. Cathedral. First half of the 7th century.
(Photo: Edition Leipzig)

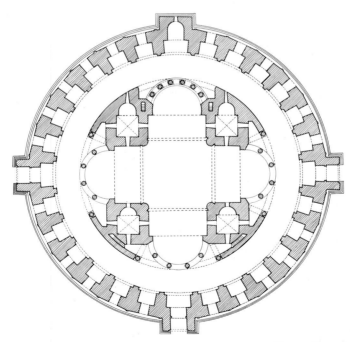

Bana, Georgia. Cathedral.
Architectural plan.
First half of the 7th century
(Photo: Edition Leipzig)

Ateni, Georgia. The 7th century church of Sioni
(Photo: Edition Leipzig)

535 to patriarch Epiphanius of Constantinople. It was, in fact, a set of detailed ecclesiastical by-laws enforcing existing canonical prescriptions on such issues as the marital status of the clergy, church property, episcopal residence, obstacles to ordination, and adding new rules in areas which were not covered by the canons, such as clergy selection and education, and the legal status of clerics. The emperors before Justinian exercised a similar role of managers of church order and discipline, but Justinian's legislation is much more thorough and complete, setting the pattern for the entire medieval period. In the preamble to the *Novella*, the emperor defines a formal ideological principle:

"There are two great gifts which God, in his love for man, has granted from on high: the priesthood (ἱερω-σύνη) and the imperial dignity (βασιλεία). The first serves divine things, while the latter directs and administers human affairs; both, however, proceed from the same origin and adorn the life of mankind. Hence, nothing should be such a source of care to the emperors as the dignity of the priests, since it is for their (imperial) welfare that they constantly implore God. For, if the priesthood is in every way free from blame and possesses access to God, and if the emperors administer equitably and judiciously the state entrusted to their care, general harmony (συμφωνία τις ἀγαθή) will result and whatever is beneficial will be bestowed upon the human race."[1]

What Justinian obviously could not—or would not—define is how harmony, or "symphony" was to be established between the eschatological reality of the Kingdom of God, manifested in the Church and its sacraments, on the one hand, and, on the other, such "human affairs," inevitable in any society, as violence, war, social injustice, etc., which the state by itself is neither capable, nor willing to avoid. Therefore, the preamble of the *Sixth Novella* describes nothing but an aspiration. It also makes a theological mistake: no honest reading of

[1] *Nov*, pp. 35-36. Cf. an excellent commentary on the text in F. Dvornik, *Early Christian and Byzantine Political Philsophy: Origins and Background*, (*Dumbarton Oaks Studies* 9,2), Washington, DC, 1966, pp. 815-819; see also J. Meyendorff, "Emperor Justinian, the Empire and the Church," *DOP* 22 (1968), pp. 45-60; reprt. in *The Byzantine Legacy in the Orthodox Church*, Crestwood, NY, 1982, pp. 43-66.

the New Testament can suggest that a static "symphony" can ever exist between the Kingdom of God and "this world," but rather a tension between the partial, inadequate and incomplete achievements of human history, and the absolute hope for a new world, where God will be "all in all." Under Justinian, as under his predecessors, this tension was maintained by the monastic ascetics rather than by legislation and policies, such as the *Sixth Novella*.

Be it as it may, Justinian's zeal for unity and order took the form of a radical repression of religious dissidents. Vestiges of paganism were mercilessly suppressed with all remaining pagans ordered to convert under the menace of property confiscation. The monk John of Ephesus prides himself on having converted one hundred thousand pagans in Asia Minor with direct imperial help. Temples, such as those of Baalbeck in Syria and Phile in Egypt were closed and destroyed, as well as the last surviving center of pagan education: the school of Athens. This break with the religious and philosophical traditions of antiquity was reinforced by the condemnation of Origenism, which will be discussed below, and which was anathematized precisely as a dangerous survival of "hellenic myths." Judaism continued to be tolerated, following an ancient Roman tradition, but Justinian limited the civil rights of Jews and even ordered the synagogues to use the Greek text of the Bible, rather than the Hebrew, paving the way for a tighter integration of Jews into Christian society. However, the Samaritans were threatened even more. They were not covered by laws protecting orthodox Judaism, and had organized revolts. By 555, they had suffered bloody repression in Palestine and massive executions. Christian heretics, which included Manicheans, Montanists and remnants of Gnostic movements, were treated more severely than the Jews. They were forbidden all religious activity, excluded from all liberal professions, deprived of civil rights, including the right to own property. There were also capital executions. Following the reconquest of Africa, Italy and Spain, the Arian church of the Vandals and the Goths saw its many properties confiscated and its clergy exiled.

However, by far the most serious problem was presented by the existence, in the East, of a vast number of Christians who refused to accept the council of Chalcedon and its christological definition. Radical Monophysites, like the formal supporters of Eutyches or the so-called *akephaloi* (the "headless," who, in the name of Monophysitism had refused to comply with the *Henotikon*), were persecuted like the other heretics. But the followers of Severus of Antioch, and the church of Egypt—monolithically opposed to Chalcedon—represented the popular masses, and could not be dealt with by force alone. This was the major problem of Justinian's religious policy. In dealing with it, he received the advice and cooperation of his remarkable wife, empress Theodora, who assumed the role of a major policymaker in religious matters.

The church of Constantinople—together with an unstable patriarchate at Jerusalem—was the only defender of Chalcedon in the East. But, because of the case of Acacius, it was also in conflict with the "old Rome"—the foremost hope and main political base for an eventual restoration of the empire in the West. A reconciliation between the two "Romes" was thus an urgent necessity, and was approached as a first priority by Justinian.

1. *Union with Rome*

Political and ecclesiastical elements were tightly intertwined in the settlement which brought about a resumption of communion between the churches of Rome and Constantinople in the spring of 519. Finding itself under the rule of the Gothic Arian kingdom of Theodoric, the Roman church could not be controlled from Constantinople. The Gothic rule was relatively benevolent. Arian churches were being built and richly supported in Rome, in Ravenna, and elsewhere, but the king was not limiting the activities of the catholic church. He had intervened decisively in the schism between Symmachus and Laurence, but only because he had been asked by the catholic bishops themselves to do so. Eventually he supported the choice of the clergy, Symmachus. But the Gothic ruler must have acted not without some inner satisfaction, because it was Laurence, not Symmachus, who was receiving sympathy and support from Byzantium. Although technically an "ally" (*foederatus*) of the Roman empire, Theodoric, while adopting Roman ways and legal principles, was very appreciative and jealous of his independence. He did not want the pope, who was the symbolic and moral leader of the Roman population of Italy, to take orders from Constantinople. He wanted the church and the Roman aristocracy to cooperate with him in the administration of Italy, rather than nourishing a nostalgia of Roman rule and cultivating loyalty to the Eastern emperor. No wonder that it is precisely under this benevolent Gothic rule, that Pope Gelasius could assert the apostolic claims of his church and challenge directly imperial power in his letters to Emperor Anastasius. But in Rome itself the anti-Byzantine attitude of Gelasius was opposed by a sizeable section of the aristocracy which tended to be loyal to Constantinople: it is this aristocratic party—faithful to the ideal of *Romanitas* and weary of the Goths—which had supported Laurence, pushed the election of the pro-Byzantine pope Anastasius II (496-8) and promoted a moderate attitude in the case of Acacius.[2]

The election of pope Hormisdas (514-23) reconciled the Roman parties, but the reversal of Byzantine policies in favor of Chalcedon in 518, following the death of emperor Anastasius, created a new situation which was cleverly, if somewhat brutally, exploited by the new Byzantine government. The full restoration of Chalcedonian orthodoxy corresponded, in any case, to the convictions of Justin and Justinian. But by making formal concession to papal claims (which they understood in a moral, rather than administrative sense), they also made possible the reinstatement of the Roman church within a Byzantine version of *Romanitas*, winning a diplomatic victory over Theodoric and gaining new political influence in Italy.

Following the proclamation of Justin I as emperor on July 9, 518 —the very day of Anastasius' death—a ceremony took place at St Sophia on July 15-16, during which the names of patriarchs Euphemius and Macedonius, deposed by Anastasius, were restored in the diptychs, as well as the name of pope Leo. Severus was anathematized. Furthermore, the day of July 16 was appointed for an annual liturgical celebration of the council of Chalcedon.[3] Following a council, held on July 20, an imperial edict ordered all bishops to present a Chalcedonian confession of faith. Acceptance of the council was required even from soldiers.

The new policy implied the total rejection of the *Henotikon*. Local councils reaffirming the faith of Chalcedon met at Jerusalem, at Tyre and in Syria. The Chalcedonian Paul was elected bishop of Antioch, whereas Severus escaped to Egypt, where the Monophysites remained solidly in control.

Pope Hormisdas was, of course, notified immediately of the

---

[2]For a very relevant discussion of this situation, cf. Richards, *Popes*, pp. 133-5.
[3]The feast eventually developed into a celebration of the first four, then the first six councils. It remains in the Orthodox Byzantine calendar to this day. Cf. S. Salaville,

changes by solemn letters from emperor Justin, his nephew Justinian and patriarch John. The letters were carried to Rome by count Gratus. Fully understanding that, for the moment, he held the trump card for a quick and general reconciliation sought by the new Byzantine government, the pope formulated strict conditions: that the names of all those who had been excommunicated by Rome, since the publication of the *Henotikon,* be stricken from ecclesiastical diptychs. This included not only Acacius, but also Euphemius and Macedonius, the victims of Anastasius—whose names had just been reinstated in the diptychs!—as well as all the innumerable Eastern bishops who had exercised their ministry under the *Henotikon* régime. Papal legates even brought to Constantinople a *libellus,* to be signed by Eastern bishops, which, in fact, was a solemn proclamation of the Roman doctrine, making the pope a criterion of orthodoxy. Having enumerated all the heretics from Nestorius to Acacius, each signatory had to pledge the following:

> "In following in all things the apostolic see and in professing all its constitutions, I hope that I will deserve to remain in the same communion with you which is professed by the apostolic see, in which persists the total and true strength of the Christian religion. Promising also not to recite in the liturgy the names of men who have been separated from communion with the Catholic Church which means, who do not agree with the apostolic see . . ."[4]

Welcomed solemnly ten miles from Constantinople by a delegation of state officials, including Vitalian and Justinian, the legates, in spite of some reluctance expressed by emperor Justin, obtained that the *libellus* be formally signed by patriarch John and other bishops and abbots on March 28, Holy Thursday, before the common celebration of the Eucharist which sealed the end of the schism.

The signature implied an unprecedented recognition, by Eastern-

"La fête du concile de Chalcédoine dans le rite byzantin," in *Chalkedon,* II, pp. 677-695. A detailed description of the events will be found in A. Vasiliev, *Justin I,* Cambridge, Mass., 1950, pp. 136-144.

[4]*Collectio Avellana,* ed. O. Gunther in CSEL 35, II, Vienna, 1898, *Epist,* 16B, pp. 520ff. (Cf. also PL 63, col. 393). The *Avellana* is a famous collection of letters and other documents referring to the "Acacian" schism and its aftermath. The most recent critical study on the collection is by V. Borovoy, "*Collectio Avellana* kak istorichesky istochnik," *Bogoslovskie Trudy* I, Moscow, 1962, pp. 111-139.

ers, of Roman doctrinal prestige. It would be wrong to believe, however, that both sides had suddenly acquired the same perception of
authority in the Church and an identical understanding of the events
which followed Chalcedon. For the Greeks, the text of the *libellus*
meant a factual recognition that the apostolic Roman church had been
consistent in orthodoxy for the past seventy years and, therefore,
deserved to become a rallying point for the Chalcedonians of the
East. Essentially this was for them a simple acknowledgement of an
historic achievement. Interestingly, patriarch John, before signing the
text, added a sentence, declaring that the churches of Old and New
Rome are *one church*: "I declare," he wrote, "that the see of apostle
Peter and the see of this imperial city are one."[5] The phrase, while
recognizing Rome's apostolicity and honorary priority, suggested the
identity and equality of the two sees, in the sense in which they were
defined in canon 28 of Chalcedon, as the churches of the first and
second capitals of the one empire.

What was really controversial in the text of the *libellus* was the
requirement that the names of all those who had not been in communion with Rome since 482 were to be scratched out of the diptychs,
including Euphemius and Macedonius, the two archbishops of Constantinople, who had just been acclaimed as confessors! Nevertheless,
the legates obtained the removal of their names from the diptychs,
in Constantinople. Justinian would not admit that the union with
Rome collapsed on a formality, and had further plans concerning the
Roman church . . . Elsewhere in the East, however, resistance to the
papal demands was fierce and effective. Entire synods had greeted
the restoration of the memory of Euphemius and Macedonius,[6] and
refused to comply with the Roman *libellus* which required that this
memory be dropped. In Thessalonica, one of the papal legates, bishop
John, visiting the city—which was the seat of a papal vicar—in order to
require signing of the *libellus,* was brutalized in a mob scene. The
local bishop Dorotheus refused to sign the *libellus* precisely because
it required that he renounce the memory of locally respected bishops.
Excommunicated by the pope, Dorotheus was, nevertheless, exonerated

[5]*Illam sedem apostoli Petri et istius augustae civitatis unam esse definio* in *Coll.
Avell., Epist.* 159, *ed. cit.,* p. 608 (Cf. also PL 63, col. 444A). On the implications of
this sentence, see K. F. Morrison, *op. cit.,* p. 115-6.

[6]As, for example, in Tyre, as witnessed by a letter of bishop Epiphanius to the
synod of Constantinople (Mansi, *VIII,* 1073-1082).

by a council in Heraclea and, with imperial support, unconditionally reinstated on his see.[7]

One should not be astonished, therefore, if Justin I, Justinian and patriarch John, in several letters to the pope, attempted to obtain from him a public statement, which would allow a more moderate interpretation of the *libellus*. They suggested that of all the supporters of the *Henotikon,* Acacius alone be formally blamed and his name removed from the diptychs, not the names of his successors, or the innumerable bishops who were in communion with him.[8] Justinian directly reminded Hormisdas that his predecessor, pope Anastasius, was ready to enter communion with Macedonius, if only the mention of Acacius alone was excluded from the diptychs.[9] But Hormisdas remained steadfast. He perceived that the Byzantine government needed the Roman church, and that the political circumstances presented the right opportunity for asserting the apostolic authority of Rome without compromise. In the long run, however, his attitude would prove counterproductive. The Easterners—as they had done already at the time of pope Damasus in the late fourth century—*de facto* disregarded the papal demands. This is shown in the case of Dorotheus of Thessalonica, mentioned above, and in the quick resumption of the veneration of Euphemius and Macedonius not only as canonical archbishops, but also as holy confessors. Furthermore, in hagiographical sources, Acacius himself, far from being viewed as a "heretic," is referred to as "blessed," for his defense of Chalcedon.[10] Obviously, to the ecclesiological consciousness of the East papal authority was not the only and sufficient criterion of orthodoxy.

Whatever the underlying ambiguities which the *libellus* of Hormisdas failed to solve, the union between Rome and Constantinople was now achieved. But it was only the first step in Justinian's effort to establish religious unity. Rome's insistence that the true faith was adequately and sufficiently expressed by the *Tome* of Leo and the conciliar definition, represented a difficulty for much of the East,

---

[7]The incident is discussed in several letters of pope Hormisdas, preserved in the *Avellana;* for a full account, see A. Vasiliev, *op. cit.,* pp. 185-8.

[8]The Latin text of the letters is found in no particular chronological order in the *Avellana* (*ed. cit.,* pp. 636-7; 650-1; 649-50; 701-3; 715-6; for an English translation, cf CN III, pp. 976-989).

[9]*Edit. cit.,* p. 702; English translation, p. 985.

[10]Cf. for instance the *Life of St Daniel the Stylite,* written by a contemporary, ed. H. Delehaye in *AB* 32 (1913), 70 (English translation in E. Dawes and N. Baynes, *Three Byzantine Saints,* reprt. Crestwood, 1977, p. 49).

where it was rather St Cyril of Alexandria who was seen as the criterion of orthodoxy, not only among the Monophysites, but among the Chalcedonians as well, especially among those who had so easily accepted the *Henotikon*.

The *Henotikon* had failed only because it had marginalized Chalcedon, raising ambiguities which proved unbearable to its sincere opponents, as well as its consistent defenders. In 512 the authority of Chalcedon was restored, but a question remained: if Chalcedon represented the right faith, which of the existing interpretations of the Chalcedonian definition was correct?

In the East, there were at least three distinct trends, which created division and uneasiness:[11]

1) The main trend of Monophysitism, represented by Severus of Antioch,[12] rejected Chalcedon pretending it was Nestorian, but maintained a christological doctrine closely dependent upon Cyril of Alexandria.[13] Often misunderstood, as Cyril himself, by secular historians and theologians sympathetic to a strictly "Antiochene" christology, the Severian monophysites affirmed that Christ was perfect God and perfect man after the union. They formally rejected Eutyches and agreed that the incarnate Word was "consubstantial to us," as He was "consubstantial with the Father." However, they also clung to a meaning of the word "nature" (φύσις), which gave it an exclusively *concrete* meaning, practically synonymous with the term *hypostasis*. Chalcedon, they repeated, by admitting two natures after the union, meant that Christ was concretely not one, but two beings, acting separately. Of course, Severus would make subtle distinctions. He would admit that, in Christ, there was divinity and humanity, *two essences* (οὐσίαι, an abstract concept), which could be distinguished rationally ('κατ' ἐπίνοιαν, or ἐν θεωρίᾳ), that there was a duality in the qualities (ἰδιώματα) of these two essences, but concretely, there was *one nature*, though that nature was "composite in regard to the flesh" (σύνθετος πρὸς τὴν σάρκα). Christ was one single "actor" (ἐνεργῶν), one Savior, one subject, and this was, for

---

[11]For a more detailed discussion of these trends, see Meyendorff, *Christ,* pp. 29-68; cf. also P.T.R. Gray, *The Defense of Chalcedon in the East* (451-553), Leiden, 1979.

[12]There were acrimonious internal debates *within* Monophysitism, which will be discussed in the next chapter, but the Severians represented the prevailing tendency.

[13]Cf. the classical monograph by Joseph Lebon, *Le Monophysisme sévérien,* Louvain,· 1909, and, by the same author, "La christologie du monophysisme sévérien," in *Chalkedon,* I, pp. 425-580.

Severus, what was meant by the Cyrillian formula: "one nature incarnate of God the Word."[14] Faithful to Cyril, but in a "fundamenalistic," literal way, the opponents of the council refused to see the usefulness of the Chalcedonian formula in counteracting the dangers presented by a "Eutychian" understanding of Cyril.

2) Some Chalcedonians who interpreted the conciliar decree as a rehabilitation of the old Antiochene positions of Theodore of Mopsuestia, were giving the Monophysites a pretext for suspecting the council of Nestorianism.[15] In Constantinople, the monastery of the "Non-Sleepers" (Ἀκοίμητοι) seems to have been the main proponent of such a view. The "Non-sleeping" monks had been the main critics of patriarch Acacius and of the *Henotikon* in the capital, but they also strongly opposed the "theopaschite" formulas, complaining to Rome on the subject. It is generally believed that a collection of forged letters by various bishops to Peter the Fuller originated with the "Non-Sleepers."[16] These texts specifically objected to the idea of *hypostatic* union, and to attributing the sufferings of Christ to His unique *person*. The passions, they affirmed, belonged only to His "humanity," an impersonal concept. The opponents of the "Non-Sleepers" accused them even of refusing to use the term *Theotokos*. The firm Chalcedonian stand of the monks was a great help to the Chalcedonian archbishops of the capital, successors of Acacius, and influenced their own positions as well as the views held in Rome. However, these views made the whole Chalcedonian party suspect in the eyes of Monophysites. The fears of the latter were further confirmed by the Chalcedonian reaction in parts of Syria in 519. In Cyrus there was a solemn celebration in memory of, not only the late Theodoret, but also the teachings of Theodore of Mopsuestia and Diodore of Tarsus.[17] The "Antiochene" interpretation of Chalcedon appealed to some in the West also, because it seemed to agree with the position that Chalcedon was,

---

[14]Cf. more in detail in Meyendorff, *Christ*, pp. 40 ff.

[15]These fears of the Monophysites were faithfully reported to pope Hormisdas by the intelligent Egyptian deacon Dioscoros, who was one of the papal legates to Constantinople in 519 (cf. *Coll. Avell.*, ed. cit., pp. 676, 686: *non sufficit synodus contra Nestorium*).

[16]Text published in E. Schwartz, "Publizistische Sammlungen zum Acacianischen Schisma," *München, Bayerische Akad. der Wiss., Abh., Phil-Hist. Abt.*, N.F. 10 (1934).

[17]According to documents quoted in the Acts of the Fifth Council (ed. J. Straub, ACO IV, 1 Berlin, 1971, p. 187), the name of Nestorius himself was included in the celebration—an unlikely occurrence, which must have been the product of tendentious reporting.

in itself, a sufficient christological formula and supported the struggle of Rome against the *Henotikon*. In fact this position reflected a superficial reading of the texts: "theopaschism" was affirmed in the *Tome* of Leo itself and Chalcedon had specifically endorsed the faith of Cyril.

3) The "Cyrillian" approach to the Chalcedonian formula was, as we have shown in the preceding chapter, that which had been in the mind of most Fathers in 451. It is often referred to as "neo-Chalcedonism," a designation which would be incorrect if it implied a betrayal of the Council's mind.[18] If the unfortunate polarization between "fundamentalist" Chalcedonians (who rejected Nestorius, but did not feel the danger of Nestorianism) and the "fundamentalist" Cyrillians (who rejected Eutyches, but were not immune to Eutychianism) had not occurred after 451, the true dimension of the Chalcedonian definition would not have been obscured as it was. A clarification began with the episode generally referred to as the "affair of the Scythian monks," but it came too late to avoid the final schism between Chalcedonians and Monophysites.

A group of Scythian[19] monks—already encountered by us in Chapter V in connection with their involvement in the controversies about Augustinism in the West—had come to Constantinople in March 519 in the entourage of the Chalcedonian *magister militum*, Vitalian, who had rebelled against Anastasius, but became close to the court of Justin I. They had, therefore, impeccable Chalcedonian credentials, but undertook to correct the Chalcedonian position, as it was expounded by the "Non-Sleepers," by placing it in Cyrillian christological context. Their busy activism and some sloganeering were annoying to the Constantinopolitan establishment, but the substance of their position was undoubtedly correct: the Chalcedonian definition had not revoked the Cyrillian doctrine, according to which the person, or *hypostasis* of Christ was the pre-existing *hypostasis* of the Logos, that his assumption of the flesh did not imply the assumption of another subject, that there were not "two sons," but one, and that, therefore, it was perfectly correct and necessary to say—in the context of an orthodox view of redemption—that "One of the Holy Trinity suffered in the

---

[18]The term "neo-Chalcedonism" was coined by Joseph Lebon, whereas the pejorative implication is emphasized in more recent studies by Charles Moeller, and others.

[19]In the sixth century the term "Scythia" designated the region on the lower Danube, known today as Dobrudja. It was populated by descendants of the ancient Dacians, the ancestors of the modern Romanians. Both Latin and Greek were spoken in the region (Cf. Jones, *Roman Empire*, II, pp. 986, 988).

flesh." In favor of their position the Scythian monks could, of course, point not only to the *Twelve Anathemas,* contained in the Third letter of St Cyril to Nestorius, but also to the Nicene creed itself, in which the subject of the verb "suffered (παθόντα) under Pontius Pilate" is indeed the Son of God. The formula "One of the Holy Trinity suffered in the flesh" has also been used in the *Tome of Proclus* to the Armenians (435).

The theopaschism of the Scythian monks did not, in fact, affirm any christological doctrine different from that which was implied by the title of *Theotokos* applied to Mary: only *somebody* (not "something") can be born of a woman, and only *somebody* (not "something") can suffer and die. In Christ there was no personal subject, except the Logos, who remained personally the same in assuming the flesh and in suffering on the cross.[20] It is the hesitation of some Chalcedonians, under the lingering influence of the christology of Theodore of Mopsuestia, to admit "theopaschism" which allowed the Monophysites to accuse them of betraying the faith of Nicaea itself.

Since, in 519, the settlement approved by the imperial court between Constantinople and Rome was unclear on this point, a part of the Scythian group, headed by John Maxentius, travelled to Rome, in order to convince pope Hormisdas that the soundness of the Chalcedonian position required a formal acceptance of "theopaschism." Justinian was at first disturbed by their mission, presumably fearing that it would compromise peace with Rome. He asked the pope to expel the monks.[21] However, the Scythians, who stayed in Rome for fourteen months, received some support, especially from their Scythian compatriot, the famous canonist Dionysius Exiguus ("the Small"), who translated the Third letter of Cyril to Nestorius into Latin,[22] and from the theological expert of the African episcopate, St Fulgentius of Ruspe.[23] Justinian then changed his mind. He wrote a new, and rather peremptory letter to Hormisdas requesting that the pope "per-

---

[20]It is really surprising to find this orthodox "theopaschism" being sometimes confused with "Patripassianism" (*i.e.* the monistic, non-Trinitarian doctrine according to which it was God the Father, being identical with the Son, who suffered on the cross) and even labelled "the touchstone of Monophysite orthodoxy" (Frend, *The Rise,* p. 168).

[21]*Coll. Avellana,* ed. cit., p. 644-5; English translation CN III, p. 968-9; "Certain persons, monks by name . . . introduce in the Church novelties which neither the former venerable synods nor the holy pope Leo's letters are known to contain" and "excite disturbances in every district."

[22]PL 67, col. 11.

[23]Cf. *supra,* p. 137.

form those things which confer peace and concord on the holy churches," and asking for a "speedy reply," which would "satisfy the religious monks."[24]

In 520, nevertheless, pope Hormisdas still decided to expel the monks, declaring the theopaschite formula unnecessary. From Constantinople, John Maxentius wrote a violent protest to the pope,[25] and Justinian maintained his support of the Scythians. Indeed, from then on, the emperor's religious policy, aiming at uniting the pope, the church of Constantinople and the anti-Chalcedonian East will focus on the theopaschite formula, which, as he was now convinced, was necessary for "peace and concord."

Meanwhile, the Gothic king Theodoric, aware of the threat to to his control of Italy created by the new and friendly relationship between Rome and orthodox Constantinople, became increasingly suspicious of the papacy. In 506 Clovis, King of the Franks, had converted to orthodox Catholicism and was followed by Theodoric's son-in-law, Sigismund of Burgundy (510). In 523, Thrasimund, king of the Vandals and husband of Theodoric's sister—a fierce Arian—died. These events put the Arian Theodoric increasingly on the defensive. In 524, Boethius, the renowned Christian philosopher and an eminent member of Roman aristocracy, was accused of plotting with Byzantium against Gothic rule. Together with another senator, Albinus, he was eventually executed. Almost simultaneously Justin I published an edict banning the Arian church in Byzantine territories. It is then, in 526, that pope John I, who had succeeded Hormisdas (523) and was a friend of Boethius, had to travel to Constantinople in a humiliating mission of intercession with the emperor on behalf of the Arians, under the menace of retaliation against Italian Catholics. Gradually loosing its position of arbiter, the church of Rome was becoming a contested political tool, to be used for the control of Italy, either by the Gothic kings or the emperor.

Justinian was determined to win the contest. The pope was met with great solemnity in Constantinople and presided over the eucharist, celebrated in Latin. He was even allowed to crown emperor Justin anew.[26] But Justin refused amnesty to the Arians. Having thus failed

[24]*Coll. Avell.,* ed. cit., p. 648-9; Engl. tr., CN III p. 971.

[25]PG 86, col. 93 ff.

[26]*LP* I, p. 274 (tr., p. 134). For the history of the relations between Byzantium and the West during the reign of Justin I, see J. Richards, *Popes,* pp. 100ff.

in his mission, John and the bishops who had accompanied him were arrested by Theodoric upon their return. The pope died in prison in 526, and his death was followed by a retaliatory edict allowing Arians to occupy catholic churches. Theodoric himself died before the edict could be applied (August 30, 526), but he was, of course, execrated by the Catholics.

These tragic events in Italy were staging the scene which would serve to justify the policies of Justinian, who became convinced that Christian orthodoxy had no more any other defender, either in the West or in the East, than the only and God-established Roman emperor of Constantinople. The union with the papacy, achieved in 519, was now to receive its full political justification, with the pope entering back into the imperial system, with the five patriarchates acting as its "five senses," with the Arian barbarian kingdoms being suppressed by force, and with necessary theological clarifications being made to assure the acceptance of Chalcedon in Egypt and Syria.

2. *Justinian and Theodora*

Proclaimed co-emperor with Justin I on April 4, 527, Justinian quite naturally succeeded his uncle on the throne, following the latter's death on August 1 of the same year. He was then a mature and experienced man of forty-five, ready to begin a long personal reign (527-565). At the beginning in 532, he almost lost his throne in the midst of a popular protest against taxation, known as the "Nike revolt."[27] Almost never leaving his palace and leading the life of a quasi-ascetic, he spent days at work on administrative matters and often engaged personally in theological debates.[28] At all times, he enjoyed the constant support of his remarkable wife, Theodora, whose humble origins and hazy past (she was the daughter of a circus performer, and for a time had lived from prostitution) did not prevent

[27]The possible connections between this combined rebellion, involving both major circus parties—the Blues and the Greens—with religious groups is discussed by J. Jarry, *Hérésies et factions dans l'Empire byzantin du IVe au VIIe siècles*, Le Caire, 1968.

[28]As is well known, the court historian Procopius, who had composed histories, full of praise for Justinian, glorifying the emperor as politician, war-leader and builder, is also the author of *Anecdota*, or "secret history," where he describes the same Justinian, and his wife Theodora under the darkest colors, as selfish, greedy and cruel tyrants. It is generally agreed today that the true picture of Justinian's reign stands somewhere between these two extremes.

her from assuming the role of main advisor to her husband, especially in religious affairs. Many historians refer to her as a "Monophysite." That designation is incorrect, because Justinian and his court had always been formally Chalcedonian. But the empress was undoubtedly convinced that Severian Monophysites stood in substantial conformity with orthodoxy and could be made to accept the council if they were treated as equals and with respect. With Justinian's knowledge and approval, she cultivated personal relations with Monophysite leaders, gave them shelter at crucial times and engaged in political schemes aiming at helping their reconciliation with the official orthodox church.[29] Justinian and Theodora were a very united couple: the empress gave her husband the courage and zest needed to overcome the Nika rebellion in 532, and they actively cooperated in religious policies by distributing roles, and thus keeping in touch with otherwise divided ecclesiastical parties.[30]

Already during the reign of Justin, Justinian had become convinced —as we have seen from his support of the Scythian monks—that the theopaschite formula ("One of the Holy Trinity suffered in the flesh") must be accepted by the Chalcedonians, in order to remove all suspicion of Nestorianism. Therefore, he included it in an imperial profession of faith, which served as a preamble to his famous *Code of Laws*, and was published in 528.[31] However, this religious policy in the East was closely connected with Justinian's military projects. Counting on a stabilization of the Eastern borders of the empire, facing Persia, he embarked upon a systematic reconquest of the West. It began with a rapid destruction of the Vandal kingdom in Africa by Justinian's great general Belisarius and the occupation of Ceuta in Spain (533-4). This initial victory was followed by the invasion of Italy in 535. The total occupation of that country would take a series of protracted, bloody campaigns ending only in 561.

The wars of reconquest immediately followed the repression of the Nika rebellion (532). It is then that Justinian began the rebuilding of the center of Constantinople which had been burnt down during

---

[29]Cf. the description of the imperial couple in R. Browning, *Justinian and Theodora,* New York, 1981, pp. 63-69. But the author does not discuss the religious dimensions of the events he describes.

[30]On this last aspect of their cooperation, see Bolotov, *Lektsii,* IV, pp. 378-80. The favors given to Monophysites by Theodora are remembered with gratitude by authors like John of Ephesus, Michael the Syrian, and Severus himself.

[31]*CJ* I, 1, 5.

the disorders. He undertook the construction of a "Great Church," *Haghia Sophia*, which he intended to become the church of all his Christian subjects. In this atmosphere of optimistic anticipation, following Theodora's advice, he organized, at the imperial palace of Hormisdas, a formal conference between Chalcedonians and Monophysites. Each party was represented by six bishops, accompanied by clerics and experts. The emperor himself presided over the third and last session. This interesting conference was one of the rare known official occasions, when competent representatives of both parties discussed the issues in a sufficiently calm and rational atmosphere.[32] The Severians agreed that Eutyches was a heretic, that Dioscoros, while personally orthodox, made a mistake in 449 in accepting him to communion, that therefore emperor Marcian had sufficient reasons to call together a new ecumenical council at Chalcedon. The Chalcedonians fully accepted the theopaschite formula. But disagreement persisted on the terms used in the Chalcedonian definition. The Severians repeated their usual objections against the "novelty" of the expression "in two natures," which Cyril did not use, and against the rehabilitation, at Chalcedon, of Theodoret and Ibas. They produced numerous patristic quotations, including passages by Athanasius, popes Felix and Julius, and St Gregory the Wonder-worker. The Chalcedonians objected to these because they were Apollinarian forgeries.[33] The Severians also produced references to the writings of "the blessed Dionysius the Areopagite" (this is the first known mention of those writings in history): the orthodox side expressed doubts as to their authenticity, since they were known neither to Athanasius, nor to Cyril, nor to the council of Nicaea.[34]

Only one bishop of the Severian side joined the Chalcedonian camp after the debates, but the peaceful atmosphere which had prevailed during the consultation was immediately capitalized upon by Justinian and Theodora in their efforts to conciliate the Monophysites. Two imperial letters were soon published expressing the views of Justinian on the religious situation. The first was forwarded to all the major

[32]An account of the meeting has come to us in a letter of one of the orthodox participants, Bishop Innocent of Maroneia (ed. E. Schwartz, ACO IV, 2, 1914, pp. 169-184). For the date 532 (rather than the frequently cited 533), see Stein, *Histoire*, II, Paris, 1949, p. 378.

[33]On the Apollinarian forgeries, see H. Lietzmann, *Apollinaris von Laodicea und seine Schule*, Tübingen, 1904.

[34]*Ed. cit.*, p. 173.

churches (except Alexandria, held by the Monophysites) ; the second—to Epiphanius of Constantinople, addressed already as "ecumenical patriarch."[35] Giving once more the imperial sanction to the condemnation of Nestorius, Eutyches and Apollinaris, the emperor solemnly proclaimed that none of the four ecumenical councils, including Chalcedon, will ever be removed from the diptychs. Having thus reaffirmed his Chalcedonian commitment, he also sanctioned the orthodoxy of the theopaschite formula: "One of the Holy Trinity suffered in the flesh." The use of the hymn "Only-Begotten" ('Ο μονογενὴς υἱός), which contains the theopaschite formula, was included in the *ordo* of the eucharistic synaxis in Constantinople.[36] The intention was, of course, to popularize "theopaschism" by using it liturgically, as the Monophysites have done by chanting their interpolated *Trisagion*. However, in the hymn "Only Begotten," there was no doubt that "suffering" was attributed to the Son alone without any possibility to imply that passion could be attributed to the Trinity, as it could have appeared in the case of the interpolated *Trisagion*.[37]

As Justinian was proclaiming principles of imperial policies, Theodora took charge of ecclesiastical personel to be elevated to the highest positions in the episcopate. According to the sources, it is she who arranged for the election of Theodosius, a friend of Severus, to the see of Alexandria (February 10, 535) and for the transfer of Anthimus, bishop of Trebizond, to the patriarchal see of Constantinople, following the death of Epiphanius, in June of the same year. Anthimus, although he had been a Chalcedonian participant of the colloquium of 532, agreed to exchange confessions of faith with both Severus (still in exile, but claiming to be the legitimate patriarch of Antioch) and Theodosius. Severus himself came to Constantinople

[35]The letters were included in *CJ* (I, 1, 6 and 7; English translation in CN, III, pp. 1125-31).

[36]Its authorship is traditionally attributed to Justinian himself, although the text is probably of the late fifth century, cf. V. Grumel "L'auteur et la date de la composition du tropaire 'Ο μονογενής," EO 22, 1923, pp. 398-418.

[37]There is no doubt, however, that the interpolated *Trisagion*, introduced by Peter the Fuller of Antioch ("Holy God, Holy Mighty, Holy Immortal *who was crucified for us,* have mercy on us") was also meant to be addressed to Christ, and not to the Trinity, and was, therefore orthodox in its intention. This fact was recognized by moderates on both sides (cf. Severus, *Hom.* 125, PO 29, p. 241-7; Ephrem of Antioch, in Photius, *Bibliotheca* 228, ed. P. Henry, vol. 4, Paris, 1965, p. 115). This christological meaning of the *Trisagion* remains alive in the Byzantine liturgy (cf. its use on Good Friday and in funeral services; also *doxasticon* of Lauds, First Sunday of Lent; Lite, 2d. stikheron, Ascension day). On this, see V. S. Janeras, "Les Byzantins et le trisagion christologique" *Miscellanea in honor of G. Lercaro,* II, Rome 1967, pp. 469-499.

and agreed with Anthimus on the substance of christology. These arrangements, which created a situation similar to the period of the *Henotikon* of Zeno, remained tentative and private because the imperial decrees, affirming Chalcedon, were clearly in force. Plans to arrange a union, which would include some form of acceptance of Chalcedon by the Monophysites were in the making,[38] but they could not be put into effect immediately.

In Alexandria, a sharp conflict arose in the Monophysite camp, with the opposition of the Julianist *aphthartodocetae* (believers in the incorruptibility of the body of Christ) to the election of Theodosius.[39] The opposition was led by archdeacon Gaianus. A contingent of 6000 imperial soldiers, headed by the famous general Nerses, was sent to Egypt. It restored Theodosius on his see at the cost of 3000 dead among Gaianites, but now the archbishop, compromised by the support he received from the empire, was hardly in a position to make concessions on the Chalcedonian question, as the imperial couple expected him to do.

The efforts of Theodora to support ecclesiastical leaders whom she hoped would become artisans of unity, proved ineffectual also because of opposition from Rome.

Momentous events had shaken the Gothic throne in Ravenna following the death of Theodoric in 526. After a short reign of his young grandson Athalaric, under the regency of the pro-Byzantine queen Amalasuntha (526-534), the latter was murdered by her cousin, Theodahad who proclaimed himself king. All this served Justinian's plans for reconquest, which would be undertaken by general Belisarius in 535, under the pretext of avenging Amalasuntha's death.

No eminent personalities occupied the papal throne during this stormy period, dominated by corruption and political intrigue.[40] However, Justinian continued to attribute the greatest importance to the episcopal see of Rome, both because of his vision of a "Roman" church unity, in which the Roman church had to occupy a leading position, and because of his need to use the church in his reconquest plans. In 534, on the eve of the invasion, a high-level Byzantine ecclesiastical

[38]On such hopes concerning Theodosius, see J. Maspéro, *Histoire des patriarches d'Alexandrie,* Paris, 1923, p. 128.

[39]On aphthartodocetism, which was opposed by both Severus and Theodosius, and its important christological implications, see below, Chapter VIII, p. 274.

[40]Cf. the careful discussion of papal history during this period in Richards, *Popes,* pp. 120ff.

delegation, headed by Hypatius of Ephesus, the chairman of the colloquium of 532, travelled to Rome and obtained from pope John II—whom Justinian addressed humbly as his "most pious son"—a formal excommunication of the "Non-Sleepers," who were friends of the papal see and the main adversaries of "theopaschism" in Constantinople. Justinian's position on theopaschism was thus confirmed by John.[41] It did appear, at this point, that the policies of reconciliation, followed by the imperial couple, were proceeding according to plan.

In 535, however—as the invasion was beginning—Agapetus, an elderly deacon ordained by Symmachus and a follower of the tradition of Gelasius and Felix III, was elected pope. In a fascinating repetition of the situation of 525, when pope John I had to act as ambassador of Arian Goths in Constantinople, Agapetus was dispatched to the Eastern capital by Theodahad to request from the emperor the recall from Italy of the invading armies of Belisarius. The mission was, of course, a hopeless one. Being so close to his goal, Justinian could only reject it with triumphant self-assurance. But, as in 525, he paid all the mandatory respects to the pope, as head of the Roman church. Met with great pomp on his arrival on February 2, 536, the pope was able to reverse—temporarily—Theodora's union plans, which, in any case, were too dependent on shaky personal changes. Anthimus, who actually seems to have become a convinced Severian, resigned his throne,[42] and Agapetus personally consecrated his successor Menas.

Having obtained this new remarkable confirmation of Roman prestige, Agapetus did not have to face the wrath of the Goths, as did John I; he died in Constantinople on May 2. The conditions of the election of his successor, the sub-deacon Silverius on June 8, 536, are described thus in the *Liber Pontificalis*: "He was appointed bishop by the tyrant Theodahad without discussion of the appointment. For Theodahad had been corrupted by bribes and he terrified the clergy so that they believed that whoever did not support the ordination of Silverius would suffer by the sword."[43] Silverius' only distinction was that he was pope Hormisdas' son, but this did not add much to his prestige or popularity. It is therefore understandable that, as the

---

[41]The correspondence between the emperor and John II is included in the Code (I, 1, 8); English translation in CN III, pp. 1149-54.

[42]In addition to Monophysite convictions, his position was weakened by the fact of his transfer from one episcopal see (Trebizond) to another, a practice which was formally uncanonical.

[43]*LP*, p. 290 (tr. p. 146).

Byzantine armies were advancing towards Rome, a successor was being groomed by Theodora. He was found in Constantinople itself in the person of Vigilius. A prominent Roman artistocrat, the deacon Vigilus had been nominated by Pope Boniface II (530-2) to succeed him, but the election went to John II, so that the unsuccessful candidate was given the compensation price of being appointed *apocrisiarios,* or papal representative, to the imperial court. Acquainted with Theodora, he gave her a promise to follow the imperial ecclesiastical plans if he was elected pope.[44] The empress was soon able to fulfill her part of the bargain: in 537, following the murder of Theodahad by Wittiges, Belisarius occupied Rome. Silverius was summarily exiled, and Vigilius was elected pope.

It is clear, therefore, that the resignation of Anthimus, under the pressure of Pope Agapetus, was not yet the end of the union attempts in the East. Actually, Agapetus had not cancelled his predecessor's endorsement of the "theopaschite" formulae, and the future was now in the hands of a friend of Theodora, Vigilius. With the elimination of Gothic power in Italy, the cooperation of the Roman church seemed assured. However, Theodora's personal diplomacy, which had made possible the agreements between Anthimus, Theodosius of Alexandria and Severus, was facing difficulties: it had given too much influence to otherwise divided Monophysites, and remained formally unacceptable to Rome. The course of imperial policy, therefore, shifted again, in an attempt to quench Monophysite opposition. Severus and all his friends were forced to leave Constantinople. Theodosius of Alexandria was called to the court and ordered to accept Chalcedon. Upon his refusal, he was exiled and replaced in Alexandria first by Paul, the abbot of the Chalcedonian monastery of Canopus, who acted so brutally towards the Monophysites and even towards imperial officials, that he was soon deposed and given, as a successor, the more colorless Zoilus.

In Antioch, the see was given to Ephrem of Amida, a former *comes Orientis,* who proceeded to impose the Chalcedonian faith by

---

[44]This information—in itself quite plausible—is given, with derogatory exaggerations, by an irate enemy of Vigilius, archdeacon Liberatus of Carthage (*Breviarum causae Nestorianorum et Eutychianorum,* 22, ACO II, 136-8 (= PL, 68, col. 1039D-1042A; Fr. tr. in F. X. Murphy and P. Sherwood, *Constantinople II et Constantinople III,* Paris, 1973, pp. 300-2). It is confirmed by information, contained in the *Liber Pontificalis,* about personal correspondence between Vigilius and Theodora (*ed. cit.,* pp. 296-7).

the staunch methods he had learned as an imperial official.[45]

This temporary pro-Chalcedonian reaction did not imply that the imperial couple had given up plans of reconciliation with the Monophysites. Personal protection continued to be given by Theodora to the leaders of the opposition. This protection would have tragic consequences: the establishment of a permanently separate Monophysite church.

The idea of setting up an "underground" hierarchy had appeared among the opponents of the Council during the reign of Justin I. It had far-reaching ecclesiological implications. The office of bishop, since the sub-apostolic period, implied presidency in a stable and permanent eucharistic community or local church, and all clerical ordinations presupposed a ministry within such visible and recognizable local churches. The canonical legislation of the fourth and fifth centuries was unanimous in denouncing ordinations *ad personam,* which would give sacramental powers to a person with the right to exercise them "at large." A fundamental ecclesiological principle always defined Christian ministry as an ecclesial function and not a privilege belonging to an individual.

Since 451, the struggle between Chalcedonians and Monophysites was always conceived as a conflict *within* the Church, or between local churches, and the principle of "one bishop in one city" was always maintained. If one disagreed with the doctrinal position of one's local bishop, one could either abstain from the sacraments, or move to a neighboring region, where the "right faith" was preached, but one would not set up a parallel church. Of course, imperial authorities generally took the necessary measures to preserve this "local" unity, by exiling dissidents. As we have seen, in this and the preceding chapters, both Chalcedonian and Non-Chalcedonian bishops enjoyed, in turn, imperial recognition. The vast majority of the population remained in communion with local bishops, whatever their doctrinal position at a given time.

This order, however, broke down in 537. Already under Justin, the exiled Severus of Antioch wrote to Julian, the abbot of Mar Bassus in Syria: "In times of persecution anyonesoever of the God-loving bishops who is *of the same confession and the same communion with us in everything* (Italics mine, J.M.) may properly supply the need

---

[45]On Ephrem, see J. Lebon, "Ephrem d'Amida, patriarche d'Antioche" in *Mélanges Ch. Moeller,* I, Louvain 1914, pp. 197-214.

(including performing ordinations, J.M.) of any among the Orthodox who is in need."[46] The new principle was applied, on a grand scale, by John, Monophysite bishop of Tella, during the early days of Justinian. In spite of the advice given to abbot Julian, Severus and the more responsible part of Monophysite leadership seemed to have been aware that the policy of massive ordinations *ad personam* implied a new ecclesiological perspective and permanent schism, and hesitated initially to condone it without reservation. Eventually, however, John went ahead. The result was that "every day fifty, a hundred and sometimes as many as two or three hundred men came to him for ordination."[47]

In 537, therefore, there already existed, in remote parts of Syria, a parallel Monophysite hierarchy, although the major sees were all given to Chalcedonians. Severus and John of Tella both died in 538. Theodosius of Alexandria, however, who was first exiled in Derkos, was brought to Constantinople and given shelter in a suburban residence, under the auspices of the empress. He was surrounded by numerous staff and clergy and began to act as the head of the Monophysite church worldwide. In Theodora's quarters at the Great imperial palace itself, there was a monastic community, composed primarily of anti-Chalcedonian monks and ascetics. The protection thus provided to the Monophysite leadership was obviously meant by Theodora—with her husband's agreement—to secure a future reconciliation once a universally acceptable formula would be found. But Theodosius, still recognized by his followers as the legitimate patriarch of Alexandria, instead of planning union, pursued the policy of John of Tella with even greater authority and prestige. Under the very tolerant eyes of the empress, he began to ordain Monophysite bishops. Others, like John of Hephaiston, did the same elsewhere. Political considerations were also involved. The Roman and Persian empires were competing for the allegiance of Christian Arab tribes which populated the desert between Palestine and the lower Euphrates.[48] The Lakhmid tribe of Hirah accepted Nestorianism and Persian protection, whereas the

---

[46]Severus, *Letters* I, 59, ed. and tr. E. W. Brooks, PO 12, 2, Paris, 1916, pp. 178-9.

[47]John of Ephesus, *Lives of Eastern Saints,* ed. and tr. E. W. Brooks, PO 18, Paris, 1925, p. 518. According to John of Ephesus the number of ordinations performed by John reached 170,000, an obvious exaggeration. Whatever the exact number, however, the conditions of these massive ordinations, the training of candidates, etc. must have been quite "charismatic," changing both the normal canonical order and the psychological atmosphere in which Church ministry was exercised.

[48]Cf. above, Chapter IV, pp. 110-2.

Ghassanids, predominantly Monophysite, asked and obtained the Roman alliance. In 541 the Ghassanid chief Al-Harit sent to Constantinople a request for a new bishop, which was necessarily to be a Monophysite. The ordination, therefore, could not be performed by the Chalcedonian patriarch of Constantinople, so that the presence of Theodosius of Alexandria in the capital suddenly answered an immediate concern of imperial policy. By direct request of the government, Theodosius ordained Theodore, as bishop of Bostra, and Jacob Bar' Addai,[49] as bishop of Edessa. The latter's underground missionary activity, with the title of "ecumenical metropolitan" being applied to him by later sources[50] lasted thirty-five years (542-78), and consisted in ordaining Monophysite bishops and clergy throughout Asia Minor, Syria, Armenia and even Egypt.[51] Henceforth, a new church—which will be known as "Jacobite"—will exist independently of the vagaries of imperial policies and basically distrustful of all union attempts.

It was obvious, therefore, that Theodora's policy of salvaging her—and her Chalcedonian husband's—contacts with the Monophysites after 536 proved counterproductive and led to a permanent schism. As Justinian continued, even after Theodora's death (548), to promote his solution to the problem—a formal recognition that Christian orthodoxy implied accepting Cyrillian and Chalcedonian christologies as compatible and complementary—he will face not only the disagreement of a few theologians, but the resistance of the masses, led by "underground" leaders, proud of their martyrdom and gradually beginning to identify their religious cause with the cultural non-Greek and non-Roman identity of Syrians, Armenians, Arabs and Copts.

3. Origenistic controversies

It is not easy to determine the exact connections which existed between the sudden eruption of a debate on the theology of Origen,

---

[49]His surname Bar' Addai, meaning "a rag," comes from his later travels throughout the East, disguised as a beggar.

[50]In the accepted canonical terminology of Nicaea, a "metropolitan's" main duty and right was in confirming and performing the ordination of bishops *within his province.* The title "ecumenical," in the case of Jacob, implied that he exercised this right everywhere, without respect for civil or ecclesiastical borders.

[51]The main source for Jacob's life is John of Ephesus, *Lives of Eastern Saints,* ed. and tr. E. W. Brooks, PO 18, Paris, 1925; cf. also E. Hönigmann, "Evêques et évêchés monophysites d'Asie antérieure au VIe siècle," CSCO, 127, Louvain, 1951; A. van Roey "Les débuts de l'église jacobite," *Chalkedon,* II, pp. 339-360.

and the other ecclesiastical and political events of the reign of Justinian. What is known for sure, however, is that, in 531 St Sabbas, the great Palestinian ascetic, who had contributed much towards saving the Chalcedonian cause in the patriarchate of Jerusalem, came, at the age of 92, to Constantinople, officially to request the emperor's help for the victims of a Samaritan rebellion, but also to complain against disorders created by Origenistic monks in his monastery, the famous *lavra* of Mar-Saba.[52] Indeed, a sizeable group, headed by abbot Nonnus, had seceded from his community to create a *New Lavra* near Bethlehem. The mission of St Sabbas did not result in an immediate curbing of Origenistic activities. Quite to the contrary, St Sabbas discovered an Origenist, Leontius of Byzantium, among the monks who had accompanied him to the capital! After the return of the great old man to Palestine and his death on December 5, 532, the Origenists attempted to storm his *lavra*. They also acquired high-level protection in Constantinople through the mediation of Leontius who had access to the emperor. Some of them, including Theodore Askidas, the leader of the Origenistic *New Lavra,* became influential in wide ecclesiastical circles. Theodore was even consecrated archbishop of Caesarea in Cappadocia.

Both Leontius of Byzantium and Theodore Askidas became directly involved in christological debates. Leontius was present at the colloquium between Chalcedonians and Monophysites in 532 and a signatory of the acts of the Council of 536,[53] where new imperial policies towards the Monophysites were determined. He was also the author of several theological tracts in defense of Chalcedon against the Nestorians and the Monophysites.

However, following more Origenistic disturbances in Palestine and a council meeting against them in Gaza (539), more requests reached Constantinople for measures to be taken against the Origenists. Finally, in 543, a treatise against Origen and the Origenists was published by Justinian himself.

Was there a clear theological rationale behind these events which involved not only obscure monastic personalities, but the emperor himself?

[52]The main source for the events is the *Life* of St Sabbas by Cyril of Scythopolis, ed. E. Schwartz, *Kyrillos von Skythopolis* (= TU XLIX, 2), Leipzig, 1939, pp. 85-200; French tr. by A. J. Festugière, *Les Moines d'Orient,* Paris, 1961-64, III, 2, pp. 13-130.

[53]On his identification as one of the participants, see E. Schwartz, *ibid.,* pp. 386-408,

The theology of Origen had been controversial in his lifetime and had remained so ever since.[54] Indeed, his genius had consisted in defining the essential elements of the biblical faith in terms understandable to intellectuals, trained in Hellenistic, primarily Neo-Platonic thought. Without his decisive influence, the achievements of the great Cappadocian Fathers of the fourth century would have been unthinkable. However, his notion of an "eternal creation" by God of a world of souls (or "intellects," νόες) united in the contemplation of the essence of God, but divided and diversified in the fall; the corresponding idea of a "preexistence" of souls and their eventual and universal restoration in God (*apokatastasis*); were hardly compatible with either the biblical message or the orthodox tradition. Nevertheless, they represented the very heart of Origen's metaphysical system. Popular among the monks who were particularly inspired by the spirituality of Origen's greatest disciple, Evagrius Ponticus, Origenistic ideas were condemned at the council of Alexandria (400) by archbishop Theophilus, but remained very much alive in monastic circles, as the Palestinian incidents of 530-43 clearly show. Origenists saw themselves as a spiritual and intellectual élite, privately aware of the fact that their ideas were unacceptable to many and covering up their philosophical and mystical convictions by the use of ambiguous vocabulary. The publicity given by St Sabbas to their teachings could only displease their leaders greatly. They counterattacked by offering positive help in an area which was of great interest to Justinian and which urgently needed a constructive solution: the christological conflict between Chalcedonians and Monophysites.

The Origenistic tradition, represented especially by Evagrius, had developed a peculiar christology based upon the fundamental metaphysical presuppositions mentioned above. Since creation is a pre-eternal reality, every soul exists eternally in "essential" communion with God before its manifestation in the visible and fallen world. This is, therefore, also the case for the human soul of Christ, with the only difference that His is the only soul, or "intellect," which *never fell* and never became subject to division and diversification connected with sin. In Christ, therefore, one discovers the pre-existing "perfect" humanity.. In this system, however, the Incarnation ceases to be seen

and D. Evans, *Leontius of Byzantium. An Origenist Christology,* Washington, D.C., 1970, pp. 159-185.

[54]Cf. my discussion of Origen and Origenism, in the theological context of the sixth century, in *Christ*, pp. 47-68, where further bibliography is available.

as an assumption of humanity by God, but only as a manifestation, within the fallen material world, of a pre-existing union of God and man. Christ's humanity, or "soul," is united essentially (κατ' οὐσίαν), or substantially (καθ' ὑπόστασιν) with the Logos.[55] Origenistic theologians approached Justinian with this solution of the christological issue and nourished the hope that their notion of "essential" union would please the Severian Monophysites, whereas their use of the word *hypostasis* would reconcile the Chalcedonians. Their spokesman, Leontius of Byzantium attacked both the Nestorians and the Eutychians, and eventually came up with christological terms which would become quite useful to St Maximus the Confessor and St John of Damascus in their development of the Chalcedonian concept of hypostatic union in a purely orthodox Cyrillian context.

In 531-543, however, Origenistic christology appeared primarily as a revival of the "Antiochian" ideas of Theodore of Mopsuestia. Thus, St Sabbas uncovered "Nestorianism" and ideas "held by Theodore of Mopsuestia" among the Origenistic monks who came with him to Constantinople in 531.[56] Indeed, for the Origenists, the humanity of Christ—his pre-existing "soul"—was as distinct from the Logos as the soul of any human being, and there was no distinct hypostatic union in Christ different from the original state of all souls and from their eternal destiny in the "eschaton." Origenistic and Evagrian spirituality even interpreted the goal of prayer and of monastic life, in particular, as leading every human soul to that restored state of union with God, which was "originally created,"—a state which would make it "equal to Christ."[57]

Justinian and his advisors discovered the inappropriateness of Origenism as a solution to the christological debates and its overall incompatibility with the mainstream of Tradition. With his customary tendency to solve theological debates by authoritative statements when-

---

[55]Further discussion of the Origenistic metaphysics and terminology being impossible here, readers are referred to such studies as M. Harl, *Origène et le fonction révélatrice du Verbe incarné* (Paris, 1958); A. Guillaumont, *Les "kephalaia gnostica" d'Evagre le Pontique et l'histoire de l'Origénisme chez les Grecs et les Syriens* (Paris, 1962), and D. Evans, *op. cit.*

[56]Cf. Cyril of Scythopolis, *Vita Sabae*, ed. Schwartz, p. 176; French tr. by Festugière *op. cit.*, pp. 104-5.

[57]The Origenistic monks of the "New Lavra" were called "Protoktists" (πρωτό-κτιστοι—"first created") and "Isochrist" (ἰσόχριστοι—"equal to Christ"); cf. Cyril of Scythopolis, *Vita Sabae*, ed. cit., p. 197, French tr. p. 127; *Vita Cyriace*, ed. cit., p. 230, French tr. pp. 39-52.

ever this was practically possible, Justinian, not only wrote his anti-Origenistic treatise, but addressing it to Patriarch Menas, suggested that Origenism be condemned in a series of ten anathemas.[58] Inevitably, a local council presided by Menas endorsed the imperial demand. The condemned propositions included the doctrine of the pre-existence of souls—and specifically the idea that the human soul of Christ pre-existed the Incarnation, so that only His "body" came from the Theotokos. Also condemned were various other aspects of Origenistic eschatology, such as the doctrine of the *apokatastasis,* or restoration of all things, angels, demons, stars, and human beings, as identical "spherical" spirits united to God's essence.

In Constantinople, however, Theodore Askidas, the Origenistic monk mentioned earlier, who had become bishop of Caesarea-in-Cappadocia, needed to clear himself of suspicions which associated him and his fellow-Origenists with Nestorianism. He began to stir up the court circles in favor of new measures against the "Antiochene" christology.[59] This fitted exactly the framework of Justinian's own concern with the Monophysite accusations which were voiced particularly at the Colloquium of 532 and according to which Chalcedon had rehabilitated "friends of Nestorius"—Ibas and Theodoret. Thus, the Origenistic crisis became somehow artificially connected with the issue of the "Three Chapters."

The troubles caused by the Origenists in Palestine did not cease with the condemnation of Origenism in the capital by the synod of Menas in 543. Sources hostile to the policies of Justinian indicate that Theodore Askidas continued to protect his Origenistic friends of the "New Lavra." Following the death of the Origenistic head of the New Lavra, Nonnus (547), his most radical followers, known as "isochrists," succeeded in having a supporter, Macarius, elected Patriarch of Jerusalem (552). The orthodox abbot of the main Lavra of Mar-Saba, Conon, reported directly to Justinian asking for help. It came at once, in the form of a deposition of Macarius, replaced by

[58]Text of the Letter to Menas, ed. E. Schwartz, in ACO III, Berlin, 1940, pp. 189-214 (cf. also PG 86, cols. 945-989); English tr. of the anathemas in NPNF 14, pp. 318-20.

[59]On the role of Theodore Askidas, see Liberatus, *Breviarium* 24, ACO, II, 5, p. 140; Evagrius, *Hist. eccl.* IV, 38, *ed. cit.,* pp. 186-9; Facundus, *Defensio III Capitulorum,* IV, 4, PL 67, col. 627. The Latin authors explain the actions of Askidas by his desire to avenge the attacks against Origen by Theodore of Mopsuestia—not a very likely motivation—and his crypto-monophysitism.

Eustochius,[60] and by a new imperial letter to the bishops assembled in the capital, in view of the condemnation of the "Three Chapters." The letter contained fifteen anathemas, reproducing the substance of the propositions condemned in 543,[61] and suggested their endorsement by the larger episcopal assembly now present in the capital.

The Latin version of the Acts of the Fifth ecumenical council—the only one preserved—does not include the text of these anathemas, but only a condemnation of Origen, whose name follows in a list of heretics including Arius, Eunomius, Macedonius, Apollinaris, Nestorius and Eutyches.[62] Some historians have supposed that the name of Origen was interpolated later, that his condemnation did not take place at the council itself, and that even if the council did condemn him, the condemnation did not receive formal papal approval. However, an overwhelming collection of witnesses[63] proves the opposite: Origen was condemned in 553. A practically unanimous tradition considers this Fifth Council as a council against the "Three Chapters," as well as against Origen, Didymus[64] and Evagrius, even if the formal minutes of the session, where the decision was taken, are not extant.

4. *The "Three Chapters," pope Vigilius and the Fifth ecumenical council*

In the abundant literature dealing with christological debates in the sixth century the expression "Three Chapters" (κεφάλαια, *capitula*) first designated the *statements*, contained in the anathemas, published against them by Justinian and reflecting the opinions of Theodore of Mopsuestia, Theodoret of Cyrus and Ibas of Edessa. Eventually, the term "chapter," because of its closeness in Greek and Latin with the word meaning "head" (κεφαλή, *caput*), was applied

---

[60]Eustochius was so occupied with the Origenistic troubles in Palestine, that he could not attend the Council of 553 in Constantinople.

[61]Cf. text in F. Diekamp, *Die origenistische Streitigkeiten im sechsten Jahrhundert und das fünfte allgemeine Konzil*, Münster-in-W., 1899, pp. 90-97 (cf. also PG 86, cols. 989-993).

[62]ACO IV, 1, p. 218; English tr., NPNF, 14, p. 314.

[63]It was assembled by F. Diekamp, *op. cit.*, pp. 98-112, and it includes the authoritative witness of Cyril of Scythopolis (*Vita Sabae*, ed. cit., p. 119), and the opinion of later popes, who consider that Vigilius *did* approve Origen's condemnation together with the other decisions of the council.

[64]Didymus, the "Blind," a fourth century successor of Origen as head of the Alexandrian school.

to the person of each of the three condemned theologians.

We have already noted, that the Monophysite opposition against Chalcedon never stopped accusing the council of Nestorianism, not only in connection with the definition itself, but also because many Chalcedonians were reluctant to admit Cyrillian "theopaschism," and because the council had formally rehabilitated two critics of Cyril: the bishops Theodoret and Ibas. These accusations had to be refuted, if Justianian's hope to achieve a truly theological agreement between the parties was to be fulfilled. His support of the Scythian monks in their affirmation that, indeed, "the One of the Holy Trinity suffered in the flesh" was the first step. The second step came when, in 543, having decisively rejected the "Origenist solution," Justinian published a treatise against the "Three Chapters," forcing a formal ecclesiastical debate on the subject which will result in the conciliar decrees of 553.[65]

The rather naive and malevolent interpretation of this imperial move as a result of singlehanded intrigues of Theodore Askidas[66] must be rejected. The status and authority of Antiochene christology in its relation to Cyril's was challenged systematically not only by the Severians at the colloquium of 532, i.e. the party with which Justinian needed an agreement, but in Chalcedonian circles as well. The christology of Theodore of Mopsuestia had been characterized already in 435 by Proclus of Constantinople in his authoritative *Tome to the Armenians,* as a "weak spider web" and "words written with water."[67] At the height of the pro-Chalcedonian reaction in 520, Theodoret is mentioned by Emperor Justin I, as a man "everywhere accused of error of faith," being, together with Theodore of Mopsuestia, associated with Nestorius.[68] As in other cases, therefore, Justinian was not raising a new issue, but trying to solve a standing difficulty in his relations with the Monophysites. It remains, however, that the condemnation of the

[65]The text of Justinian's treatise has not been preserved, although its general contents are known. The disappearance of the text is most likely due to the fact that the emperor intended to preserve only the "last word" on the subject, i.e. the decisions of 553 which did not coincide in every way with his own text. This instance, as many others, actually shows the limitations of imperial power over church decisions in Byzantium.

[66]This interpretation, based upon the accounts of Facundus of Hermiana and Liberatus of Carthage—two staunch Western defenders of the "Three Chapters," interested in presenting their condemnation as accidental—often appears in textbooks; cf. for instance, Jedin-Dolan, *History,* III, pp. 450-1.

[67]Ed. E. Schwartz, ACO IV, 2, pp. 191-2.

[68]Mandate to Hypatius, Mansi IX, col. 364; English tr., CN III, p. 981.

"Three Chapters" involved figures who had died, like Theodore of Mopsuestia (d. 428), in full communion with the Church, or who, as Theodoret and Ibas, were personally rehabilitated at Chalcedon. Could one condemn their memory without disavowing the council itself? And was it legitimate to anathematize persons who had lived more than a century earlier, although that was already done in the case of Origen? And, finally, was not Justinian, like Zeno and Anastasius, using his imperial power to impose a policy favoring the Monophysites?

Such objections were raised in Chalcedonian circles in the East, but were rapidly overcome: patriarchs Menas of Constantinople, Zoilus of Alexandria, Ephrem of Antioch and Peter of Jerusalem all signed an approval of Justinian's edict. There was reluctance on the part of Ephrem and Peter but they were convinced both by imperial pressure and by the consideration that Justinian had specifically reaffirmed the authority of Chalcedon: Ibas and Theodoret, rehabilitated at Chalcedon, were not condemned personally, but only their writings, where the council of Ephesus (431) and the christology of St Cyril were specifically criticized. Since both Ibas and Theodoret had anathematized Nestorius, it could be maintained that they had themselves rejected whatever might have been "Nestorian" in their earlier writings or thought.

More serious resistance came from the West. The deacon Stephen, papal delegate (*apokrisiarios*) in Constantinople, broke fellowship with Patriarch Menas. Two Western bishops, Datius of Milan and Facundus of Hermiana in Africa, who as refugees were residing in the capital, expressed their opposition to the condemnation of the "Three Chapters." Their attitude will be that of the vast majority of bishops in Italy and Africa. Pope Vigilius, a friend and appointee of Theodora, hesitated, but the Roman deacons Anatolius and Pelagius, worried by his indecision, tried to force his hand. They wrote to Africa requesting a conciliar deliberation on what appeared to them as a new plot against the authority of Chalcedon. The response to their request was drafted by the Carthagenian deacon Fulgentius Ferrandus and declared that Theodoret and Ibas were absolutely covered by their Chalcedonian rehabilitation and that all the decisions of the council were directly inspired—as Scripture is—by the Holy Spirit.[69] The West seemed committed to a Chalcedonian "fundamentalism" comparable in every

[69]PL 68, cols. 921-8.

way to the Cyrillian "fundamentalism" of the Monophysites.

At this crucial moment, Justinian could not fail to realize that the further progress of his policies depended upon one person—pope Vigilius—and that the enhancing of papal authority, which was condoned and promoted during the reign of Justin I, could be effective again: the pope's role was now to "deliver" Western compliance with the condemnation of the "Three Chapters," and to fulfill the personal promise he had given to Theodora at the time of his elevation on the papal throne.

Vigilius could not resist the imperial invitation to visit Constantinople: a detachment of troops saw to it that he took a boat to Sicily on November 22, 545. He was given the possibility to consult with a gathering of bishops in Syracuse, where he received the most negative advice from Datius of Milan, who had come to meet him there on his way home from Constantinople. The opinion of the Africans was also made known to him through the text of Ferrandus. While stopping in Patras, the pope consecrated Justinian's appointee to the see of Ravenna, Maximian, who, during the absence of the pope from Italy, enhanced the prestige of his see as the residence of the imperial administration and, therefore, surpassing Rome in prestige.[70] Vigilius was cornered between the opinion of a majority of his Western flock and the threat of imperial retaliation.

The arrival of the pope in the imperial capital took place only on January 27, 547. Met with great pomp, he decided, at first, to resist imperial will, in conformity with the advice received from his Western colleagues. Lodged in the palace of Placidia, he was surrounded by Western advisors, which included Datius of Milan and the bi-lingual African theologian, Facundus of Hermiana. He also received a visit of deacon Pelagius. All suggested resistance. The pope refused to concelebrate with patriarch Menas, and the latter retaliated by suppressing the name of Vigilius in the diptychs.

However, after six months of tension and debates, the pope began to realize the hopelessness of his situation: morally committed by his promises to Theodora, stranded in Constantinople—especially since the recapture of Rome by the Gothic king Totila on December 17, 546—

---

[70]For this attempt, supported from Constantinople, to build up Ravenna as a competitor to Rome, even to the point of making it an "apostolic" see, see F. Dvornik, *The Idea of Apostolicity in Byzantium,* Cambridge, Mass., 1958, pp. 151-2, and J. Richards, *Popes,* pp. 154-6; cf. also below, p. 298.

he finally concelebrated with Menas on the day of Sts Peter and Paul, June 29, 547, and submitted new secret pledges to the emperor promising to condemn the "Three Chapters," provided this condemnation would follow ecclesiastical procedures and would not consist simply in his signing of Justinian's edict.

What Vigilius implied then by correct procedure, was the possibility for himself, as bishop of Rome, to render a sentence on the matter, following a consultation with the episcopate. Justinian agreed to give him that opportunity. A conference of seventy bishops, who had not yet accepted the condemnation, was thus held under the pope's presidency. It included Facundus of Hermiana, who is the major primary source about these events and who, in the midst of the debates in Constantinople, began to draft his *Twelve Books for the Defense of the Three Chapters.*[71] As a result of the conference, Vigilius, fulfilling the promises given to the imperial pair, submitted a *Judicatum*—or papal "adjudication"—to patriarch Menas on Holy Saturday, April 11, 548, which contained a formal condemnation of the "Three Chapters,"[72] together with a strong reaffirmation of Chalcedon. Justinian must have felt satisfied, but he soon discovered that papal authority was not recognized in the West as he thought it was. Facundus continued to resist and challenged the *Judicatum.* His book received wide distribution and even the Roman clerics who had accompanied the pope to Constantinople, refused to concelebrate with him at St Sophia on Christmas Day, 549. His nephew, the deacon Rusticus, and another deacon, Sebastian, circulated letters accusing Vigilius of having betrayed the council of Chalcedon. There were widespread protests by bishops of Italy, Africa, Dalmatia, Illyria and Gaul. The bishops of the Illyricum deposed the bishop of Justinina Prima, because he had accepted the *Judicatum,* while in Africa a council presided by Reparatus of Carthage deposed pope Vigilius himself and excommunicated him until repentence.[73]

Vigilius tried to appease the opposition by writing—particularly to Aurelian of Arles—that no harm was done to the council of Chalcedon; but the strength of the Western opposition convinced

[71]Text in PL 67, cols. 527-854. On Facundus, see the monograph by the Russian scholar A. Dobroklonsky, *Sochinenie Fakunda, episkopa Germianskogo v zaschitu trekh glav,* Moscow, 1880.

[72]The full text of the *Judicatum* is lost, cf. fragment quoted in the *Acts* of the council of 553, ed. Straub, ACO, VI, 1, Berlin, 1971, pp. 11-12.

[73]Victor of Tunnuna, *Chronicon,* a. 550, MGH, *Auctores antiquissimi,* XI, p. 202.

Justinian (Theodora had died in 448), that papal authority was insufficient and that the issue of the "Three Chapters" had to be brought before an ecumenical council. Vigilius was thus allowed to take back his *Judicatum*.

These events were only the beginning of a tragic conflict between a vacillating and compromised Vigilius, and the emperor Justinian, convinced of the rectitude of his course and using force and intimidation to reach the assigned goal. The details of the story have been often told.

In order to assure the success of the council, imperial authorities took measures to eliminate the leaders of the opposition. Reparatus of Carthage was deposed under a political accusation. A successor, Primosus, was imposed by force and an imperial official, Mocianus Scholasticus, was sent to Africa to recruit docile bishops to attend the projected council.[74] A less expected opposition came from Zoilus of Alexandria who was also deposed and replaced by Apollinarius. But Justinian was also pushed by his advisors, particularly Theodore Askidas, to intimidate public opinion further. He published a personal *Confession of faith,* which, being an imperial document, had automatically the legal authority of an edict. It proclaimed the authority of the four councils, reaffirming particularly Chalcedon, but also included anathemas against the "Three Chapters." Vigilius, understandably, considered this publication as a breach of confidence since it had been agreed that the issue would be discussed at a council. He again broke relations with patriarch Menas and excommunicated Askidas. In spite of his obvious weaknesses, the pope was at times capable of a firm stand!

Fearing imperial wrath, he left the palace of Placidia and symbolically took asylum—together with Datius of Milan—in the church of St Peter at the Hormisdas palace. Police officers tried to dislodge him physically. The pope—who was a big and strong man—held firm to the altar table, which fell upon him. A crowd of indignant faithful demonstrated in his favor and the officers left. It took a mission of Justinian's great general, the conqueror of Italy, Belisarius, to convince the pope to return to the palace of Placidia and to give him proper assurances of security.

Following this moral victory, the pope was soon isolated and

[74]Cf. the second writing by Facundus of Hermiana, *Adversus Mocianum,* PL 67, cols. 853-868.

placed under virtual house arrest. A campaign was launched against his reputation in Italy. On December 23, 551, he escaped again, this time—also symbolically—finding refuge on the other side of the Bosphorus at the church of St Euphemia in Chalcedon, where the great council had been held. Another mission by Belisarius and several other attempts were unable to convince him to return. Furthermore, he published an encyclical to all Christians complaining against the violence being done to him and proclaiming his faithfulness to the four ecumenical councils. He did have friends in the city, so that imperial police were unable to prevent the circulation of the encyclical and even its posting in prominent public spots.[75] Justinian had to retreat and although he himself did not withdraw his edict, Menas and Theodore Askidas were encouraged to apologize to the pope and reaffirm their unity in faith with him. The pope considered this sufficient and returned to the city. He also approved the confession of faith of a new patriarch of Constantinople, Eutychius, with whom he entered communion (January 553).

It appeared that the preparation of the council could proceed as planned. But there was no agreement as to the projected attendance. Vigilius, understandably worried by the Western opposition, demanded that, since few bishops from the West were likely to come, preliminary synods be held in Sicily or Italy. But Justinian was now in a hurry, and a council of merely one hundred and forty five bishops—only six of them from Africa—met at the *Mega Sekreton* of St Sophia on May 5, 553. The patriarchs of Constantinople, Alexandria and Antioch were present, as well as a delegate of the patriarch of Jerusalem, but Vigilius refused to attend or even to be represented, because, in his view, not enough Western bishops participated in the debates.

In the history of the Church, this was the second time (the first being the council of 381) that a council claiming ecumenicity met not only without the presence of a delegate of Rome, but also in contravention to the pope's wishes.

Under the circumstances, the outcome of the council was a foregone conclusion. There were eight sessions in all (May 5 to June 2). At the first session, presided by Eutychius of Constantinople, the Fathers heard a somewhat apologetic letter from Justinian explaining that his previous actions—edicts, confession, etc.—were equivalent to a consultation of the episcopate, similar to the one undertaken by Emperor Leo

[75]Text in PL 69, cols. 67-68.

I; that he had consulted the patriarchs, including the pope; that all agreed to condemn the "Three Chapters," and that what remained now was to have that decision formally endorsed by the council.

It was decided to make a new attempt at assuring the presence of Viligius. Three patriarchs went to him, inviting him to attend, unsuccessfully. A second visit by the same patriarchs, accompanied this time by high imperial officials, was also in vain. As the council continued its deliberations—consisting essentially in a series of speeches calling for the condemnation of the "Three Chapters"—pope Vigilius submitted to the emperor his own opinion—or *Constitutum*—on the subject, signed by sixteen other bishops and three Roman clerics, including the learned deacon Pelagius.[76] The *Constitutum* condemned sixty propositions from the works of Theodore of Mopsuestia, but the pope still adamantly refused to condemn Theodore personally, because he had died in communion with the Church and because the dead could not be excommunicated. Furthermore, neither Theodoret, nor Ibas could be liable to condemnation because the council of Chalcedon had exonerated them. Finally, Vigilius anathematized those who were condemning the "Three Chapters."

Justinian refused to accept the *Constitutum* as sufficient, declaring that he possessed written evidence from Vigilius that he had already condemned the "Three Chapters," and that, by producing the *Constitutum* now, he was only condemning himself. Indeed, at the seventh session of the council, the evidence was produced. It included several letters of Vigilius, where the pope was defending his *Judicatum* of 548, or otherwise rejecting the "Three Chapters," and his solemn vow "on the four Gospels" given on August 15, 550, where he solemnly promised to Justinian that he would do his best to have the "Three Chapters" condemned.[77] Following the reading of these documents, Justinian, in a letter to the council, proposed that the name of Vigilius be deleted from the diptychs and he himself be "separated from comunion," since, after having condemned the "Three Chapters" for a period of seven years, he was now opposing the consensus of the Church. The council unanimously complied, declaring that, by doing so, it was "serving unity with the apostolic see of Old Rome"— by removing its unworthy incumbent!

[76]Text in Mansi, IX, col. 61-106.
[77]Cf. ACO IV, 1, pp. 198-9. *Hoc velle, hoc conari, ita agere, quantum possumus, ut ista tria capitula . . . condemnentur et anathematizentur.*

The eighth session on June 2 was consecrated to the approval of a rather lengthy definition followed by fourteen anathemas,[78] which formally sanctioned Justinian's policies of the past years. It endorsed the Four Councils once more, but affirmed the "Cyrillian" (or "Neo-Chalcedonian") interpretation of Chalcedon: the "theopaschite" formulae were used, the Twelve anathemas against Nestorius were approved, and the famous, ambiguous Cyrillian formula—"one nature incarnate of God the Word"—was even mentioned as legitimate, provided the Chalcedonian "two natures" formula was admitted also. The condemnation of the "Three Chapters" had the form which Justinian had given it: it applied to the *person* of Theodore of Mopsuestia, to the *writings* of Theodoret, directed against the council of Ephesus (431) and St Cyril, and to the *Letter* of Ibas of Edessa to Maris the Persian, where the condemnation of Nestorius was called unjust.

It took Pope Vigilius six more months to change his mind again. Still in Constantinople, on December 8, 553, he wrote to patriarch Eutychius a letter formally repenting having written the *Constitutum*. Invoking the example of St Augustine—who also had written *Retractions!*—he declared that further study of the Fathers had convinced him of the heresy of the "Three Chapters," and that he was now anathematizing them.[79] On February 23, 554, he published a *Second Constitutum*, where he maintained the same attitude, reaffirming fidelity to Chalcedon and declaring that the Ibas' letter was not authentic. This latter view on the letter, aimed at safeguarding the authority of Chalcedon, had been held by Justinian himself, and is admitted, as a possibility, in the conciliar decree of 553.[80] These actions of Vigilius were followed by his reconciliation with the emperor and the restoration of his name in the diptychs of Constantinople. Since the Byzantine general Nerses had reoccupied Rome in 552, the pope was ready to return home and to accept the new Roman order in Italy as defined by Justinian's *Pragmatic Sanction*, published in 554, with new privileges granted to catholic bishops. He did not reach Rome, however, but died in Syracuse in Sicily, on June 7, 555.

The conciliar decree of 553 was accepted without major problems

---

[78]Text in Mansi IX, cols. 367-675; ACO IV, 1, pp. 208-220; English tr. in NPNF XIV, pp. 306-316.

[79]Text in Mansi IX, cols. 419 ff; English tr. in NPNF XIV, pp. 321-23.

[80]Cf. the fourteenth anathema: *epistolam quam dicitur Ibas ad Marim Persam haereticum scripsisse.*

throughout the Chalcedonian East, although it failed to convince the Monophysites that the acceptance of Chalcedon was not a betrayal of St Cyril: the schism had taken root, and the necessary mutual confidence between the "imperial" church and the Monophysite communities was not present anymore after so many government interferences in episcopal appointments and depositions, and the even more tragic, bloody clashes in the streets of Alexandria. In the West, the opposition came from the Chalcedonian camp, whose "Chalcedonism" was of a different kind than in the East. Latin theologians understood better the language of the *Tome of Leo* than that of St Cyril. They saw no need and only danger in condemning obscure figures of long-departed bishops of Syria, about whom they knew next to nothing, except that they opposed Monophysitism and supported Chalcedon. Furthermore, while respecting the church of Rome, the bishops of the West did not consider that the approval of the council by Vigilius was in any sense a guarantee of truth.

In order to secure the recognition of the Fifth council, Justinian employed drastic measures, precisely in those provinces which had been recently recovered by his armies. We have seen that in Africa, the legitimate bishop of Carthage, Reparatus, had been deposed; but the government-appointed successor, Primosus, was rejected by many. Several African clerics—Victor of Tunnuna (the author of the *Chronicon*), Theodore of Cabarsussi, Primasius, abbot of Hadrumetum, and others—were sent to distant places of exile in the East. Facundus of Hermiana went into hiding, but was discovered and sentenced in Constantinople, together with other bishops in 564. In the Illyricum too, bishops were exiled, but others succeeded in finding refuge in Northern Italy where the metropolitan of Aquilea, Paulinus, was leading the opposition. The bishops of Liguria, Emilia, Venetia, Istria and Dalmatia supported him. Since the imperial reconquest of the area did not last and was overpowered as early as 568 by the Lombards, the schism of Aquilea could not be repressed by force, and continued until the seventh century.

In Rome itself, a new pope was installed in the person of deacon Pelagius, who had been with Vigilius in Constantinople and had strongly advised him to resist imperial will. In 553, he had been arrested. But by 555 he accepted the condemnation of the "Three Chapters." Of course, he became highly unpopular in the West and, on April 16, 556, only two bishops were found to perform his consecration as pope, under the protection of the Byzantine general Nerses. He could do nothing to prevent the secession of the Northern Italians from Roman communion under the leadership of Paulinus of Aquilea.

5. *The Legacy of Justinian*

It would be anachronistic to interpret the direct involvement of emperor Justinian in the theological debates of his time as actions of a cynical political leader interested only in administrative order and effective government. The christological issues themselves were seen by him—and by his wife Theodora—as essential to the true and spiritual well-being of society and to their own eternal salvation. The coercive measures which he considered necessary to take so often against opponents of his policies, were themselves expressions of what he understood to be his responsibility as Christian emperor, i.e. to reward the virtues and to correct the mistakes of his subjects. He did not believe to be personally infallible—and, therefore, changed tactics frequently —but neither did he consider anyone else to be immune from error. He undoubtedly accepted the traditional Christian concept that bishops in council were the highest and the most reliable witness to Truth, although he sometimes presumed to know in advance what this witness should be and attempted to take shortcuts to save time and energy, by publishing his own edicts about the faith. Significantly, none of these edicts was accepted as authoritative by itself and all were eventually debated by episcopal assemblies.

Perhaps the best indication of Justinian's personal involvement in theological issues was his sudden attempt, at the very end of his life, to impose on the Church the doctrine of *aphthartodocetism*. Recounting the episode, the historian Evagrius reports tragically: "Justinian, departing from the right path of the doctrines (of the Church), fell into thorns and was walking on ways foreign to the apostles and the fathers."[81] There was no political reason for this move at all. Aphthartodocetism was a doctrine held by some Monophysites, which affirmed that the body of Christ was incorruptible (ἄφθαρτος), even before His resurrection, and that, therefore His human life on earth was radically different from that of other humans. This view had been violently opposed by Severus himself, in his confrontations with the

[81]*Ed. cit.*, p. 190.

"Gaianites" in Egypt, and was not connected with Monophysitism as such, since some of its adherents were, as Justinian himself, Chalcedonians.[82]

The old emperor was ready to publish an edict in favor of aphthartodocetism, and even had patriarch Eutychius exiled for his opposition to the project. In Antioch, Patriarch Anastasius gathered a council of one-hundred and eighty bishops, who also opposed the imperial move. It appears that the edict never saw light, because Justinian died on November 14, 565, at the age of 82.

This personal commitment to theological matters—obviously quite misguided in the case of aphthartodocetism—explains the general consistency of his religious thinking. Modern historians are not kind to Justinian, noting particularly the "zig-zag" quality of his policies. However, except for the case of apthartodocetism, the "zig-zags" concerned tactics and methods, not substance. There has never been, on the part of Justinian, any intention to disavow Chalcedon, but from the very beginning of his reign, he considered that it was historically and theologically wrong to interpret Chalcedon as a disavowal of St Cyril of Alexandria. We have seen in the preceding chapter that such a disavowal was not the intention of either the Fathers of 451, or St Leo of Rome. But, in spite of this Chalcedonian Cyrillism, the old christology of Theodore of Mopsuestia, which was indeed incompatible with Cyril's, continued to flourish in some circles, and its adherents were finding comfort by interpreting the Chalcedonian definition in their own way. Actually, Theodore of Mopsuestia—not Nestorius—was the real teacher and leader of what in the fifth and sixth centuries was vaguely called "Nestorianism," and these Christians, schooled in Edessa or Nisibis, who left for Persia after Cyril's triumph in 431, and whom we call "Nestorians," did not refer to the name of the unfortunate patriarch of Constantinople, as their doctrinal authority, but, almost exclusively, to Theodore.[83]

Since, on the other hand—as modern research has confirmed—the Severian Monophysites held no other christology than that of Cyril, was Justinian not justified in attempting to erase suspicions of "Nestorianism" from Chalcedonian orthodoxy? And was it not inevitable

[82]For a more detailed discussion, see the next chapter.

[83]On the Nestorian church, see next chapter. It is therefore quite logical that modern authors who consider the christology of Theodore to be in fact orthodox (including especially Devreesse, Moehler and, among the Orthodox, A. V. Kartashev) interpret Justinian's Fifth council as a *de facto* betrayal of Chalcedon.

to do so precisely by condemning Theodore, as the Monophysites were doing for their own extremist Eutyches, and by rejecting those writings of Chalcedonian theologians, like Theodoret and Ibas, who were if not "Nestorian," as least clearly "Mopsuestian"? This solution which, in the sixth century, was accepted by such respected figures of Chalcedonism as patriarch Ephrem of Antioch, the Alexandrian Nephalius and Leontius of Jerusalem, is that which was endorsed by the Fifth council. It allowed for the full weight of Cyrillian soteriology—which affirmed that the God of the New Testament is not simply a celestial Creator and Judge, but in His love for creation, personally makes the "flesh" His own in its fallen state and in death itself, in order to bring it back to communion with Himself—to remain part of the Christian *kerygma* and theology. But it also allowed for the best achievements of Antiochian exegesis, in the person of the blessed Theodoret of Cyrus—whose person and overall position as a critic of Eutyches was not in jeopardy—to be preserved as part of Tradition, together with the Athanasian and Cyrillian doctrine of "deification."

This implied, of course, the recognition of a certain methodological and terminological pluralism. According to the Fifth council, one could speak of "one nature incarnate," as well as use the obviously preferable Chalcedonian terminology. One could also accept the Severian way of speaking of two natures, distinguished "mentally" (ἐν θεωρίᾳ), provided one admitted that each nature preserved its characteristics or energies, manifested concretely in the life of Jesus. The whole approach to theology was a "catholic" one, which implied the limitations of all languages and all methods in their attempts to express the One Truth.[84] In this sense, the decisions of 553 could be called "ecumenical" (in the modern sense of the word) since they were made partially *for the sake of the separated,* correcting omissions and explaining in a better way that which had been a cause of scandal in the past.

What is less defensible, of course, is Justinian's use of coercion and Theodora's deceptive diplomacy. But here, the indictment should fall not so much on them personally, as on the entire Byzantine imperial ideology and system, and on those forms of theocratic society, which were common to the East and the West until the Enlightenment.

[84]On this issue, see the more extended comments in my article "Emperor Justinian, the Empire and the Church," *DOP,* 22 (1968), pp. 45-60; repr. in *The Byzantine Legacy in the Orthodox Church,* Crestwood, New York, 1982, pp. 43-66.

It remains, however, that the religious policies of Justinian in the East were a failure, and that the methods used by the imperial pair were largely responsible for it. Because of the tactical protection bestowed by Theodora upon the establishment of separate Monophysite church, it became immensely more difficult to reestablish unity, while the use of military force and administrative measures in religious matters transformed what was, at times, a loyal opposition into a fanatic resistance movement. In fact, the diplomatic or coercive methods used by the imperial authorities neutralized the possible effect of the substantially "ecumenical" attitude approved by the council of 553.

The results were tragic. The Monophysites entrenched themselves within the formal boundaries of Cyrillian christological language, refusing to admit that Chalcedon, by maintaining the integrity of a distinct and active human nature of Christ, only confirmed Cyril's affirmation that One of the Holy Trinity was truly (i.e. humanly) born of Mary, and truly (i.e. humanly) suffered on the cross. Those who refused to accept Chalcedon were, therefore, opposing that "catholic" terminological flexibility, which makes the Tradition of the Church to be a living Tradition, always charitably open to problems raised by brethren in need of salvation. This "brotherly" spirit—which also presupposed concern for unity with the orthodox West—was implied by Chalcedon, and was well expressed by the Fifth council. But it came too late and with much too much clumsy politicking to prevent the schism.

Often spoken of as the last "Roman" emperor and the first "Byzantine" *basileus,* Justinian entered history not only as the emperor-theologian, but also, and primarily, as legislator. His famous *Code*—whose second and final version was published in 534—together with the *Digest,* the *Institutes,* and a long series of *Novellae,* or "new laws," reflected his dream of a universal and Christian Roman order. It is through those texts, especially the *Code*, that Roman law became available in the East and the West, throughout the medieval and modern periods. Since large sections of this legislation were concerned with the Church, it is difficult to underestimate Justinian's impact on the history of ecclesiastical institutions, on dicipline and morals, on the Byzantine and medieval understanding of Church and society. The main lines of that legislation followed the principles, established since the time of Constantine and Theodosius I, and have been discussed above (Chapter I and II). But Justinian's contribution was much more exhaustive. Extraordinarily minute details are conveyed in the several sections of the *Code* dealing with ecclesiastical property, clerical duties, episcopal rights in various civil suits, monastic discipline, or the disabilities imposed on heretics.[85] *Novellae* 6 and 123, on the other hand, represent full by-laws of the imperial church, based essentially on existing canonical legislation issued by councils, but also going beyond and legislating in areas which the councils did not cover. Thus, for instance, Justinian forbade the ordination to the episcopate of men living with their wives or being fathers of children,[86] and formalized the famous system of "Pentarchy," according to which the universal church was to be ruled by five patriarchs—Rome, Constantinople, Alexandria, Antioch and Jerusalem—a system which was prevented from functioning effectively by some measures of Justinian himself (the granting of autocephaly to the church of his birthplace) and by the Monophysite schism. What resulted is a *de facto* supremacy of Constantinople in the East and a radically reduced authority of the other "melkite" (or imperial) orthodox patriarchs.[87]

Perhaps, the most striking way to understand the grandiose vision of Justinian is to visit the astounding remnants of his construction program, which have survived the centuries even to this day. The most famous of these include the church of San Vitale in Ravenna, where a beautiful mosaic representation shows Justinian and Theodora carrying gifts and being introduced to a eucharistic celebration by their appointee to the see of Ravenna, the bishop Maximian.[88] Also, the monastery on the Sinai peninsula, known today as the monastery of St Catherine, but originally dedicated to the Transfiguration of Christ, was built by Justinian on the traditional spot where Moses saw the burning bush. Virtually still intact today, the monastery was meant to be an outpost of Christian and Chalcedonian presence in the deserts surrounding the Red Sea and populated by Arab tribes, a symbol of Justinian's extended policies in *Arabia felix* and Ethiopia. An almost invisible inscription on the roof beams of the Church reads: "For the memory and repose of our late empress Theodora"[89] a touching, secret reminder of Jus-

---

[85]Numerous texts translated and commented CN III, pp. 908-1178.

[86]Code I, 3, 47 (531); English text in CN, III, p. 1096. Only the first condition eventually received ecclesiastical sanction by the council in *Trullo* (692).

[87]Cf. *supra*, p. 58.

[88]Cf. *supra*, p. 238.

[89]G. H. Forsyth and K. Weitzmann, *The monastery of Saint Catherine on Mount Sinai. The Church and Fortress of Justinian*, Ann Arbor, Mich., 1965, PL. LXXX-LXXXI, C.

tinian's faithfulness to his helpful and powerful consort buried in 548 at the church of the Holy Apostles in Constantinople.[90]

But by far the most extraordinary monument to Justinian's reign is unquestionably the "Great Church," St Sophia of Constantinople.

The main basilica of the imperial capital, dedicated to Christ, as Wisdom of God (cf. I Cor. 1:24), was first built by Constantine and Constantius. It burned down in 404, during the riots which marked the exile of Chrysostom. Rebuilt by Theodosius II, it was totally destroyed again during the Nika rebellion of 532. With a speed illustrating the incredible economic power of the empire, a totally new church was erected by the architects Anthemius of Tralles and Isidore of Miletus, and consecrated on Christmas day, 537. The vast space of the Great Church, filled with light, was covered with an immense dome symbolizing the descent of heaven on earth. The walls were covered with golden mosaics and marble plates of different colors. Immense columns, used in the building, were brought from as far as the destroyed temple of Zeus in Baalbeck in Syria. The architectural achievement and the message was so strong, that St Sophia—which remained the largest church of Christendom until the building of the Gothic cathedrals of the twelfth century in the West—was seen as the spiritual center of Eastern Orthodox Christendom until the fall of Byzantium.

---

[90]Also commissioned by Justinian and inaugurated officially in 550, already after Theodora's death, this huge church disappeared with the Turkish rebuilding of the city after 1453.

CHAPTER VIII

THE CHRISTIAN EAST AFTER JUSTINIAN: ARE THE DIVISIONS FINAL?

The failure of Justinian's attempt to bring about religious unity in the East was not merely a political one. It showed that neither theological arguments nor coercion were able to overcome the deep distrust of the masses of Syria and Egypt towards the Chalcedonian definition—a distrust which had been planted once and for all by the first opponents of the Council. Never in the entire history of doctrinal controversies East and West, it seems, had so many theological overtures and concessions been made to dissidents by the official ecclesiastical establishment for the sake of unity. Actually, most Western historians resent these concessions and are critical of Justinian and his successors not only for the violence which they used occasionally against the opposition, but also for their supposed betrayal of Chalcedon. We have tried to show that no such betrayal occurred. Rather, the Orthodox Church was made to reaffirm that the same mysterious truth of the Incarnation could be expressed in different terminologies; that Cyrillian terminology was needed, to exclude Nestorianism; that Chalcedon was equally necessary as a barrier against Eutyches; that, in order to avoid any hint that Chalcedon disavowed Cyril, not only the term *Theotokos,* but also the theopaschite formulas ("The Logos suffered in the flesh") were to be included in confessional and liturgical texts; that the Chalcedonian definition ("in two natures") did not invalidate the Cyrillian "of two natures"; that the formula of Severus of Antioch, admitting the distinction of "two natures" in Christ, but only "men-

251

tally" (ἐν θεωρίᾳ) corresponded to the faith of the Church.

It appears therefore that, after the council of 553 which endorsed these positions, no real christological differences remained between the imperial church and the moderate "Severian" Monophysites. Indeed, even modern scholarship agrees that the christology of Severus is indeed the christology of St Cyril, who was recognized by all, and especially the council of 553, as the most prominent criterion of orthodoxy.

Was the opposition then based on cultural, national and ethnic factors only? Were doctrinal issues artificially used, as cover for the cultural separatism of Syrians, Armenians and Copts, and their hatred for the Greeks and the Byzantine empire? This view was widely held until recently, and is still defended by many,[1] but only at the price of indulging in serious anachronism. Cultural differences were contributing to the schism, but not decisively. As we have shown earlier, the anti-Chalcedonian opposition was, if not justified, at least understandable on purely christological grounds, during the second half of the fifth century, because of a persistent "Antiochian" interpretation of Chalcedon among some leading Chalcedonians.[2] Almost all the spokesmen of the opposition were Greeks deeply loyal to the Empire, like Dioscoros, Timothy the Cat and Severus of Antioch. The clumsy attempt at avoiding the problem, instead of solving it, engineered by Acacius of Constantinople and Peter Mongos (the *Henotikon*), was doomed to failure. But why did the opposition remain alive even after 553?

The basic conservatism of the masses and their profound distrust of an often vacillating ecclesiastical leadership should be seen as the main motivation of those who opposed Chalcedon during and after the reign of Justinian, though growing cultural and ethnic differences should not be excluded altogether as factors contributing to the spirit of opposition. The "monophysite" position consisted essentially in a sort of "Cyrillian fundamentalism" which allowed no compromise at all. The Chalcedonian orthodox camp was making major terminological concessions and clarifications: the antichalcedonians were making none. Even the great Severus of Antioch, who undoubtedly saw the dangers of unabashed Monophysitism and understood the importance of affirm-

---

[1]See, for example Azi S. Atiya, *History of Eastern Christianity,* Notre Dame, Ind., 1967, pp. 69-74.
[2]Cf. above, pp. 191-2.

ing the full reality of Christ's manhood, stopped short from accepting "two natures after the union." Several individual leaders of Monophysitism eventually accepted Chalcedon, but they were disavowed by their flocks.[3]

Essentially a conservative or "fundamentalist" schism, Monophysitism rejected the "catholic" dimension of Chalcedon. Indeed, in the view of Chalcedonian and Neo-Chalcedonian orthodoxy, the catholicity of the Church requires that the one Truth be expressed in different terminologies; that some legitimacy be granted not only to Alexandrian expressions of salvation in Christ, but also to the Antiochian and the Western Latin tradition found in the *Tome* of Leo (provided there was agreement in substance); that a clearly "diphysite" christology was necessary to refute Eutychianism, and that it did not amount to a disavowal of St Cyril. By standing for *their* theology, *their* formulas only, the Monophysites were moving in the direction of deliberate and exclusive sectarianism. This trend resulted in further groupings and splits, each group affirming its own exclusivity, rejecting other groups by always remaining opposed to Chalcedonian unity.

However, at least until the Persian and Muslim conquests, this tragic divisiveness of the Christian East did not preclude a lingering sense of ecclesiastical and imperial unity. Both sides were using violence against each other, but also nourished hopes for the conversion of their opponents. Such contradictory feelings always existed in Constantinople and explain the many deliberate inconsistencies of imperial policy, such as the apparently contradictory attitudes of Justinian, repressing the Monophysites, while Theodora harbored the "pope" of Alexandria, Theodosius, in her palace. Later the pattern was repeated by Justin II and Empress Sophia. In fact, the imperial couples were consciously assigning roles, but there was never any doubt that both Theodora and Sophia formally belonged, to the official Chalcedonian church together with their imperial husbands. Similarly ambiguous attitudes were adopted by some ecclesiastical leaders not only in the *Henotikon* era (Peter Mongos, Acacius), but later as well. Chalcedonian patriarchs John Scholasticus of Constantinople (565-577) and Anastasius I of Antioch (559-569) presided over meetings between

---

[3]A. Van Roey is right in speaking of two "convergent movements"—"Cyrillian" among the Orthodox and "Chalcedonian" among the Monophysites, but it remains that the first became official policy of the Church, whereas the second was systematically disavowed by the Monophysite masses (See "Une controverse christologique sous le patriarcat de Pierre de Callinique," OCA, 205, 1978, p. 357).

opposing Monophysite parties, trying to reconcile them. Other leaders of official Orthodoxy—John the Faster of Constantinople (582-595), John IV of Alexandria (570-581)—were highly praised by Monophysite historians John of Ephesus and John of Nikiu for their asceticism, piety and tolerance of dissent.[4] Moreover, there is another sign showing that neither side had yet accepted the reality of a final schism. A strong Monophysite, Peter the Iberian, continued to be venerated as an ascetic saint by Chalcedonian Georgians. Emperor Maurice, less notable than his predecessors, or successors, as a compromiser with Non-Chalcedonians, is remembered as a "God-loving" emperor by the Monophysite John of Ephesus, and is venerated as a Saint by Monophysite Syrians.[5] Similarly, the Chalcedonian patriarch of Alexandria, St John the Merciful (612-617) appears as a Saint in Coptic and Ethiopian calendars.[6]

Two factors, however, contributed strongly to the perpetuation of the schism: the existence, since the consecration of Jacob Bar'Addai as bishop by Theodosius of Alexandria (542-3), of a separate parallel Monophysite church, which was, ecclesiastically and sacramentally, providing an illegal, but readily available alternative to Chalcedonian unity; and the internal divisions of the Monophysites, which made it impossible, even for the most respected leaders, like Theodosius or Jacob Bar'Addai, to speak, or negotiate on behalf of all the Non-Chalcedonians.

1.   The internal splits of Monophysitism

In Egypt alone, by the end of the sixth century, the anti-Chalcedonian opposition was split into twenty groups, each claiming canonical and doctrinal purity, and, in many cases, counting adepts in Syria, Arabia and Persia.[7] Some groups like the Akephaloi ("Headless," who had rejected the Henotikon of 482 and, therefore, the hierarchy, set up by Peter Mongos and all his successors) and the Dioscorians (who

---

[4]On these and other cases, see P. Allen, "Neo-Chalcedonism and the patriarchs of the later sixth century," Byzantion L, 1980, pp. 5-17.

[5]Hist. eccl. V, 14 (ed. and tr. E. W. Brooks, CSCO, Scriptores syri III, 3, Paris-Louvain, 1935-6); Légende syriaque de Maurice, in PO V, pp. 773-8.

[6]Cf. J. Maspéro, Histoire des patriarches d'Alexandrie, Paris, 1923, p. 328.

[7]Cf. Timothy, presbyter of Constantinople in a treatise "On those who return to the Church" (PG 86, 1, col. 11-74); crit. ed. in V. Beneshevich, Syntagma XIV titulorum, I, St Petersburg, 1906, pp. 707-738.

rejected all the patriarchs since 454, date of Dioscoros' death, because his successor Timothy "the Cat" had not reordained repenting Chalcedonian clerics) had seceded from mainstream Monophysitism on disciplinary grounds. Others, like the *Agnoetai,* without accepting Chalcedon, were nevertheless critical of extreme Cyrillism which insisted upon the total deification of Christ's humanity. Their spokesman was the Alexandrian deacon Themistius. He maintained that Jesus, as man, shared human *ignorance.* Other splits resulted from certain serious theological debates of the sixth century which are known in even greater detail.

The first of these had opposed Severus of Antioch and Julian of Halicarnassus, as both were living in exile in Alexandria during the reign of Justin I. Julian affirmed that since death and corruption (*phthora*) resulted from sin, Christ's body was not corruptible, because He was the New Adam assuming a humanity without sin. The implication was that, by virtue of the hypostatic union, Jesus's humanity since His conception by Mary, was not the "fallen" humanity of Adam, but the new, incorruptible humanity of the Kingdom of God. The doctrine of Julian—labelled *aphthartodocetism* by its opponents— was therefore linked to the concept of original sin and its consequences. It contained no elements which were specifically "monophysite" and attracted Chalcedonians, as well, including, in his later days, emperor Justinian himself. It was resolutely opposed by Severus on the grounds that if Christ's humanity was "incorruptible," His passion and death were only "apparent" ("docetism").[8] For Severus, the *voluntary* death of Christ implied His assuming *our* mortal humanity. For He was indeed foreign to personal sins, because He was God. But the assumption of *our* humanity by the Logos presupposed that Christ experienced the consequences of sin—the "blameless passions" (ἀδιάβλητα πάθη)—such as hunger, disease, suffering, corruptibility, and death. The incorruptibility of His body was manifested at His resurrection, not His birth! The firmness of Severus in defending those obvious aspects of orthodox christology illustrates the distance separating his

---

[8]On aphthartodocetism, see especially R. Draguet, *Julien d'Halicarnasse et sa controverse avec Sévère d'Antioche sur l'incorruptibilité du corps du Christ,* Louvain, 1924. Julian himself denied the accusation that, in his view, the passion of Jesus was only an "appearance." He affirmed its reality, but not as a necessity for Jesus: it resulted from a special decree of divine will and condescension. Severus agreed, of course, that the passion was voluntary, but he also maintained that the divine will, leading to it, was implied in the very act of incarnation itself. Cf. V. V. Bolotov, *Lektsii,* pp. 343; Meyendorff, *Christ,* pp. 87-88, 165-6.

view of salvation from extreme, Eutychian Monophysitism.

The debate between Severus and Julian was not limited to the narrow circle of professional theologians. The aphthartodocetae, also known as Phantasiasts, became an influential party. In Alexandria, following the death of pope Timothy III (Feb. 535) and with the government's toleration, another Monophysite and friend of Severus, the deacon Theodosius, was elected patriarch. However, immediately following his enthronement, he was removed by the force of a mob, led by monks. Archdeacon Gaianus, a Julianist, was installed in his stead, until order was restored by imperial troops, led by the famous general Nerses. Thus, Theodosius, although a Monophysite, recovered the patriarchate under imperial protection (May 535). However, the heresy of Julian remained very much alive not only in Egypt, where it would cause further troubles under Justin II, but "in the countries of the Romans, the Persians, the Indians, the Kushites [i.e. Ethiopians], the Himyarites [in Arabia], the Armenians."[9] Its success among the "Romans" was illustrated, as we have seen already, by the conversion of Justinian himself, whereas the Armenian Church formally approved a moderate form of Julianism in 551 and even anathematized Severus, as an enemy of aphthartodocetism [see below pp. 282-3].

Another equally involved debate opposed Monophysite theological factions to one another on the so-called issue of *tritheism*.

A central monophysite position in the debate with the Chalcedonians was the refusal to distinguish between the terms *nature* (φύσις) and *hypostasis*. Indeed, it was precisely the council's definition of Christ's *two natures* and *one hypostasis,* which the Monophysites rejected, relying on the patristic saying: "there is no nature without a *hypostasis*" (οὐκ ἔστι φύσις ἀνυπόστατος). There was therefore some logic in affirming that since there were three *hypostaseis* in God, there was also "three natures," i.e. "three Gods." This logic was adopted in Constantinople, around 557, by a certain John Asconaghes,[10] who was one of a number of Monophysite ecclesiastics, including Theodosius of Alexandria, hosted by the imperial court. The views of John were accepted by someone no less than Sergius, whom Theodosius, in Constantinople, had consecrated as Monophysite patriarch of Antioch

---

[9]Michael the Syrian, *Chron.*, IX, 30, (ed. II, 251). On the crisis of 535, see J. Maspéro, *op. cit.*, pp. 110-119.

[10]The name referred to his habit of wearing shoes made of leather, otherwise used to make water bottles. On the origins of tritheism, see especially A. Djakonov, *Ioann Efessky i ego tserkovno-istoricheskie trudy,* St. Petersburg, 1908, pp. 125-144.

(557). Other "tritheists" were Eugenius of Seleucia and Conon of Tarsus, as well as Athanasius, a grandson of empress Theodora (through an illegitimate daughter). These were real extremists of the Monophysite cause: Conon and Eugene had been the first bishops to be consecrated, sometime before 553, by Jacob Bar'Addai, and were therefore among the founders of the Monophysite "underground." Realizing the errors of some of his followers, the old pope Theodosius published a refutation of tritheism. Also, by contrast, he rejected another possible consequences of the identification of the terms "nature" and *hypostasis*: a doctrine which would claim that God, since He is one nature, has also one hypostasis. The Incarnation of such a unique hypostasis would imply confusion of natures. The result was obvious pantheism, which was actually professed by another Monophysite author of the period, Stephen Bar-Sudaili.

Theodosius' negative reaction did not end the debate. Indeed, tritheism found a powerful and authoritative proponent in the person of an Alexandrian scholar, John Philoponos, who produced a series of arguments, based on Aristotle—for whom indeed both hypostasis and physis expressed concrete reality—to defend the theory.[11] The movement spread and Athanasius, mentioned above, was consecrated by tritheists as patriarch of Alexandria after the death of Theodosius (566). Nevertheless, by 569, Philoponos and his tritheism was condemned by other major Monophysite authorities, including Jacob Bar'Addai himself. Even then, the influence of the sectarians at the court was strong enough to provoke a public debate in Constantinople between leaders of Monophysitism on the issue of tritheism presided by the Chalcedonian orthodox (!) patriarch John Scholasticus, acting as arbiter. The debate—which remained inconclusive—was morally detrimental to the cause of Monophysitism. The extreme, separatist undercurrent gained influence, and the moderates lost. The historian Michael the Syrian, who generally sympathized with the moderates, reports the story with understandable bitterness.[12]

At the time of Justinian's death (565), the Monophysite movement was still not only impressive in numbers, but also strong intellectually and politically. The numbers were represented by the popular masses of Syria and Egypt. The theological strength came from intel-

---

[11]On the date and circumstances, see A. Van Roey, "Les débuts de l'église jacobite" in *Chalkedon*, II ,p. 358.

[12]*Chron.*, IX, 30, (ed., II, 258-60).

lectuals and high ecclesiastics, most of whom still thought and wrote in Greek often using Greek philosophical categories to justify their positions. The constant readiness of the imperial court, supported by the Chalcedonian episcopate, to negotiate common formulas and unifying confessions, and also to provide shelter and security to those members of the Monophysite leadership—including especially pope Theodosius of Alexandria—who gave some hope for accomodation, kept possibilities of union always alive.

But the bitter divisions within Monophysitism made union negotiations difficult. The majority was less and less inclined to trust the "moderates," i.e., those who, headed by Theodosius of Alexandria, represented the mainstream of Monophysitism and agreed with the positions of Severus. Perhaps, if these moderate prelates had provided a more prominent leadership at the right time, the obvious basic christological consensus expressed in "Neo-Chalcedonism," would have prevailed. But the existence of the "parallel" church, created by Jacob Bar'Addai, the sloganeering directed against "the synod" (of Chalcedon) which was lasting now for over a century, and which represented the Chalcedonian faith as a "novelty," and, finally, the painful remembrance of Chalcedonian patriarchs imposed upon Alexandria or Antioch by imperial soldiers, following the exile of "confessors" like Dioscoros, or Timothy the "Cat," made union look like a betrayal. There was no *conscious* reaction against the empire and the Greek church. Higher ecclesiastics and theologians of Monophysitism continued to speak Greek. The liturgy, used by Syrians, and in particular the Copts, remained largely bilingual. Imperial loyalists were still strong, especially among the bishops. But the masses and the monks were once and for all set in the "old ways," which, according to them, had been abandoned by Marcian, Pulcheria and pope Leo; they rejected any formulas different from those of the great Cyril.

2. Imperial policies after Justinian

The prevailing view among contemporary historians[13] is that the death of Justinian and the accession of his nephew Justin II to the

[13]Cf. for instance, Frend, *The Rise*, pp. 317-319; and H. G. Beck in Jedin-Dolan, *History*, II, p. 457; also P. Goubert "Les successeurs de Justinien et le Monophysisme" in *Chalkedon*, II, pp. 179-192.

imperial throne (565) were marked by a return to a policy of theological compromise, similar to that of Zeno and Anastasius, and that
both the new emperor and his wife Sophia—Theodora's niece—were
"well-disposed towards Monophysite theology." This view is primarily
based upon the account of John of Ephesus, a "moderate" Monophysite,
whose *Ecclesiastical History* represents one of the major sources for
the period. John generally nourished strong devotion and loyalty to
the empire, and it is therefore understandable that he placed all his
hopes in a possible shift of imperial policies under Justin II. The same
John recognizes, however, that the patriarchs of the capital—first John
Scholasticus, then Eutychius—were staunch Chalcedonians: he places
the blame for an eventual resumption of the anti-Monophysite persecution on them.

John of Ephesus reports—on the basis of hearsay only, as he himself recognizes—that empress Sophia, in her youth, took communion
with Monophysites and secretly involved her husband in the same,
formally illicit, sacramental practice.[14] However, according to the same
historian, both Justin and Sophia had to become formally Chalcedonian
in order to reach the imperial throne. This recognition by John that
one could not become emperor, except by recognizing Chalcedon, is
significant and reflects the real situation in Constantinople by 565.

Indeed, it was unthinkable for anyone in power in the capital to
return to the situation which prevailed, before 518, under Zeno and
Anastasius. As we have seen earlier, a solemn yearly liturgical celebration was established by Justin I on July 16 to commemorate the council
of Chalcedon.[15] Furthermore, there could be no question for Justin II
to cancel the decrees of the "Fifth" council of 553, which confirmed
Chalcedon, even less to erase the mention of Chalcedon, which was
found in the very preamble of the Justinianic *Code*. There existed,
therefore, a formal and irreversible state sanction given to Chalcedon,
which makes one understand better the joy of John of Ephesus, and
other Monophysites, when they saw Justin, *in spite of* this official
commitment, pursue a policy of conciliation and dialogue.

The possibility of a "secret" Monophysitism of Justin and Sophia
is made even less probable by the available information on the close
personal and political ties which existed between the new emperor and

[14]*Hist. eccl.* II, 10 (ed. and tr. E. W. Brooks, CSCO, *Scriptores Syri*, III, 2-3, Paris,
1933-5).

[15]Cf. S. Salaville, "La fête du concile de Chalcédoine dans le rite byzantin," in
Chalkedon, II, pp. 667-695; cf. above, p. 212.

patriarch John Scholasticus, who may have facilitated Justin's enthronement.[16]

In spite of some ineptitude in foreign policy marked by a resumption of war with Persia, the reign of Justin II (565-574), before it ended pathetically in the emperor's madness, was marked by a strong patronage of the arts, building projects, and a distinct concern for religious affairs, not only in the East, but also in the West.[17] In its attitude towards the Monophysites, the new government and church leadership could afford to be quite conciliatory, precisely because the formal recognition of Chalcedon as the official faith was taken for granted and publicly sanctioned by law, so that there was no need to mention it directly in specific agreements with dissidents. This clarity of the official stand explains the assurance with which offers of dialogue were made—without the fear of a Chalcedonian, or Western-papal backlash—and the stern reactions of the government to Monophysite stubborness.

A learned lawyer from Antioch, John Scholasticus (565-577), assumed the patriarchate still under Justinian, after the emperor had deposed and arrested patriarch Eutychius for his refusal to condone the heresy of aphthartodocetism. John had therefore accepted the position in rather ambiguous circumstances. Well versed in palace intrigues and diplomacy, he nevertheless managed to avoid condoning aphthartodocetism formally until Justinian's death in November 565. He is particularly known for his codification of canonical texts—which were to parallel the codification of state laws accomplished under Justinian.[18] Unavoidably, he also became involved in relations with Monophysites.

The reign of Justin II began with a strong reaffirmation of the faith of Chalcedon, which is witnessed by Western authors and based upon public policy established under Justinian. But, at the same time, measures of personal attention and clemency favored the Monophysites. The titular and respected senior leader of the anti-Chalcedon-

---

[16]The information is found in the *Life* of St Symeon the Stylite, the Younger; cf. P. Van den Ven, "L'accession de Jean le Scholastique au siège patriarcal de Constantinople," *Byzantion* I, 1965, pp. 320-352.

[17]Cf. A. Cameron. "The early religious policies of Justin II," in D. Baker, ed. *The Orthodox Churches and the West* (Studies in Church History, 13), Oxford, 1976, pp. 51-67.

[18]John's work includes the *Collection of canons* (Συναγωγὴ κανόνων) *in Fifty Titles* (ed. V. Beneshevich, *Joannis Scholastici synagoga L titulorum*, München, Bayer, Akad. des. Wiss., Abh., NF, 14, 1937), and the *Collection* in 87 chapters (ed. J. Pitra, *Jur. Eccl. Graecorum Historia et Monumenta*, II, Rome, 1868, pp. 385-405).

ian opposition, Patriarch Theodosius of Alexandria, was still residing in the capital, under the court's protection since the time of Theodora. He was granted a personal audience with Justin and, when he died in 566, was buried with great honors. The moral leadership of the Monophysites in the capital was passed on to John of Ephesus, author of the well-known *Ecclesiastical History*, a moderate, and personally close to the court.[19] To placate Monophysite conservatism, Justin ordered the Nicean creed to be recited at each Eucharist to demonstrate that the Chalcedonians had not betrayed the ancient faith of the Church.[20] Several of the Monophysite leaders, exiled under Justinian, received amnesty. The emperor even offered his help in reconciling the conflicts existing between Monophysite factions on the issue of Tritheism, so that John Scholasticus presided over a debate on the issue—a rare case of fraternization between a Chalcedonian patriarch and prominent dissidents. The leaders of the schism, including the old Jacob Bar'Addai himself, were invited in the capital to hold consultations. Although the debates, held in 566-7, remained inconclusive, the emperor attempted to placate the opposition in a series of statements affirming that the only creed of the Church was that of Nicaea-Constantinople (since Chalcedon did not produce a "creed," but only a "definition"); that one should avoid quarrels about "persons" and "syllables"; that, in case of union, all anathemas, including those against Severus, could be abolished; that the decrees of 553 against the *Three Chapters* had eliminated all real christological differences between the two parties, etc.[21]

[19]Michael the Syrian, *Chron.,* IX, 30 (ed. cit., p. 257).

[20]This measure is reported by the Spanish chronicler John of Biclar, who was present in Constantinople at the time. Extreme Monophysites were accusing the council of Chalcedon of betraying the creed by attributing "double consubstantiality' to Christ, whereas the creed spoke of His consubstantiality to the Father only.

[21]These proposals, reported by the twelfth-century Monophysite chronicler Michael the Syrian (X,2, ed. cit., II, 289-290) are generally labelled, by most historians, as the "first Henotikon" of Justin II. However, neither one of the two contemporary historians (John of Ephesus, a Monophysite and Evagrius, a Chalcedonian) mentions any formal edict. The text reported by Michael actually looks more like a draft than a formal imperial decree. If a text was published by Justin at all in 566-7, it was indeed a draft memorandum for use in negotiations first in the capital, then in Callincium (on this, see the pertinent comments by A. Cameron, *ibid.,* pp. 62-4). Michael's reference to Justin, calling upon the protagonists to avoid discussing "syllables," is typical of the usual orthodox Chalcedonian attitude in the face of Monophysite "fundamentalism." The offer to forget about "persons" obviously refers to a possible rehabilitation of old and respected Monophysite theologians like Severus. Even if stricter Chalcedonians, like John Scholasticus, were not ready to go that far, the offer remained in the draft resulting from the many encounters between the two parties in the first years of Justin's reign.

These proposals of union could not be discussed fruitfully in the capital—even in the presence of Jacob Bar'Addai—because the Monophysite leaders felt too far removed from their popular "base" and unable to act as responsible spokesmen. Consequently, the proposals were entrusted to an imperial ambassador en route for Persia, John Commentiolus, who, on his return trip, met with a representative group of Monophysite ecclesiastical leaders in Callinicum on the Euphrates, at the borders with Persia (567 or 568). It seemed that the moderates, including even Jacob Bar'Addai—and certainly John of Ephesus, who is full of praises for the emperor's efforts—were ready to settle for union. The internal divisions of Monophysitism, manifested particularly in the debates of tritheism, had made unity more attractive to at least some Non-Chalcedonians. But the masses refused to follow: during the meeting in Callinicum, a monk grabbed the text of the imperial proposals from the hands of the reader and tore it apart. Still venerated as a Saint and a Confessor, the old Jacob Bar'Addai himself could not control his numerous, fanaticized followers.

Upon the return of John Commentiolus to the capital, more consultations were held, but no concrete results were achieved. In 571, finally, Justin II published a "program" addressed to all Christians (τοῖς ἑκασταχοῦ χριστιανοῖς πρόγραμμα),[22] which was a new manifesto of "Neo-Chalcedonian" theology. It affirmed that orthodox christology can be expressed both in Cyrillian ("one incarnate nature of God the Word") and Chalcedonian ("the difference of the natures is not annulled by the union . . . but each being distinctly existent . . .") languages. In his conclusion, the emperor calls all to union on the basis of "right doctrine," avoiding "unnecessary disputes about persons or words, since the words lead to one true belief and understanding, while the usage and form (ἔθος καὶ σχῆμα) which have hitherto prevailed in the holy catholic and apostolic Church of God, remain for ever unshaken and unchanged." The last sentence presumably alludes both to the various existing terminological systems and to liturgical and canonical traditions.

Never before, it seems, were the terms of union between Chalce-

---

[22]Text in Evagrius, *Eccl. hist.*, V, 4 (ed. Parmentier, pp. 197-201); tr. in Frend, *The Rise,* pp. 366-368 (the author systematically translates *hypostasis,* as "subsistence"). This text is often referred to as the "second *Henotikon*" of Justin II. But we have seen earlier that there has been no "first *Henotikon*" and that the term *Henotikon* itself, establishing a parallel with Zeno's, is hardly justified in either case.

donians and Monophysites spelled out in more realistic terms. There was an appeal to agree on substance, not words, and the reference to "unnecessary disputes on persons" hinted again at a possible disregard for past excommunications. There were no ambiguities, as in the time of the *Henotikon* of Zeno. Not only was Justin II celebrating the memory of Chalcedon every July 16, but his interest in contacts with the West excluded a betrayal of the council, so dear to Rome. The Latin poets Corippus and Venantius Fortunatus celebrate his orthodoxy. He was in correspondence with the king of the Franks and sent a reliquary with pieces of the True Cross to the former queen, St Radegunda, now a nun in Poitiers, as well as a beautiful cross, with his own portrait and Sophia's, to the pope. These events were taking place simultaneously with the union negotiations in the East.[23]

But Justin remained unable to persuade the Monophysite leadership, and therefore felt entitled to use some force as well.[24] In Constantinople and Asia Minor, all Monophysites were required to accept the "program." A number complied and, even some formerly anti-Chalcedonian bishops, who occupied sees in competition with orthodox incumbents, were reordained. Eventually, the practice of re-ordination was formally prohibited, and converts were only required to accept a "formula of union," in which reference was made to the agreement between Cyrill of Alexandria and John of Antioch in 433.[25] Among those who for a time accepted union was Paul the "Black," Monophysite patriarch of Antioch, who resided in Constantinople,[26] but the resistance of the majority of the Jacobites led to a renewed synodal anathema in Constantinople against Severus.[27]

Under Justin's designated successor Tiberius II (regent, 574-8; sole emperor, 678-82), the death of the staunchly Chalcedonian patriarch John Scholasticus (577) was followed by a new relaxation

[23]On these contacts with the West, see A. Cameron, *ibid.*, pp .51-59. The chronology of the events of Justin's reign is rather confused in the sources. I am following the sequence of events as proposed by Cameron.

[24]John of Ephesus was held under arrest until the death of John Scholasticus (Aug. 31, 577), whom he considers as the initiator of the repression.

[25]Characteristically, a similar procedure with the same reference, has been suggested, as a solution, by the theological consultation between Chalcedonians and Non-Chalcedonians held in our own time (Cf. the minutes in *GOTR*, 10, 2 (Winter 1964-5), and 13, 1 (1968).

[26]On these events, see particularly I. Djakonov, *op. cit.*, pp. 99-111.

[27]Cf. A de Halleux, "Trois synodes impériaux au VIe siècle dans une chronique syriaque inédite," in R. Fischer, ed., *A Tribute to Arthur Vööbus*, Chicago, 1977, pp. 302-307.

of imperial policies towards the Monophysites. The old patriarch Eutychius, who had occupied the throne under Justinian (552-65) and presided over the council of 553, was invited back to his see (577-82). He possessed the aura of a confessor, since he had been the victim of Justinian's infatuation with aphthartodocetism. He seems to have resisted Tiberius' tendency towards relaxing administrative measures taken by Justin against the dissidents. Indeed, the emperor was again recognizing *de facto* the existence of the two churches side by side. Jacob Bar'Addai was again visiting the capital. It is true that John of Ephesus, freed in 577, was rearrested in 578-9. Actually, Tiberius' moderation was motivated politically, and the Arab Christian state of the Ghassanids again played a decisive role in shaping imperial attitudes. We remember how, under Justinian, the Arab "phylarch" Al-Harith, had obtained the establishment of a Monophysite hierarchy in 543. Al-Harith's son, the Ghassanid Arab "phylarch," Al-Mundhir was now also solemnly received by Tiberius in 580. Acting as protector of the Monophysites, he obtained freedom for several clerics, who had refused union with the Chalcedonians.

Tiberius and patriarch Eutychius both died in 582. Before his death, Eutychius became involved in a debate with the *apocrisiarios* (delegate) of the Roman bishop in the capital, the deacon Gregory, who would later become pope, as Gregory the Great. Gregory reproached Eutychius for believing that the human body, in the resurrection, was "impalpable,"[28] and maintained that the risen Christ was indeed physically *touched* by Thomas, so that the same physical reality would appear in all those who will rise on the last day. Eutychius described the bodies of the resurrection in a more spiritual dimension. The debate found no solution. Gregory wisely decided to drop the issue following the death of Eutychius, whose name is found among the saints of the Church.

With the enthronement of John the Faster as patriarch (582-95) and of Maurice as emperor (582-602), the roles were reversed in terms of policies towards the Monophysites. The patriarch, a pious ascetic, is credited by the Monophysite sources with asking: "What did the dissident (διακρινόμενοι) do or say, which deserves persecution? If pagans have been justified and amnestied, how can I persecute Christians, who are blameless in their Christianity and, so it seems, have

---

[28]Cf. Gregory the Great, *Moralia in Job XIV*, 72-74; ed. A. Bocognan, 3 (SC, 212), Paris, 1974, pp. 433-439.

more faith than we?"[29] In Constantinople, the patriarch tolerated the presence of Monophysites who entered in partial concelebration with the Orthodox, without taking communion. Some monasteries, formally orthodox, were using the interpolated Trisagion.[30]

The new emperor, however, while not pretending to be a theologian, tried, during his entire reign, to enforce Chalcedonian unity, not only by force or persuasion, but also through diplomatic skill. "One of the most outstanding of Byzantine rulers,"[31] he made peace with Persia (591) and stabilized the internal structure of the empire. In 584, he abolished the Ghassanid "phylarchy," thus depriving the Monophysites of powerful political support.[32] The expansion of the empire's influence in Armenia and the Caucasus allowed for the move of the Georgian catholicosate of Mtskheta towards Chalcedonian Orthodoxy and an ecclesiastical union between the imperial church and a large segment of the Armenian church. At the same time, Maurice, as did his immediate predecessors, entertained cordial relations with the Roman bishop who in return was fully loyal to the imperial exarch, residing in Ravenna. In the religious policy of Maurice, a leading role was played by the emperor's cousin, bishop Domitian of Melitene, remembered by the Monophysites as a stern persecutor, but also by pope Gregory the Great, as "a man of prudence and shrewdness." Together with patriarch Gregory I of Antioch (570-93) Domitian helped Maurice to achieve peace with Chosroes of Persia.[33]

As shown earlier in this chapter, the world of Eastern religious dissidents was not a united entity. Not only were there schisms based on theological differences, but also, culturally and institutionally, Syrians, Egyptians, Armenians and Persian Christians faced the problem of church unity differently. Their history during the sixth century must therefore be examined separately.

[29] John of Ephesus, *Hist., eccl.,* V, 15 (*ed. cit.*).

[30] *Ibid.,* II, 13, 47; III, 19.

[31] G. Ostrogorsky, *History of the Byzantine State,* 2nd ed., New Brunswick, NJ, 1960, p. 80.

[32] It is true that the price paid for this measure by the empire was expensive: in future confrontations with Byzantium the Arabs tended to side with either Persia or Islam.

[33] Y. R. Paret, "Domitianus de Melitène et la politique religieuse de l'empereur Maurice," REB 15 (1957).

3. *Antioch and the Jacobites*

During the period of tolerance and "dialogue," instituted by Justinian in the first years of his reign (527-536), the anti-Chalcedonian opposition had the opportunity to organize itself by establishing a separate church, parallel to that which was ruled by the official imperial episcopate. In their view, Severus—who had been patriarch of Antioch under Anastasius since 512, but exiled under Justin (518) —was the last "orthodox" patriarch in the official line. Following his deposition, the imperial government secured the appointment of a series of Chalcedonian patriarchs (Paul, 519-21; Euphrasius, 521-6; Ephrem, 527-45; Domninus, 545-59; Anastasius, 559-570). Opposing them, a certain Constantine of Laodicea was the first to be recognized, in Monophysite circles, as the acting patriarch.[34] Following his death in 553, the Monophysite patriarch of Alexandria, Theodosius—living in exile, but under the court's protection, in Constantinople—consecrated Sergius of Tella (557) as patriarch of Antioch. In 561, Paul the "Black" succeeded Sergius.

The existence of a parallel line of patriarchs provided the opposition with a rallying point, especially since Justinian—and particularly his wife, Theodora—never fully gave up attempts at reaching agreement with the Monophysite leadership. Gradually, the Monophysites moved beyond the mere tactic of maintaining a nominal "orthodox" patriarchate, and began to create a parallel hierarchy wherever they could. The first step in that direction was taken around 530 with the initially very reluctant blessing of the exiled patriarch Severus. John, bishop of Tella in East Syria, began to perform ordinations not only for his diocese, but for any group anywhere who sought anti-Chalcedonian "orthodoxy." The historian John of Ephesus was himself ordained deacon by him and reports the probably exaggerated number of 170,000 ordinations performed by John of Tella.[35] These clandestine ordinands included not only lower clerics. There were also well attested cases of episcopal consecrations, performed by John of Tella together with other Syrian Monophysite bishops, for Persia.[36] Whatever their number—and it must

---

[34]E. Hönigmann, "La hiérarchie monophysite au temps de Jacques Baradée, 542-578," CSCO, Subs. 2, Louvain, 1951, p. 170.

[35]Cf. John of Ephesus, *Lives of Eastern Saints,* ed. Brooks, PO 18, pp. 515-521. There is every reason to believe that John of Tella was not the only Monophysite bishop engaged in such ordinations, predominantly secret (cf. A. Van Roey, *op. cit.,* p. 353).

[36]Elias, *Vita Iohannis ep. Tell.,* ed. Brooks, CSCO 7, Paris, 1907, 58-61, 38-40.

have been great—such ordinations were schismatic by their very nature, because they implied that the Chalcedonian church was not the Church anymore, and that one had to abstain from its sacraments at all costs. Furthermore, most of the ordinands must have been rather uneducated persons, but they were strongly committed to oppose the "synodites" (supporters of the council of Chalcedon) and psychologically set for struggle against the imperial establishment. It is understandable, therefore, that moderate leaders like Severus and Theodosius of Alexandria were reluctant to follow the path made by John of Tella; indeed, union negotiations would become incalculably more difficult once two separate and parallel hierarchies were established.

The activity of John of Tella lasted no more than six or seven years. Captured by agents of the Chalcedonian patriarch Ephrem in 536-7, John died in seclusion in Antioch in 538. Indeed, after 536, Justinian had adopted strong administrative measures against the Monophysites everywhere.

However, the emperor and his wife also tried to secure the future. Patriarch Theodosius of Alexandria, who was living in honorable exile in the capital, was permitted to fulfill a petition received from air imperial ally, the Monophysite Arab Ghassanid "phylarch" Al-Harith; who was requesting bishops for his country. In 542 or 543 Theodosius, with the knowledge of the court, consecrated two monks, Theodore and Jacob Bar'Addai, as bishops.[37] Theodore seems to have limited his pastoral activities to the lands of the Arabs, especially Palestine, whereas Jacob, made metropolitan of Edessa, is famous for his remarkable missionary activity, which consisted in consecrating Monophysite clergy throughout the whole of the Eastern empire. Later sources apply to him the title of "ecumenical metropolitan," although it seems that it was rather the popes of Alexandria, who, in that period, used the title of "oecumenical patriarch" for themselves (the usage is attested for Dioscoros and Theodosius).[38]

It is interesting, however, that Theodosius refused to multiply a "parallel" episcopate further and that Jacob had to go to Egypt, sometime before 553, to find co-consecrators for Eugene and Conon, well-known for their involvement in tritheism. With these colleagues in the

[37]On these events and the activities of Jacob, see D. D. Bundy, "Jacob Baradaeus," *Le Muséon* 91 (1978), pp. 45-86.
[38]For Dioscoros, see above, p. 114; for Theodosius, see *Documenta ad origines monophysitarum,* ed. Chabot, CSCO, *Scriptores Syri,* II, 37, Louvain, 1933, pp. 63 ("ecumenical patriarch"), 87 ("ecumenical teacher").

"truly orthodox" episcopate, Jacob soon proceeded with the consecration of two patriarchs and twenty-seven archbishops and bishops.[39] It is from James (or Jacob) Bar'Addai, that the Monophysites of Syria became known as "Jacobites."

Earlier in this chapter we discussed the theological debates which occurred within the Monophysite community on the issue of tritheism. But there were also other conflicts which were partially created by the unavoidably clandestine, and therefore chaotic, way in which the "Jacobite" hierarchy was being established and by its dependence upon the personal prestige of a few "charismatic" leaders. There were also cultural divisions between Syrians and Egyptians, and a basic difference of mentality between bishops residing in Constantinople, loyal to the empire, and still hoping for a reversal of official policies (Theodosius of Alexandria, John of Ephesus) and the monastic and popular elements constituting the majority of the clergy ordained by Jacob Bar'Addai. The latter were ready to struggle against imperial agents to the end.[40]

These various factors were all combined in the controversial stories of two Monophysite patriarchs of Antioch: Sergius of Tella and Paul the "Black."

Sergius, consecrated by Theodosius of Alexandria in 557, was in conflict with the latter on the issue of tritheism (which he supported). Following the early death of Sergius (560-1), Theodosius, concerned with the unity of the Church, waited for three years before choosing a successor. He finally approved the candidacy of his own secretary, an anti-tritheist and an Alexandrian, Paul the "Black." He also requested Jacob Bar'Addai and his colleagues to consecrate him as patriarch, which was done in 564.[41] To Paul, Theodosius—who was acting as a *de facto* head of the Non-Chalcedonians worldwide, although with little real control over the masses—confided the mission to visit Egypt and restore a dissident hierarchy there. Following this relatively unsuccessful mission to Alexandria and the death of his patron, Theodosius, in Constantinople (566), Paul returned to Syria, where he discovered that, as representative of the conciliatory "Theodosian" trend and as a staunch opponent of tritheism, he was not welcome among the followers of Bar'Addai, although the latter had been his consecrator and was not

---

[39]John of Ephesus, (*Lives of the Saints,* PO 19, pp. 156-8) gives their names and titles.

[40]On this, see A. Diakonov, *op. cit.,* pp. 95-108.

[41]On Paul, see particularly E. W. Brooks "The patriarch Paul of Antioch and the Alexandrian schism of 575," *BZ,* 30 (1930), pp .468-76.

opposing him personally. He was received more favorably by Al-Harith
however, and set up residence with him in Arabia. Eager to recover his
jurisdiction in Syria, and enjoying the political support of the Arab
chief, he took advantage of his imperial connections, and accepted the
"program" of Justin II, communicating with the Chalcedonians.[42] Seeing
that the mass of the Monophysites were not following, he recanted, was
arrested, but escaped and again received the hospitality of the Arab
"phylarch"—Al-Harith's son, Al-Mundhir, only to find refuge again in
his native Egypt. Involved in local ecclesiastical affairs, he organized
the clandestine consecration of a Syrian monk, Theodore, as patriarch
of Alexandria. The latter proved unacceptable to the local Monophysites, who elected and consecrated their own candidate Peter (576).
Peter was recognized as legitimate patriarch by Jacob Bar'Addai.
Excommunicated both in Egypt and in Syria by both the Monophysites
and, of course, the Chalcedonians, Paul the "Black" never recovered
his patriarchate. He was back in Constantinople, when Al-Mundhir
visited emperor Tiberius II in 580. Under the auspices of the Arab
king, supporters of Paul and Jacob Bar'Addai were temporarily reconciled,[43] but Paul himself died in obscurity in Constantinople in 581.

During the years of conflict between "Jacobites" and partisans of
Paul the "Black," there was much confusion, even bloodshed among
the Syrian Monophysites. More and more, the conflict appeared to
reflect a growing incompatibility between the more moderate, still
"imperial-minded" bishops, like Paul, and the Syrian masses, whom
even Jacob Bar'Addai was unable to control and who were definitely
set against all compromise with the "synodites." The interventions of
the Alexandrians in the Syrian affairs did not help either.[44]

Following the death of Jacob Bar'Addai (578) and the unglorious
disappearance of Paul the "Black," the new Monophysite patriarch of
Alexandria, Damian (578-604), successor of Peter, consecrated Peter
of Callinicum as his colleague in Antioch, a candidate who could hope
to reconcile the opposing parties. This did not happen, however. Damian
and Peter quarrelled with each other on theological technicalities related
to tritheism, which they both rejected. Peter of Antioch was seen in

---

[42]Michael the Syrian, *Chron.*, X, 6 (ed. cit., p. 304).
[43]John of Ephesus, *Hist. eccl.* IV, 40-1 (ed. cit.).
[44]Distressed by these interventions and disappointed with the lack of Egyptian support for Paul the "Black," with whom he sympathized, John of Ephesus expresses his anger
against the "Pharaonites," capable only of "struggle, confusion and barbarism" (*Hist.
eccl.* IV, 11; *ed. cit.*).

Alexandria as a challenger to the supreme prestige of Alexandria in theological matters.[45]

During the period between 581 and 611—the year of the Persian conquest—the Jacobite patriarchs of Antioch resided in the monastery of Gubba Barraya, East of Aleppo, since Antioch, as well as other major cities, were controlled by the Chalcedonian hierarchy. In spite of all the internal disputes, the great majority of Syriac-speaking monasteries and villages were faithful to Monophysitism. It is then, on the eve of the Persian invasion, and following the activities of Jacob Bar'Addai, that confessional loyalties became interwoven with ethnicity: words such as "Syrian" and "Egyptian" turned into normal designations for opponents of Chalcedon, whereas the term "Greek," more often than not, became synonymous with "Melkite" (the "emperor's man") and reflected Chalcedonian loyalty.[46]

This does not mean that the orthodox Chalcedonian patriarchs of the period were always simply imperial agents. While the former *Comes Orientis* Ephraem (527-545) and his successor Domninus (545-559) faithfully applied the policies of Justinian, by promoting a strongly "Cyrillian" Chalcedonism,[47] but also repressing the dissidents, Anastasius I (559-601, 593-8) stood up against Justinian's intention to enforce Aphthartodocetism, and was saved from deposition only by the emperor's death (565). He also came into conflict with Justinian's successor, Justin II, for reasons which seem to have been of an administrative and economic nature,[48] and forced to leave the patriarchate, to be restored only under Maurice. Respected for his theological competence, and a correspondent of pope Gregory the Great, he wrote against the tritheism of John Philoponos. This stand gained him some recognition in moderate Monophysite circles, also opposed to tritheism. During his second patriarchate, he took part in debates between Monophysites, in particular those provoked by the views of the Alexandrian "sophist" Stephen.

Stephen was reducing *ad absurdum* the fundamental affirmation of Severus that divinity and humanity in Christ were fully distinct, but that nevertheless it was necessary to speak of only one nature in Him.

---

[45]On this quarrel, see below, p. 275.

[46]Cf. Frend, *The Rise*, p. 334.

[47]Ephrem was a good theologian in his own right; cf. J. Lebon, "Ephrem d'Amida," in *Mélanges Ch. Moeller* I (Louvain, 1914), pp. 197-214.

[48]Sources and discussion in G. Downey, *A History of Antioch*, Princeton, 1961, p. 560-1.

For Stephen, it was impossible to distinguish "natural qualities" in Christ without admitting also a duality of natures. In the case of the "Sophist," the basic Chalcedonian logic was re-emerging in Monophysite circles. Under his influence, the Monophysite monk Probus, in 595-6, turned Chalcedonian.[49]

Patriarch Gregory I (570-593), who replaced the temporarily exiled Anastasius, was able to win a spectacular conflict with the *Comes Orientis* Asterius, who had attempted to discredit the head of the Church.[50] Later, together with Domitian of Melitene, he played a major diplomatic role on behalf of emperor Maurice by escorting the Persian king Chosroes on his way back to Persia, and receiving the latter's lavish gifts for the shrine of St Sergius at Resafa.[51] He also gave indirect support to Paul the "Black" by preventing Damian of Alexandria from consecrating a patriarch of Antioch, rival to Paul.[52]

It does appear that the increased civic role played by the Chalcedonian patriarchs coupled with their theological competence and diplomatic skill, could have eventually led to ecclesiastical peace with at least some of the divided Monophysites. But this possibility depended heavily on political stability in Constantinople and on peace with Persia. Unfortunately, this peace, happily arranged by Maurice, was broken by his murderer, Phocas. Renewed hostilities brought catastrophe: a Persian invasion and the capture of Antioch (611). With the invasion, "the memory of the Chalcedonians disappeared from the Euphrates to the Orient [*i.e.* Syria],"[53] and the Jacobite patriarch Athanasius of Qennesrin (known as the "Camel driver," 595-631) wrote to his collegue in Alexandria: "The world rejoiced in peace and love, because the Chalcedonian night has been chased away."[54]

---

[49]Cf. on the christology of Probus, A. Van Roey "Une controverse sous le patriarcat de Pierre de Callinique" in *Symposium Syriacum* 1976 (OCA, 205), Rome, 1978, pp. 354-7. On the personality and writings of Anastasius I, see G. Weiss, *Studia Anastasiana,* München, 1965; and P. Allen, *op. cit.,* pp. 13-15.

[50]Evagrius, *Eccl. hist.,* VI, 7, ed .cit., pp. 225-6.

[51]*Ibid.,* VI, 18-21, ed. cit., pp. 234-5.

[52]John of Ephesus, *Hist. eccl.* IV, 42 (ed. cit.). On St Anastasius I and St Gregory I, Chalcedonian patriarchs of Antioch, see P. Goubert, 'Patriarches d'Antioche et d'Alexandrie, contemporains de St Grégoire le Grand," REB 25, 1967, pp. 65-76.

[53]Michael the Syrian, *Chron.* X, 25, ed. cit., II, pp. 380-1.

[54]Severus of Asmounein, *Hist. of the Patriarchs,* ed. and tr. B. T. A. Evett, PO 1, Paris, 1907, p. 481.

4. Alexandria and the Copts

The unique role of Egypt—and of its capital, Alexandria—within the Roman world has been already described earlier. This cultural and historical identity was acknowledged by outsiders—Persians, Arabs— as well as, of course, by the Egyptians themselves.[55] The sense of cultural superiority, characteristic of the Egyptians, was based upon their awareness of being heirs of the ancient pharaonic civilization. Until the fourth century, this awareness was inseparably linked to syncretistic paganism, which combined strong elements of the ancient Egyptian religion with Hellenistic cults. However, the Christian faith came to Egypt with both intellectual and political strength: Clement and Origen on the one hand, and the forceful bishops of Alexandria —Athanasius, Theophilus, Cyril—contributed to making Christianity, more rapidly than elsewhere, the faith of the majority. The young and powerful Egyptian church assumed much of the old Egyptian cultural self-awareness. Its readiness to define itself as "Egyptian" probably contributed to its success throughout the entire population of the country.

Throughout the fourth, fifth and sixth centuries, there existed a vivid contrast between the city of Alexandria, a great intellectual center where the Greek language and the Greek intellectual tradition were dominant, and the rest of the country—the country of Egyptian peasants speaking Coptic, a peculiarly simplified and hellenized form of the ancient Egyptian tongue. Sometimes, people leaving Alexandria for the countryside, would say that they were "going to Egypt." But, in the consciousness of contemporaries, the cultural contrast between Alexandria and the rest of the country, was also felt as the country's strength. The Greek-speaking Alexandrians were no less proud of the Egyptian cultural inheritance, and readily attributed to Egypt the invention of all philosophy, all science, and all wisdom of the ages, whereas the Coptic masses followed Alexandria's leadership faithfully in both political and ecclesiastical matters. This was particularly the case of Egyptian monasticism, which counted, perhaps as many as half a million monks and nuns.[56] This huge monastic community fol-

---

[55]The most comprehensive treatment of this Egyptian selfawareness is still that of J. Maspéro, *Histoire des patriarches d'Alexandrie,* Paris, 1923 (Chapter II: "Le peuple égyptien aux VIe et VIIe siècles"), pp. 23-64.

[56]Maspéro, *ibid.,* p. 55.

lowed blindly the leadership of the "pope" of Alexandria, whose personal influence in the entire country was incomparably stronger than that of the provincial episcopate, or of the largely uneducated, and much less numerous married clergy.

The episcopal see of Alexandria, however, never defined itself as a national, or ethnic institution. The archbishop called himself "judge of the universe" (κριτὴς τῆς οἰκουμένης), a title which is used even today by both the Greek and the Coptic incumbents. Aware of the fact that the council of Nicaea itself (canon 6) had established a parallel between Alexandria and Rome, as possessing special "privileges" on the basis of "ancient customs," the archbishops of the Egyptian metropolis justified their position both by the cultural heritage of Egypt, by their ancient right to determine the annual date of Easter for all the other churches, as well as by the victories won by St Athanasius and St Cyril over what they saw as the two most dangerous heresies of Christianity: Arianism and Nestorianism. They claimed jurisdiction not only over Egypt, Lybia and Pentapolis (as defined in Nicaea), but over the whole of Africa, including Ethiopia, Arabia, Carthage, and occasionally even Jerusalem. They resented bitterly the establishment of a "new Rome" in Constantinople, and tried, whenever they could, to restrain the influence of this unwelcome ecclesiastical upstart. Thus, the Alexandrian bishop did not define his role merely in terms of an Egyptian "ethnarch," but rather as a guardian of orthodoxy and church order in the empire and the whole Christian world.

This is the reason why the condemnation of Dioscoros at the council of Chalcedon was interpreted as an unacceptable scandal engineered by Constantinople and Rome, and in need of redress.

After the unhappy and bloody attempts by Marcian to impose Chalcedon by force, emperors Zeno and Anastasius settled with Monophysite patriarchs in Alexandria and attempted to reestablish religious unity through compromise (the *Henotikon*) between the major patriarchates. The Chalcedonian firmness of Rome prevented the success of this policy. Justinian and Theodora gradually developed more subtle tactics, often criticized as devious. In fact, however, they were trying to solve the christological issue in its substance, while being tolerant of personalities and popular sensibilities. Their partial success was due also to divisions within the anti-Chalcedonian Egyptian majority. Following the death of Patriarch Timothy III (535), empress Theodora was instrumental in the appointment of Theodosius, a friend of

Severus, and thus belonging to the mainstream of the Monophysite movement, with which Justinian was seeking agreement. However, a "Julianist" rebellion, promoting aphthartodocetism, overthrew Theodosius and installed another patriarch, Gaianus. These events almost coincided with the adoption by Justinian of a new hard line against the Monophysites. Gaianus was arrested in the midst of street riots and massacres, and exiled to Carthage. Theodosius was brought to Constantinople, urged to accept Chalcedon and, upon his refusal, exiled to Derkos, in Thrace.

This sharp division of the Monophysite clergy in Alexandria between "Theodosians" and "Gaianites," and the tritheistic controversies which occurred later, made Chalcedonian control of the patriarchate easier. From 537 to 641, for more than a century, until the capture of Egypt by the Muslim Arabs, a "melkite," or Chalcedonian patriarch resided, almost without interruption, in Alexandria. Justinian's own appointees included the energetic Paul the Tabennisiot (537-539), formerly the abbot of the great Pachomian monastery of Canopus, the more passive Zoilus (539-51), and Apollinarius (551-570). During most of this period, however, Theodosius, the Monophysite incumbent lived in honorable exile under the court's protection in Constantinople, acting as the spiritual head of the entire Monophysite "underground" in the empire. His activities in restoring a Monophysite hierarchy have been discussed above. In Egypt, however, his real influence was limited. At the end of the reign of Justinian (565), there were no more than four Monophysite bishops left—all residing in remote parts of the country. It would seem, therefore, that Justinian's policies had borne some fruit. Still holding in the countryside, Monophysitism had lost control of the ecclesiastical establishment in Egypt.

The exiled Theodosius was strong in his opposition to Chalcedon, but remained basically loyal to the empire, sharing with the emperor some hopes for reconciliation. Significantly, at least some of the Coptic monks of the desert seemed to have accepted ecclesiastical peace during this period. The Chalcedonians were strong among the Pachomian monasteries, in addition to holding the major churches of Alexandria.[57]

Following the death of Theodosius (566), the Monophysite party was not in a position to elect a patriarch for nine years. In 575 the vacancy ended, but only clandestinely, and in a controversial manner.

[57]On the respective strength of Chalcedonians and Monophysites in Egypt at the end of Justinian's reign, see E. R. Hardy, *Christian Egypt*, pp. 135-139.

One patriarch, Theodore, was consecrated secretly in the desert by the exiled patriarch of Antioch Paul the "Black," together with Longinus, bishop of the Nobadae in Nubia.[58] But Theodore's election was challenged by the majority of the Egyptian Monophysites, who, in the same year, elected Peter as patriarch. The two groups exchanged anathemas and theological accusations, which divided their partisans both in Egypt and in Syria. Whereas Paul left for Constantinople, his friend Longinus continued his successful mission work in Black Africa: he succeeded in converting the tribe of the Alauah, on the upper Nile.[59] The other more "anti-imperial" party, following Peter's death (574), was headed by Damian (578-604), a learned, but also controversial leader of Monophysitism. Challenged by tritheists, then by Stephen the Sophist, who had criticized the very foundations of Severian monophysitism (identification of *physis* and *hypostasis*), Damian tried unsuccessfully to reconcile the various Monophysite factions. Travelling to Constantinople, he worked out a temporary reconciliation with the partisans of Paul the "Black" (580), together with the phylarch Al-Mundhir and emperor Tiberius. But theological debates continued between Damian and Peter of Callinicum, Monophysite patriarch of Antioch. Always afraid of tritheism, Damian, in his writings tended to relativize the hypostatic identity in the Trinity, and was accused of Sabellianism by Peter. His partisans were sometimes labelled *Tetradites* for introducing a 'fourth" reality in God—the "common God," distinct from the three Persons.[60]

For contemporaries, the controversy between the two patriarchs gradually acquired cultural overtones, as a struggle between "Syrians" and "Egyptians." It resulted in a schism between Monophysite Antioch and Monophysite Alexandria, which was resolved only in 616, when Peter's successor, Athanasius the "Camel Driver," known for his asceticism and holiness (595-631), came to Egypt in the last year of the reign of Damian's successor, the learned patriarch Anastasius (604-616). There is every reason to believe that their reconciliation was encouraged by Nicetas, cousin and close friend of emperor Heraclius, who was present in Egypt on that date and busy organizing a united Christian front against the impending Persian invasion. A

---

[58]Cf. supra, p. 268.

[59]John of 7phesus, *Hist. eccl.*, IV, 51-3 (ed. cit.).

[60]For the respective positions of Damian and Peter, see Bolotov, *Lektsii*, pp. 354-5; and also R. Y. Ebied "Peter of Antioch and Damian of Alexandria," in R. H. Fischer, ed. *A Tribute to A. Vööbus*, Chicago, 1977, pp. 277-82.

theological consultation took place between representatives of the two parties, but in the absence of the two patriarchs. After animated debates, a remarkable solution was worked out: recognizing the differences and the mutual excommunications of the two "blessed archbishops," Peter and Damian, in the past, the two parties—now that the said archbishops "had gone to God"—declared that their faith was one. The two patriarchs issued a *Synodikon* stating agreement in faith and entered into eucharistic communion with each other, disavowing both "tritheism" and "tetradism," the two heresies of which Damian and Peter had accused each other.[61] It appears, however, that a group of "Damianites" rejected the agreement, and even elected an "antipope," John, to lead them.[62]

During these episodes, the Monophysite patriarchs of Alexandria were forbidden by law to reside in the city, or to use the main ancient basilicas: the *Caesareum*, the martyrium of St Mark, and others. Since the schism, however, they had built new churches for their faithful—the *Angelion* and the church of Sts Cosmas and Damian—and could live at the monsatery of the Ennaton on the cost, west of the metropolis. Among the Chalcedonian patriarchs of the period, some managed to acquire a real personal prestige, and to avoid direct confrontations between Chalcedonians and Non-Chalcedonians. The most prominent and influential among them, in the late sixth and early seventh centuries, were St Eulogius (581-608) and St John V, the "Merciful" (612-617).

St Eulogius, under the able reign of Maurice, acted as the *de facto* highest authority in Egypt, successfully opposing, where necessary, local imperial officials and even assuming the leadership of civil government.[63] He was the author of several theological treatises—six books against the Severians, three books in defense of the *Tome of Leo,* a treatise dealing with the struggle between Theodosians and Gaianites, and other writings related to the christological and trinitarian issues of the day.[64] The polemics contained in these treatises strictly follow the "Cyrillian-Chalcedonian" position, and the conciliatory attitude

---

[61]Michael the Syrian, *Chron,* X, 26 (ed. cit. II, pp. 381-393). There is no doubt that a similar solution of the struggle between Chalcedonians and Monophysites (who were accusing each other of Eutychianism and Nestorianism respectively) was the one promoted unsuccessfully by Justinian and all the so called "Neo-Chalcedonians."

[62]On the reconciliation, see Maspéro, *op. cit.,* pp. 319-342.

[63]Cf. *Ibid.,* pp. 267-8.

[64]Unfortunately, none of these writings has been preserved in its original text. Their content is known through a very detailed analysis given by Photius in his *Bibliotheca*

towards the Monophysites, which characterized the imperial policies of the period. Eulogius has left no reputation as a persecutor. On the contrary, as he sent, upon his election, his letter of communion to the other patriarchs, pope Gregory I, receiving it in Rome, answered with a criticism: Eulogius had failed to mention Chalcedon explicitly or to condemn any Monophysite by name, or to define a "two natures" christology with all necessary clarity.[65] Clearly, Eulogius was writing in the spirit of the "program" of Justin II, avoiding issues of wording, or personalities, and limiting himself to the orthodox substance of christology. The subsequent writings of Eulogius must have quieted Gregory's apprehension: the two patriarchs exchanged regular and friendly correspondence (several letters of St Gregory to St Eulogius are preserved). Gregory even complained to his colleague in Alexandria against the assumption of the title of "ecumenical patriarch" by John the Faster of Constantinople.[66] The reaction of Eulogius to that complaint is discussed below.

The chaotic and bloody reign of emperor Phocas disturbed the relative peace which prevailed in Egypt under Maurice. Following the death of Eulogius (608 or 609), a former member of the imperial guard, or *Skribon* (σκρίβων), Theodore, was made Chalcedonian patriarch, and entrusted with the task of repressing the Monophysites and other dissidents by force, a policy followed by Phocas throughout the empire.[67] A rebellion followed which was led by Nicetas, cousin of Heraclius. Theodore was killed in 609, together with other officials faithful to Phocas, as Nicetas entered Alexandria (609).[68]

The Chalcedonian patriarchate remained vacant for several years. The vacancy was presumably due to the general chaos resulting from the Persian War, provoked by Phocas, and the need for Heraclius, who assumed the throne in 610, to consolidate his power. The new patriarch was the right candidate for restoring confidence in the new regime: John, known as "the Merciful," or "the Almsgiver" (ἐλεήμων), who held the throne from 611 to the capture of Alexandria by the Persians in 617.

(cod. 182, 208, 225, 226, 227, 230, 280); ed. R. Henry (Paris, 1965-77), vols. 2, 3, 4, 5 and 8.

[65]Cf. the content of these criticisms in Photius, *Bibl.* 230, ed. cit. 5, p. 8.

[66]Cf. *Ep* V, 41, MGH, *Ep* I, 331-5, cf. below, pp. 305-6.

[67]Cf. Maspéro, *op. cit.,* pp. 275-77, 326.

[68]The circumstances are well described in J. Kulakovsky, *Istoriya Vizantii,* III, Kiev, 1912, pp. 20-21; cf. L. Bréhier, in Fliche-Martin, *Histoire de l'Eglise* 5, Paris, 1947, p. 76.

A widower and family man, son of a former governor of Cyprus, John was promoted to the patriarchate from the lay state upon the recommendation of the prefect Nicetas. His *Life,* composed soon after his death, is a valuable source of information not only about St John himself, but also the state of the Church in his time.[69] The fact that he was eventually venerated as a Saint by the Copts, shows that he discontinued the repressive policies of Phocas and Theodore. We have seen that the prefect Nicetas had sponsored a reconciliation between Monophysite factions in 616. Patriarch John, who was godfather of the prefect's children and a close friend, must have had sympathized with his actions, at least indirectly. His *Life* presents him, of course, as a faithful Chalcedonian, who accepted many Monophysite clergy back into the Church, but never reordained them. The harvest of such meekness was a tenfold increase of his flock in Alexandria.[70] However, the greatest achievement of John lies in the way he secured social justice, fed the poor and, especially, cared for the masses of refugees which had flocked into Alexandria from Palestine and Syria, invaded by Persians. The means of the church of Alexandria were considerable: the patriarchate owned ships, businesses, and a huge constantly replenished treasure. On his arrival, John found 8000 pounds of gold in the bishop's house, and the exact figures, attested in the *Life,* of the gifts he sent to Jerusalem, following the burning of the Holy City by the Persians, are quite impressive. Although the prefect Nicetas found some of John's generosity to be exaggerated, there is no doubt that the social activity of the "Merciful" patriarch did much to unite the population of Egypt and raise the prestige of the "melkite" patriarchate. The relative peace which prevailed under the holy patriarchs Eulogius and John was interrupted by major catastrophies: the Persian and Arab invasions of Egypt.

Lasting twelve years (617-629), the Persian occupation was unpopular with the Copts, and the restoration of Roman rule by Heraclius was greeted as a liberation. The relative success, after 631, of the policies of unity between Chalcedonian and Non-Chalcedonians must have been caused at least in part, by the memories of the peace between communities which existed under Eulogius and John the

[69]Cf. an English tr. in E. Dawes and N. H. Baynes, *Three Byzantine Saints,* London, 1948 (reprt. Crestwood, NY, 1977).

[70]According to the *Life, there* were only seven Chalcedonian churches in 611 (probably a consequence of the patriarchal vacancy in 609-11), but John succeeded in increasing their number to seventy (*Life,* 5; tr. cit., p. 201).

Merciful. Unfortunately, that union was vitiated theologically ("mono-energism") and, soon morally compromised by the brutality of patriarch Cyrus (see below).

Be it as it may, the overall history of Christian Egypt in the years preceding the Muslim conquest (642) leaves one with the impression that religious unity remained possible. There was inconsistency and brutality in the Byzantine rule. But most Egyptians continued to feel that their "popes" were not only called to defend local cultural identity, but also to preserve the orthodox faith in the entire world and thus in the empire. Their opposition to Chalcedon was motivated by misguided stubbornness, but their "catholic" self-awareness left hope for the future. It was exemplified not only in the memory of the great archbishops Athanasius and Cyril—whom the Chalcedonians also venerated—but also in the personality of Theodosius, friend of Justinian and Theodora. Only the Muslim conquest, by establishing an age-long barrier between Constantinople and Egypt, sanctioned the Coptic sense of self-sufficiency and isolation. But even then, the mainstream of Coptic Christianity, forgetting the "Gaianite," the "Tritheist" and other aberrations, remained faithful to the "Cyrillian" heritage, whose central place in orthodox christology was never denied by the Chalcedonians.

The strong sense of Christian—and "imperial"—unity also expressed itself in missionary expansion (see above, chapter 4) in East Africa and Southern Arabia, areas which naturally fell into the orbit of Alexandria. Although this expansion was carried out primarily by Monophysites, the empire, throughout the sixth century, gave it protection and support, obviously counting on the success of its unionist policies towards the anti-Chalcedonian opposition. Thus St Longinus, the great missionary to Nubia, had been ordained by patriarch Theodosius in Constantinople (566). The recent excavations in the region indicate that the Christian communities in Nubia used Greek in their liturgy (together with Coptic and Nubian), and that their architecture and art imitated Constantinopolitan models.[71] Similarly, just as they maintained close friendship with the Arab Ghassanid "phylarchs" of Northwestern Arabia, the emperors of the sixth century cultivated relations with the Axumite (Ethiopian) kingdom, and supported its con-

---

[71]Cf. K. Michalowski, *Faras: die Kathedrale aus den Wüstensand,* Zürich, 1967; E. Dinkler, ed. *Kunst und Geschichte Nubiens in christlicher Zeit,* Recklinghausen, 1970; cf. also Frend, *The Rise,* pp. 297-303.

quest of the Yemen, where Persian-supported Nestorians and Jews, not Monophysites, represented the opposition to Byzantine influence.

It is therefore only the Muslim conquest which gave the anti-Chalcedonian schism its real permanence not only in Egypt itself, but also the entire Red Sea region.

5. *Christianity in Persia: Armenians, Jacobites and Nestorians*

Since the very origins of their communities, Armenian and Syrian Christians had suffered from the age-long competition between the Roman and the Sassanian Persian empires, whose borders—constantly modified by wars or by diplomacy—crossed through Armenia and Mesopotamia, dividing Christian populations living on both sides. Since the emperors of Constantinople acted as protectors of Chalcedonian Orthodoxy, it was in the obvious interest of Christians in Persia to define their own ecclesiastical affiliation, in terms which would not make them appear as foreign agents in the eyes of the Persian kings. This encouraged a self-determination by Syrians against the council of Ephesus (431) and by Armenians against Chalcedon (451).

Since the time of St Gregory the "Illuminator" the Armenians seem to have "indigenized" Christianity very rapidly, by making it an integral part of the life of the nation as a whole, and of the various clans within it. Of course, the Christian tradition going back to St Gregory and continued by St Mesrop, was catholic and missionary in scope: both Scripture ad liturgy were translated in all the languages of the region,[72] but the episcopate—and later the Armenian catholicosate —became a hereditary function. The primatial see was closely linked to the Arsacid dynasty, whereas "the most effective limitation of royal control over the ecclesiastical hierarchy stemmed not from as yet unformulated canonical regulations, but from the irrevocable hereditary privileges that united the Armenian secular and ecclesiastical magnates against any encroachment on the part of the crown."[73] If the catholicos was the head of the national church controlled by the king, the bishops felt themselves to be pastors of individual clans and even signed

[72]Cf. supra, p. 104.
[73]N. G. Garsoian, "Secular jurisdiction over the Armenian church (fourth-seventh centuries)," in *Harvard Ukrainian Studies* VII (*Okeanos*, Essays presented to Ihor Sevcenko), 1983, p. 250; see the significant texts, quoted *ibid.*, pp. 233-4.

conciliar acts accordingly, without territorial titles of cities, as was commonly accepted elsewhere.[74] The councils of the Armenian church were actually assemblies of bishops together with aristocratic clan rulers,[75] which determined the faith of the nation not only in religious, but also in political and cultural terms. These conditions were created by the imperative to survive, as a minority, within Persian Zoroastrian culture, but it also set a pattern for relations with Byzantium. Although the Persian rule was hated—it manifested itself frequently in violent persecutions of Christianity—the Armenians had no choice but to remain loyal to the Sassanians, and even make formal use of Persian protection, whenever they had to oppose the Chalcedonian emperors of Constantinople. But they also occasionally sought Roman help against the Persians, although their appeals to Constantinople were often unsuccessful. Significantly, both pro-Chalcedonian and anti-Chalcedonian texts signal direct interventions by Persian kings in such issues, as Armenian ecclesiastical independence from the Greek church and the gathering of councils rejecting Chalcedon.

These facts do not imply that the acceptance of Monophysitism by the Armenian church was exclusively a matter of Persian political pressure. Indeed, the main Christian church in Persia, whose contacts with the Persian court were constant and immediate, was the Syrian Nestorian catholicosate of Seleucia-Ctesiphon. Nestorianism was therefore a politically acceptable option for the Armenians, and pressures from the Syrians in that direction were strong in the first decades of the fifth century. Among the reasons which determined Armenian religious options, fear of Syrian Nestorianism played an important role. This fear had been instilled in them already in the aftermath of the council of Ephesus (431) at the time of the translation activity of St Mesrop, under the catholicos Isaac (390-439). Temporarily deposed in 428, Isaac was replaced by several catholicoi appointed from Ctesiphon. But resistance to Nestorianism was instigated by letters from Cyrillian theologians like Acacius of Melitene, whom the exiled Isaac had consulted specifically on the matter (433). The efforts of Isaac and Mesrop to create a distinct Armenian literature and culture were motivated, at least in part, by the need to protect Armenia (and Georgia) from Syrian Nestorian monopoly in Persia.

[74]Cf. for the council of 505/6: Mersapuh, bishop of the Mamikonean; Xabbary, bishop of the Arcruni; Sahe, bishop of the Amatuni; cf. ibid., pp. 223-4.

[75]Cf. Karekin Sarkissian, *The Council of Chalcedon and the Armenian Church*, London, 1965 (repr. New York, 1975), p. 205.

Following the period of direct contacts with Constantinople, the Armenians were cut off from the empire by war in 451. They were not involved at all in the events of the council of Chalcedon. In 451, the Armenian rebellion against Persian rule was vanquished in Avarayr, and in 454 catholicos Joseph and several bishops were killed by the Persians. No help came from Byzantium.

During the second half of the fifth century, Nestorianism continued to be promoted vigorously in Persia by the famous bishop Barsauma of Nisibis, and was strongly supported by the Persian court. Meanwhile, since emperors Zeno and Anastasius began interceding for the Monophysites in Persia, new contacts were established with the Armenians. In 505-6, as relations between Byzantium and Persia were improving, the Armenian catholicos Babgen, at a council held in Dvin, took delight in repudiating Nestorianism and affirming a traditional Cyrillian confession, while of course, rejecting Eutyches. He condemned the great leaders of the Antiochene school, in particular Theodore of Mopsuestia, Ibas, Theodoret and Nestorius, as well as Barsauma, and affirmed that "the Greeks, the Armenians, the Georgians and the Aghouans have the same rule of faith."[76] This was in essential agreement with the policies of Zeno's *Henotikon* which prevailed at that time in Byzantium, so that the Armenians rightly considered themselves at that moment as being part of a universal consensus, opposed to the isolated Nestorians. Several councils meeting in Dvin confirmed this attitude, even after the rejection of the *Henotikon* by Justin I in 518.

In 551-5, however, the Armenian Church came in closer contact with distinctly Monophysite Syrian communities of Mesopotamia, which happened to belong to the Julianist anti-Severian trend, and maintained the doctrine of incorruptibility of Christ's body before his resurrection ("aphthartodocetism"). Excommunicated by the mainstream Severian Monophysites, the "aphthartodocetists" asked for the protection of the Armenian catholicos Nerses II (548-557). The latter

---

[76]Cf. long extracts of the texts in Sarkissian, *op. cit.,* pp. 196 ff. Together with many historians, the author considers the council of 505-6 as an official rejection of Chalcedon by the Armenians. For problems of text authenticity and other controversial issues, see also V. Inglisian, *Chalkedon,* II, p. 364-370; J. Mécérian, *Histoire et institutions de l'église arménienne,* Beirut, 1965, pp. 64-66. The problem is that a critical mention of Chalcedon (not really different from that which is found in the *Henotikon*) is found not in the synodal letter itself, but only in a second, personal letter of the catholicos, the authenticity of which is in doubt. Otherwise, the faith defined at Dvin is in perfect conformity with that of the Byzantine empire at the time *i.e.* the *Henotikon.*

agreed to consecrate them a bishop, named Abdisho and, holding a new synod in Dvin (555), formally condemned not only Eutyches, the *Three Chapters,* Nestorius and—this time quite explicitly—the *Tome of Leo* and the council of Chalcedon, but also Severus of Antioch, for his doctrine of "corruptibility" of Christ's body. After this council, the Armenian catholicosate of Dvin firmly adopted the Monophysite position, together with a moderate form of Julianism or "aphthartodocetism"[77]

Theological, historical, cultural and political factors were thus involved in this evolution of the official position of the Armenians in Persia. These included the necessities of survival, a theological and cultural defensiveness towards the Syrian catholicosate of Seleucia-Ctesiphon, and the confusion created by the contradictions of imperial policies in Constantinople, as well as the difficulty, faced by all non-Greeks, to understand the technical terminology of the christological disputes.

Nevertheless, throughout this period of the Byzantine empire, ethnic Armenians occupied a social position second only to that of the Greeks.[78] The fact that the two greatest Byzantine generals of Justinian's time, Belisarius and Nerses, were Armenians illustrates their role among the Byzantine military. Emperors Maurice and Heraclius, as well as several of their successors, were themselves of Armenian descent. Obviously, Armenians who were part of the imperial establishment, belonged to the official orthodox Chalcedonian church, as did many Armenian communities in Eastern Asia Minor, who were under Roman rule. Armenian ecclesiastical affiliation was, of course, of some political importance for both the Byzantines and the Persians, especially since Armenia was the field of battle between the two empires. It is quite probable, therefore, that if the Byzantines had been more successful in their wars with Persia, Chalcedonism would have prevailed in Armenia.

In 572, an Armenian rebellion, led by Vardan Mamikonean, temporarily destroyed Persian power in Dvin, receiving help from emperor Justin II. A forceful Persian counter offensive forced prince Vardan, the catholicos John II and the other leaders of the rebellion

---

[77]Armenian scholars and theologians do not agree even today, as to the exact significance of this "Julianism" (cf. references in Sarkissian, *op. cit.,* p. 215). It remains, however, that the condemnation of Severus became a part of official Armenian doctrine, precisely because of this "Julianist" commitment.

[78]Cf. P. Charanis, *The Armenians in the Byzantine Empire* (Lisbon, 1963).

to flee to Constantinople, where Justin II had recently published his "program," strongly reaffirming Cyrillian christology, while maintaining Chalcedon. In 573, the Armenians, including the catholicos, accepted Church union and took communion with the Chalcedonians. The catholicos John II died in Constantinople the next year.

The extraordinary settlement between Byzantium and Persia reached in 591 emperor Maurice, through his support and friendship with Chosroes II, gave the Roman empire control over most of Armenia. The river Azat served as the dividing line, with Dvin, the residence of the Catholicos, still on the Persian side, but right at the Byzantine border. Invited to participate in a council of union, the catholicos Moses II, issued a famous rebuttal: "I shall not cross the Azat river, to eat the baked bread of the Greeks, nor will I drink their hot water."[79] However, a majority of Armenian bishops, who were living on the Byzantine side of the border, met at Theodosiopolis (Erzerum) in 593 and elected a new Chalcedonian catholicos, John III Bagarantsi, who resided in Avan, across the river from Dvin, until his arrest and deportation by the Persians in 611. The formal acceptance of Chalcedon by the Georgian catholicos of Mtskheta, Kirion (600-1), a former secretary of Moses II, and the difficulties faced by anti-Chalcedonian Armenians in electing a successor to Moses, even in Persian occupied lands, seems to indicate that, under Maurice, there was a close chance for a total Chalcedonian restoration in Armenia—and in the whole of the Caucasian region.

As in Egypt, however, the Persian invasion interrupted the efforts at reunification, until the new and significant initiatives taken by Heraclius, following his victory over Chosroes II.

Since Persia served as a refuge for all dissidents from the Roman empire, and since Syriac-speaking Christian communities had always existed on both sides of the border, it was inevitable that all the various factions, found among the Syrians, including Jacobites and Nestorians, would spread to Persia as well. There is information that christological disputes were taking place in 497, under Nestorian catholicos Babai, when two bishops, Papa of Beit-Lapat and Yazad of Rew-Ardasir, opposed the dominant Antiochian (*i.e.* "Nestorian") position and

---

[79]Quoted in G. Garitte, *La Narratio de rebus Armeniae.* Ed. critique et commentaire. CSCO 132, Subsidia 4, Louvain, 1952, pp. 226-7. The allusion is obviously to the use of the leavened bread and the *zeon,* or hot water, poured in the chalice before communion, by the orthodox Greeks. Armenians use unleavened bread and unmixed wine in the liturgy.

refused to attend the council in Seleucia-Ctesiphon.[80] Other sources inform us of the activities of Simeon, bishop of Beit Arsham, known as the "Persian Sophist," who was travelling around Persia, struggling against Nestorianism.[81] Simeon was among the Syrians who came to Dvin in 506, seeking protection from the Armenian catholicos Babgen and provoking the solemn declaration by which the Armenian church opposed Nestorianism and confirmed a Cyrillian confession, consonant with the *Henotikon*.[82]

The author of the *Life* of John of Tella informs us that, by 536, in spite of support received from the Armenians, the "true faith," i.e. Monophysitism, was almost extinct in Persia, because of Nestorian persecutions. With the approval of Severus, John then consecrated Monophysite bishops for Persia.[83] The clandestine activities of Jacob Bar'Addai and his followers further reinforced the Monophysite communities in Persia. In 559, Jacob consecrated Abudemneh as bishop of Taghrit. The latter's missionary activities included the baptism of a son of king Chosroes I. Some of the Syrian Monophysites were followers of Julian of Halicarnassus, and their impact on the Armenian Church was mentioned earlier, but the majority remained faithful to the Severian patriarchs of Antioch. By the end of the sixth century, a Jacobite metropolitan resided in the monastery of Mar Mattai in Mesopotamia. In 629, with the approval of the patriarch Athanasius, the "Camel Driver" of Antioch, a "great metropolitan," or "catholicos" with jurisdiction over twelve diocese of "the East," was established at an assembly held in Mar Mattai. The first "great metropolitan" was Marutha (629-49), who resided in Taghrith. The prestige and influence of the "great metropolitan," later called "maphrian," greatly increased with the Arab Muslim conquest of the area. Indeed, the Muslim rule extended over the formerly Byzantine Syria, where Monophysitism was strong, and allowed it to unite and expand. It also effectively ended the special privileges enjoyed, under the Persians, by

[80]Elias, *Vita Johannis Tellae,* ed. E. W. Brooks, CSCO, *Script. Syri,* III, 25, Paris, 1907, p. 39.

[81]Michael the Syrian, *Chron.* IX, 9-10, ed. cit., p. 165. His *Life* was written by John of Ephesus (*Lives of Eastern Saints,* 10).

[82]Cf. texts in Sarkissian, *op. cit.,* pp. 196-213. This author interprets this confession as already deliberately anti-Chalcedonian; for the problems connected with this view, see above, note 66.

[83]*Synodicon Orientale,* ed. J. B. Chabot, *Notices et extraits des manuscrits de la Bibliothèque Nationale,* 37, Paris, 1902, p. 314.

the Nestorian catholicosate of Seleucia-Ctesiphon.[84]

It is understandable therefore, that this continued presence of Monophysite communities was felt by the leaders of the catholicosate as a threat to their position in Persia and encouraged them to reaffirm their doctrinal commitments to what they considered as true orthodoxy: the christology of Theodore of Mopsuestia.

Rooted in Judeo-Christian traditions brought directly from Palestine, as early as the second and third centuries,[85] the church in Persia, constantly cut-off from the Roman world by wars and political competition between the empires, accepted the Nicaean definitions and principles of church order at its council of Seleucia in 410. The city of Seleucia served as residence to its supreme metropolitan, or catholicos. Situated on the Tigris, 20 miles southwest of the modern Bagdad, capital of Irak, it constituted a twin-city with ancient Ctesiphon, capital of the Persian "king of kings." The decisions of 410 were formally confirmed by the king, and the catholicosate came to be viewed as the official headquarters of Christianity in the Persian empire. This reorganization, which followed a period of fierce persecutions of Christianity by the Zoroastrians, was welcomed by the Syrian-speaking catholicosate as a model for future survival under the Persian kings, whose mood could be appeased by political loyalty. In order to show that loyalty was quite exclusive, the catholicos Dadisho (421-456) presided over another council in Markabta (429) which defined the catholicos as "successor of Peter" and the only head of the Church, without any dependence upon "Western Fathers." The "West" included Antioch, Alexandria and Constantinople, as well as Rome.[86]

These proclamations of religious self-sufficiency and political loyalty did not prevent the catholicos Babowai to be formally executed in 484 by king Peroz under the simple accusation of correspondence with the Byzantine emperor Zeno. The violent opposition to any contacts with the "West" was promoted by the famous bishop Barsauma of Nisibis, who must have been—at least indirectly—responsible for the death of Babowai. Councils, opposed to the dominant positions of the Church in the Roman empire—who then lived under the regime of the *Henotikon,* favorable to Monophysitism—were held, in Beit-

---

[84]On the Jacobites in Persia, see T. Dautiller "L'expansion de l'église syrienne en Asie centrale et en Extrême Orient," *L'Orient Syrien* 1 (1956), pp. 76-87.

[85]Cf. above, chapter IV.

[86]Cf. J. Labourt, *Le Christianisme dans l'empire perse sous la dynastie sassanide (224-632),* Paris, 1904, pp. 119-125.

Lapat (484), Beit-Adrai (485) and Seleucia (486), under the catholicos Acacius. Some of the decisions were directly sponsored by Barsauma, others he denounced before his death (*ca.* 495), as too moderate in terms of his own Nestorian convictions.

The council of Seleucia (486) confirmed a strictly "Antiochian" confession of faith about a union of two natures in Christ in one *prosopon*,[87] and also changed church discipline by forbidding celibacy to anyone, except monks; bishops, priests and deacons were required to marry. Barsauma himself contracted marriage with a nun. Second marriage was allowed for priests.[88] It appears that these measures were directly provoked by the Persian kings who, on the one hand, considered celibacy unacceptable and, on the other hand, were fighting Zoroastrian sectarians advocating community of women. A strict code, enforcing a middle road, was thus promulgated by the Persian church at the council of 497 under catholicos Babai (who was married himself): all clergy would be husbands of one wife.[89]

It remains, however, that the church suffered several decades of confusion, partly due to scandalous marital conduct of the clergy, such as consanguineous marriages, admittedly common in Zoroastrianism. Order returned with the election of Mar Aba as catholicos in 540.

A convert from Mazdeism and later a student in Nisibis, Mar Aba was an ever-curious and well-informed mind. He travelled to Roman territories and learned Greek in Edessa. In Alexandria, he met with Cosmas Indicopleustes, the famous traveller who, in spite of his Monophysite commitment, showed great admiration for Mar Aba. The latter also visited Egyptian monasteries and later travelled to Constantinople, where he stayed at least a year and made friends. The reign of Justin I (518-527) and the first years of Justinian were marked by anti-Monophysite reaction. Persian-Nestorians were apparently quite welcome in high places and included men like Paul the Persian, who was charged with conducting a debate with the Manichean Photinus. Paul's exegetical methods, adopted from Theodore of Mopsuestia, remained popular in later centuries. Mar Aba's trips to Alexandria and Constantinople illustrate the continued influence of Syrian Christians in the Byzantine world, independently of their confessional affiliation. Upon his return to Persia, he taught for a time at

[87]Cf. W. F. Macomber, "The Christology of the synod of Seleucia-Ctesiphon, A.D. 486," OCA XXIV, 1958, pp. 142-54.

[88]Cf. *Synodicon orientale,* ed. cit., pp. 302-3.

[89]*Ibid.,* p. 321.

Nisibis before being elected catholicos in 540. He became one of the most eminent leaders of the Persian church. His activities included the restoration of discipline among the married clergy and of unity among the bishops, which had been disturbed since the chaotic activities of Barsauma. Arrested in 541, when it was found that he was a convert from Mazdeism (such conversions were seen as capital offenses by the Persian authorities), he was saved from execution only by his extreme popularity among the Christians. Appearing personally before king Chosroes, he was able not only to secure forgiveness, but even to help the king stop a rebellion, in which many Christians had taken part. He died in 552, having greatly strengthened the church in Persia.

There is evidence that Justinian, having re-established a peace treaty with Persia in 561, obtained stipulations protecting the rights of Christians. Hoping to reunite the Nestorian catholicosate with Orthodoxy, he received a delegation of theologians, headed by Paul, bishop of Nisibis.[90] The negotiations failed. In 585, catholicos Ishoyabh (567-85) presided over another council in Seleucia, which marked a further and definitive estrangement from Byzantium. Reacting against the activity of Jacobites in Persia, the council published thirty-one canons which expressed the final doctrinal commitment of the Persian church. Not only did it confirm "Antiochene" christology, but—in direct opposition to the condemnation of the *Three Chapters* in Byzantium—declared that "it is forbidden to anyone, in secret or in public to criticize the Teacher of the Church [i.e. Theodore of Mopsuestia], to reject his holy writings and to adopt other commentaries of Scripture . . ." (canon 3).[91] No personal mention of Nestorius was made by the Persian councils of the period; by canonizing Theodore, the church defined itself as "Mopsuestian," rather than "Nestorian," which, in terms of doctrinal content is certainly a more accurate description of its basic christological stand. After the Fifth council (553), however, which had formally condemned Theodore, the Persian church was placed in direct conflict with Byzantine orthodoxy.

In spite of its isolation and the difficult conditions of its survival, the Persian church was extraordinarily rich in theological minds. The exegetical tradition of Theodore of Mopsuestia was continued and

---

[90]Not to be confused with "Paul the Persian," received in 527. On the episode, see A. Guillaumont, "Justinien et l'église de Perse," DOP 23-24 (1969-70), pp. 49-50, 62-66.
[91]*Synodicon orientale*, ed. cit., p. 400.

developed by dozens of writers. Their commentaries on both the Old and the New Testament are mostly known only by their titles,[92] but many manuscript treasures in the Syriac language have not been studied yet. The doctrine of the Incarnation, on which all contemporary Christian divisions were focused, was also reexamined by theologians. One of them, Henana, a famous teacher at the school of Nisibis seems to have protested against the exclusive authority of Theodore of Mopsuestia, and preferred the exegesis of St John Chrysostom. His ideas, obviously closed to Chalcedonian orthodoxy, were criticized by the Nestorian theologian Babai the Great (569-628), who, as abbot of Mount Izala, near Nisibis, was one of the leaders of the remarkable revival of monasticism, following the catholicosate of Mar Aba. At a council held in 612, the church confirmed the views of Babai, whose *Book of Union* (i.e. of divinity and humanity in Christ) became the standard confession of Nestorianism in Persia: Christ possessed, not only two natures, but also two *hypostases*.[93]

Following the failed attempts at restoring Christian unity in the East by emperor Heraclius after his victory under Chosroes II (see below), the Muslim conquest froze all the Christian communities in their isolation for centuries.

Opposed by the Jacobites and rejected by the Armenians, the catholicos of Seleucia-Ctesiphon preserved for a time his jurisdiction over the Arab Christian Kingdom of Hira, until the latter's disappearance after the Muslim invasions. But the church expanded further East. Throughout the Middle Ages, the Nestorians maintained the extraordinary zeal, which had characterized Syrian Christianity from the beginnings. As the most accessible Christian center for Indian Christians, the catholicosate continued for centuries to appoint bishops in India where the East Syrian liturgy and language would be preserved until the Portuguese conquest of the late fifteenth century. Nestorian missionaries evangelized Hephthalite Huns on the river Oxus, and, in 549, the catholicos Mar Aba consecrated a bishop for them. If the famous "Nestorian stone" of Sianfu in China is authentic, its inscription, dated 781, witnesses to the presence of a mission sent by catholicos Ishoyabh II (628-643) to that country. In the eighth to

---

[92]Cf. a list in R. Duval, *La littérature syriaque*, Paris, 1907, pp. 71-4, and *passim*. Recently, a great number of Syriac manuscripts were studied by Arthur Vööbus, making that rich branch of ancient Christian literature more easily accessible. On Vööbus' work and innumerable publications, see R. H. Fischer, *A Tribute to Arthur Vööbus*, Chicago, 1977.

[93]Cf. A. Guillaumont, *op. cit.*, p. 61.

tenth centuries there is countinued evidence of the presence of Nestorian Christian communities in Central Asia, with bishops in Samarkand
and Bukhara. Marco Polo found a church in the Mongol capital of
Karakorum. The court of the Tatar Khans, who invaded Europe in
the thirteenth century, had Christian priests accompanying it in its
travels. This extraordinary missionary enterprise seems to have ended
only with the establishment of the Ming dynasty in China, late in the
fourteenth century. In the sixteenth century, following the end of
Portuguese occupation of India, the Malabar Christians reestablished
their hierarchy through the Jacobite patriarch of Antioch, which involved a change from Nestorianism to a Monophysite confession and
the West-Syrian liturgical tradition.

The modern history of the Nestorian Christians is a tragic one.
Often designated as "Assyrians," they saw their numbers greatly
reduced by Western proselytism (the creation of the "Chaldean"
church, united with Rome) and through massacres perpetrated by
Muslim Kurds. A group, headed by a bishop, joined Chalcedonian
Orthodoxy through the offices of the Russian Church in Urmia in 1898,
but it was dispersed in the aftermath of World War I and the Russian
revolution.

*   *   *

What, then, were the main reasons for the tragic divisiveness of
Eastern Christianity in the fifth and sixth centuries? We have already
referred to several factors usually mentioned by historians: the ethnic
and cultural differences, opposition to Byzantine imperial rule, the need
for survival under Persian and, later, Islamic occupations. All of these
elements did undoubtedly contribute to the perpetuation of the schisms.
By themselves, however, they were never used as formal justification
for divisions and, therefore, cannot be considered in isolation, as
sufficient explanations. It is a fact, for instance, that while Persian rule
encouraged Christians to break ties with the "West," not all of them
took the same option: Nestorians, Jacobites and Armenians established
themselves as distinct groups. Within the Roman Empire, on the other
hand, the socio-cultural factor was not decisive either, since the leadership of all the factions de facto belonged, throughout this period, to
educated Greek-speaking theologians. It is unavoidable, therefore to
recognize that those of them who rejected unity within the Orthodox

Church (whose position was both Chalcedonian and Cyrillian and which refused to be tied up by one single terminological system) did so not through misunderstanding, but through stubborn conviction—"Cyrillian fundamentalism" in the case of the Monophysites.

In practice, there existed no other external form of Church unity than the one provided by the imperial system, defined by Justinian. The Monophysites knew this well and, although they had suffered from its brutality, they nevertheless constantly tried to swing the imperial system in their favor. Occasionally, they succeeded, and were then happy to profit from its political power themselves. But the empire was not always brutal. Indeed, it would be unfair to simply forget the wide use of "ecumenism" (in the modern sense) by both the emperors and the Chalcedonian orthodox Church, *i.e.* the attempts at terminological compromises, the favors bestowed upon leaders of the opposition, the readiness to correct and clarify previous definitions (even to the point of condemning the dead, as in the case of the *Three Chapters*), the willingness—as under Justin II—to forget former anathemas against leaders of Monophysitism. Many contemporary historians, who dislike Cyrillian christology, view all these episodes as Machiavellian and "caesoro-papistic" betrayals of Chalcedon. We have tried to emphasize the fact that such an outlook is, in our opinion, generally wrong.

Without denying the dangers and the abuses of imperial power, which occurred in particular instances, the system as such, which had been created by Theodosius I and Justinian, did not deprive the Church from its ability to define dogma through conciliarity. But conciliarity presupposed the existence of a mechanism, making consensus possible and effective. Local churches needed to be grouped into provinces and patriarchates, and patriarchates were to act together to reach an agreement valid for all. The empire provided the universal Church with such a mechanism. The emperors, while they believed to be God's appointees, did not consider themselves infallible, and were not considered such by anyone. The imperial system was showing its imperfection every day, but had no practical alternative, at least in the East.

Such an alternative, however, was gradually taking shape up in the Latin West in the form of the Roman papacy. Seen in the perspective of the sixth century, the papal alternative to imperial unity was, of course, quite unrealistic. The Roman church was seen very much as part of the imperial system, and the popes themselves were not yet denying their loyalty to it. However, the concept of "apostolicity" which they also defended, gradually raised, before the consciousness of world Christendom, the issue which would dominate it during the Middle Ages: did Christ Himself provide the Universal Church with an obligatory structure, based on Rome's apostolicity, or did He confide Church unity to a responsible consensus of local churches, which were left to actualize it in conformity with changing historical requirements?

CHAPTER IX

ST GREGORY THE GREAT AND THE BYZANTINE PAPACY

The reconquest of Italy by the armies of Justinian was a long and bloody enterprise which resulted in the devastation of the country. Among many destroyed cities, Rome itself suffered greatly. Occupied by the imperial general Belisarius (536), unsuccessfully besieged by the Gothic king Wittigis (537), it faced a long and painful blockade by Totila (543-546), which ended with its falling back to Gothic rule. The population was decimated by hunger, disease and massacres. Only in 553 did Roman troops, under the command of Nerses, reenter the city after finally defeating Totila.

In the now ruined old capital, the Church represented the only remaining moral and economic power. Although the revenues from its lands in central Italy had been drastically reduced by the devastations of the war, the pope could secure income and supplies from immense possessions in Provence, Africa and, especially, Southern Italy and Sicily, where the Byzantine reconquest had occurred rapidly without ruining the countryside.[1] Furthermore, since the ruling classes had been decimated and since the administrators sent from the East were rather ill-prepared to master the chaotic situation of Italy, the pope, the bishops and the clergy represented by far the most efficient administrative structure remaining in the country. In his *Pragmatic Sanction*, Justinian formally restored Roman rule in Italy (Aug. 13, 554), but

[1]Cf. the figures in P. Llewelyn, *Rome in the Dark Ages,* London, 1970, p. 80-81, 168-9. The lands owned by the Roman church covered more than 500,000 hectares (G. Le Bras, "L'église romaine et les grandes églises occidentales après la mort de Grégoire le Grand," *Settimane di studio del Centro di Studi sull'altro medioevo,* V, 1958, p. 199).

doubting the competence of the imperial administrators, he entrusted the bishops with the task of supervising the civil, educational and financial systems. This crucial role to be assumed by the Church after the reconquest had been foreseen by the imperial government even before the event. This explains why Justinian sought to reestablish normal relations with the popes since the beginning of his reign.

Thus, the Church alone was in a position to serve the Italian population by giving it food and securing public order, but it now fulfilled those functions within the framework of the imperial system, of which the "old Rome" was a part again. At the same time, beyond the borders of reconquered Byzantine Italy, the Roman bishops, until their "defection" to the Franks in 754, continued the task initiated by their predecessors of the fifth century in contributing wherever they could to the Christianization of the Barbarian kingdoms in Britain, Gaul, Spain, and Germany. Compared to the East, Western Christendom in the sixth and seventh centuries was not greatly preoccupied with doctrinal issues. Even the schism of Aquileia, connected with the debate on the *Three Chapters,* actually involved Church authority, rather than the substance of Christology. Among the leaders of the Church, few were theologians. After the gradual disappearance of the Roman educated class, represented by men like Boethius, executed by Theodoric in 524, and Cassiodorus, who had established a famous monastery school, the *Vivarium,* and died *circa* 585, there could be little concern for the preservation of the Greco-Latin philosophic tradition. Latin Christian literature was confined largely to liturgical poetry, hagiography and history. Educated clerics like St Gregory the Great and St Isidore of Seville, had little ambition beyond moral teaching and encyclopedic compilation of patristic or scientific data. No minds of the ability of a Leo the Great, a Cassian, a Caesarius of Arles, or a Fulgentius of Ruspe—who in the fifth century, still exposed Latin thought to the challenges of the patristic age—appeared in the sixth or seventh centuries.

The young and dynamic forces of Western Christendom were rather directed at mission, monastic asceticism and the organization of the Church within the new "barbarian" world. The result of their efforts would eventually evolve into the new medieval Latin civilization.

1. *Rome, Ravenna and Byzantium; St Gregory the Great*

Residence of the last emperors of the West and later of the Gothic kings of Italy, the city of Ravenna, where Theodoric had built beautiful palaces and churches, became again, after the reconquest, the center of the imperial administration, while the ancient capital, still governed by a *praefectus urbis,* was dominated by the pope and his court. Until 567 vice-regal powers were exercised in Ravenna by general Nerses, the vanquisher of Totila. In 568, however, his successor, Longinus, was threatened by an invasion of the Lombards—a Germanic, still Arian people who soon dominated most of Northern Italy, with a capital in Pavia. The Lombards also established the duchies of Spoleto and Benevento further South. The Byzantine authorities tried, with very limited success, to fight the Lombard power by securing the alliance of Childebert II, the Frankish catholic king of Austrasia (575-596). But Frankish attacks did not succeed in destroying the Lombards. In order to consolidate imperial power in Italy, emperor Maurice then created the so-called exarchate of Ravenna, with all civil and military powers concentrated in the hands of the exarch (*ca.* 584). The actual power of the exarch covered dispersed cities and provinces, *i.e.* Liguria (with capital in Genoa), Istria-Venetia (with the city of Aquileia), Aemilia (with Ravenna and the seaport of Ferrara), the area of Pentapolis, whose link to Rome was protected by the fortress of Perugia, and, finally, in the South, Naples, Apulia, Lucania and the Bruttium. Between these dispersed imperial possessions, the country was controlled by the Lombards, so that communications·were possible largely by sea.

Political divisions and constant wars made the position of the popes an even more important element in the preservation of *Romanitas* in Italy. However, their moral, canonical and economic powers were challenged by the Lombards' allegiance to Arianism and by the schism of Aquileia, provoked by the condemnation of the *Three-Chapters* at the Fifth council, which was seen by many in the West as a betrayal of Chalcedon.

The population of Rome had been greatly reduced during the Gothic wars. It was now concentrated primarily around the Lateran palace, where the pope resided, and the *basilica aurea* ("Golden Basilica"), which served as the bishop's cathedral. Also, in the area of the Vatican hill, the "Leonine city" with its huge martyrium built upon the tomb of St Peter, its hospices and hostels, which surrounded the sanctuary, was visited annually by thousands of pilgrims. If, in the earlier period, popular piety always united Peter *and Paul*, as patrons of the church of Rome, the rise óf a Petrine ecclesiology, so well developed and professed by St Leo the Great, tended now to single out St Peter's basilica, as the real symbol of Rome's prestige. Nevertheless, St Paul's tomb, "beyond the walls" to the South of the city, never ceased to be venerated also. The fourth major papal basilica was, of course, that of St Mary's on the Esquilin. There were also twenty-eight parishes, or *tituli,* headed by priests. Whether he celebrated in one of the basilicas, or at a parish church, the bishop of Rome proceeded there with solemnity, accompanied by his clergy and stopping on the way for prayers at churches or holy places. These processions and "stations" became a characteristic of Roman (and Constantinopolitan) liturgy.

The city was divided into seven sections with a deacon in charge of ecclesiastical administration in each of the areas. An archpriest and an archdeacon headed the college of priests and the college of deacons respectively. The archdeacon was often considered as the presumptive successor of the reigning pope, although the close ties which existed with the imperial court also gave some advantages, in achieving papal succession, to the *apocrisiarius*—or permanent delegate—of the Roman church in Constantinople. In the seventh century, the number of refugees coming from the East increased the proportion of Greek clergy, so that, at times, Greek was becoming the language of the papal court and the synods.[2] Greeks, Syrians and Illyrians, as well as native Italians, were elected to the papal throne.

The administration of the church also used laymen, especially to manage the huge papal estates. These included the *primicerius,* head of the *defensores* (or solicitors for church interests) and the management of the *secretum,* or office of papal correspondence.

The remaining great wealth of the Church, made it into a banker of the imperial administration and allowed it, on several occasions, to provide crucial supplies to the embattled imperial armies, which were far away from their Eastern sources of money and equipment. St

[2]P. Llewelyn, *op. cit.,* p. 183; cf. also by far the most comprehensive recent study on Greek clergy in Rome by J. M. Sansterre, *"Les moines grecs et orientaux à Rome aux époques byzantine et carolingienne (milieu du IVe—fin du IXe s.),"* I-II, Bruxelles, 1980.

Gregory the Great, in one of his letters, called himself the paymaster of the imperial troops in Rome. This role of imperial ally did not prevent the Church from using its resources for extensive social work, especially when it was led by holy men like Pope Gregory, and from being viewed as the "treasury of the poor."[3]

Ecclesiastical affairs were discussed at annual synods of bishops, generally held on the anniversary of the reigning pope's consecration. We have seen earlier that direct jurisdictional powers of the Roman bishop over the West were actually much more restricted than those of the great Eastern patriarchs (particularly Constantinople and Alexandria), over their respective territories. The chaotic events of the sixth century did not contribute to any expansion of papal administration. In practice, papal power was limited to the bishops of the vicinity of Rome (*suburbicarii*), the South of Italy and the three big islands of Sicily, Sardinia and Corsica. Over those areas, the pope exercised the right of a metropolitan. He consecrated the bishops, following their election locally. Only in cases of disputed elections was the pope in a position to impose a candidate of his own choice.[4] Beyond those limits, the papal authority was primarily a matter of moral and doctrinal prestige. The church in Africa, in Spain and the provincial metropolitans of Northern Italy—Milan and Aquileia—were totally self-governing. The "patriarchal" powers of the pope over his vicars in Gaul and the Illyricum were limited to occasional appellate resolution of local conflicts.

The relations between the Roman bishops and the court of Constantiple were cordial—at least until the reign of Emperor Constans II and the monothelite crisis—but they were also marked by ambiguity. According to the strong local Roman tradition, which had been so distinctly formulated by St Leo I, the pope enjoyed authority by virtue of the Petrine apostolicity of his see, whereas the emperors tended to treat him as one of the two major "imperial" patriarchs, together with his colleague of the "New Rome" on the Bosphorus. No one, of course, objected against imperial control over papal elections, which had been exercised earlier by the Western emperors of the fifth century and by the Gothic kings as well. But the tension between the two conceptions of the Roman primacy manifested itself in such cases as

[3]Cf. for these different aspects of the role of the Church, P. Goubert, *Byzance avant l'Islam, II. Byzance et l'Occident sous les successeurs de Justinien*, 2.
[4]Cf. Richards, *Popes*, pp. 323-38.

the lingering conflict over the role of the bishop of Ravenna.

The city had been established as a major ecclesiastical center by Justinian's appointed bishop, Maximian (546-56), who was instrumental in completing several of Ravenna's churches, including St Vitalis, with its famous mosaic of Justinian and Theodora. Although tradition required that Ravenna's bishop be consecrated by the pope, his role soon became special because the city also served as the exarch's residence. Against objections by St Gregory the Great, he began wearing a *pallium,* in the Eastern manner, affirming his Eastern connection, while such a piece of episcopal ornament was seen in the West as a particular distinction granted only by the pope.[5] In 666, emperor Constans II formally established Ravenna's autocephaly,[6] a move which was immediately opposed by the popes. A succession of bishops of Ravenna (Maurus, Reparatus, Theodore, Damian) were nevertheless consecrated independently of Rome. The schism ended by a recognition of the pope's rights in 692, and later lost its *raison d'être* with the disappearance of imperial power in Italy.

This attempt of Constans II to formally establish Ravenna as the center of "imperial" Christianity in Italy was, in fact, an isolated incident. Since Justinian, the emperors consistently relied on Rome in their Western ecclesiastical policies, even when this required the use of the exarch's power to force the popes into compliance.

Except in Ravenna, the emperors did not interfere in local episcopal elections, but the appointment of the right person as bishop of the Roman church was seen by them as essential to the perpetuation of their rule in Italy. We have seen earlier how Belisarius deposed pope Silverius in 537, whose election had been approved by the Gothic king Theodahad and who was therefore accused of cooperation with the enemy. The unfortunate pontiff had good local credentials, being the son of pope Hormisdas, but he had refused to follow Theodora's policy of conciliation with the Monophysites. The appointment and

[5]Cf. P. Goubert, *op. cit.,* pp. 158-60; cf. also Y. Congar, *L'ecclésiologie du Haut Moyen-Age de St Grégoire le Grand à la désunion entre Byzance et Rome,* Paris, 1968, pp. 204-5.

[6]Doelger, *Reg.* 232-3; the story is also found in Agnellus, *Liber pontificalis ecclesiae Ravennatis,* MGH, *scr. rer. Longobardorum,* pp. 112-24; cf. Richards, *Popes,* pp. 196-6; P. Lemerle "Les répercussions de la crise de l'empire d'Orient au VIIe-siècle sur les pays d'Occident," *Settimane* V, 1, Spoleto, 1958, pp. 723-6; and, especially A. Simonini, *Autocefalia ed esarcato in Italia,* Ravenna, 1969, pp. 63-116. The term "autocephaly" implied an archbishop's independence from the regional metropolitan (*i.e.* the Roman bishop in the case of Ravenna) and a direct connection with Constantinople.

subsequent fate of his successor Vigilius illustrated the new dependence of the papacy upon Justinian's regime.

The normal procedure for papal elections followed four distinct stages: 1) Upon the death of the incumbent, the archpriest, the arch-deacon and the lay *primicerius* formally informed the emperor (or the exarch) of the see's vacancy, asking for permission to proceed with an election. 2) The election itself took place at the *basilica aurea* of the Lateran with the participation of the clergy and the people. 3) A formal document, signed by the archpriest and the candidate himself was submitted to the emperor (or the exarch), soliciting authorization to perform the consecration. 4) On the Sunday following the receipt of the imperial confirmation, three bishops under the traditional presi-dency of the bishop of Ostia, ordained the candidate and installed him as the new pope.

Since government action was required twice and since at least some elections were stormy, the vacancies frequently lasted for months.[7]

Following the death of Vigilius (555), the imperial authority played a decisive role in the election of Pelagius I (556-61). A deacon of the Roman church, Pelagius had distinguished himself—as pope Vigilius was absent in Constantinople—by protecting the population during the siege of Rome by Totila (543-6). He also played a role in seeking peace terms. Later, he joined the pope in the Eastern capital and became a staunch opponent of the condemnation of the *Three Chapters,* strongly advising the pope accordingly. After having been arrested in 553, he changed his mind on the issue of the *Three Chapters* and thus became a logical candidate for the papacy in 555.[8] In Italy, however, he was viewed as a turn-coat, and hostility to his election was so strong that only two bishops could be found to perform his consecration, with the bishop of Ostia being represented only by a priest. The rather short pontificate of Pelagius was marked by the be-ginning of the protracted "schism of Aquileia" (see below, pp. 310-4). However, his general record as a pastor, fighting corruption and

---

[7]Cf. the list of the vacancies in Richards, *Popes,* p. 365-6; significantly, in 468-536, under Gothic rule, vacancies were quite short—normally a week—because confirmation by the Gothic kings was readily available. Following the Byzantine reconquest, the need to obtain Constantinople's approval required vacancies lasting sometimes more than a year. Cf. the procedures of election in Llewelyn, *op. cit.,* pp. 130-2.

[8]Pelagius was a competent theologian and the evolution of his mind can be studied in his writings. Louis Duchesne has published his treatise *For the defense of the Three Chapters* (Studi e testi, 7, Vatican, 1932); cf. also by the same author, *L'Eglise,* pp. 219-25.

attempting to restore the church after the Gothic war, remained a good one.

His successors, John III (561-74), Benedict I (575-9) and Pelagius II (579-90) had to face the tragedies that accompanied the Lombard invasion (568). They were consistently loyal to the empire, in spite of the failure of the imperial authorities to provide active protection. In 589, there was also a natural catastrophe. The Tiber left its banks and flooded the center of Rome, destroying buildings and graineries, provoking hunger and a ravaging plague. Pope Pelagius II himself died of the disease and a unanimous popular demand brought St Gregory I to the "throne of Peter."

It is difficult to determine the one single reason why the title of "Great" was attached by tradition to the name of pope Gregory. In the Barbarian West, his sponsorship of the mission to England and the popularity of his writings[9] (he was the only pope of the period with writing abilities) explains his popularity, although, in Rome itself, the monastic style of his government and spirituality was rather detrimental to his prestige, so that he received a relatively brief notice in the *Liber Pontificalis*. No formal *Life* was composed until pope John VIII (872-882) commissioned a deacon John to write one.[10] In the East, St Gregory's popularity is entirely due to the Greek translation by pope Zacharias (741-52) of his *Dialogues,* containing lives of Italian saints. The book received wide distribution, and earned Gregory the surname of *Dialogos* in the Greek (and Slavonic) worlds.[11] It is the overall record of his life and his pontificate; his personal contacts with churchmen of the entire world from Georgia to Spain, and from England to Egypt; his correspondence with barbarian kings and queens; his asceticism and moral incorruptibility; his diplomatic wisdom and balanced personality; his pastoral concern for the poor; his feeling for the catholic nature of the Church—which made him one of the greatest and least questionable "icons," or models of a Christian bishop.

[9]These include an important collection of Letters, the *Dialogue,* the *Pastoral Rule* and several ethically oriented commentaries on Scriptures.

[10]This *Life,* written by John the Deacon, used local Roman traditions and archives and, in spite of its verbosity, represents—together with Gregory's own writings—a major source on his activities (text in P.L. 95, cols. 59-242). An anonymous English author and Bede the Venerable testify to the early veneration of St Gregory in England.

[11]The Slavonic equivalent of *Dialogos* is *Dvoeslov.* The Byzantine tradition—apparently only since the tenth century—attributes to Gregory the authorship of the Liturgy of the Presanctified Gifts. The reasons for this attribution have never been firmly established.

Born around 540 in a noble and pious Roman family, he inherited his parents' mansion on the *Clivus Scauri*—the slope of the Caelian hill —and large revenues. Still a young man, he was named prefect of the city, and experienced the problems of administering a ruined community, constantly menaced by Lombard raids and utterly underadministered by the distant imperial government of Constantinople. About the year 573, he resigned his position, used his revenues to establish six monasteries in Sicily and transformed his own house on the Caelian hill into a monastery dedicated to St Andrew, where he himself became a simple monk, under abbot Valentio. The *Rule* was similar to that of St Benedict, for whom, as founder of the monastic tradition in the West, St Gregory always nourished the greatest admiration.[12]

Although little is known about Gregory's education, which must have been limited to the basics of grammar and rhetoric,[13] he was among the rare educated persons in Rome, and was soon called to service at the papal court. In 579, pope Pelagius II ordained him a deacon and sent him as his *apocrisiarios* to Constantinople, where he stayed seven years. Except for a normal and articulate support for Chalcedonian orthodoxy, Gregory had little understanding of the theological problems besetting the East. He never learned Greek well,[14] and continued, even in Constantinople, to live in a community of Latin-speaking monks. This did not prevent him from befriending high-positioned people at the imperial court (where Latin was still spoken) and in the ecclesiastical world of the time. Thus, the Spanish, Visigothic bishop Leander of Seville, who was also sojourning in the imperial capital, encouraged Gregory to write his *Moralia* on the book of Job.

Having returned to his Roman monastic retreat, Gregory was

[12]The second book of Gregory's *Dialogues* is our primary source on St Benedict's life and work (*ca.* 480-*ca.* 547). His memory was very much alive both in the mind of St Gregory and in that of his contemporaries. This does not make it right to call Gregory a "Benedictine," a technical term which was not used before the fifteenth or sixteenth centuries.

[13]Gregory has been praised by this biographer John as a scholar in the liberal arts, but was judged severely by some modern historians, as an obscurantist. Such judgments, positive or negative, have a meaning only in the context of his times, in which educated people were quite rare in the West. For an overall objective discussion, see P. Riché, *Education et culture dans l'Occident barbare, VIe-VIIIe siècles*, Paris, 1962, pp. 187-200.

[14]Against the opinion expressed by most historians of the period, an attempt to show that Gregory knew *some* Greek was made by Joan M. Petersen "Did Gregory the Great Know Greek?", in Baker, D., ed., *The Orthodox Churches and the West* (Studies in Church History, 13, Oxford, 1976), pp. 121-34.

called in 590 to succeed Pelagius II, who had died of the plague. In order to escape the honor, he vainly requested emperor Maurice not to approve his election.

During his relatively short reign as pope (590-604) and in spite of an increasingly failing health, Gregory maintained a constant and intense pastoral activity. In Rome itself, he used the vast resources of the church to help the sick and the poor. The first monk ever to become bishop of Rome, he strengthened the discipline and morals of the clergy in the spirit of monastic strictness, discouraging worldliness and secular interests (even in the area of education). Greatly concerned with the good order of the liturgy, he encouraged the preservation of old local traditions and developed new ones. The *Sacramentary* and the *Antiphonary,* known under his name, reflect the evolution of the Roman liturgy during his period, although their text, as it is known today, is a version reedited under later popes. The musical system, known as Gregorian chant, is also traditionally connected with his reign. However, the pope was aware of the dangers of pure aestheticism. He forbade deacons to sing anything except the Gospel, in order to avoid the temptation—which obviously existed already at his time—to have men ordained to the diaconate for their voice only, rather than on the basis of their spiritual or administrative qualifications.

The "suburbicarian" dioceses, where the bishop of Rome exercised the rights of a metropolitan, continued, during the reign of Gregory, to elect their own bishops. The rights of the pope were limited to the canonical approval he gave to such elections, and to papal interventions occurring only when the local electors were unable to agree on a suitable candidate, as, for instance, during the long conflict in the church of Naples (591-601). The obligation of the bishops to attend the annual synod in Rome was generally upheld, except in the case of distant Sicily, whose bishops were allowed to come every three, or even five years only. In order to secure episcopal conciliarity in the big island, pope Gregory allowed in 591 the bishop of Syracuse to act as a papal vicar and hold disciplinary synods in Sicily—an obvious step towards decentralization and the development of a separate "metropolitan" province in Sicily. The papal liberality in the case of Sicily did not extend to Ravenna, whose archbishop—as we have seen earlier—wore the pallium, and sought independence from

Rome. Gregory's strong resistance succeeded, temporarily, at limiting his ambitions.

Pope Gregory had neither the power, nor the desire to exercise administrative jurisdiction beyond the "suburbicarian" dioceses. However, the moral prestige of his see was strong throughout the Christian West. His large correspondence contains numerous letters addressed to the bishops of Africa, particularly on the issue of Donatism, the old schism of the early fourth century, which still challenged the church. Since most of the West was now in the hands of "barbarian" kingdoms, the relations of those kingdoms with the church were, of course, a high priority in the pope's pastoral activities. We will discuss later the famous mission to distant England, sponsored by Gregory, and his contacts with Gaul. His most immediate concern, however, was the Lombard power in Italy—a rather brutal occupation of traditionally Roman lands by Arian Germanic kings and dukes, who not only fought directly the armies of the imperial exarch of Ravenna, but also opposed the spiritual authority of the pope among the Orthodox population by giving protection to the "schism of Aquileia." Frustrated by this situation and expressing the natural human reaction of a former Roman patrician, Gregory, in a letter to a friend in Constantinople, exclaims ironically: "I was made a bishop not of Romans, but of Lombards."[15] Elsewhere, he compares Rome to an eagle which has lost its feathers.[16] This Roman patriotism of Gregory justifies his total political loyalty to the empire. He writes to emperor Maurice as his "unworthy servant" (*indignis pietatis vestrae famulus*) and, since papal influence was more widely spread in the entire West than that of the exarch, he acts as a distributor of imperial decrees, even in cases when he disagrees with their content, as in the case of an order to refuse ordination to civil servants without their settling their obligations to the state.[17] This role of the papacy in the West, as a *de facto* imperial representative, will later serve as a psychologically important precedent for the assumption of independent civil powers by the popes.

However, Gregory did not always behave as a passive instrument of imperial policies. In his relations with the Lombards he adopted an independent attitude. Emperor Maurice and his exarch Romanus did not, for a long time, envisage any peaceful settlement. The pope

[15]*Epp.* I, 30, MGH, *Ep.* I, 43.
[16]*Hom. on Ez.* 2, 6, 23; P.L. 76, col. 1011 B.
[17]For a good discussion of this issue, see P. Batiffol, *Saint Grégoire le Grand,* fifth ed., Paris, 1931, pp. 195-7.

nevertheless established contacts with the Lombard king Agilulf through his orthodox wife Theodelinda. Using bribes and conciliation, he prevented the capture of Rome (592). He was denounced as a traitor by Romanus and mildly chided by emperor Maurice for his independent initiatives in Italy. But after 598 his policies won the day when, under the new exarchs Callinicus and Smaragdus, peaceful settlements were reached with the Lombards. Adaloald, son of Agilulf and Theodelinda, even received orthodox baptism (603). The policies of peaceful settlements were continued by emperor Phocas, the murderer of Maurice (602), who was facing a new war in the East with Persia. This partially explains, but hardly justifies, the joy of Gregory at the installation of this bloody tyrant as emperor in Constantinople. As a response to the pope's support, Phocas issued a special decree in favor of Roman primacy and was glorified in Rome by the erection of a column in the forum in his honor. The column still stands today.

The relationships which prevailed at the time of Gregory, between the church of Rome and the other major centers of Christendom show that, while clearly maintaining the moral authority of his see, the pope understood his ministry in terms of service, rather than power. In letters addressed to Dominicus, archbishop of Carthage, he formally acknoweldged the rights, i.e. the total judicial independence, of the African church. He also maintained a routine correspondence with Eastern patriarchs, especially Eulogius of Alexandria, Anastasius of Antioch, and even Kirion of Georgia. His donations to monasteries in the Holy Land and Sinai were remembered for centuries.

Some difficulties arose, however, between Gregory and the church of Constantinople. In 595, the pope formally canceled the condemnation for heresy issued by patriarch John the Faster against the two Greek clerics, John and Athanasius, who had appealed personally to Rome. The case illustrates the fact that Gregory was fully aware of the Roman *principatus* defined by his predecessors. He was ready to give a somewhat extended meaning to the canons of the council of Serdica (343) which allowed Rome to cancel judgments of other metropolitans and establish courts of appeals with bishops of the neighborhood. In the case of the above mentioned clerics, Gregory adopted more direct procedures and had the case judged in Rome.

It is significant, however, that he did not deny that the bishop of Constantinople ranked second, after Rome, and above Alexandria, among the major sees. This traditional Byzantine order, which had been established by the council of Constantinople (381), but challenged by St Leo in the fifth century, appears in Gregory's synodical letter, announcing his election in 590.[18] But this realism of the pope concerning the position of the "New Rome" did not prevent his famous protest against the title of "ecumenical patriarch" used by John the Faster. Already challenged by Gregory's predecessor, Pelagius II in 588, the title was used repeatedly by patriarch John in his correspondence with Rome in 595 concerning the presbyters John and Athanasius. In letters addressed to John the Faster himself, to emperor Maurice and to empress Constantina, St Gregory shows a surprising misunderstanding of the title's true significance. Used previously by patriarchs of Alexandria, Constantinople, and other sees, as well as Rome, the title "ecumenical" (οἰκουμενικὸς) affirmed a certain authority within the framework of the *oikoumene*, the "inhabited earth."[19] It was *de facto* applied primarily to the bishop of Constantinople. In the mind of the Byzantines, it certainly did not imply any challenge to the "apostolic" and moral authority of the Old Rome, since the title was readily used in the case of the bishop of Rome as well. Its more regular adoption in the late sixth century may have derived from the desire of the bishops of Constantinople to assert their "imperial" influence against the monophysite resistance. Be it as it may, St Gregory gave the issue an ecclesiological dimension which proves, on the one hand that, even after his long sojourn in Constantinople, the exaggerated use of titles by the Byzantines remained foreign to his straightforward Latin mind, and, on the other hand, that he understood all primacies, including his own, in a way which excluded the existence of a "universal" bishop.

Always translating (rather incorrectly) the word "ecumenical" as "universal," he accused patriarch John of unpardonable pride and power-seeking. Anyone aspiring to be a "universal bishop," he wrote to the emperor, is playing the role of the Antichrist, since even Peter the Apostle, to whom Christ confided His sheep, was never called "universal apostle."[20] If one bishop is *universal*, the others are no bishops at all.[21] This last idea he tried to impress in letters addressed to his colleagues, the patriarchs Anastasius of Antioch and Eulogius

[18]*Ep* I, 24, MGH, *Ep* I, 28.
[19]Cf. a discussion of the title with abundant bibliography in Beck, *Kirche,* pp. 63-4.
[20]*Ep* V, 37; MGH, *Ep* I., 323.
[21]*Ep* IX, 156; MGH, *Ep* II, 158.

of Alexandria. The results were mixed. In his answer, Anastasius directly reproved the pope, suggesting that he was acting out of jealousy. Eulogius, in a more conciliatory mood, promised, "in obedience to Gregory's commands" not to use the title any more when writing to his colleague of Constantinople. Also, trying to please Gregory, Eulogius addressed him as *universal pope,* another unexceptional title frequently used for the Roman bishop. But the good St Gregory protested again:

> "I beg you never let me hear that word again. For I know who you are and who I am. In position you are my brother, in character my father. I gave therefore no commands, but only endeavoured to point out what I thought was desirable . . . I said you ought not to use such a title [*i.e.* "universal bishop"] in writing either to me or to any one else; yet now, in your last letter, notwithstanding my prohibition, you have addressed me by the proud title of Universal Pope. I beg your Holiness, whom I love so well, not to do this again . . . I do not consider that anything is an honour to me, by which my brethren lose the honour that is their due. My honour is the honour of the Universal Church, my honour is the united strength of my brethren. Then and then only am I truly honoured when no one is denied the honour which is justly his. But, if your Holiness calls me Universal Pope, you deny that you are yourself that which you say I am universally. God forbid! Far from us be the titles which inflate men's pride and deal a wound to charity!"[22]

Following the death of John the Faster (595), his successor, Kyriakos (596-606) continued to use the title of "ecumenical patriarch" and emperor Maurice directly ordered the pope to close the debate. Nevertheless, whatever the misunderstandings, the episode provided St. Gregory with the clear opportunity to express an ecclesiology and a theology of the episcopate, which were precisely those maintained by the Orthodox East against the papal claims in the later period of church history.

[22]*Ep* VIII, 29, MGH, *Ep,* II, 31; tr. Frederick Homes Dudden, *Gregory the Great,* London, 1905 (repr., New York, 1967), II, p. 223. There is no historical basis for the suggestion often made, that Gregory, in reception of Constantinople's claims, began the use of the title *servus servorum Dei* for himself. This use became standard only in later times.

It would probably be an exaggeration to say, with Hans Küng,[23] that Gregory I "recasted in a crucial way the authoritarian conception of the primacy which had been held by his predecessors Victor and Stephen, Damasus, Innocent, Leo and Gelasius," and that he should be compared with pope John XXIII. Neither Gregory, nor John XXIII stood really in opposition to the prevailing views of their contemporaries. And Leo the Great himself was not fully consistent in asserting the "apostolic" privileges of Rome. But it is true that the incipient papal ecclesiology, expressed in the *Decretum Gelasianum*, was foreign to St Gregory the Great. Like all the popes of the period, he viewed himself as a successor of Peter, and he saw Peter, as the source (*origo*) of episcopal power, but he did not consider that this power was communicated to other bishops from Rome only.[24] He is, therefore, a major witness to the "ecclesiology of communion" which kept the East and the West together during the first millenium of Christian history.

Close relationship between Byzantium and the Roman bishops continued throughout the seventh century, although no major personalities appeared among the popes of the times. Gregory's successors Boniface III (607) and Boniface IV (608-15) maintained friendship with Phocas, who rewarded them by transforming the Roman Pantheon into a church. Under Heraclius (610-641), pope Honorius I (625-38) was popular among the Romans, because, according to his epitaph, he "followed the steps of Gregory," and was seen as the "leader of the people" (*dux plebis*).[25] He reestablished a monastically inspired, pious and disciplined régime at the Lateran. Unfortunately, he was compromised, in the memory of the Church, by his ill-fated letter to patriarch Sergius of Constantinople, supporting Monotheletism (634). As a result, he figured among the heretics condemned by the Sixth ecumenical council (680), and later popes were required to anathematize his memory at their consecration.

[23]*The Church,* tr. by Ray and Rosaleen Ockenden, New York, 1967, pp. 470-1.
[24]Cf. the pertinent and well-documented observations of Y. Congar, *L'ecclésiologie du haut Moyen-Age,* Paris, 1968, pp. 142-6, 151-63. Gregory's objections to being called "universal pope' by Eulogius are truly extraordinary. The title was used routinely by the Easterners in letters to the popes, together with such appellations as "archbishop of the universal church," "head of all priests," etc. (Cf. L. Magi, *La Sede romana nella corrispondenza degli imperatori e patriarchi bizantini,* Louvain, 1972, pp. 37, 54, 111, etc.). For an opposite and apologetic view, trying to show that Gregory was a consistent upholder of papal power, see N. Sharkey, *Saint Gregory the Great's Concept of Papal Power,* Washington, D.C., 1950.
[25]*LP,* p. 325, note 2.

This "fall of Honorius" was followed, however, with a direct rebellion of his successors against the Monothelite policy of emperor Constans II. In 648, the papal *apocrisiarius* in Constantinople refused to sign the imperial *Typos*. Following pope Theodore's death (649), pope St Martin I, also a former *apocrisiarius* in the imperial capital, more aware of Eastern affairs, was elected without imperial confirmation. He welcomed orthodox refugees from the East, including the great St Maximus the Confessor, and held a council of 105 bishops which condemned Monotheletism. Dragged to Constantinople by the exarch Theodore Calliopas, the pope was tried, condemned, tortured and exiled to the Crimea (653), where he died in 655. The Roman church recognized his deposition, and a successor, Eugenius I, was elected and confirmed by the heretical emperor (654). The new pope's *apocrisiarii* communicated with the Monothelite Patriarch Peter.[26] However, the synodical letter of the patriarch, which Eugenius was ready to approve, provoked a riot in Rome, and the pope sided with his orthodox flock. He was saved from Martin's fate by his sudden death in 657. His successor, pope Vitalian (657-672) was again elected with imperial approval and sent a synodical letter to the Monothelite patriarch. Furthermore, he solemnly welcomed the emperor himself, as Constans II visited Rome in 664. In later tradition, in particular the Acts of the Sixth council, the ambiguous behavior of pope Vitalian was justified by the fact that the emperor always made orthodox statements in his presence. This subservient attitude of the popes during this period of Byzantine control of Rome stood in sharp contrast with their independence and intolerance of doctrinal ambiguity in the fifth century, as Italy was in the hands of the Ostrogoths. The assassination of Constans II (who meanwhile had tried to weaken the papacy further by establishing autocephaly in Ravenna) in Syracuse in 668 put an end to the Monothelite crisis, and to further doctrinal embarrassment of the popes. Orthodoxy was sanctioned in 680 by the Sixth council, where the delegates of pope Agatho I were present.

The following decades were marked by close cooperation between Constantinople and the papacy. The *theme* system, which prevailed in the empire, implied that the imperial exarchs were given full administrative and financial autonomy in Italy. As a result, the exarch's approval was sufficient to legitimize papal elections and no recourse to Constan-

---

[26]*Acta Maximi*, 7, PG 90, col. 122 B. (Tr. George C. Berthold, New York, 1985, p. 23).

tinople was needed. Since the pope remained the "paymaster" of the imperial troops, the Byzantine military authorities treated the Church with respect. Most of the popes elected during this period were of Eastern origin. The remarkable embellishments made by them in Roman churches—always in the Byzantine style (Sts Cosmas and Damian, Santa Maria Antiqua, St Agnes, and many others)—illustrate the increasingly "Eastern" character taken by the Roman church during the period of the "Byzantine" papacy.[27]

The only major incident which marred this period was the refusal by pope Sergius I to sign the decrees of the so-called Quinisext council, which was held in Constantinople in the presence of papal legates (692). The reason for the refusal was the criticism raised in some of the council's decrees against liturgical practices accepted in Rome, and other disciplinary matters (fasting on Saturdays, celibate clergy). Emperor Justinian II tried to reenact against pope Sergius the drastic action of his predecessors Justinian I and Constans II against popes Vigilius and Martin, but failed. The imperial commissioner Zacharias, sent to force papal compliance with the conciliar decrees, faced a rebellion of the troops, who stood up in defense of the pope. Eventually, Zacharias had to hide under the pope's bed, until Sergius himself calmed the rebels.

This moral victory of Sergius did not prevent his successor, John VII in 706, from giving approval to the Quinisext council. Of course, the formally anti-Roman decrees were never really applied in the West. However, in decorating the church of Santa Maria Antiqua in Rome, John VII avoided the representation of Christ, as a lamb, because such representations were forbidden by the Quinisext.[28] In 711, pope Constantine paid a solemn visit to Constantinople, an event which had not occurred for almost a century.

The radical change in Byzantine imperial policies which would occur under the iconoclastic emperors Leo III (717-741) and Constantine V (741-763)—forceful imposition of iconoclasm, confiscation of the pope's Sicilian revenues, and cutting all military support of the papacy against the Lombards—put an end to the period of "Byzantine" papacy. Pope Stephen II looked for support elsewhere and switched

[27]Cf. P. Llewelyn, "Constans II and the Roman Church," *Byzantion* 46, 1976, pp. 120-6.

[28]Cf. J. Brekinridge, "Evidence for the nature of relations between Pope John VII and the Byzantine emperor Justinian II," BZ 65, 1972, pp. 364-74; cf. also Meyendorff, *Christ,* p. 177-8, for the theological issue involved.

his loyalty to the Franks (754). These events will have their long-term disastrous consequences for the relations between East and West.

2. The Arian Lombards and the schism of Aquileia

Although Justinian's Fifth council (553) proposed a significant and needed christological clarification when it reaffirmed the authority of both Cyril of Alexandria and the council of Chalcedon, its practical results were minimal in terms of reconciliation of Christendom in the one faith. The Cyrillian "fundamentalism" of the Monophysite masses in the East remained as staunch as before. In the West, meanwhile, the final acceptance of the Fifth council by Pope Vigilius provoked the sharp resistance of Chalcedonian "fundamentalists" who viewed the *post mortem* condemnation of Theodore of Mopsuestia as inappropriate and the criticism of Theodoret and Ibas, who had been rehabilitated at Chalcedon, as totally unacceptable. To these Western churchmen, the condemnation of the *Three Chapters* was a betrayal of Chalcedon. In their view, pope Vigilius rejected the faith of Leo, through whom "Peter had spoken" once and for all.

This Western movement of opposition placed the cause of the true faith, as it understood it, clearly above the authority of the Roman bishop. Their theological creed was the *Defense of the Three Chapters* published in 547-8 by the African bishop Facundus of Hermiana. They rejected the *Second Constitutum* of pope Vigilius, finding widespread support in their opposition among the bishops of Africa and Illyricum. However the repressive measures taken by the imperial authority imposed the acceptance of the Fifth council in these two regions.[29] But since the Lombard invasion of 568 had made much of Northern Italy inaccessible to the imperial administration, the opposition, strengthened by refugees from the Illyricum, persisted there for over a century.

Upon his enthronement as pope in 555, Pelagius I tried to placate the opposition by making a profession of faith, which proclaimed adherence to four councils only, without mentioning the Fifth. Such an attitude was presumably considered as admissible in the eyes of Justinian for the sake of Church unity. Indeed, in the East, the Cyrillians who preferred speaking of the Incarnation without mention-

[29]Cf. above, p. 244.

ing Chalcedon, were also welcome to do so. But Pelagius did not gain anybody's trust and many, in Rome itself, withdrew from his communion.[30] To win them back the pope made gestures; publicly, at St Peter's, he took a solemn oath of innocence and orthodoxy in order "to dispel suspicions about the orthodoxy of the Roman see."[31] He also sent around confessions of orthodox faith.

Outside of Rome, the provinces of Milan and Aquileia, headed by their independent metropolitans, broke fellowship with the pope, formally proclaiming their opposition to the condemnation of the *Three Chapters*. The resulting schism was canonically limited to North Eastern Italy, and is known as "Aquileian," or "Istrian." But its doctrinal stand found much sympathy elsewhere in the West, where the Alexandrian christology sanctioned by the Fifth council, with its implied doctrine of "deification" of humanity, was little understood. On the other hand, the opposition of so many against the papacy showed that, at that time, Western Christians were still far from accepting, as absolute, the doctrinal authority of the see of Rome. We will, in turn, describe the political background, and the schism itself.

The Lombards who invaded Italy in 568, headed by king Alboin (*c.* 560-573), were formally Arian, although some had remained pagan. Actually, only recently, had the king decided in favor of Arianism, just before the invasion of Italy, in order to secure the loyalty of another Arian Germanic tribe, the Gepids. In Italy, the Lombards established their own "kingdom" (*regnum*), clearly distinct from the Roman empire (*imperium*), with which the Roman church was in full solidarity. The conquest began a long series of military, cultural and religious conflicts. Orthodox Christianity was making progress among the Lombards, but very slowly. In 589, king Authari married the catholic queen Theodelinda, but, in 590, he formally prohibited the baptism of Lombard children in the Catholic Church. Nevertheless, king Agilulf—who also married the same Theodelinda after Authari's death—allowed for the catholic baptism of his son Adaloald (603). This became possible not only because of the peaceful initiatives of pope Gregory I, but also because of the fact that the catholic Church in the Lombard kingdom was in schism with both

[30]*LB*, I, p. 303.

[31]Cf. A. Grillmeier, "Vorbereitung des Mittelalters. Eine Studie über das Verhältnis von Chalkedonismus und Neu-Chalkedonismus in der lateinischen Theologie von Boethius bis zu Gregor dem Grossen," in *Chalkedon*, II, p. 824-30.

Rome and the empire.[32] The baptism of Adaloald did not imply submission to the imperial church. The Irish monk St Columban, who founded the famous abbey of Bobbio under the patronage of Agilulf and Theodelinda, would write to pope Boniface IV (608-615): "The name of God is, through you and your controversy, blasphemed everywhere among the nations," and would call on the pope to clear "the ill-repute of St Peter's chair" through a council.[33]

In general, it is still the peaceful approach, engineered by the diplomacy of St Gregory the Great, and adopted by the imperial exarch Smaragdus after 602, which was producing slow but sure results. Actually, the military weakness of the empire in Italy made peace inevitable and peace gradually contributed to Church unity. Abbot Attala, successor of St Columban, abandoned the schism, and so did queen Gundeperga, daughter of Agilulf and Theodelinda. Finally, the Lombard crown itself fell to a Catholic, Aripert (652-661), and the last Arian bishop of the Lombard capital of Pavia, Anastasius, converted to orthodoxy. The papacy was further strengthened by the end of Monotheletism under Constantine IV (668-84). The *de facto* extinction of Lombard Arianism paved the way for the end of the schism also.

Formally begun by a council of bishops in Aquileia in 555 which rejected the Fifth council, the "Istrian" schism originally involved the entire metropolitan provinces of Milan and Aquileia. As the Lombards invaded Italy, Paulinus, bishop of Aquileia, found refuge in the fortified island-city of Grado (569). Honoratus of Milan together with a part of his clergy and flock fled to Genoa, still occupied by the Byzantines.

In Genoa, following the death of Honoratus (570), the exiled Milanese elected another bishop, Laurence, who entered in communion with Rome on the basis of an ambiguous agreement, which allowed him to keep mental reservations concerning the Fifth council. Meanwhile, in Milan, under the Lombard occupation the remaining community elected another bishop, Fronto, who remained in schism. The final restoration of catholic unity in Milan, with a metropolitan in

[32]On the connections between the Lombard kingdom and the schism of Aquileia, see P. Goubert, *Byzance avant l'Islam, II. Byzance et l'Occident sous les successeurs de Justinien, 2. Rome, Byzance et Carthage*, Paris, 1965, pp. 82-121; and Jedin-Dolan, *History*, II, pp. 574-85.

[33]*Ep* 5, PL 80, col. 274-84; cf. J. Rivière, "St Columban et le jugement du pape hérétique," *Revue des sciences religieuses*, 1927, p. 277.

residence, did not occur before the tenure of Mansuetus (672-81).

In Grado, the schism continued under metropolitans Paulinus, Elias and Severius. Against Severius, the exarch Smaragdus used force. Coming to Grado in person, he arrested the metropolitan—who had begun to use the title of "patriarch"—and three bishops, brought them to Ravenna and forced them to communicate with the orthodox archbishop John (586). However, upon their return, a council meeting in Murano (589), restored the schism as it existed previously. In 591, pope Gregory I tried also to pressure Severius, but the council of bishops of Istria appealed to emperor Maurice. The latter "ordered" the pope to leave the schismatics alone until "all the regions of Italy are pacified and the other bishops of Istria and Venetia restore the traditional order."

During his entire reign, pope Gregory I was understandably preoccupied with the Aquileian schism. His confession of faith, published at his entronement (590) reflects this concern. It is not as ambiguous as that of Pelagius I, but it still proclaimed only *four councils* and compared them to the four Gospels. The text eventually mentions the "Fifth council" against the *Three Chapters,* as if in an afterthought.[34] Following Gregory's example, it became rather common, in the West, to emphasize the particular and eminent authority of "four councils," and consider the other three as somewhat lower in rank and concerned with "Eastern" problems only.

It remains, however, that the correspondence of St Gregory with queen Theodelinda, and the appeals he and his successors made to the bishops leading the schism, began to bring results, especially as the Lombard kings and dukes converted one by one from Arianism to orthodoxy. In 679, heeding the appeals of pope Agatho for a demonstration of catholic unity, as a preparation for the ecumenical council convoked by emperor Constantine IV in Constantinople, a synod met in Milan to condemn Monotheletism. A Greek deacon, Damian, drew the minutes of the synod and soon became bishop of Pavia, replacing the Arian Anastasius. The mission to the Lombards, which was conducted mainly by schismatic bishops, was now undertaken by the oriental personnel of the Roman church (as was also the case with the mission of Theodore of Tarsus in England). The last Istrian resistance to the now catholic *regnum* of the Lombards was defeated militarily, and king Cunincpert (678-700) presided over the synod

---

[34]Text in ACO IV, 2, p. 136-7.

of Pavia (698-9), at which ecclesiastical peace, in full sacramental unity with both Rome and Constantinople, was restored. Politically, however, the Lombard kingdom remained totally independent from the empire, and continued to be a challenge to the Roman papacy also.

This relatively happy resolution of the long Aquileian schism illustrates the remarkable role played by the "Byzantine papacy" during that period of history. Occasionally brutalized by the emperors of Constantinople, faced with fierce resistance of the various Barbarian kingdoms against normal ecclesiastical order and deprived of real political, or canonical powers, St Gregory the Great and his successors succeeded in providing moral leadership and in maintaining unity between East and West. Their role was equally positive in channeling and directing the missionary expansion in the West which, as in the East, originated mostly from local initiative and the witness of a few zealous monks.

3. The Mission to the Anglo-Saxons: the Irish monks and St Augustine

The sixth century was a critical one in the history of Christianity in the British Isles. An invasion of Angles, Saxons, Jutes and other pagan Germanic tribes swept through most of the eastern and central parts of Britain. The new Anglo-Saxon kingdoms destroyed Roman administration and interrupted existing contact with the Roman world. However, the old Celtic church survived not only in Ireland, where the legacy of St Patrick remained strong, but also in Wales and in Scotland. Other Celts emigrated to Brittany. We have spoken earlier of the peculiar role of the Irish monasteries and their abbots, and their connection with local tribal structures. "The abbot of the tribal monastery was usually of high birth and often a relative of the tribal chief; the connection between tribal and ecclesiastical rule was close, but the abbot was not necessarily a bishop."[35] In the latter part of the century, the activities of St Columban, an Irish monk who had to leave Ireland, as a result of local clan battles, is most extraordinary. With a few companions, he established a monastery on the island of

[35]M. Deanesly, The pre-conquest Church in England, London, 1963, p. 39. A somewhat similar parallelism between ecclesiastical and tribal structures existed, in the same period, in the remote Christian countries of the Caucasus, Armenia and Georgia (Cf. supra, p. 281).

Iona (563) and converted the neighboring Picts. After his death (597), his disciples moved south and began working on the conversion of the Anglo-Saxon invaders in Northumbria, where the mission of St Augustine (see below) was challenged by a pagan revival. Following the baptism of prince Oswald at Iona, a daughter-house was established on the "holy island" of Lindisfarne, near Bamborough, the capital of Northumbria, with St Aidan as bishop (635). One of Aidan's women-disciples, St Hilda, founded a mixed abbey at Whitby, where monks and nuns lived under the direction of the abbess. Whitby soon became a major spiritual and intellectual center.

Other Irish abbots extended their missions far from the British Islands. St Brendan (d. 577) was known as the "Navigator," and reached various islands in the North Sea; St Columban the Younger, an unrelated contemporary of St Columban the Older, founder of Iona, left his mother-house of Bangor with twelve companions (592) and founded several monasteries in Frankish lands, of which the most famous was Luxeuil in Burgundy. The introduction of Irish ways by St Columban created problems: he insisted on the total canonical independence of his communities, refused the jurisdiction of local bishops and performed pastoral functions without referring to them. Expelled from Burgundy in 610, he found support in Lombardy, where he established the abbey of Bobbio, siding with the Aquileian schism against Rome (cf. *supra,* p. 312). On his way from Burgundy to Italy, he was active among the Allemani, in today's Switzerland, where his disciple St Gall (d. after 629) created the great abbey, known under his name.

In their tireless voyages and activities, the Irish abbots were spreading a Christian tradition somewhat distinct from the patterns which prevailed within the Roman world of the sixth century. This Celtic tradition preserved some of the legacy of the fourth century missions, including especially the use of Latin in the liturgy, but it used a different calendar and developed its own discipline and spirituality. In the fifth century, as we saw in the case of St Patrick, the influence of the Gallic churches on the Irish had been quite strong, including the monastic spirituality of Lérins (St John Cassian). But Rome had played practically no role in the origins of Irish Christianity, and the idea of any administrative dependence upon any disciplinary structure, other than that of the abbots, was quite foreign to the Celtic church. Although a tradition of pilgrimages to the tombs of Sts Peter and Paul was alive among the Celts, as it existed also among Eastern Christians, they had not assimilated at all the concept, promoted by pope Leo I, that the bishop of Rome was the exclusive "successor of Peter." St Gildas, a monk of Bangor and a founder of the monastery of Rhuys in Brittany (d. 570) and one of the few Celtic abbots to be also a writer, specifically upholds the view, which was also widely accepted in the East, as well as in earlier period in the West (cf. St Cyprian of Carthage, third c.), that "the whole episcopal order exercises spiritual authority in the Church and inherits the power which Christ first granted to Peter."[36] Thus the authority of the papacy carried little weight in the eyes of the Celtic abbots and, in any case, was not sufficient to convince them that their disciplinary and liturgical tradition had to be discarded for the sake of the Roman practice.

The Irish practices included some [unknown] peculiarity in performing baptism, a different form of clerical tonsure[37] and, most importantly, a particular system of paschal computation. Whereas everybody accepted the Nicaean condemnation of the "Quattrodecimans," who celebrated Easter with the Jews, there was no consensus as to the alternative date, which, according to tradition, had to be a Sunday, following the 14th of Nisan, the lunar month following the vernal equinox. Some placed the equinox on March 21st, and some on the 25th. Also, there were several methods of calculating months, which had been debated in Rome at the time of the Laurentian schism (see above, p. 163). The Celts had received a faulty old Roman system, based on a cycle of 84 years, which had been replaced in Rome in 457 by a different cycle, that of Victorius of Aquitaine. The latter was further modified by the calculations of Dionysius Exiguus (the "small") in 525, which were those of the church of Alexandria. Thus, after 525, Rome was in accord with the East, but at least two other systems were followed in different areas of the West. The "old" system was passionately defended by the Celts and would be followed in some

---

[36]K. Hughes "The Celtic Church and the Papacy," in C. H. Lawrence, ed., *The English Church and the Papacy in the Middle Ages*, London, 1965, p. 9 [with translation of texts by Gildas]. This view was also widely held in Gaul until the ninth century with the Petrine text (Matt 16:13-19) serving as the reading for the rite of episcopal consecration; cf. A. Dold, *Das älteste Liturgiebuch der lateinische Kirche. Ein altgallikanisches Lektionar des 5/6 Jahrhunderts aus dem Wolfenbuttler Palimpsest.* [*Codex Weissenburgensis 76*] (= Texte u. Arbeite, Erzabtei Beuron, I. Abt., 26-28); and Y. Congar, *op. cit.*, pp. 138-154.

[37]Instead of shaving their head completely and keeping a circular crown of hair, as did the clerics in the Roman world, the Irish were shaving only the front part (*"from ear to ear"*) and maintaining a semi-circular "crown of hair."

regions of Gaul until the eighth century, and in remote parts of Britain until the twelfth.

In Britain, there was violent animosity and permanent warfare between the Celtic Christians and the pagan Anglo-Saxon invaders. Mission work by Celts was therefore difficult and although, as we have just seen, the Iona monks would eventually establish Christianity in Northumbria, the most famous Christian enterprise among the English would come from Rome. It has been described for future generations by the Venerable Bede (672-735) in his *Ecclesiastical History*. That mission, however, would not be really successful beyond the borders of the Southern Anglian kingdom of Kent.

Bede reports a legendary account explaining the sudden interest of pope Gregory for the Anglo-Saxons. We are thus told that upon his return from Constantinople and before his election, Gregory noticed handsome slaves on a Roman market. Asking about their origin and informed that they were "English" (*Angli*), he lamented that such "angelic" (*angeli*) looking faces were not Christian. His mind became set upon an eventual English mission, which would be a specifically monastic enterprise. Indeed, as he was pope already (595), he ordered the priest Candidus, who was going to Gaul, to buy young English slaves in Marseille, so that they might be sent to a monastery, baptized, tonsured and trained as missionaries to their country.[38] It is unlikely that the improvised recruits could be supplied on time, because the mission left Rome already in 596. It was composed of forty monks from St Gregory's own monastery of St Andrew, on the Caelium, and headed by one Augustine, as *praepositus*.

It is likely that St Gregory had made preliminary contacts with England. The most likely channel was queen Bertha, the Christian wife of the *bretwalda* (or king) of Kent, Aethelbert. Daughter of a king of Paris, she had married Aethelbert in 560 and had gone to Doruvernum (Canterbury), the residence of Aethelbert, accompanied by the Frankish bishop of Sens, Liuthard, as chaplain. This initial Christian presence at the court made the coming of a papal mission possible. But Augustine and his companions faced some difficulties as they crossed Gaul. The local bishops did not approve of a Roman intervention in Britain, which they considered as territory belonging

[38]The letter to Candidus is preserved (Greg., *Ep* VI, 10, MGH, *Ep* I, 388-9). These were obviously quite original initiatives of St Gregory. Had he heard of the success of the former slave St Patrick among the Irish? Was he inspired by the missionary work of Syrian monks, about whom he might have learned in Constantinople?

canonically to the metropolitan of Arles. Only the strong support of Gregory allowed the mission to go through and reach the island.

According to Bede, the preaching of Augustine and his companions was immediately successful and "thousands" were baptized in 597. As the king himself was seeking baptism, and this ceremony required the presence of a bishop, St Augustine travelled to Arles, where he was consecrated by the metropolitan, in accordance with the old Gallic order, which had placed Britain under Arles' jurisdiction. King Aethelbert was baptized in 601. In the same year, answering queries by Augustine, pope Gregory provided the new church with a set of instructions, establishing a permanent link with Rome. The instructions contain broad guidelines concerning discipline and liturgy, but they also reflect the perspective in which the pope viewed Britain: the mission of St Augustine was meant to reestablish the old Roman structure which had disappeared in the fifth century. Two metropolitans were to reside in the previously existing two Roman provinces with sees in the old provincial capitals of Eboracum (York) and Lundinum (London). Each province was to be organized as twelve dioceses. Both metropolitans were to receive a *pallium* from the pope, signifying direct allegiance to Rome (and not to Arles).

However, this Gregorian scheme hardly corresponded to British reality in 601. There would be no bishop in York until 625, and Augustine alone wore the *pallium*. Unable to settle in London, he stayed in Canterbury, which will thus remain as the permanent ecclesiastical center of Britain. But his greatest challenge, in addition to the reluctance of other Anglo-Saxon kings to receive baptism, was the old Celtic church in Cornwall, Wales and Northern Britain. The pope certainly knew of its existence, but had no information about either the names, or the number of its bishops, who were actually submitted to the abbots of large monasteries. He ordered Augustine to "instruct" them, which implied their integration into the new Roman ecclesiastical system. In this particular task, St Augustine failed miserably in spite of two special meetings with the Celts. They refused to recognize him as their metropolitan and to change their ways, particularly to modify the date of Easter. The difficulties were not only ecclesiastical, but also political: the Roman mission was linked to the Anglo-Saxon court of Canterbury, considered as foreign and hostile by the Celts.

In 604 Augustine alone (by special permission of the pope) consecrated Mellitus and Justus as bishops of London and Rochester. He also ordained Laurence, as his successor in Canterbury. No Celtic bishops took part in the consecrations. Apparently, the legitimacy of their apostolic succession was in doubt.

Following the death of Aethelbert (616), the pagan reaction was so strong that the mission barely survived. The king's own son returned to paganism. The only significant success was the consecration of bishop Paulinus for Northumbria and the baptism of king Edwin (627), who became the most powerful leader among the English. The Christian faith spread throughout the country for a few brief years until Edwin was killed at the battle of Heathfield (633). Except in Kent, where the dynasty of Aethelbert returned to Roman Christianity, the progress of Christianity, in the midst of bloody battles between the leaders of the various kingdoms, was assured not by Roman missionaries, but by the Celtic hierarchy, especially St Aidan and St Finian of Lindisfarne. The latter sent missionaries to Wessex and East Anglia, and baptized Peada, the son of Penda, the powerful pagan king of Mercia (655).

The further progress of Christianity required a solution to the division between the Celtic "church of St Columban" and the see of Canterbury. Union, on the basis of the Roman practice, was finally achieved at the synod of Whitby (664), organized by Oswy, king of Northumbria. Representatives of both churches held animated debates on the correct date of Easter, with an important role played by St Wilfrid, former monk of Lindisfarne and now abbot of Ripon, who had travelled to Rome and became convinced of the necessity to celebrate Easter together with the rest of Christendom. The king was also convinced by references to the apostolic "Petrine" tradition kept in Rome. But, even after Whitby, the old Celtic practice remained in force for a while at Iona (until 716) and in Wales until 755, and competition between the two cultures and mentalities continued, with some doubt as to the canonicity of the "Columban" apostolic succession often expressed by the Anglo-Saxons. The conflict was illustrated by the long struggle for the see of York between the pro-Roman Wilfrid, who went to be consecrated bishop in Compiègne in Gaul, and Ceadda (or Chad), who got his episcopate from British bishops, under the auspices of king Oswy.

The pro-Roman mentality in Kent was so strong that, in 664, it was decided that the candidate for the see of Canterbury should be consecrated in Rome. Unfortunately the candidate, Wighard, after reaching Italy, died of the plague. Another Roman candidate, Theodore, was then selected locally in Rome by pope Vitalian and consecrated in 668. The predominance of Greek personnel at the papal court which, as we saw earlier, also influenced the papal missions to the Lombards, explains the fact that the new archbishop of Canterbury was a Greek, from Tarsus. An old man already—he was sixty-six at his consecration—Theodore developed a remarkable energy travelling throughout the country, establishing the Roman practice for the celebration of Easter, presiding over councils (Hertford, 673; Hatfield, 680), and founding a number of new dioceses, all organized on a territorial basis. His zeal in having the patterns and practices of the catholic Church accepted in England led him to perform a *reordination* of bishop Chad, the Celtic aspirant to the see of York, installing him as bishop of Lichfield, while the see of York went to St Wilfrid. The latter, however, had to appeal twice to Rome against attempts by Theodore to divide his huge diocese. Theodore died in 690 at the age of 98. He left a church solidly integrated in the Roman and imperial system. His legacy also included a *Penitential,* reflecting an Eastern sacramental theology. His foreign origin, however, may have been the reason why he was never added to the catalogue of English saints, as was St Wilfrid of York, who, in spite of his efforts at obtaining papal support, never recovered his see and died at Ripon (709).

The English church, now finally controlled by Anglo-Saxons and accepting Roman jurisdiction more directly than the church in France, remained faithful to one major aspect of the old Celtic tradition: its missionary zeal extended not only to the British Isles, but also to continental Europe. Following the example of the great St Columban, the Scot St Fridolin evangelized Southern Allemania. Monks coming from Luxeuil, the great foundation of Columban, worked in Bavaria, and were succeeded by an Irishman, St Rupert (d. 715). Another Irish abbot, St Kilian, consecrated bishop by pope Conon, worked in Thuringia, where he died a martyr (689). In Frisia, on the North Sea coast, St Wilfrid of York himself preached on his way to Rome (678), and was followed by St Egbert and, particularly St Willibrord, a monk of Ripon, who in 695 was consecrated by pope Sergius as first bishop of Utrecht. Even the old monastery of St Benedict in Monte-Cassino, South of Rome, was revived in 729 by the English monk Willibald, Finally, Wynfrid, another Englishman, born near Exeter, but renamed

Boniface during a visit to pope Gregory II in Rome, became in the eighth century the great apostle to Germany.

Established originally as an extension of Gallic Christianity, the British church, after a difficult period of inner struggle between the old Celtic tradition and the Germanic Anglo-Saxon newcomers, became itself the mother-church of Central Europe. The Roman patterns of church life, so painfully accepted at the council of Whitby (664), were followed strictly by the missionaries to the continent. In almost every case, they sought papal sanction for the establishment of new churches, appealing to "Petrine" apostolicity. In general, these new churches contributed to the growth of the medieval papacy, which was seen as the main representative of Roman universalism. The older principle of essential identity between local churches, which had been so stubbornly (and somewhat peculiarly) maintained by the Celtic "Columban" church, would persist in Spain and in France, rather than in Britain and Germany.

4. *National churches in Spain and France*

As we have seen earlier, Nicaean catholicism was adopted as the official religion of the Visigothic, previously Arian, kingdom of Toledo under king Recared (589). Since that date and until the Arab Muslim conquest (711), church and state, the metropolitan of Toledo and the king, exercised the religious and political leadership of society, so much so that Toledo was seen by some almost as a restoration of the Western empire. This isolationism of the Visigothic kingdom was partly due to its defensive attitude towards the Byzantine empire, which held control over Southeastern Spain, with the cities of Carthagena and Malaga. At their installation, the kings acquired a sacred character by being anointed with chrism. They approved the elections of bishops and the decrees of the councils which repeatedly met in Toledo to solve local issues, both political and religious. Presided by the kings, these councils were actually national assemblies and included not only bishops, but also lay dignitaries of the realm.[39] The Spanish church possessed its

[39]A very similar system predominated in other Eastern and Western distant off-shoots of the "imperial church" (Armenia, Georgia, Ethiopia, Merovingian Gaul and, later, Slavic Christian countries) where the local rulers assumed the role played within the empire by the Christian emperors. The major difference between the "imperial" and the "national" variants of this church-state formula, lies in the *universal* scope of the

own ancient "mozarabic" liturgical tradition. It developed a peculiar way of christianizing the laws, inherited from its barbarian Gothic past (*Lex Visigothorum*), and produced its own canonical collection (*Hispana*), which, through the Carolingians, influenced canonical developments in the Latin Middle Ages.

St Leander of Seville, the main architect of the conversion of Recared, had sojourned in Constantinople, where he met St Gregory the Great. He was therefore undoubtedly familiar with the spirit and the affairs of world Christianity. However, the council of 589 took place without any formal contacts with Rome. It is in a private letter, that St Leander informed his friend Gregory, who had become pope in 590, of the event which had taken place. Only three years later, did the king himself formally notify Rome, and received, in return, a gift of relics. Pope Gregory was undoubtedly interested in extending the influence of Rome upon catholic Spain and sent a *pallium* to Leander, but this sign, which elsewhere implied some symbolic dependence upon the papacy, did not have much concrete significance in Spain. St Isidore, brother and successor of Leander as bishop of Seville (d. 636), occasionally mentions the Roman primacy, but specifically denies the pope's infallibility and speaks only of conditional obedience: "Our duty of obedience is affected on no point, except that he order something directly against the faith."[40] There was practically no Roman intervention in the affairs of Spain, and no appeals to the pope by Spanish bishops. To the contrary, having in 683 received, from pope Benedict II, the decisions of the Sixth ecumenical council of Constantinople of 680, the Spanish bishops accepted it only conditionally and produced "explanations," composed by St Julian of Toledo. These explanations (*Apologeticum fidei*) were not really substantial, but reflected clearly a sense of doctrinal independence. Upon receiving them, the pope made some critical remarks before the Spanish envoy. The council of Toledo (688) approved a new, rather trenchant *Apology,* which clearly signified that the faith in Spain did not depend upon any external authority, not even that of Rome.

This rather distant attitude adopted in Spain towards Rome was certainly connected with the fact that the "Byzantine papacy" of St Gregory and his successors appeared very much as a close ally of the

imperial formula whereas national churches inevitably carried the danger of provincialism and separatism.

[40] *Ep* 6, 3, PL 83, col. 903A.

empire, which occupied the South of Spain and was politically intoler-
ant of the Visigothic kingdom. One notes that in Byzantine territory
the authority of the pope was acknowledged much more distinctly than
in Toledo: in 603, for example, a papal legate, the *defensor* John,
came especially to judge a case involving the bishop of Malaga,
Januarius.

Under such circumstances, it is understandable that no authority,
whether Roman, or Constantinopolitan, was able to do much about a
fateful event: the inclusion of the *Filioque* in the Creed, as an anti-
Arian affirmation, in connection with king Recared's conversion (589).
It was later reaffirmed by other councils, held in Toledo (particularly
633 and 653). While reflecting primitive ecclesiology, the regional
autonomy of Christian Spain lacked permanent channels of communication and conciliarity with the rest of the Universal Church.

We have already seen above (p. 133) how the conversion of
Clovis to orthodox Christianity in 493 led to the development of a
national Frankish church sanctioned *de facto* by the council of Orléans
presided by the king (511).[41] Although the Frankish church generally
showed solidarity with the bishop of Rome in doctrinal questions,[42]
there were no permanent administrative ties. Appeals to Rome were
extremely rare. At the time of St Gregory the Great (590-604), the
metropolitan of Arles still received a delegation of power from Rome,
as papal vicar, judicially responsible to the pope and not to the local
episcopate, but in practice, his role was only honorary, and is not
mentioned since that time. There were also several other ecclesiastical
centers. At the time of king Gontram of Burgundy (561-93), the
bishop of Lyons even used the title of "patriarch."[43] Since the Frankish
kingdom was not, like the Visigothic kingdom of Toledo, a permanently
unified state, church organization had to adapt itself to the shifting
borders of the various sub-kingdoms. The old Gallo-Roman metropolitan sees, originally responsible for the filling of episcopal vacan-

[41]The major source for the knowledge of ecclesiastical history of the Frankish
kingdom is the honest account of a contemporary, St Gregory, bishop of Tours (*ca.* 538-
594), in his famous *History of the Franks.*

[42]There was nevertheless some sympathy for the opposition against the Fifth council
and its confirmation by Rome. One does not find reference to the condemnation of the
Three Chapters in Frankish ecclesiastical documents until the council of Saint-Jean-de-
Losne (673-5).

[43]Cf. L. Duchesne, *Fastes épiscopaux de l'ancienne Gaule,* I, Paris, 1907, p. 140-1.
Eventually, and until our own days, the bishop of Lyons would enjoy the honorific position of "primate of the Gauls."

cies, lost their authority, which now *de facto* belonged to regional kings and the bishops of their realm. The cohesion of the Frankish church was nevertheless preserved by frequent councils, which were not, as in Spain, national assemblies with large lay participation, but episcopal gatherings, convoked by kings for the solution of church problems. The Frankish episcopate of the period was not prominent in the field of intellectual pursuits or theological competence, but, in spite of its dependence upon local kings, it produced a number of authentic saints and heroes of the faith, which maintained its moral authority among the people. Monastic life, strengthened by the activities of leaders coming from the British Isles, contributed much to the propagation and integrity of the faith.

At the death of Clovis (511), the kingdom was divided between his four sons, then briefly reunited again by one of them, Chlotar I (558-561), only to be divided again, at Chlotar's death, between several representatives of the Merovingian dynasty. The period of second reunification (after 613), the Golden Age of the Merovingians, occurred under Chlotar II (584-629) and Dagobert I (629-639), with Paris becoming the center of political and ecclesiastical life of the kingdom.

Since, according to Gregory of Tours, only 3000 Franks were baptized with Clovis in 493, it is clear that some time elapsed before Christianity became accepted by society at large. The *Salic Law* of Clovis contains hardly any Christian elements, whereas the *Ribuarian Law* of Chlothar II and Dagobert, as well as the Germanic collections of the early eighth century, include privileges for clergy, sanctification of Sunday, protection of Christian marriage, and a certain role of the Church in freeing slaves.

In the life of the royal courts, marked by bloody dynastic feuds, both saints and criminals were remembered by posterity, including formidable women figures. St Radegunda, reluctant captive wife of Chlothar I, obtained permission to leave the court (after Chlotar had assassinated her brother) and founded the monastery of the Holy Cross near Poitiers. The pious St Radegunda stood in contrast to Fredegunda, successively the mistress, wife, divorcée, and wife again of Childebert II, and especially to Queen Brunehilde (or Brunehaut), whom Chlothar II had indicted and executed for murdering ten kings. The somber image of Brunehilde, painted by St Gregory of Tours and the author of St Columban's *Life,* is however, contradicted by the praises sent to her by pope Gregory I.

In the midst of these bloody episodes, holy men tried to maintain Christian integrity and suffered for it. St Pretextat, bishop of Rouen, was assassinated on orders from Fredegunda while celebrating the liturgy in 586. St Desiderius (Didier), bishop of Vienna, suffered a similar fate, because he had displeased Brunehilde.

The only Merovingian who entered history with the reputation of having been a "good king" was Dagobert I (629-639). Advised by friends like St Eligius (Eloi), an artist and jeweler, who later became bishop of Noyon, Dagobert travelled throughout the country patronizing the poor and protecting them from an exacting aristocracy, promoting arts and building projects. He rebuilt the monastic center which existed around the tomb of St Denys, whom tradition designated as the first bishop of Paris (and whom Carolingian divines will later identify with St Dionysius the Aeropagite).[44]

Monastic foundations, influenced by Lérins, existed in Gaul before the Frankish conquest. As in the East, these monastic communities were canonically dependent upon local bishops. A new trend was started with the arrival of the Irish. In 592, St Columban and his twelve companions founded the abbeys of Luxeuil and Fontaine, acting in total independence from the bishops and local canonical order. Initially patronized by Brunehilde, St Columban was soon asked to leave the country. The ascetic severity of Irish monasticism was soon mitigated at Luxeuil by the moderating influence of the rule of St Benedict. In this new form, the foundation itself became a major center of monastic and missionary revival, preserving its tradition of independence from local episcopal supervision. This regime of monastic independence was facilitated by the "proprietary church" system, which allowed founders and patrons to control the economy of ecclesiastical foundations. Thus, new monasteries were often *de facto* independent churches under secular law.

While contacts between the Frankish church and the papacy were rare, diplomatic contacts between the Merovingian monarchy and Byzantium were frequent. Emperor Maurice (582-602) solicited the alliance of Childebert II (575-596) against the Lombards. Coins

---

[44]The personal, political and religious merits of Dagobert did not prevent him from being a man of his times, and his private life was rather disorderly. He was successively the husband of four queens, and entertained an untold number of concubines.

with the emperor's image were struck in Gaul, clearly showing the recognition of the universal Christian empire by the Franks.[45] King Dagobert's ambassadors visited Constantinople to conclude an agreement with Emperor Heraclius. Although the alliance was not very successful in crushing the power of the Lombards, it served as an opportunity for cultural and religious connections between Byzantium and the Franks. The Gallican liturgy contained Eastern elements, such as the chanting of the Trisagion, in both Latin and Greek, before the Scripture readings. In Poitiers, a relic of the True Cross was venerated at the monastery founded by Radegunda. In 565, the retired queen herself had requested it from emperor Justin II and empress Sophia. The relic came enshrined in a special imperial reliquary, and the poet Venantius Fortunatus wrote verses for the occasion; they included a special poem in honor of Justin and Sophia, glorifying their orthodoxy, and two of the most popular medieval Latin hymns about the Cross: the *Vexilla regis prodeunt* and the *Pange lingua*.[46]

In the late seventh and early eighth centuries, following the death of Dagobert, the Merovingian dynasty entered a period of notorious decadence. "Do-nothing kings" (*rois-fainéants*) delegated power to "palace mayors" who actually ruled the kingdom. One of them, Charles Martel, successfully stopped the Arabs at the famous battle of Poitiers (732). His son, Pepin the Short, took several steps which changed the course of history in a radical way. In 751, he formally deposed the last nominal representative of the Merovingian dynasty, Childebert III, and had himself anointed king by St Boniface, the English apostle to Germany. With the help of Rome, Boniface was in the process of restoring canonical order in Bavaria and the Rhineland. Even before his anointment as king, Pepin had given to Boniface the latitude to extend his reforms to his realm. It included in particular a restoration of "metropolitans" (now called "archbishops") in major cities, ending the arbitrary elections of bishops which had become the pattern under the Merovingians. The reform was effected in the name of the apostolic mission of Rome, whose authority St Boniface was invoking constantly.

This new connection between the Frankish church and Rome would find its culmination in the famous meeting in Ponthion between

[45]Cf. P. Goubert, *Byzance avant l'Islam. II. Byzance et l'Occident sous les successeurs de Justinien. 2. Byzance et les Francs*, Paris, 1955, pp. 12-26.

[46]The most recent study on these events is by A. Cameron, "The early religious policies of Justin II" in *Studies in Church History* 13, 1976, pp. 55-59.

king Pepin and pope Stephen (754), The Byzantine emperors, by promoting the iconoclastic heresy, by refusing help to the pope against the Lombards, and finally by depriving him from his jurisdiction (and revenues) in Southern Italy and Illyricum forcibly ended the period of "Byzantine papacy." The pope searched for a new protector, and found one. The king of the Franks had been a supporter of catholicism against the Arians, and an ally of the empire against the Lombards. He was now called to save the See of Peter abandoned by its legitimate protectors in Constantinople. But in doing so, he also gradually assumed the imperial legacy itself, in opposition to Byzantium, with the pope becoming a crucial factor in this new version of *Romanitas.*

None of the main actors of this fundamental change of political geography realized the future consequence for the fate of Christendom: the religious and cultural polarization between East and West.

5. A "patriarchate of the West"?

Already at Chalcedon (451), and certainly at the two following "ecumenical" councils of Constantinople II (553) and Constantinople III (680), the assembled bishops were seen as representing five *patriarchates.* Authentic ecumenicity required the participation of these five patriarchs, either in person, or by proxy, or, at least, as in the case of pope Vigilius and the council of 553, in the form of a *post factum* approval. This system of "pentarchy," the governing of the universal church by five rulers, equal in dignity, but related to each other by a strict order (τάξις) of precedence, was a Byzantine vision, enshrined in the legislation of Justinian.[47] The order of precedence was never truly accepted in Alexandria, however, and the refusal by the "popes" of Egypt to recognize that they had to stand below Constantinople, was a factor in the Monophysite schism.[48] In Rome, especially during the period of the "Byzantine papacy," which was discussed earlier in this chapter, the system of pentarchy was accepted *de facto,* although

[47]Cf. especially *novella* 131 of 545 A.D. *ed. cit.,* p. 655; the imperial edicts concerned with the Church were addressed to the five patriarchs (cf. for instance, the edict of 543 against Origenism, PG 86, cols. 945 D, 981 A).

[48]In fact, the pentarchy was always more an ideal than a reality. It functioned in practice in the fifth century, when it had not yet been legally defined. In the sixth century, as it was enshrined in legal texts, only the "melkite" Chalcedonian orthodox patriarchs of the East were part of it, but they were hardly equal, except in name, to the powerful archbishops of the two Romes.

reservations were generally made about the apostolic, rather than the imperial origin of the Roman primacy, which always implied that the Roman bishop ranked first in the pentarchy.

Outside of Rome, however, the pentarchic system was hardly even known in the West. Although Byzantine texts tend to view the entire West as constituting the territory of the Roman "patriarch," just as the various parts of the East were seen as divided between his four colleagues, this vision did not correspond to the realities of Western Christendom of the the fifth, sixth or seventh centuries. In the West, the title of "patriarch" never acquired a very specific sense.

The bishop of Rome was occasionally addressed as "patriarch," especially by Easterners, and his residence at the Lateran was designated as the "patriarchate," but the title never became the specific privilege of the church of Rome. It was occasionally assumed by other important sees of the West, like Aquileia and Lyons, without necessarily implying a challenge to Rome. In the East, the canonical rights of all four patriarchates had been defined with some clarity by the councils. Thus, the highly centralized Alexandrian "papacy" had been condoned, as a local "ancient custom" by canon 6 of Nicaea, whereas the rights of Constantinople were clearly described both geographically and canonically in canon 28 of Chalcedon, as a right to consecrate metropolitans in the imperial dioceses of Thrace, Pontus and Asia. The canons also implied that Antioch and Jerusalem enjoyed similar rights within defined areas. In the case of Rome, there was only custom and a certain moral prestige, but no conciliar definitions on rights, territory, or jurisdiction. Rome itself never either exercised or claimed to exercise "patriarchal" rights over the entire West.

Such "patriarchal" jurisdiction of Rome existed *de facto* over the so-called *suburbicarian* dioceses, which covered a relatively large territory—ten provinces—which were within the civil jurisdiction of the prefect of Rome.[49] The power of the pope upon this territory was, in every way, comparable to the jurisdiction of Eastern patriarchs. It consisted in presiding over regular synods and consecrating metropolitans in each province. It was clearly an expression of the parallelism between civil and ecclesiastical structures, which were taken for granted in the empire and concerned territories where imperial traditions and administration were stronger and more permanent than elsewhere in Italy.

[49]Cf. *supra,* p. 64.

Beyond the "suburbicarian" dioceses, the Christian West included churches which were, in every way, as independent ("autocephalous," as we would say today), as their sister-churches in the East: the church of the Visigothic kingdom of Spain, the Frankish church, the Celtic "Columban" church, and, of course, the church in Africa. Even the English church, created by the Roman mission of St Augustine of Canterbury, a staunch supporter of Roman prestige, was administratively independent: of 376 episcopal ordinations in England between 669 and 1050, not one required papal intervention.[50] There was only one case of appeal to Rome during the entire Merovingian period in Gaul, and even this case was, in fact, an uncontested one, approved by king Guntram (561-93).[51] Each of these churches had its own liturgical tradition and could, as was the case with the Merovingians, establish contacts with the East, independently from Rome. Their relationships with Rome were in a way similar to those maintained by distant Eastern churches—the Armenian, the Georgian, the Persian, the Indian—with their mother-church in Antioch, even if, fortunately, no doctrinal controversies, as violent and divisive as in the East, interfered in those relationships in the West.

The Barbarian invasions and the establishment of new national churches, a remarkable achievement of the Christian mission carried on by Irish monks as well as by Roman missionaries, had weakened the idea of an "imperial" unity, or *Romanitas*. Still quite strong with the Ostrogoths in Italy, it was openly challenged by the Spanish Visigoths and the Italian Lombards.

The loyalty to Constantinople, unpopular in some barbarian kingdoms, but consistently pursued by the popes of the "Byzantine" period, led to a further limitation of papal authority. Of course, all Western Christians preserved varying degrees of pious concern for the tombs of the great apostles Peter and Paul. In the entire West, Rome possessed a unique claim to holiness and was a place of pilgrimage, which had been exalted already by Irenaeus, Tertullian and Cyprian. But was there a connection between the presence of venerated apostolic tombs in Rome, and ecclesiastical structures? The answer to this question depended upon one's ecclesiological understanding of the roles of the apostles, as described in the New Testament, and upon the problem of their "succession."

[50]Cf. Y. Congar, *op. cit.*, p. 133.
[51]Duchesne, *L'Eglise*, p. 531-2.

There were *de facto* two distinct approaches to this issue which had not been debated, as such, either in the East or in the West, since the time of St Cyprian of Carthage. For Cyprian, Peter was the model and origin of the episcopal ministry, exercised in each local church in unity with all other churches. This first approach was generally taken for granted in the East, and also by many authorities in the West, including local Gallic councils, Isidore of Seville and the Venerable Bede.[52] This perspective encouraged pilgrimages to Peter's tomb and justified a certain moral authority of the church where he preached (Rome was the church "close to Peter," *propinqua Petro*), but did not imply any power of the Roman pope over the other bishops. The other perspective was firmly and stubbornly maintained in Rome itself. As expressed by Leo the Great and Gelasius, it affirmed that Peter speaks through the bishop of Rome in a particular, personal way, so that Rome alone is truly the "see of Peter." Therefore, the "Petrine" nature of the episcopal ministry required the recognition of the bishop of Rome as the "head" (*caput*) of the episcopate and therefore, of the universal Church.

This second interpretation of the "Petrine" ministry could not, of course, be applied uniformly in practice: the concrete historical reality was that of a decentralized church. We have seen that even St Leo the Great, who never lost an opportunity to affirm the Petrine Roman primacy, was, in fact, inconsistent with it and rather appealed to Nicaea in his protests against canon 28 of Chalcedon. St Gregory the Great emphatically affirmed the equality of bishops, when he stood up against the title of "ecumenical patriarch" assumed by the archbishop of Constantinople, but also expressed his belief that Peter, even *now*, is present in his [Roman] successors.[53] An inner mystical conviction seemed to be always present, whenever the popes, in spite of many historical inconsistencies, affirmed to be successors of Peter, with Paul, the traditional co-founder of the Roman church, being somewhat relegated to the background.

It is this conviction that gradually acquired an institutional and juridical authority. It can be said, indeed, that all the actions and

---

[52]Cf. the texts gathered and brilliantly interpreted by Y. Congar, *op. cit.*, p .138-63; for ecclesiological perspectives, see J. Zizioulas, *Being as Communion*, Crestwood, NY, 1985, pp. 171-260; for the consensus on the issue in Greek and Byzantine patristic thought, see J. Meyendorff, "St Peter in Byzantine theology," *The Primacy of Peter in the Orthodox Church*, ed. J Meyendorff, London, 1963, pp. 7-29.

[53]*Letter to Eulogius, Epp* VII, 37, MHG *Ep* I, 485-6.

pronouncements made by the Roman bishops and addressed to churches beyond the borders of their "suburbicarian" patriarchate were motivated by the concept that their primacy was Petrine and, thus, universal. This is true of the motivations behind the establishment of papal "vicars" in distant places like Arles and the Illyricum, and the distribution of the *pallium* to certain chosen metropolitans. Also, there is no doubt that the papal "decretals," which were published as early as the fifth century to answer issues raised throughout the West, were written in the same spirit.

This does not mean, however, that the papal vicars themselves, or the recipients of *pallia,* shared an absolute view of papal primacy. Both Gaul and the Illyricum occasionally opposed Rome. The factors which contributed most to give a formal and juridical dimension to papal authority, were the victory of "Roman" practices at the council of Whitby (664) and the subsequent activities of St Boniface in Western Germany and the Frankish kingdom. "Roman" order was now promoted as a program of church reform, following the chaotic conditions in France under the Merovingians. In 742, under Boniface's inspiration, the council of Soissons decreed that *all metropolitans* were to receive a *pallium* from Rome. The *pallium* thus came to symbolize canonical jurisdiction coming by delegation from Rome.[54] The idea will actually be imposed by Charlemagne, establishing indeed a "patriarchate of the West," a phenomenon of the Carolingian age.

To the question, therefore, whether or not there was a "patriarchate of the West" before Whitby and St Boniface, the answer must be a negative one. The other important observation to be made is that the "patriarchate," which appears in Carolingian times, is based on the concept of the *universal* Petrine authority of Rome. It is not, therefore, a patriarchate of the Eastern type, with clear territorial limitations and sharing in the fellowship of a pentarchy, but an extension of Roman authority over those parts of Christendom which were ready to accept it, *i.e.* the barbarian West. But the claims themselves were universal and had to include the East as well. Thus a potentially dangerous tension with the East would lead to open conflict in the Carolingian period.

In the sixth and seventh centuries, the Roman church was still playing the role of a link between East and West, as shown with particular clarity by St Gregory the Great. It did so, however, at the

[54]Cf. texts and comments by Y. Congar, *ibid.,* p. 204-5.

price of certain inner contradictions. Accepting the "pentarchy" by participating in the imperial Byzantine system, it was, at the same time using the argument of Petrine apostolicity, wherever it could be used to assert jurisdiction. Perhaps, this Janus-like equilibrium could have been maintained much longer, if the arrogance and carelessness of the iconoclastic emperors of Byzantium had not condemned the papacy to become a Western institution, tied to the Carolingian monarchy, first as an instrument and then as a fierce competitor for the rule of a centralized and culturally uniform Latin Christendom.

CHAPTER X

EMPEROR HERACLIUS AND
MONOTHELETISM

Heraclius I (610-641) was the most prominent imperial figure
to occupy the Byzantine throne since the death of Justinian. A man
of energy and vision, he restored the empire shattered during the reign
of the murderous Phocas (602-610). Peace with Persia had been one
of the major achievements of the reign of Maurice (582-602), the
predecessor of Phocas. Maurice had given shelter to the exiled Persian
"king of kings" Chosroes II and the latter, having married his
daughter, considered him as his father and protector. After Chosroes
was restored on his throne, the Byzantine empire gained significant
territorial advantages in Armenia. It was the murder of Maurice by
Phocas in 602 which served as the signal of an all-out attack of the
Persians on the Roman empire. In 610, a Persian detachment supported by Avar allies had already reached Chalcedon, across the
Bosphorus from Constantinople. It is then that Heraclius, son of the
exarch of Africa, led a fleet to rescue the city. Almost immediately he
was crowned emperor himself, as Phocas was executed. Since Chosroes
refused to conclude peace, the new emperor became engaged in a war
which lasted practically without interruption for eighteen years. Both
sides considered the war as a religious struggle between two world
religions: Christianity and Zoroastrianism. Each side fought not for
some passing political gain, but for the final triumph of what it
considered as universal and absolute Truth. Although religious values
had been invoked in all wars of the ancient world, never before was
the confrontation as explicit and as conscious.

333

On the Byzantine side, the religious dimension of the war was emphasized by the new emperor himself, who received constant advice from his friend, patriarch Sergius (610-638). Both emperor and patriarch were of oriental origin: Heraclius belonged to a prominent Cappadocian family, probably of Armenian stock, and Sergius was a Syrian. Their cooperation was a decisive element both in the conduct of the war and in the definition of religious policies. The Byzantine armies marched against the Persians, carrying, for the first time, icons of Christ and the Virgin, as symbols of heavenly protection.[1] The religious symbolism of the war was enhanced by the importance given on both sides to the relic of the True Cross, which had been venerated at Jerusalem since its unearthing by St Helen, mother of Constantine. As the Persians captured Jerusalem in 614, they massacred the population, took patriarch Zacharias prisoner and carried away the True Cross as a present to Chosroes.[2] However, the relic was restored to Jerusalem by Heraclius after his victory, most probably in March, 631.[3] The feast of the Exaltation of the Cross (September 14) was celebrated in Jerusalem with particular solemnity that year, and Heraclius was made into a legendary hero, remembered as a glorious precursor by the French crusader of the twelfth century, William of Tyre.

More significantly still, Heraclius inaugurated the use of a new title for Byzantine emperors: πιστὸς ἐν Χριστῷ βασιλεὺς ("basileus —or king—faithful in Christ"), to replace the traditional Roman title of emperor (Gr. αὐτοκράτωρ). The change is all the more significant, because, by Roman imperial standards, it could be interpreted as a lessening of imperial dignity. The title *emperor* belonged to the one and universal Roman emperor, whereas there were many "kings"

[1]On this, see A. Grabar, *L'iconoclasme byzantin. Dossier archéologique,* Paris, 1957, pp. 47-8.

[2]As compensation for the loss, two other exalted relics—the spear and the sponge, used by soldiers at Christ's crucifixion—were saved from the disaster, and brought to Constantinople (Cf. *Chronicon paschale,* PG 92, col. 988).

[3]The most detailed historical study of the relic is by A. Frolow, *La Relique de la Vraie Croix,* Paris, 1961. Cf. the discussion of the date in V. Grumel, "La reposition de la vraie croix à Jérusalem par Héraclius. Le jour et l'année," *Byzantinische Forschungen* I, 1966, pp. 139-149. On the chonology of Heraclius' return from Persia, see also V. Bolotov, "K istorii imperatora Irakliya," VV, 14 (1907), pp. 94-7 (restoration of the cross in Jerusalem dated 630). Byzantine chronicles also report some contradictory information about a further transfer of the True Cross to Constantinople. The tradition might have originated from the fact that Heraclius after the victory returned briefly to the capital with the Cross, before going to Jerusalem (cf. below note 26). In any case, the history of the relic, of which innumerable pieces circulated both in the East and in the West throughout the Middle Ages, defies any reliable historical investigation.

(*reges*) of individual nations, claiming only regional, or tribal juris-diction.[4] The change of the imperial title is often interpreted as a sign of the new "hellenic" consciousness of the Byzantines, or, on the contrary, as an imitation of the Persian "king of kings." In reality, the more decisive factor was that *basileus* was a biblical and messianic term: in the New Testament, Christ is the true and unique *basileus*, or king, so that the emperor being "faithful" (πιστὸς ἐν Χριστῷ) was now associating himself to Christ's royal ministry. Thus, the change reflected primarily a further integration of a Christian theocratic ideology with official Roman political philosophy. Henceforth, the title *basileus* became the exclusive privilege of the one universal sovereign of New Rome, and was denied to Frankish, or Slavic pretenders.[5]

The military challenge faced by the empire provoked Heraclius to an aggressive reaffirmation, in theory and in practice, of the universal vision inherited from Constantine, Theodosius I and Justinian. Having begun his career in the Latin West, as his father was exarch in Carthage, he always remained conscious of the Western dimension of his empire, using the papacy as a necessary element of his religious policies, even when the latter were determined primarily by Eastern imperatives. This universalist legacy was maintained by his successors. Constans II even travelled to Italy and envisaged the transfer of the capital there, away from Constantinople threatened by Arabs.

In 610, the situation of the empire was so tragic, that Heraclius himself thought of returning to more secure Carthage. Slav and Avar tribes had occupied practically the entire Balkan peninsula, leaving only isolated cities under imperial control. The Persian advance con-tinued. Antioch and Damascus were taken in 613, and the tragic sack of Jerusalem—symbol of Christian rule in the East—occurred in 614. Persian armies crossed Asia Minor and arrived again at the Bosphorus in 615. Egypt fell to them in 619. It is then that Heraclius, personally leading his troops, began his celebrated counter-offensive. Leaving Constantinople to the care of a provisional government under patriarch Sergius (622), he landed on the Eastern shores of the Black Sea,

---

[4]Cf. Ostrogorsky, "Avtograror i Samodrzac," in *Glasnik Srpske Akademiie,* 164, Belgrade, 1935, pp. 95-187. The title of *basileus* is used by Heraclius in a novel of 629 (J. and P. Zepos, *Jus graecoromanum,* I, Athens 1931, p. 36)

[5]Eventually, the emperor began to combine both titles, the religious and the secular, designating himself, as "basileus faithful in Christ God, and emperor of the Romans" (ἐν Χριστῷ τῷ Θεῷ πιστὸς βασιλεὺς καὶ αὐτοκράτωρ ʽΡωμαίων).

attacked the Persians in Armenia, and succeeded in liberating Asia Minor. For years, he continued operations South of the Caucasus, allying himself with the Christian kingdoms of the Lazi, Abasgi and Iberians (Georgians). In 626, however, as the emperor was campaignings in the East, the army of Chosroes II attacked Constantinople, supported by the Avars and Slavs. Patriarch Sergius animated the defense of the city. The great attack failed, and this salvation of the New Rome was attributed to the special protection of the Virgin Mary, associated particularly with the icon and church of the Virgin near the Blachernae Gate.[6] Meanwhile, Heraclius was continuing his offensive in Armenia. In 627, he invaded Persian territory and, in 628, occupied Dastagerd, the residence of the Persian "king of kings." Chosroes himself was murdered by his son Kawadh. Armenia, Mesopotamia, Syria and Egypt returned to Byzantine rule. The relic of the True Cross was restored to Jerusalem and Heraclius returned in triumph to Constantinople.

These dramatic events constitute the background of the religious policies of emperor Heraclius and patriarch Sergius. The Byzantine armies were fighting—with extraordinary success—for the external, physical preservation of the universal Roman empire. But the emperor and the patriarch could not avoid being concerned also with its internal, ecclesiastical unity, which, as we saw in the preceding chapters, was challenged by the schism between Chalcedonians and Monophysites. This issue was of crucial importance precisely in those areas— Armenia, Syria, Egypt—where the battle was taking place: a decisive battle not only for territory and political control, but also for the souls of the Eastern Christian population.

1. The Union Policy of Heraclius and Sergius: Monoenergism

In taking initiatives towards the reconciliation of the Monophysites, Heraclius followed the example of his predecessors who, for almost two centuries, had tried to achieve the goal of ecclesial unity in

---

[6]The author of the famous *Akathistos* hymn to the Virgin Mary is unknown. Some scholars support the authorship by Romanos the Melode, under Justinian. However, the popularity of the Kontakion, calling Mary a "victorious general" (ὑπέρμαχος στρατηγός), and the particular veneration of the Blachernae icon go back to the siege of 626 (cf. arguments and bibliography by S. S. Averintsev in Udal'tsova, Z.V., ed., *Kul'tura Vizantii*, Moscow, 1984, pp. 322-27).

the East. However, his policies were not based on simply avoiding issues, as did the *Henotikon* of Zeno. Rather, he attempted to uphold a christological development, based (so he thought) on the progress made already under Justinian, when the meaning of the Chalcedonian doctrine of the two natures was redefined in a Cyrillian context. This did produce limited results. We have seen earlier, that, as internal divisions were disturbing the Monophysite camp, at least some leaders of Syrian Monophysitism were tempted to join the orthodox Church, particularly during the reigns of Justin II and Tiberius. Patriarch Sergius himself was born in a Jacobite Syrian family,[7] and could therefore be considered a convert from Monophysitism. It is he who acted, discreetly and skillfully, as the emperor's theological advisor. Unfortunately, he does not seem to have been a truly great theological mind, and did not realize at once the implication of the formula which he proposed, as basis for unity. The formula consisted in affirming that the *hypostatic unity* of two natures in Christ, since it implied the unity of *one active subject,* presupposed one *divino-human energy,* or "activity" (μία θεανδρικὴ ἐνέργεια) in Christ.

The advantages of proposing this "monoenergism" as a formula of union were many. Severus of Antioch himself—who had accepted a distinction of the two natures of Christ "in thought" (ἐν θεωρίᾳ), affirmed the concrete unity of the Agent: "One is the agent (ἐνεργῶν), he wrote, *i.e.* the incarnate Word; one is the activity (ἐνέργεια), but the works (τὰ ἐνεργηθέντα) are varied."[8] The Fifth council also had admitted that in Christ there are not two concrete beings, but two natures to be distinguished only "in thought" (τῇ θεωρίᾳ μόνῃ, anathema 7).[9] Was it not then logical to conclude, that Christ was one "in activity" (ἐνεργείᾳ)? Was it not appropriate to think so, especially if one used the Cyrillian expression—whose legitimacy was fully admitted in 553—of "one nature incarnate of God the Word"? Aristotelian logic and terminology always connected the terms "nature" (φύσις) and "energy" (ἐνέργεια)—"energy" represented the concrete manifestation of any "nature." One could therefore legitimately speak of one energy, since one also spoke of one

---

[7]Anastasius of Sinai, *Hom. 3 on the image of God,* PG 89, col. 1153 CD; on Sergius, see J. L. Van Dieten, *Geschichte der Patriarchen von Sergios I. bis Johannes VI,* (610-615), Amsterdam, 1972, pp. 1-56.

[8]*Letter to Sergius,* CSCO, *Scriptores Syri,* IV, 7 (Louvain, 1949), p. 60.

[9]*Conciliorum ecumenicorum decreta,* 3rd ed., Bologna, 1973, p. 117; Engl. tr. in NPNF, XIV, p. 313.

nature, provided, of course, one also admitted the importance and orthodoxy of Chalcedonian "diphysitism" as an antidote against Eutyches.

The Chalcedonians could refer to some recognized authorities (especially Syrian) in favor of "monoenergism." First among these was Pseudo-Dionysius, who wrote in one of his rare christological passages of "one theandric energy."[10] The promoters of Mono-energism also made use of a spurious treatise of Menas of Constantinople to pope Vigilius. A respected theologian of the late sixth century, St Anastasius I of Antioch (559-570, 593-599)—who had opposed the aphthartodocetism of the old Justinian—was known to have used the same expression.[11] Furthermore, and paradoxically, Monoenergism was not only a bridge towards the Monophysites; it could be useful in approaching the Nestorians, whom Heraclius met in Persia. Indeed the Antiochian, pre-Chalcedonian theologians, teachers of Nestorius, formulated their christology precisely by affirming that the two natures, or hypostaseis of Christ, were united by the one activity (ἐνέργεια) of their unique "prosopon of union." Unfortunately the formula also had doubtful antecedents, since it had been used by Apollinaris.[12]

It is understandable, therefore, that patriarch Sergius did not begin his promotion of Monoenergism without hesitations and precautions. We actually know very little about the chronology of events which finally led to the adoption of the formula, as official theology in Constantinople. The rare available sources[13] clearly point to Sergius as the architect of the new policies. He took pains to seek advice, around 615-617, from the Chalcedonian bishop Theodore of Pharan (on the Sinai peninsula) and the Monophysite bishop Macaronas of Arsinoe in Egypt, and obtained their approval of his ideas.[14] He made further contact—in spite of protests by St John the Merciful of Alexandria—with another scholarly Egyptian Monophysite, Georges

---

[10]Ep IV, PG 3, col. 1072 C; of course, no one suspected that the author of the Corpus Areopagitcum was himself probably a Severian monophysite.

[11]Cf. G. Weiss, "Studien zum Leben, zu den Schriften und zur Theologie des Patriarchen Anastasius I, von Antiochien, 559-598," Miscellanea Byzantina Monacensia, IV, 1965, pp. 240 ff.

[12]"We worship Him in one nature, one will and one operation (ἐνέργεια)," in H. Lietzmann, Apollinaris von Laodicea und seine Schule (Tübingen, 1904), p. 248.

[13]The most reliable are a passage of the Disputation of St Maximus the Confessor with Pyrrhus (PG 91, cols. 332 B-333 B) and the letters of Sergius himself to pope Honorius and to Cyrus of Phasis.

Arsas (*ca.* 619), requesting patristic documentation favoring Mono-energism. When Heraclius, in 622, held his first meetings with Armenians in Theodosiopolis (Erzerum), Sergius was discreetly help-ing him by trying—this time unsuccessfully—to convince the Mono-physite theologian Paul, the One-Eyed, to accept Chalcedon on "monoenergistic" premises. In 626, as Heraclius was in Lazica, in Western Caucasus, which had been evangelized only at the time of Justinian (*i.e.* much later than the period of St Gregory "the Illumin-ator" and St Nino of Georgia, the apostles of Armenia and Eastern Georgia), the local Metropolitan Cyrus of Phasis (mod. Poti, on the Black Sea) was also gained over to Monoenergism through an exchange of letters with Sergius.[15] The recent reunion of the neighboring Georgian catholicos Kirion of Mtskheta with Chalcedonian orthodoxy (*ca.* 600) had strengthened the emperor's hand in the region.

Although our information about all these contacts is fragmentary, their importance was becoming quite obvious to contemporaries. The policy of church union began bearing fruit both during the campaigns of Heraclius and after his final victory in 628. No opposition seemed to have been voiced from any circle before 633, when St Sophronius finally raised his voice in Alexandria, provoking a retreat of Sergius. At the same time, the great St Maximus, the future Confessor, in a letter to the abbot Pyrrhus, who solicited his opinion on, and approval of, the doctrine of the "one energy" of Christ, answered with warm praises to the doctrine of the *Psephos* of Sergius (see below), (p. 349) and with an avowal of incompetence: he only asked Pyrrhus to explain what is meant by "energy" in the ongoing debate. Significantly how-ever, he stressed the point that the meaning of theological terms is more important than the words themselves.[16]

It is obvious therefore that even the best minds of the Church trusted the policies of Sergius and Heraclius over two decades, under-standably rejoicing in the great victory over the Persians and hoping for a new beginning in unionist efforts.

---

[14]It does appear that Theodore of Pharan was the real intellectual author of "monoenergism." Fragments of his writings were presented (and condemned) at the Sixth council in 680 (Cf. F. X. Murphy and P. Sherwood, *Constantinople II et Constantinople III*, Paris, 1973, pp. 143-6, 303-4).

[15]Texts in Mansi XI, cols. 525-8, 560-1.

[16]PG 91, col. g96 AC; cf. comments and translation of the letter in F.-M. Léthel, *Théologie de l'agonie du Christ*, Paris, 1979, p. 59 ff.

2. *Church unions in the East and in Egypt*

The Persian conquest of the entire Middle East, which lasted eighteen years in Syria (611-629) and eleven years in Egypt (618-629) caused fundamental changes in the relationships between various religious groups. The large Jewish population of Palestine and Egypt, whose rights were restricted within the Christian empire, welcomed the arrival of the Persians. It even appears that, following the capture of Jerusalem in 614, Jews not only participated in the massacres of Christians, but obtained a privileged position in the local administration. This privileged status was eventually ended by a decree of Chosroes II, expelling Jews from the city.[17] As compared to many of his predecessors, Chosroes had not planned deliberately to humiliate or suppress Christianity. Not only had he become familiar with the Christian world during his exile, under the protection of emperor Maurice, but his two preferred wives—Maria, daughter of Maurice, and Shirin, a Jacobite—were Christians, and he is known to have honored them by building Christian churches and monasteries at their request.[18] The conquest of large territories with a Christian population presented him with the challenge faced by all multi-cultural empires: to establish social harmony through toleration, since immediate religious unity could not be imposed by force.

In 614, after the capture of Jerusalem, Chosroes took the unusual —but very "imperial"—step of convoking representatives of the major three Christian groups to Ctesiphon. Presidency at the meeting was given to the Armenian prince Sembat Bagratuni. The Nestorians, who previously held a dominant position in Persia, presented a confession of faith.[19] However, the Armenians later reported that it is their faith which was given the upper hand at the meeting.[20] In fact, it appears that—any doctrinal agreement being obviously impossible—Chosroes decided to maintain the Nestorian predominance among Christians in former Sassassid territories and to support the Monophysites, where they held clear majority, i.e. in former Byzantine territories of Syria,

[17]Cf. in particular the Armenian chronicler Sebeos, *History of Heraclius,* ed. and Fr. tr. by F. Macler (Paris, 1904), pp. 71-2.
[18]Cf. M. J. Higgins, "Chosroes II's votive offerings at Sergiopolis," BZ 48 (1955), pp. 89-102.
[19]Text in Chabot, *Synodicon,* pp. 580-98.
[20]Sebeos, *ibid.,* pp. 113-16.

Armenia and Western Mesopotamia. The Chalcedonians were obviously less favored because of their attachment to the Roman empire. They were not represented at the meeting in Ctesiphon, but were nevertheless allowed to restore their churches in Palestine where they held the majority. They did so under the leadership of Modestus, the *locum tenens* of the patriarchate of Jerusalem, since the incumbent Zacharias had been led to captivity. The work of restoration received generous help from St John the Merciful, patriarch of Alexandria.

The overall result of the Ctesiphon meeting was to give a big boost to the Monophysite establishment, both in Armenia and in Syria.[21] Following the death of Anastasius II, Chalcedonian patriarch of Antioch, which occurred during the riots of 611, even before the Persian conquest, the see remained vacant for decades until after the Muslim occupation. When the Persians came, the Monophysite patriarch Athanasius, the Camel-Driver (595-631), wrote to his colleague in Alexandria: "The world rejoiced in peace and love," because the "Chalcedonian night" had vanished.[22] The Monophysite chronicler Michael the Syrian also reports with satisfaction how the Persian king ordered "all Chalcedonians to be expelled" and that "the memory of the Chalcedonians disappeared from the Euphrates to the Orient (*i.e.* Syria)."[23]

But then came the victory of Heraclius and the restoration of Byzantine rule, followed by new attempts at ending the schism. During his own six year stay in Transcaucasia and Persia (622-8) and in the years which followed the victory, Heraclius, advised by Sergius of Constantinople, actively pursued a policy of church union. He needed it not only politically, but also to justify the religious character of the war and the miraculous victory of 628.

Just as Justinian, Heraclius could not envisage a religiously pluralistic empire. He took drastic measures to suppress small minorities, like the Jews, who had compromised themselves by cooperating with the Persians. In 634, he published an edict ordering all Jews to be baptized.[24] To escape forced conversion, Palestinian, Syrian and Egyptian Jews fled in great numbers to the protection of either Persia or the invading Muslim Arabs. But we know that the edict was effectively

[21]Cf. Frend, *The Rise*, pp. 335-9.
[22]Severus of Asmounein, *History of the Patriarchs*, ed. and tr. B.T.A. Evetts, PO I, Paris, 1907, p. 481.
[23]X, 25, *ed. cit.*, II, pp. 380-1.
[24]Cf. Michael the Syrian, *Chron.*, IX, 4, *ed. cit.*, II, pp. 414.

applied in Africa.[25] A different approach—especially after the tolerant policies of Chosroes II—was needed in relations with both the Monophysites and the Nestorians. The Monoenergism of Sergius was offered as a solution, and produced several spectacular results. The chronology of events is obscure,[26] but the facts themselves are well established.

Following the victory, solemnly announced on April 8, 628, problems of implementation required long negotiations between Heraclius and the Persians, now represented by king Kawadh—son and successor of the murdered Chosroes—and the general Shahrbaraz, whose armies were still stationed in Syria, and who pursued independent ambitions of his own. Before his untimely death, already in October 628, Kawadh sent to Heraclius an embassy headed by the highest Christian official of Persia, the Nestorian catholicos Isoyabh II. Received by the emperor, probably in Theodosiopolis, the catholicos was "greatly honored" by Heraclius.[27] After presenting a confession of faith—and presumably some brief discussion—the catholicos celebrated the divine liturgy in an orthodox church, at which the emperor and his court received Holy Communion. A christology of two natures, acting as "one energy," could be accepted easily by both Chalcedonians and Nestorians! This remarkable—and first—great success of unionism would be even more understandable if the hypothesis made by V. V. Bolotov, according to which it was Isoyabh who returned the relic of the True Cross to Heraclius, could be verified: a gesture of this magnitude, sealing reconciliation and peace, would make sacramental communion even more appropriate.[28] Contacts of the Nestorian catholicosate

[25]Cf. the Jewish document known as *Doctrina Iacobi* (ed. Bonwetsch, Berlin, 1910, p. 88).

[26]Interpreting Syriac, Armenian and Greek sources, scholars disagree on whether the meeting with the Nestorian catholicos Isoyahb II, the return of the True Cross and the council of Theodosiopolis with the Armenians occurred before the triumphal return of Heraclius to Constantinople in 630 or 631 (cf. V. Bolotov, *Lektsii,* pp. 88-91), or during his other voyage to Syria and Jerusalem in 631-33 (cf. L. Bréhier in Fliche & Martin, *Histoire,* V, Paris, 1947, pp. 98-101, 111-117).

[27]Μεγάλως ἐτίμησε, Nicephorus, *Breviarium,* 20, ed. Bonn, p. 23.

[28]The hypothesis is presented, with rather solid arguments (V. V. Bolotov, *Lektsii,* pp. 85-88). Sources are very contradictory on the fate of the relic after its capture in Jerusalem in 614, and on the circumstances of its return to Heraclius. These silences and contradictions can be explained by the reluctance of chroniclers to attribute this gesture to Kawadh (who was not recognized as king by Shahrbaraz), and to a Nestorian catholicos. The same reluctance exists concerning the place, where the relic was kept after its capture. Why was it not destroyed, or publicly profaned to show the triumph of Zoroastrianism over Christianity? Could it not have been offered, as a pious present, by Chosroes to one or both of his Christian wives, which would make its return by Isoyabh quite natural? The True Cross actually would never have left Christian hands.

of Seleucia-Ctesiphon with Heraclius continued. In 631, a second Persian embassy sent by queen Boran and including again Isoyahb II met the emperor in Berrhoe(Aleppo).

Once in possession of the True Cross, Heraclius, travelling through Armenia, "gave many fragments [of the relic] to Armenian dignitaries," trying to gain their loyalty and induce them to ecclesiastical union.[29] We have seen (above, p. 284) that, since 591, the Armenian Church had been divided between a Chalcedonian catholicosate on Byzantine territory, and the Monophysite center in Dvin, under the Persians. With Chosroes' conquest in 607-8, the Chalcedonian catholicos John was arrested and died in captivity, as the church was again reunited under Monophysite catholicoi Abraham and Komitas. After the latter's death (628) and the brief tenure of a successor, Christopher, the catholicos Ezr (Esras) was contacted by Heraclius, who now controlled the whole of Armenia, and was offered union. He met the emperor in Edessa (probably in 630) and was satisfied with the emperor's "monoenergistic" orthodoxy. Eucharistic communion took place, and the catholicos returned to Dvin, gratified with many imperial favors. Facing opposition among Armenian clerics and theologians, Ezr, urged by Heraclius, convoked a formal council of 193 Greek and Armenian bishops in Theodosiopolis (Karin, Erzerum), where union was formally discussed and signed, including a formal acceptance of the council of Chalcedon by the Armenians.[30] Resistance to the union was limited to a few theologians, headed in particular by John Mavragometsis. In 640, John was formally condemned by Ezr's successor, catholicos Nerses III, the Builder, who remained Chalcedonian until a new council held at Dvin (648-9) where union was rejected again. At that time an anti-byzantine alliance with the Muslim khalifate dominated Armenian politics. But a forceful return of Byzantine armies to Armenia reversed the situation once more. In 654, Emperor Constans II personally came to Dvin: the liturgy was celebrated at the cathedral of St Gregory the Illuminator, at which the emperor received communion with the catholicos Nerses, who recognized Chalcedon again. It is the Arab conquest which ended the union for good in 660.

More difficult still were the contacts of Heraclius with the Jacobites of Syria and Mesopotamia. As the emperor was visiting

[29]Ovhannes Mamikonean, as quoted in Bolotov, *Lektsii,* p. 88.
[30]The date of the council is a debated problem, the most likely being 632-3.

reconquered Edessa, he seems to have taken for granted a state of union with the Monophysites. According to Michael the Syrian, he attended the Eucharist celebrated by the local (Jacobite) bishop Isaiah, but was publicly rebuked from the chalice by the latter, who requested a preliminary anathema to Chalcedon and the *Tome* of Leo.[31] In spite of this setback, further contacts continued, this time with the old ascetical and learned Jacobite patriarch of Antioch, Athanasius, the Camel-Driver (595-631). Athanasius had a record of theological moderation and imperial loyalty. He had been deposed by the Persians, travelled to imperial-held Egypt in 616, and accepted the imperially-sponsored unity with the Egyptian "Theodosian" Monophysites (see above, p. 275-6). The patriarch and twelve of his bishops met emperor Heraclius in Hierapolis (Mabbugh). Sergius of Constantinople sent letters explaining Monoenergism, and Cyrus of Phasis came in person to promote union. According to Monophysite sources, the debates were inconclusive and Heraclius began persecuting the opponents. In fact, it does appear that some understanding was reached.[32] The death of patriarch Athanasius, which followed almost immediately (July 631), may have prevented the implementation of the union. No Chalcedonian successor was named, presumably in expectation of a joint election. Many monasteries and communities in the area of Antioch, accepted Chalcedon with "monoenergistic" understanding. One of these was the monastery of St John Maron near Emesa, where Heraclius was met with solemnity, making land donations to the monastery. From that time, an isolated community of "Maronites," faithful to the Monoenergism of patriarch Sergius of Constantinople, survived persecutions and massacres by escaping to the mountains of Lebanon and establishing there their own patriarchate. Eventually, with the help of the Latin crusaders, the Maronites joined the communion of the Roman Catholic Church (1182).[33]

The relative success of the imperial policies in Armenia, Persia and Syria was overshadowed by the even more significant union which occurred in Egypt. St John the Almsgiver, Chalcedonian patriarch of

---

[31] *Chron.* XI, 4, *ed. cit.*, II, 411-12.

[32] Cf. Duchesne, *L'Eglise*, pp. 397-8; L. Bréhier, *op. cit.*, pp. 115-6; Frend, *The Rise*, p. 347.

[33] Apologetic attempts have been made to defend the perpetual "orthodoxy" of the Maronites, but there cannot be any serious challenge to the contemporary scholarly consensus on the original Monophysitism of the Maronite community, and its Monoenergism between the seventh and the twelfth century.

Alexandria had left the country, fleeing the Persians (617). Under the Persian régime, the Monophysite patriarch Andronicus occupied the *Caesareum*, the main church of Alexandria. Following his death, he was succeeded by a young and able man, Benjamin (he was 35 at his election), whose popularity and ascetical prestige unified the Christian Copts in this crucial period of their history. He is the first to be designated in sources as the "Coptic patriarch" and his tenure lasted thirty-nine years (623-662). Meanwhile, Heraclius inaugurated in Egypt the tactics which were serving him so well in other territories recovered from the Persians.

In autumn 631, a new Chalcedonian patriarch arrived in Alexandria, invested with extraordinary powers: that of archbishop and of prefect of Egypt. This combination of church and civil functions was contrary to ecclesiastical canons and quite exceptional in the history of the Byzantine church. In making the appointment, Heraclius may have been inspired by the successful political role played by patriarch Sergius in Constantinople, during his own absence in the East, and also by the civil role formally entrusted by Justinian to the Church in Italy, after the reconquest of the sixth century. In Egypt, since Athanasius and Cyril, there already was a tradition for the archbishop of Alexandria to play the role of national leader for the country as a whole. This time, however, such powers were entrusted by imperial appointment at a very critical moment, to a foreigner, Cyrus, formerly metropolitan of Phasis in the Caucasus, who already had a record as one of the architects of ecclesiastical unions, based on "monoenergism." His main mission was the one in which so many other Chalcedonian patriarchs had failed: to reestablish the religious unity of Egypt within imperial orthodoxy. At the time of his appointment, however, he could not have foreseen that his mission would be a short one, and that already in 639, the forces of Islam would take over Egypt, cutting off the Egyptian church from the empire and transforming it for centuries into an isolated minority.

Upon the arrival of Cyrus, the Monophysite patriarch Benjamin went into hiding and lived in remote desert monasteries until the Arab conquest.[34] In order to achieve his goal, the new "pope" Cyrus used both persuasion and force. The policy of persuasion had produced

---

[34]The *Life* of Benjamin, which is part of *History of the Patriarchs* by Severus of Asmounein, (ed. cit. above, note 22) is one of the most important historical sources for the history of Christian Egypt during this period.

at least some limited results before the Persian occupation, under the respected and competent Chalcedonian patriarchs Eulogius and John the Almsgiver.[35] Furthermore, the government of Heraclius had helped resolving the "tritheist" disputes between Monophysites, and it is under imperial sponsorship that the union of 616 between patriarch Athanasius the Camel-Driver of Antioch, and the "Theodosian" patriarch of Alexandria Anastasius, had been concluded. There is no doubt, therefore, that the church of Egypt, in spite of the Monophysite loyalty of the majority, nourished some positive predispositions towards the government of Heraclius, especially after its specatcular victories over the Persians, whose occupation of Egypt had not been popular.[36] Now, Cyrus came up with what he presented as "fresh" proposals, which at least some Monophysites could—with some justification—interpret as a Chalcedonian capitulation. Some of them exclaimed: "It is not we who commune with Chalcedon, but rather Chalcedon is coming to us."[37] But this report about the joy of Monophysites is by a Chalcedonian enemy of monoenergism. In practically all Coptic sources, the memory of Cyrus is associated exclusively with blood and coercion, not with theological compromise. They do not even mention the "monoenergistic" stand of Cyrus, or the *Ekthesis* of Heraclius, but only the persecutions suffered by the opponents of Chalcedon. Indeed, among many others, the brother of patriarch Benjamin, Menas was tortured and executed,[38] and the Roman troops kept mutilating dissident Copts, even as they themselves were besieged by Arabs in Babylon (contemporary Cairo) in 641. The terror lasted for ten years, the entire length of Cyrus' tenure.[39] Being the head of both civil and ecclesiastical administrations in Egypt, he was held responsible by the Copts for all the brutalities of his administration. Known as the "'Caucasian" (Al-Muqauqas, in Arabic) because he came from Lazica on the Black Sea, he entered history as the great persecutor of the Monophysites and a skilled—though unsuccessful—diplomat, respected by the Muslims.[40]

[35]See above, pp. 276-8.

[36]Although the Persians did not molest the Monophysite Patriarch Andronicus, many Copts were slaughtered by the occupiers. Also, the cooperation between the large Jewish population of Egypt and the Persians had not been popular among the Copts (Cf. Butler, *The Arab Conquest* pp. 80-82).

[37]Theophanes, *Chron.*, ed. De Boor, p. 330.

[38]Severus of Asmounein, *op. cit.*, pp. 489-92.

[39]Butler, *op. cit.*, pp. 184-93, 274.

[40]In nineteenth century scholarship, there was some confusion as to the identity

It must be said, however, that terror followed a serious attempt at conciliation, which is not mentioned in Monophysite sources, precisely because it was, in large part, successful. On June 3, 633, Cyrus presided over a solemn Eucharist at the Caesareum, the great cathedral of Alexandria. Reporting to Sergius of Constantinople, he affirms that "all the clergy of the Theodosians," received communion from his hands.[41] By "Theodosians," he meant, of course, the main Severian party of the Monophysites. The report is ambiguously exaggerated, but it seems probable that most of the urban Alexandrian clergy and, at least two influential "Theodosian" bishops—Victor of Fayum and Cyrus of Nikiu—, accepted union. The basis of the agreement was expressed in nine chapters (κεφάλαια), or anathematisms, which were solemnly read from the ambo by the patriarch. They contained the usual Cyrillian-Chalcedonian formulae, which represented official christology since the reign of Justinian. Thus, chapter 6 affirmed the Cyrillian expression "one nature incarnate of God the Word" (μία φύσις Θεοῦ λόγου σεσαρκωμένη) with the explanation that it actually meant "one hypostasis, composed of two natures." Then, in order to avoid the impression that the traditional formula of Dioscoros and Severus (*"of* two natures") was condoned unconditionally, the seventh chapter introduced explicitly Chalcedonian language, affirming "the one Lord Jesus Christ consisted *in* two natures." The text continues by proclaiming a Chalcedonian understanding of "Theopaschism": the same Christ, One of the Holy Trinity, "suffered humanly in the flesh as man, but remained impassible in the sufferings of His own flesh, as God." Then, the text of the Seventh anathematism uses the key expression: "the one and the same Christ and Son, acted divinely and humanly through one divino-human energy (μιᾷ θεανδρικῇ ἐνεργείᾳ), as the divine Dionysius has said."[42] Chapters 8 and 9 contain lists of heretics to be anathematized—essentially the critics of Cyril, in accordance with the decisions of the Fifth council (553).

In reporting of the union to Constantinople, Cyrus paraphrased

of the Al-Muqauqas mentioned by Arabic texts on the conquest of Egypt. The identification has been independently, but firmly established by V. Bolotov, who died in 1900, but whose article on the subject appeared posthumously (cf. *Lektsii*, pp. 68-73) and A. J. Butler (*op. cit.,* first published, Oxford, 1902, pp. 137ff.).

[41]Letter included in the *Acts* of the Sixth council (Mansi, XI, col. 561D-564A).

[42]Mansi, XI, col. 565 D. Cf. a detailed analysis of the text in Hefele-Leclerq, *Histoire des conciles*, III, 1, pp. 339-41; the reference is, of course, to Pseudo-Dionysius the Areopagite.

the famous letter of St Cyril to John of Antioch, written exactly two centuries earlier: "Even the heavenly beings rejoiced."[43] In 633, as in 433—so Cyrus thought—a common christological confession was finally agreed upon, and the peace of the Church was achieved. Indeed, the policy of Sergius, applied by Cyrus in Egypt, had succeeded in showing that shrewd approaches, combining theological initiative and military pressure, could still be effective in reconciling Eastern Christians within the imperial system. The new arrangement did not imply a renunciation of Chalcedon: the authority of the council and the union in two natures were solemnly reaffirmed. But Sergius and Cyrus overlooked the fact that they were also raising an issue which had represented the real point of separation between Chalcedonian and Monophysite christologies from the beginning: the problem of maintaining, within the "hypostatic" union, an existentially real, and therefore *active* created humanity, assumed by the Logos. They also discovered that within Chalcedonian orthodoxy there were those for whom the issue of the true faith transcended all considerations of ecclesiastical and political (today we would say "ecumenical") expediency, and who opposed the imperial policies.

3. Sophronius of Jerusalem and Honorius of Rome: Monotheletism

Precisely in 633, as the Union was being proclaimed, Sophronius, an old monk more than eighty years old, was present in the Egyptian capital. As he enjoyed wide spiritual prestige, patriarch Cyrus showed him the nine "chapters," asking for his authoritative support. "At first reading, [Sophronius] implored, supplicated and demanded from Cyrus, falling at his feet, not to proclaim any such thing from the ambo, for, he said, these were the doctrines of Apollinaris."[44] The objections of Sophronius were directed exclusively against what he considered as a misuse and a misquotation of the Dionysian expression "one divino-human energy" in chapter 7 of the Union document. The protest of Sophronius did not stop the plans of Cyrus in Egypt and the Union was proclaimed. However, the old man travelled to Constantinople immediately, to meet Sergius. His intervention had immediate effect in a gesture which seems to indicate the patriarch's diplo-

---

[43]Mansi, *ibid.,* col. 564 A; cf. Cyril's letter in ACO I, 1, 4, pp. 15-20.
[44]The episode is reported by St Maximus the Confessor in his *Letter to Peter,* written in 643-4 (PG 91, 143 CD).

matic flexibility, but also his probably sincere concern for orthodoxy. Sergius published a patriarchal *Psephos* ("authoritative opinion"), which was handed to Sophronius, and a copy sent to Cyrus. It amounted to a partial disavowal of the terms of the Alexandrian union: no one was to speak any longer about "one" or "two" energies in Christ, such expressions being "impious." The right approach would be to speak of one Divine subject, as agent, which excludes the existence in Christ of two wills contrary to each other. The text stopped short of proclaiming one will in Christ, but affirmed that "at no time did His flesh, animated by a [human] intelligence, accomplish its natural movement separately, or on its own initiative, contrary to the consent of God the Word, hypostatically united with it, but it acted as God willed."

The original complete text of the patriarchal *Psephos* has not been preserved, but long quotations were forwarded by Sergius himself to his colleague in Rome, pope Honorius. In this letter to the pope, Sergius also affirms that Sophronius was content with the text and "accepted not to speak anymore of either one, or two energies, limiting himself to tradition and to the certain and habitual teachings [of the Fathers]."[45]

This agreement with Sophronius may have been embarrassing to Sergius—and certainly to Cyrus—but it shows real concern for theological integrity on the part of Sergius, and an initial moderation on the part of Sophronius. Indeed, the *Psephos* is both a moderate and an innovative document. Although it abandons Monoenergism, it introduces a new concept in the theory of one will in Christ. Without making the theory too explicit, it excludes "two wills," and suggests that the existence of "two wills" would imply the possibility of a conflict, or opposition between them.

Who was that old man Sophronius, who intervened so forcefully in the "ecumenical" schemes of the patriarchs of Constantinople and Alexandria?

Born around 550 in Damascus, in a family of perhaps Syrian origin, he is known, by 578, as Sophronius "the Sophist," a title which reflects secular education and proficiency in Greek rhetorical skills.[46]

[45]Mansi, XI, 536 C.

[46]On the life of Sophronius, and particularly his identification as a "Sophist," see S. Vailhé, "Sophrone le Sophiste et Sophrone le Patriarche," *Revue de l'Orient Chrétien* 7 (1902), pp. 360-85; 8 (1903), pp. 32-69, 356-87. The fundamental study of Vailhé has been developed and updated by Ch. von Schönborn, *Sophrone de Jérusalem, Vie*

Feeling attracted by Palestinian monasticism, but still remaining a man of the world, Sophronius visits the Lavra of St Theodosius near Bethlehem, where he meets a friend, who would remain his companion until his death in 619, John Moschus. The two men travel to Egypt together (after 578), where John begins the composition of a famous description of Egyptian and Palestinian monasticism known as "The Spiritual Meadow" (λειμών, λειμωνάριον, or "New Paradise," Νέος Παράδεισος; Lat: *Pratum Spirituale;* Slav.: *Lug dukhovny*). They share in the intellectual atmosphere of Alexandria, visiting Stephen the Sophist, a former Tritheist,[47] and being received by patriarch Eulogius. But the most lasting impression left on the two friends is that produced by the Egyptian monks, many of them still Chalcedonian. Returning to Palestine, Sophronius becomes a monk himself at the *Lavra* of St Theodosius; then, again with John, he stays ten years on Mt Sinai, only to return again to Palestine in 594. A second trip to Egypt of the two friends, puts them in touch with the holy patriarch, St John the Almsgiver. Healed through the intercessions of two locally venerated martyrs, the "unmercenary doctors" Cyrus and John, Sophronius composes a book about their miracles, which contains interesting information on the relationships between Chalcedonians and Monophysites in Egypt at the time.

Hearing the news of the fall of Jerusalem to the Persians (614), John and Sophronius travel to Rome, where John puts the last hand to his "Spiritual Meadow" and dies in 619. Sophronius then returns to his mother-house of St Theodosius (bringing the body of John to be put there to its final rest) and remains in Palestine under Persian occupation, at least for a while. Eventually, however, he resumes his travels. In 627-8, we find him in Africa, where he makes the truly fateful encounter with another monk, also a refugee from the Persian invasion, Maximus. The future great Confessor becomes the spiritual son of Sophronius by joining his monastic community, known as the *Eukratades.*[48]

Maximus did not follow Sophronius to Alexandria, where the

monastique et confession dogmatique, Paris, 1972. See also J. Phokylides, Ἰωάννης ὁ Μόσχος καὶ Σωφρόνιος ὁ σοφιστὴς καὶ ὁ πατριάρχης Ἱεροσολύμων," Νέα Σιών 13-14 (1913-14) and especially H. Chadwick, "John Moschus and Sophronius the Sophist," JTS (25 (1974), pp. 41-74.

[47]See above, p. 275.

[48]Eukratas has apparently been the family name of John, while Moschus was his surname.

old man confronted Cyrus in 633, or to Constantinople, where he met Sergius. The letter he addressed to the abbot Pyrrhus at that time indicates that he was not yet clearly taking sides in the debate, and was even attracted by the concilitory tone of the *Psephos*.[49] Later, however, he would always remember his "blessed lord, his father and master, the lord abbot Sophronius,"[50] and there cannot be any doubt that it is indeed the example and the thought of St Sophronius, which would make St Maximus aware of the dangers of both Monoenergism and Monotheletism.[51]

Following his contacts with Sergius in Constantinople, the old Sophronius returned to Palestine, where he was elected patriarch of Jerusalem almost immediately.

The Union in Alexandria was an event of far-reaching dimensions, which made it inevitable for Sergius to inform his colleague of the "old Rome." This announcement, made in a letter written in 634, included a note of embarrassment: Sergius had to report a protest by Sophronius—now a patriarch—against the term "one energy," and admit of the content of his *Psephos,* which by forbidding to speak of "energies" could jeopardize the future of the Union, since "Mono-energism" was precisely the point which made union possible. He attempted to by-pass the issue of terminology (actually, Chalcedonians had often criticized the Monophysites for being picky about words and expressions), and to make two strong points: 1) The Union in Egypt was an unprecedented success: "The people of Alexandria had become one flock of Christ our God, and with it almost all of Egypt, Thebais, Lybia and the other provinces of the Egyptian dioceses . . ." Consequently, how can the protests of Sophronius be allowed to annul that unity in regions "which never, until today, accepted to commemorate the name of our divine and holy father Leo [the Great, author of the *Tome to Flavian*], or of the holy and great ecumenical council of Chalcedon, and which now proclaim them loudly and clearly during the celebration of the divine mysteries?" 2) The second point of Sergius reflected the content of his *Psephos*: the uncontroversial affirmation of a unity of Christ's divine subject, which excluded any conflict of "two wills" and actually made it unnecessary to insist upon counting "energies." To this point, Sophronius himself—still called

---

[49]Cf. PG 91, col. 596 AC; Cf. above, p. 339.

[50]PG 91, col. 533 A.

[51]Cf. P. Sherwood, *An annotated date-list of the works of Maximus the Confessor,* (*Studia Anselmiana,* 30), Rome, 1932, p. 6.

a "holy man" by Sergius in his letter—raised no objections. Of course, Cyrus in his nine chapters of union, had used the "one energy" terminology, but this was to be interpreted as an *oikonomia*, for the sake of the salvation of a multitude, without implying any infringement upon the exactitude (ἀκρίβεια) of the right teachings of the Church.[52]

Clearly—and with ostensible sincerity—Sergius wanted the pope to join the newly-founded consensus, insisting on his faithfulness to Chalcedon and Pope Leo. The *Psephos* seemed to have reached that goal at the price of some ambiguity to which even Sophronius had not formally objected. But the answer of Honorius, pronouncing that *Monotheletism* was to replace the now abandoned "Monoenergism" would make further consensus impossible.

In terms of Italian church history of the period, pope Honorius I (625-638) appears as a zealous, energetic and pious bishop. He built churches in Rome, including St Agnes on the Via Nomentana, with its famous mosaic, and restored in his own house the monastic traditions, so dear to St Gregory the Great. He cooperated with the exarch Isaac in facing the still Arian Lombard kings Arioald and Rothari. He was successful in struggling against the remnants of the Aquileian schism, and hospitable to numerous Eastern monks and clergy who were fleeing to the West before the Persian invasions. But he was obviously unprepared to solve the sophisticated imbroglio implied in the letter of Sergius.

His reply to the Byzantine patriarch[53] congratulates the architects of union policies, based on Monoenergism, and criticizes those who raise sophisticated problems of terminology (implying obviously St Sophronius). Giving his full approval to the policies of Cyrus and their results, he makes a significant step by clarifying further the implications of the letter of Sergius. The latter had rejected "Monoenergism" as ambiguous and controversial, but strongly emphasized that, in Christ, there was One divine Agent, which excluded "two wills" [contrary to each other]. This was a clear suggestion that the hypostatic union presupposed one will, *i.e.* the doctrine known as Monotheletism. Honorius moves from this suggestion to a clear statement: "Indeed, he writes, the Deity could neither be crucified, nor

[52]Cf. these passages of the letter in Mansi, XI, cols. 532 B-536 D.

[53]The Latin original of the letter is lost, but a Greek translation, checked against the original found in the archives of the patriarchate of Constantinople, is included in the Acts of the Sixth council, at which Honorius was condemned as a heretic (Mansi XI, cols. 537-44).

experience human passions. But [according to the hypostatic union], one says that the Deity suffered and that humanity came from heaven with the Deity. Therefore, we confess the one will of our Lord Jesus Christ (ὅθεν καὶ ἕν θέλημα ὁμολογοῦμεν τοῦ Κυρίου ἡμῶν Ἰησοῦ Χριστοῦ)."[54]

This direct step into Monotheletism, which he was first to make, is the famous "fall of Honorius," for which the Sixth ecumenical council condemned him (681)—a condemnation which until the early Middle Ages, would be repeated by all popes at their installation, since on such occasions they had to confess the faith of the ecumenical councils. It is understandable, therefore, that all the critics of the doctrine of papal infallibility in later centuries—Protestants, Orthodox and "anti-infallibilists" at Vatican I in 1870—would refer to his case. Some Roman catholic apologists try to show that the expressions used by Honorius could be understood in an orthodox way, and that there is no evidence that he deliberately wished to proclaim anything else than the traditional faith of the Church.[55] They also point out—quite anachronistically—that the letter to Sergius was not a formal statement, issued by the pope *ex cathedra,* using his "charisma of infallibility," as if such a concept existed in the seventh century. Without denying the pope's good intentions—which can be claimed in favor of any heresiarch of history—it is quite obvious that his confession of one will, at a crucial moment and as Sergius himself was somewhat backing out before the objections of Sophronius, not only condoned the mistakes of others, but actually coined a heretical formula—the beginning of a tragedy, from which the Church (including the orthodox successors of Honorius on the papal throne) would suffer greatly.

Upon receipt of the letter from Rome, Sergius felt quite relieved. The terminological problems seemed to be resolved. There was no need any longer to use the ambiguous doctrine of "one energy," since the formal endorsement of the concept of "one will" by Honorius opened the door for a christological position which seemed quite appealing: how can the one person, or hypostasis of Christ possess

---

[54]*Ibid.,* col. 540 BC.

[55]Cf. for instance, V. Grumel, *op. cit.,* EO, 32, 1929, pp. 274-7, or the rather blind acceptance of infallibility in Murphy-Sherwood, *op. cit.,* p. 102 ("Il ne peut y avoir de nouveau dans la doctrine de l'Eglise, ainsi dans celle d'Honorius"). Other Roman Catholic authors are, of course, more candid, admitting that he was an "abettor of heresy." (Karl Baus in Jedin-Dolan, *History,* p. 634), and even regretting that historians made patriarch Serguis—a promoter of church unity—"suffer for what people are unwilling to charge pope Honorius with" (H. G. Beck, *ibid.,* p. 458).

more than one will? Eventually a crucial document, drafted by Sergius with the cooperation of the abbot Pyrrhus, was presented to the signature of emperor Heraclius:[56] the *Ekthesis* of 638. Rejecting Mono-energism and repeating almost word for word the text of the *Psephos* concerning Christ as the unique Agent and Subject of His divine and of His human acts, the text also picks up the sentence from the letter of Honorius: "We confess one will of our Lord Jesus Christ."[57] Sergius died in the same year, after having the *Ekthesis* endorsed by the synod of Constantinople. His succesor, patriarch Pyrrhus—the correspondent and future adversary of St Maximus—had himself been one of the drafters and, with imperial sanction, proclaimed the *Ekthesis* to be the official faith of the empire.

There is no doubt that Sergius, who had been originally impressed by the arguments of Sophronius, felt emboldened by the perhaps un-expectedly strong support of Honorius and decided to oppose the patriarch of Jerusalem directly. The *Ekthesis* actually served as a response to a *Synodical letter* of Sophronius which the patriarchate of Constantinople refused to accept.[58]

As mentioned earlier, the election of Sophronius, already an octogenarian, to the see of Jerusalem occurred in 634. We do know that a "Monoenergistic" movement existed in Palestine, following the death of patriarch Modestus in 631,[59] and that it was headed by bishop Sergius of Jaffa. This explains the long vacancy of the patriarchate (631-4). It is probable that the government of Constantinople con-doned the election of the highly-respected Sophronius, as a reward for this promise, given to Sergius, not to raise the issue of "energies," in accordance with the *Psephos*.[60]

However, St Sophronius, in his famous *Synodical Letter* sent, according to custom, to all the patriarchs to ask their recognition in the unity of the orthodox faith and eucharistic communion, produced

---

[56]The emperor later denied the authorship. He wrote to pope John IV: "When I returned from the East, [Sergius] asked me to sign it and to promulgate it." (Mansi IX, col. 9). On the cooperation of Pyrrhus, see Mansi X, col. 741.

[57]Text in Mansi X, 992 C- 997 A; cf. a parallel French translation of the *Psephos* and the *Ekthesis* in Murphy-Sherwood, *op. cit.,* pp. 306-8.

[58]Mansi XI, col. 456 C.

[59]Administrator of the patriarchate under the Persian regime during the exile of Zacharias, Modestus was elected patriarch in 631, as Heraclius reoccupied the city, and died the same year.

[60]There is no need therefore to suppose (with Ch. von Schönborn, *op. cit.,* 89) that the election of Sophronius was seen in Constantinople as a defeat, that it happened against the will of Heraclius and Sergius.

a detailed christological treatise which, for the first time since the beginning of "Monoenergism," went beyond mere unionistic expediency and discussed not only terms, but substance itself.

Nowhere in the *Letter* is there any direct criticism of Sergius and his unionistic policies. The text does not attempt to literally "count" energies, which was forbidden by the *Psephos*. Sophronius is very careful in stressing the hypostatic unity of Christ and, consequently, His unity as the one Agent of all His acts, divine or human. Not foreseeing any problem with Rome, Sophronius shows great respect for the pope's doctrinal orthodoxy, manifested especially in the *Tome* of Leo. The inner logic of his argument, however, leads him *de facto* to affirm quite clearly that "to each nature corresponds a proper energy, that is an energy essential, natural and proper (κατάλληλον) [to that nature],"[61] and that therefore "we do not confess one, unique, essential, natural and undifferentiated energy of both (divinity and humanity), for then we would admit also one essence and one nature."[62] Sophronius does allow, however, the possibility of speaking of one "double operation" (or energy) of Christ,[63] and justifies the quotation from Pseudo-Dionysius (*Ep* IV, col. 1072 C) as referring to the "new (καινὴν) divino-human energy," the one which reflects both divinity and humanity,[64] the "synergy" manifested in the deification of creatures. But deification is possible precisely because the Logos voluntarily assumed *human* nature with human operations, the "natural and irreprehensible (ἀδιάβλητα) passions"[65] of Adam after the Fall (but not sin), so that Christ's infancy, growth, human development, hunger, thirst, fatigue, and, indeed, suffering, death and physical corruptibility were in every way similar to ours, i.e. fully human, until, "in the Resurrection, he dissolved that which in us was passible, mortal, corruptible."[66]

Thus, the thought of St Sophronius, which will be developed so brilliantly by his disciple Maximus, disclosed the fallacy of "Monoenergism," and implicitly of the still unmentioned Monotheletism. If the humanity of Christ lacked a human energy, or will, it was not

---

[61]PG 87, 3, col. 3169 D; cf. the excellent French translation and the commentary by von Schönborn, *op. cit.*, pp. 201-224.

[62]*Ibid.*, col. 3172 A.

[63]*Ibid.*, col. 3169 C.

[64]*Ibid.*, col. 3177 B.

[65]*Ibid.*, col. 3177 D.

[66]*Ibid.*, col. 3173 AD.

"our" humanity any more, but either a phantasm, or an abstraction. It is, therefore, quite understandable that Sergius of Constantinople considered that the *Synodical Letter* of Sophronius, whether or not it broke the promise given by its author not to "count energies," was a manifesto against his policies.

The *Letter,* of course, also reached pope Honorius, who seems to have been impressed by the arguments of the patriarch of Jerusalem. Only fragments of the pope's second letter to Sergius are preserved. "Monotheletism" is not mentioned any longer (at least in those fragments), but the pope repeats his appeal not to speak of energies, but rather of "two operating (or "acting") natures" belonging to One Actor. He addresses similar letters to Sophronius and Cyrus of Alexandria, declaring his readiness to maintain communion with them both, as well as with Sergius. The old Sophronius attempted to convince the pope of the dangers of his support for Sergius; an emissary of the patriarch of Jerusalem, bishop Stephen of Dora, visited Rome with this mission.[67] But Honorius died on October 12, 638, after the publication of the *Ekthesis,* without clarifying his ambiguous doctrinal stand. His successors, Severinus (reigned four months in 640) and John IV (640-2), rejected the *Ekthesis.* They escaped possible imperial sanctions only because of the general confusion caused by the Arab invasions and the dynastic troubles which followed the death of Heraclius (641).

In any case, these same Arab invasions destroyed completely the unionistic value of Monoenergism and Monotheletism: all the Monophysite communities of the East fell under the yoke of Islam, making the issue of their reconciliation with Orthodox Chalcedonians a moot question for centuries.

4.   *The Islamic invasion: Jerusalem, Syria, Egypt*

It is not possible to discuss here in detail the origins and nature of Islam. Its sudden appearance and extraordinary expansion through "holy war" (*djihad*) shocked the Byzantine empire and rapidly destroyed its domination of the Middle East. By 651, only nineteen years after the death of the prophet Muhammad, the armies of his

---

[67]As reported by Stephen himself at the council of the Lateran (649); cf. Mansi X, col. 896 D.

disciples had not only conquered Syria and Egypt, but also destroyed
the remnants of the Persian empire (which had been greatly reduced
already by the victories of Heraclius), killed the last Sassanid "king
of kings," and expanded the power of the khalifes of Islam from the
river Oxus (the modern Amu-Daria in Central Asia) to all the lands
to the East and South of the Mediterranean, reaching the Atlantic
ocean.

The conquest of Syria and Palestine began in 634. Damascus fell
in 635 and Antioch in 638. The most crucial Roman defeat occurred
on the river Yarmuk in Palestine in 636, following which Heraclius
lost means to defend the region from the invaders. Symbolically, the
most sensational event of these years was the capture of Jerusalem in
February 638. After its recovery from the Persians, the Holy City
had remained in Christian hands only seven years.

There is no documentary evidence which could make us believe
that the doctrinal conflict between Sophronius and Constantinople influenced the behavior of the patriarch of Jerusalem towards the Arabs.
He led and inspired the defense of the city as long as there was a
realistic hope of saving it. At the last moment, he sent the relic of
the True Cross to Constantinople. Finally, he decided to capitulate,
knowing that armed resistance to a direct assaut would imply massacre
and destruction, whereas submission meant survival and relative
toleration of the religious *status quo.* There are several, somewhat
contradictory, accounts of the surrender.[68] The most reliable ones
report that the old Christian patriarch met the khalife Umar on the
Mount of Olives. Surprised by the simple appearance of the khalife,
who was riding a camel, and was dressed in soiled robes of camel hair,
carrying a bag with dates, the Byzantine prelate offered him a white
sidonion (a standard nobleman's garb), which Umar kept only for
the time required to have his own old clothes washed. Entering the
city, the Muslim leader refused the invitation to pray in the Christian
basilica of the Anastasis and, instead, made a prayer in the direction
of Mecca on the location of the destroyed Jewish temple. The famous
"mosque of Umar," which is still standing today, was later built on
that place, signifying the supremacy of the Islamic revelation over the

[68]The most reliable modern treatment of these accounts is still in H. Vincent and
F. Abel, *Jérusalem. Recherches de topographie, d'archéologie et d'histoire,* II, Paris, 1922,
pp. 930-2; cf. also A. N. Stratos, *Byzantium in the Seventh Century,* II, Amsterdam,
1972, pp. 82-83, 211; and Χρ. Παπαδόπουλος, Ἱστορία Ἐκκλησίας Ἱεροσολύμων, Alexandria, 1910, p. 249.

biblical one. Moreover, the fact that Umar refused to pray in the Anastasis was not without significance: had he accepted, the basilica would have been turned into a mosque also.[69] Instead, in order to acknowledge the city's surrender by Sophronius, the khalife issued a document guaranteeing the preservation of Christian churches and the property rights of Christians, on the condition that they would not manifest their faith in the streets, avoid preaching to Muslims, would not prevent conversions of Christians to Islam, and adopt an attitude of submissiveness and loyalty to the conquerors.[70] These principles would regulate the survival of Christian communities under Islam for centuries. It is noteworthy however, that Palestine is the only area of the khalifate, where all the ancient sanctuaries remained intact in Christian hands and where the Orthodox patriarch continued to be seen by the Muslims, as the official guardian of the Holy Places. Eventually, his rights would be curtailed by other Christians, especially the Latin crusaders and also, in part, by the Armenians and the Copts, but not the Muslims. These relatively favorable conditions go back to the agreement between the Khalife Umar and the wise patriarch Sophronius. The old patriarch, who had almost reached the age of ninety, died a year later on March 11, 639.[71]

Thus the contributions of St Sophronius to history are not limited to the truly remarkable christological formulation of his *Synodal Letter* of 634. His diplomatic wisdom of 638 set the pattern of Christian survival in the Middle East. Furthermore, his sermons and, especially his poetry and prayers have become a permanent element in the liturgical tradition of the Church.[72]

The loss of Syria and Palestine by the empire was soon followed by unglorious defeats in Egypt. In spite of real hopes for church peace, the reign of Cyrus, as both patriarch and prefect, and the Union of 633, were disastrous for Egyptian Monophysitism. The Coptic sources themselves recognize that a large segment of the population

[69]This is what happened to Haghia Sophia in Constantinople in 1453.

[70]There are at least two versions of Umar's edict, none being literally authentic. Its basic contents are, however, uncontroversial.

[71]This is the most likely date; cf. Ch. von Schönborn, *op. cit.*, p. 97, note 136.

[72]The *troparia* of the so-called "Royal Hours" of Holy Friday and the eves of Nativity and Theophany are ascribed to Sophronius, as well as the main prayer of the Great Blessing of Water on Epiphany Day. All these texts are adopted from the ancient liturgy of Jerusalem; Cf. especially, E. Popovich, *"Patriarchch Ierusalimsky Sofrony"* in *Trudy Kievskoi Dukhovnoi Akademii*, 1888, nov., pp. 44-62; 1889 febr., 358-372; june, pp. 298-312; aug., pp. 617-631; 1890, aug. pp. 503-599, sept., pp. 3-42; for modern literature on the subject, see Chr. von Schönborn, *op. cit.*, pp. 107-109.

had accepted the Chalcedonian faith (in the Monoenergistic interpretation). According to Severus of Asmounein, "these were the years during which Heraclius and Al-Mugaugas (*i.e.* Cyrus, the "Caucasian") were ruling over Egypt: and through the severity of the persecution and the oppression, and the chastisements which Heraclius inflicted on the orthodox [*i.e.* the Monophysites, J.M.] in order to force them to adopt the faith of Chalcedon, innumerable multitudes were led astray, some by tortures, others by promise of honors, some by persuasion and guile."[73] The reference to "persuasion" indicates that the policies of patriarch Cyrus were more effective than the exclusively violent tactics used by imperial authorities under Marcian, Zeno and Justinian. Monoenergism seemed convincing to many. The Monophysite population of Egypt, still divided into sects, was not monolithically opposed to the empire, and the theological concession, implied in the Union of 633, must have swayed many to accept Chalcedon.[74] The Arab conquest was a gradual process, which lasted from 639 to 646, and was accompanied by massacres and pillaging, which made many people see the advantages of Roman rule. In many areas, there was popular resistance to the enemy's advances, and it is not true that "Egyptians hailed the invaders as deliverers."[75] The major weakness of the empire resided in the fact that its administration and army in Egypt depended largely upon corrupt local landowners, who pursued local interests and considered army units as private militias.[76] The appointment of Cyrus was an attempt by Heraclius to remedy the situation, and it might have produced results, both ecclesiastical and political, had the Arab invasion not come so suddenly and progressed so rapidly.

Led by 'Amr ibn-as-As, while the khalif Umar was in Syria, the Arabs entered Egypt in 639, occupied Pelusium, East of the Delta, in 640, and in September of that year, having defeated the Byzantines

---

[73]*History of the Patriarchs,* I, ed. cit., p. 491.

[74]Cf. the important observations of F. Winkelmann. "*Nekotorye zamechaniya k otsenke roli monofizitstva v Egipte v posleiustinianovskuiu epokhu;*" VV 39, 1978, pp. 86-92; "Aegypten und Byzanz vor der arabischen Eröberung," *Byzantinoslavica,* XL, 1979, 2, pp. 161-182.

[75]Butler, *The Arab Conquest,* p. 298. Other historians, however, insist upon the supposedly universal cooperation of the Copts with the invaders (cf. Stratos, *op. cit.,* II, pp. 130-33).

[76]Cf. G. Rouillard, *L'administration civile de l'Egypte byzantine,* 2nd ed., Paris, 1928; E. R. Hardy, *The Large Estates in Byzantine Egypt,* New York, 1931; *Christian Egypt: Church and People (Christianity and Nationalism in the Patriarchate of Alexandria),* Oxford, 1952.

at Heliopolis, began the siege of the fortress of Babylon, in contemporary Old Cairo. The invading army was small in numbers—4000 originally, then receiving a reinforcement of 12,000—but it provoked chaos in an underadministered and poorly protected country. 'Amr made local argreements with landlords and administrators, levied taxes and used the cooperation of local populations. Patriarch Cyrus himself, inspired perhaps by the example of St Sophronius of Jerusalem, decided to negotiate with 'Amr. Loyally, he shared his plans with Heraclius. The emperor's response was to recall him to Constantinople and to have him tried publicly and exiled for treason.

But Heraclius died on February 11, 641, after a reign of thirty years. The heroic vanquisher of the Persian empire was now a nervously sick man, deeply depressed by the extraordinary suprise of the Arab invasion, but unreconciled to the idea of a dismembered empire. His death was followed by a dynastic struggle, during the regency of his second wife Martina. The struggle ended with the deposition of Martina, the exile of her son Heraclonas and the coronation of Constans II, the eleven-year old grandson of Heraclius by his first wife, Eudoxia.[77] The regency was assured by patriarch Paul and a group of predominantly Armenian military leaders, all devoted to Monotheletism.

Meanwhile, the situation in Egypt grew worse. On April 9, 641, Easter day, the fortress of Babylon fell to the Arabs, followed by Nikiu and other important cities in the Delta.

The new imperial government formally reinstated Cyrus in his functions as both patriarch and prefect. Having solemnly reentered Alexandria on September 14, 641, he immediately began negotiations with 'Amr. Some considered capitulation to be unnecessary and again accused him of treason, since Alexandria was still quite well protected. In any case, Cyrus himself did not see the end of Byzantine rule in Egypt: he died of dysentery on March 21, 642. A Chalcedonian patriarch, Peter, was elected to succeed him (July 14, 642), but on September 29 of the same year, 'Amr entered Alexandria and wrote to Khalife Umar: "I have taken a city of which I can but say that it contains 4000 palaces, 4000 baths, 400 theaters, 12,000 sellers of green

---

[77]Constans was the son of Constantine III, elder son of Heraclius by Eudoxia. Since Martina was the niece of Heraclius, her incestuous marriage with the emperor, although blessed by patriarch Sergius, was considered as illegitimate by many. This was one of the reasons which excluded Martina's posterity from the imperial succession.

vegetables, and 40,000 tributary Jews."[78] The primitive desert dwellers of Arabia were on top of the ancient civilization of Christian Rome!

The Monophysite Patriarch Benjamin was immediately recalled by 'Amr to Alexandria and assumed control of the main churches, stabilizing the life of the church in Egypt for centuries of survival under Islam. Although numerous apostasies of Christians to the religion of the Islamic conquerors were soon taking place, the government of Constans II did not consider the defeat as final. In 645, a large Byzantine expeditionary force, led by the Armenian general Manuel, landed in Egypt and retook Alexandria. A new Byzantine defeat by 'Amr followed soon, and the remnants of Manuel's army were re-embarked in 646. The only result of the unhappy expedition was more destruction in the city of Alexandria whose population, this time, seemed to side, quite deliberately, with the Arabs,[79] and more resentment of the Copts against the empire. "The Lord abandoned the army of the Romans, writes Severus of Asmounein, as a punishment for their corrupt faith, and because of the anathemas uttered against them by the ancient fathers, on account of the council of Chalcedon."[80] Only a handful of "Melkites" remained faithful to Chalcedonian orthodoxy in Egypt.

The most visible and remarkable survival of orthodoxy in the region occurred only at the monastery of the Transfiguration (later dedicated to St Catherine) built by Justinian at the foot of Mt Sinai, where Moses spoke to God. The monastery's spiritual prestige had been enhanced recently by the leadership of a famous abbot, St John, author of a great book of monastic spirituality, entitled "Ladder of Paradise" (*ca.* 525-600). Its isolation in the Sinai desert, away from military, political and ecclesiastical upheavals, allowed this unique multi-ethnic community of Greek, Egyptian, Syrian, Georgian, Armenian-Chalcedonian and, later, Slavic monks to preserve not only themselves, but also many treasures of literature and art, going back to early Christianity.[81]

---

[78]Text in Butler, *The Arab Conquest*, p. 368.

[79]Cf. Butler, *op. cit.*, p. 471-5.

[80]*History of the Patriarchs*, II, ed. cit., pp. 492-3.

[81]For the history of the buildings, the library and the icons of Mt. Sinai, see K. Weitzmann and G. H. Forsyth, *The Monastery of Saint Catherine at Mount Sinai, I. The Icons*, Princeton, NJ, 1976; *The Church and Fortress of Justinian*, Ann Arbor, MI, n.d.

5. *St Maximus the Confessor and pope Martin*

The opposition of St Sophronius put an end to "Monoenergism" initially promoted by patriarch Sergius. Instead of this now discredited formula, pope Honorius and the *Ekthesis* of Heraclius had canonized "Monotheletism," a christological scheme which affirmed that the one and unique "subject," or hypostasis of Christ could possess only one will. How indeed, they were asking, could Christ's humanity, since it does not possess a distinct human hypostasis (this would be Nestorianism), be manifested by a distinct will of its own? The obvious flaw of their theory, however, was that since Christ's unique hypostasis was the pre-existing, divine hypostasis of the Logos, His unique "hypostatic" will could only be the divine one. Consequently, His humanity was imperfect, a passive instrument of divinity, mechanically "used" by the divine will. Monotheletism could not actually be compatible with the *Tome of Leo (agit utraque forma quod proprium est)* and the council of Chalcedon ("the characteristic property of each nature is preserved"). Indeed the property of true humanity is not passivity, but a willed realization of the divine purpose for creation. Furthermore, if a distinct will is inherent to each hypostasis, the divine Trinity itself would possess three wills. In fact, Monotheletism was a scheme not substantially different from Monoenergism: in both cases, the fullness of Christ's humanity was denied. It does appear actually, that the issue of Monoenergism and Monotheletism, as it was defined by St Sophronius and later, by his disciple, St Maximus, probably the most remarkable theological genius of the late patristic period, has been underlying the christological debates since Ephesus I (431). While the term "Monophysitism" could cover a multitude of different trends, sometimes purely Cyrillian, and therefore compatible with Chalcedon, but often mutually exclusive and contradictory, the debates of the seventh century focused on the real issue: the need to formulate a christology in which "the meaning of created being and the purpose of history" be found "in the incarnate Christ,"[82] without creation and history loosing their proper purposefulness and dynamism.[83]

[82]Cf. J. D. Zizioulas, *Being as Communion*, Crestwood, NY, 1985, p. 97.

[83]The literature on St Maximus is very abundant. For a recent summary treatment, see L. Thunberg, *Man and Cosmos. The Vision of St Maximus the Confessor*, Crestwood, NY, 1985; cf. also Meyendorff, *Christ*, pp. 131-51; and *Maximus Confessor. Selected writings*, tr. and notes by G. C. Barthold, New York, 1985.

Both patriarch Sergius of Constantinople and Honorius of Rome died in 638. The abbot Pyrrhus, one of the ideologists of Monotheletism, and also a correspondent of St Maximus, was elected patriarch of Constantinople. He had to face the rejection of the *Ekthesis* by the popes, successors of Honorius. Their protests, however, did not entail severance of communion with the see of Constantinople: the Roman bishops of the seventh century lacked the energy and steadfastness of their predecessors so clearly manifested at the time of the schism with patriarch Acacius,[84] even if the latter's compromises with the Monophysites were much more benign than those of Sergius and Pyrrhus. The successor of Sergius on the see of Constantinople was an avowed Monothelite. Invoking the authority of the late Honorius, he still hoped for a christological consensus based on Monotheletism to follow the nightmare of the Arab invasion. Unfortunately for him, he became involved in the dynastic struggle which followed the death of Heraclius (641). He ran into trouble during the short reign (three months) of Constantine III (son of Heraclius, by his first wife Eudoxia), who was opposed to Monotheletism. Siding with the cause of Martina and her children and accused of complicity in the murder of Constantine III, he followed Martina in her disgrace, after the enthronement of Constans II (November 641). Replaced by another Monothelite, Paul, at the patriarchate, Pyrrhus left the capital for an exile in Africa.

At that particular time, Byzantine Africa, with its capital in Carthage, appeared as the most secure area of the whole empire. In 610 Heraclius had used it as a base when he left with an army to deliver Constantinople from the Persian menace. As the East was invaded by Arabs and as the Lombards constantly threatened Italy, Africa was able to host numerous refugees and its exarch, Gregory, a cousin of Heraclius, combining civil and military power, tended to believe that he was holding the trump-card in the military and political struggles of the day. As he arrived in Carthage, Pyrrhus began to think of possibilities, with the help of the powerful exarch of Carthage, to recover his patriarchate, of which, as the thought, he had been unjustly deprived.

Among the Eastern refugees, also living in Africa, was Maximus, a former secretary of Heraclius, and later a monk in Asia Minor.[85] His

[84]Cf. *supra*, pp. 194-202.
[85]A. Syriac *Vita* of Maximus affirms, however, that he was of Persian and Palestinian

sojourn in Carthage had been marked by his fateful meeting with St Sophronius (633). Although he did not take sides immediately in the theological controversies in which Sophronius got involved, he seems to have begun, at least since 640, to intervene openly against Monotheletism. He was an influential person not only because of his spiritual authority and intellectual competence, but also because he had political contacts in "high places" in Constantinople.[86]

Sponsored by the exarch Gregory, a formal debate was organized in 645 between Maximus and the exiled ex-patriarch Pyrrhus.[87] The surprising result was a formal acceptance of orthodoxy by Pyrrhus, and his departure for Rome. In these events, the Monothelite government of Constantinople saw a plot involving the exarch Gregory, Maximus and the pope. Such suspicions found confirmation in the fact that Gregory indeed rebelled against Constans II in 646, being proclaimed emperor by his troops. Fate went against him however: he was killed, while resisting a forceful Arab intrusion, a prelude to the final invasion still to come (647).[88] St Maximus always forcefully denied any involvement in Gregory's rebellion. By 646 he had left Carthage following Pyrrhus to Rome. But suspicions arose, since the anti-Monothelite camp had, indeed, placed high hopes in Gregory's action. Several African councils had met in 646 and demanded, with Gregory's approval, the repeal of the *Ekthesis*.[89]

Once in Rome, Pyrrhus solemnly converted from Monotheletism to orthodoxy. He was received by pope Theodore, who recognized his patriarchal dignity and even invited him to preside at liturgical functions at the pope's place.[90] Pope Theodore (642-649) was a Greek, of Palestinian origin, which may explain in part his clearer awareness of the nature of Monotheletism. Encouraged by the decisions taken by African councils and advised by St Maximus, he formally broke fellowship with Paul of Constantinople. The latter, in return, placed

origin (Cf. S. Brock, AB 91, 1973, pp. 299-346).

[86]Cf. for instance, his letter to the eunuch John, an influential official at the court of Martina, recommending the return of exarch George to Carthage (PG 91, cols. 641-648). The attempt was unsuccessful: the appointment went to Gregory. Maximus also corresponded with Egyptian clergy, obtaining favors from patriarch Cyrus, in spite of the latter's Monoenergism (cf. *Letter to Peter Illustrius*, PG 91, cols. 533 C-536 A).

[87]Text of the debate in PG 91, cols. 288-353.

[88]On the connections between the christological debates, the ambitions of Pyrrhus and the rebellion of Gregory, see Duchesne, *L'Eglise*, pp. 436-9.

[89]Cf. the decisions of the African councils included in the *Acts* of the council of the Lateran of 649 (ACO, ser. sec., I, Berlin, 1984, pp. 66-102).

an interdict on the chapel of the palace of Placidia, which was used by papal representatives in the capital. At last the position of the Roman church became definite and clear. Meanwhile, Pyrrhus, having lost the hope of resuming his patriarchal career with the help of the exarch Gregory, who was now dead, and the anti-Monothelite party, escaped to Ravenna and reentered the Monothelite imperial establishment. The fearless pope Theodore excommunicated him, signing the act with a pen dipped into a eucharistic chalice.[91]

The futility of Monothelite policies was gradually becoming obvious even in Constantinople. Except, perhaps, in Armenia, where Byzantine influence was still strong, the hopes of using the formula as a basis for reunion with the Monophysites had been destroyed by Arab victories in Syria and Egypt, while Italy and Africa, opposed to Monotheletism, were becoming alienated from the imperial center. In 648 therefore, Constans II made an attempt to close the debate: in a formal imperial decree, known as the *Typos,* he forbade "any discussion of one will or one energy, two wills or two energies."[92] But the decision came much too late: the issue was on the table, it had become a real dilemma for Christian theological consciousness, and could not be suppressed by a simple act of political authority. In practice, the *Typos* was meant to prevent the Orthodox from fighting against official Monotheletism.

Pope Theodore died before receiving the *Typos.* The election of a successor, St Martin, was in itself an act of rebellion against the established imperial order, since the candidate did not receive approval from either the emperor, or the exarch of Ravenna. Martin, an Italian, had been in Constantinople as an envoy of pope Theodore, and had participated in negotiations concerning the fate of Pyrrhus, before the formal break between Rome and Constantinople. He was well aware of the issues and ready to face up to the empire.

In October 649, the basilica of the Lateran was the scene of a council of one hundred and five bishops, mostly from Italy and Africa. Stephen of Dora, the Palestinian bishop who earlier had been an envoy

[90]*LP*, ed. cit., I, 332.

[91]Cf. Mansi X, col. 610 BC. The unusual practice of using the Eucharist in this way was sometimes adopted in the early Middle Ages to dramatize anathemas and excommunications.

[92]Text in ACO, ibid. p. 208-10; title mentioned in the *Acta Maximi,* 8, PG 90, col. 121 D; Engl. tr. by G. C. Berthold in *Maximus Confessor, Selected Writings,* New York, Paulist Press, 1985, pp. 23-4.

of St Sophronius to Rome, was there again, as well as "many pious abbots and monks, from among the Greeks, who were either resident [of Rome] for a long time, or recent arrivals: these were John, Theodore, Thalassius, Georges, and other God-loving men."[93] These Greek monks not only inspired the debates, but were also the editors of the council's *Acts,* which were composed in Greek and, only later, translated into Latin.[94] St Maximus himself was among them, playing a decisive role in gathering patristic references and preparing the results,[95] which took the form of twenty anathematisms, reaffirming the council of Chalcedon, as well as the doctrine of two energies and two wills in Christ, as the necessary expressions of His two natures. No personal attack was directed at either Heraclius, or Constans II, but both the *Ekthesis* and the *Typos* were formally condemned, and a series of heretics were anathematized: Theodore of Pharan, Cyrus of Alexandria, and three successive patriarchs of Constantinople: Sergius, Pyrrhus and Paul. The decrees were accepted throughout the West, but opposed by Paul of Thessalonica. Although he was papal "vicar" in the Illyricum, Paul wrote the pope a letter in rough conformity with the *Typos,* and was excommunicated by Martin.[96] A bishop, John of Philadelphia (in Arabia), was sent on a mission to restore orthodoxy in the patriarchates of Antioch and Jerusalem, but the results of his activities in areas occupied by Arabs are unknown.

The clear and drastic decisions of the council of the Lateran had to provoke an equally strong reaction from Constantinople. Perhaps, pope Martin and his advisors were hoping for some political support, similar to the rebellion of exarch Gregory in Africa. Such hopes, if they existed, were not entirely without foundation, as shown in the case of exarch Olympius of Ravenna. Having received from Constantinople the order to go to Rome, arrest the pope and impose the *Typos,* Olympius, faced with popular opposition, first negotiated with the pope, then left for Sicily where, before his death in 652 from an epidemic, he plotted an alliance with the Arabs against Constans II.

[93]ACO, ibid., p. 48 For their identification, and the role of Greek monks at the council, see J. M. Sansterre, *Les moines grecs et orientaux à Rome aux époques byzantine et carolingienne (milieu du VIè siècle—fin du IXe),* Bruxelles, 1980, pp. 9-30, 117-119.

[94]Cf. R. Riedinger, "Aus den Akten der Lateran-Synode von 649," in BZ, 69, 1976, pp. 17-38. R. Riedinger is also the editor of the critical text of the Council's *Acts* in ACO, where the original character of the Greek text is firmly established.

[95]Cf. Sansterre, *op. cit.,* pp. 118-119.

[96]Mansi X, cols. 838-844.

Although both St Martin and St Maximus always denied any involvement in politics, the general atmosphere of plots and intrigue made
the religious issue inseparable from the issue of imperial loyalty.
Suspicious of the pope's political sympathies and angered by his open
opposition to the *Typos,* Constans II acted forcefully.

In 653, the exarch Theodore Kalliopas arrested the sick pope
Martin, accusing him of having been elected illegally (*i.e.* without
imperial sanction) and of having sent money to Arabs (Martin had
given support to pilgrims going to Jerusalem). St Martin was then
dragged to Constantinople, kept in prison for three months and tried
by the disciplinary court of the patriarchate of Constantinople. Indeed,
as a cleric, he was not liable to a civil court. The act of accusation
contained no religious elements, but essentially the crime of complicity
with Olympius. The pope was defrocked, publicly divested of his
episcopal ornaments, chained and humiliated. He died in exile in
Kherson in the Crimea, on September 16, 655, and is venerated by the
Church as a Confessor.

The participation of the patriarchate in these shameful events
makes this period, morally, the lowest point in the history of the church
of Constantinople. In 654, the execrable Pyrrhus succeeded in recover-
ing the patriarchal throne, and offered a deal to the legates of pope
Eugenius I. Eugenius had been elected in August 654, with the exarch's
approval, more than a year before St Martin's death and in spite of
the latter's specific warnings against such an improper usurpation.[97]
Eugenius was inclined to accept an ambiguous formula, which would
avoid the formal rejection of the *Typos,* but was prevented from falling into compromise with Monotheletism by the clergy and people of
Rome.[98] It remains, however, that both he and his successor, pope
Vitalian (657-672), were in communion with the Monothelite patriarch
Peter (654-666) who had presided over the trial of Martin. At
Vitalian's election, Constans II sent him a precious Gospel book,[99] and
the pope met the Monothelite emperor, murderer of Martin and
Maximus, solemnly as he visited Rome himself (663). Clearly, the
trial and death of St Martin had neutralized for a time the Roman
opposition to the *Typos*: the popes were neither condoning it, nor
condemning their predecessor Honorius, nor breaking fellowship with

[97]Cf. Martin's letter to Constantinople, following his arrest in Rome, PL 87, col.
199.
[98]*LP,* I, p. 341; Anastasius, the disciple of Maximus, PG 90, col. 133-6.
[99]*LP,* p. I, p. 343.

the Monothelite leadership in Constantinople, remaining loyal to the imperial system.

The resistance was therefore centered in one person, a simple monk, St Maximus the Confessor. With two of his disciples, he was arrested in Rome and sent to Constantinople. His trial followed that of pope Martin.[100] It began with political accusations, but the judges were unable to substantiate conspiracy between Maximus and the rebellious exarch Gregory. The emissaries of the emperor then came to Maximus and asked him directly: "You are not in communion with the see of Constantinople?" Maximus answered: "I am not in communion, because they have rejected the four holy councils through the Nine Chapters adopted in Alexandria [*i.e.* the Union of Cyrus in 633], through the *Ekthesis* . . ., and recently through the *Typos*." Also, Maximus quite explicitly denied the emperor any right to define dogma: "No emperor, he said, was able to convince the inspired Fathers to come to an agreement with heretics . . . It is for the priests to inquire into and define what concerns the dogmas of the catholic Church . . . During the anaphora, the emperors are remembered with the laity . . ." The emissaries then announced that the legates of pope Eugenius were in the city and would communicate with patriarch Peter the next day: "The Holy Spirit," answered Maximus, "condemns even angels who sanction anything against what has been preached (ref. to Gal. 1:8)."

Maximus and his two disciples were made to appear before patriarch Peter himself, and his colleague Macedonius, titular patriarch of Antioch. The steadfastness of the three monks made condemnation inevitable, and Maximus was exiled to Bizya on the Black Sea (655). Another attempt to break his resistance by offering him pardon, by transferring him to a monastery in Rhegium, and promising him honors in Constantinople, ended in failure again (656). Finally, together with his two faithful disciples, Maximus was judged anew by bishops and senators in Constantinople, cruelly tortured, amputated of his tongue and right hand and exiled to Lazica, the country of Cyrus of Alexandria, in the Caucasus. He died there on August 13, 662, aged more than

[100]The account of the trial known as *Acta Maximi*, was composed by one of his disciples (see the various possibilities of authorship in R. Devreesse, "La vie de St Maxime et ses recensions," *AB* 46, 1928, pp. 5-49; and J. M. Garrigues, "Le martyre de saint Maxime le Confesseur," *Revue Thomiste* 76, 1, 1976, pp. 410-52.) The text is found in PG 90, cols. 109-172; a complete English translation by G. C. Berthold in *Maximus Confessor. Selected Writings,* New York, 1985, pp. 17-28.

eighty. No protests came either from Rome, or from any other part of the Christian world.

6. The Sixth Ecumenical council

Constans II never returned to Constantinople from his Western voyage, begun in the year of St Maximus' death (662), with the purpose of organizing a counter-offensive against the Arabs. As consequence of a palace plot, he was murdered in Syracuse, Sicily, in 668. His son, Constantine IV became emperor in Constantinople. The first years of the new reign were entirely dominated by war, in which the empire was finally successful. The Arab fleet, built by the Khalife Muawija, blockaded Constantinople for four memorable years: 674-8. The "New Rome" stood directly on the way of the expansion of the Islamic *djihad* to Europe. But the siege failed, and a peace of thirty years was concluded between the empire and the khalifate. Egypt and Syria were, of course, lost to Byzantium, but the borders were set far from the capital in Eastern Asia Minor. By this victory, which will be follower by that of Charles Martel in Poitiers (732), the Christian countries to the North of the Mediterranean would be saved from the Muslim conquest.

Meanwhile, the relations between the churches of Constantinople and Rome remained ambiguous. The respective positions did not formally change. Patriarchs Thomas (667-69), John V (669-75) and Constantine (675-7) did not condemn the *Typos*, while the popes maintained an ambiguous reserve. As the war, and particularly the Arab siege of the capital, made contacts difficult, a growing estrangement arose between the two "Romes." Patriarch Theodore (677-9) attempted to force the hand of both the emperor and the pope, so that the *Typos* might be imposed by force. Instead of sending a regular "synodical" letter announcing his election to pope Donus (676-8), he asked the latter to accept unity on ambiguous and, in fact, Monothelite terms, and also suggested to the emperor that all the popes, successors of Honorius, be stricken from the diptychs in Constantinople.[101] The young emperor refrained from such drastic measures

---

[101]Curiously, all these ambiguities did not prevent most popes including Eugenius and Vitalian, and most patriarchs of this period, to be counted as Saints of the Church, *i.e.* particularly patriarchs Thomas (667-9), John V (669-75), Constantine (675-77), Theodore (677-9, 686-7), and George (679-86). The practice was to commemorate as

and immediately after the end of the Arab siege wrote to the "ecumenical pope" Donus, inviting him to send representatives of the Roman clergy and twelve bishops to a conference of theologians, which would advise as to the steps to be taken to restore unambiguous unity.[102] This initiative of Constantine IV, without the emperor having really planned it, led to the sessions in Constantinople of the Sixth ecumenical council.

The imperial letter arrived in Rome after the death of Pope Donus (April 11, 679), and was received by his successor, Agatho, a Sicilian, who, during his short reign (679-681), restored the papacy's prestige by exercising true leadership and initiative. Calling all the Western metropolitans to consult with their bishops about the issue of Monotheletism, he secured a united response of the West. Councils were held in Milan and at Hatfield in Britain. One hundred and twenty five bishops of the provinces directly dependent upon the pope met in Rome and signed a confession of faith condemning Monotheletism. The pope himself wrote a long letter to the emperor, accrediting his representatives,[103] and expressing Roman claims in terms reminiscent of the times of Gelasius and Leo, and uncharacteristic for the period of "Byzantine" papacy. The Roman church, wrote Agatho, "never departed from the way of truth" towards any even partial error (*nunquam a via veritatis in qualibet erroris parte defluxa est*); as the see of Peter and Paul, it is the beacon of true light for the universe "never obscured by any heresy" (*nulla haeretici erroris tetra caligine funebratum*). After the case of Honorius and the rather ambiguous attitude of practically all his successors (except Theodore and Martin), such pretentious utterances about Roman authority could not be taken literally by anyone.

What was obvious however is that, in contrast to the recent past, the Roman delegation was now coming to Constantinople, backed by the entire Western episcopate and strongly supporting orthodoxy against Monotheletism. Meanwhile, emperor Constantine IV had removed the rather anti-Roman Patriarch Theodore from his see. The new head of the church of Constantinople, George, was at least ready for open debate, although he still harbored Monotheletic sympathies. This new atmosphere made possible a decision taken at the first

---

Saints all the holders of major sees, who were not formally and by name condemned as heretics, and had died in communion with the Church.

[102]Mansi, XI, cols. 196-201.

[103]*Ibid.*, cols. 234-86.

session: the simple conference, originally planned by the emperor, declared itself to be an ecumenical council.

The assembly met on November 7, 680, "in a hall of the divine [imperial] palace, the so-called *Troullon*" (ἐν τῷ σεκρέτῳ τοῦ θείου παλατίου τῷ οὕτω λεγομένῳ Τρούλλῳ).[104] Until September 16, 681, there were eighteen sessions. The emperor himself wielded little influence on the debates. There were only 43 bishops in the beginning, but the final decree was signed by 174. This very small attendance reflected the state of the Christian world in 680-1. Syria, Palestine, Egypt and North Africa were occupied by the Arabs. Asia Minor itself had been devastated, and Slavs had settled in much of the Balkan peninsula. The representation of the Eastern patriarchates was nominal. Macarius, a titular patriarch of Antioch living in Constantinople, was present, but Alexandria and Jerusalem, where the Chalcedonian sees were officially vacant, were representd only by "vicars," presumably also living in the capital.

Unlike the early councils which tended to debate theological issues for their own sake, the assembly of 680-1 focused on the issue of Tradition. The only question discussed was whether the earlier conciliar decrees and the writings of the Fathers could be used to justify the doctrine of "one energy" and "one will" in Christ. Patristic authorities were brought in; the authenticity of some writings was challenged; archives were searched. This "archival" character of the debates was partly due to the fact that, since the death of the great St Maximus, no outstanding theologian was at hand to raise the christological discussion to the level which it had reached with St Cyril, St Leo, or even emperor Justinian. But the major issue was, of course, clear: the authenticity of Christ's humanity and the salvation, in Christ, not only of an abstract human "nature," but of humanity itself, as moving, dynamic and creative. This was the theological legacy of Maximus, which inspired the council's ultimate decision.

The investigation of conciliar and patristic texts began at the first session, when both patriarchs, present at the *Troullon,* George of Constantinople and Macarius of Antioch, tried to support Monotheletism and declared that the position of Sergius and his successors was in conformity with Tradition. Among the discoveries made in the debates which followed, was that the letter of patriarch Menas to pope Vigilius, which had served as a major reference in favor of

---

[104]The *Acts* of the council are found in Mansi, XI.

Monoenergism, and which had produced great impression in Rome at the time of Honorius, was inauthentic. At the eighth session (March 7, 681), patriarch George of Constantinople declared himself to be convinced by the available evidence and formally accepted the doctrine of "two wills." Henceforth, Macarius of Antioch and a handful of bishops remained alone to defend Monotheletism. A detailed examination of a confession of faith presented by Macarius was held during the eleventh and twelfth sessions. As a result, the patriarch of Antioch was deposed.

During Easter week of 681, there were demonstrations of recovered fellowship between Constantinople and the church of Rome. The bishop of Porto, John, papal legate, celebrated the Eucharist in Latin and the emperor formally suppressed the tax imposed on popes to obtain imperial confirmation at their election.[105] There were also some curious episodes illustrating a certain growth of medieval superstition, such as the declaration of the Monothelite priest Polychronius, that his convictions had just been confirmed by a vision. Asked to substantiate his claim, he offered to place his confession of faith upon the body of a dead man, who would then rise to proclaim Monotheletism. The experiment was formally authorized and performed, without the result expected by the stubborn Polychronius. Even in defeat, he nevertheless stood by his Monotheletism and was duly anathematized.

During the sixteenth session, patriarch George made one last attempt to save the honor of the church of Constantinople by arguing against the formal condemnation of his several predecessors, Sergius, Pyrrhus, Paul and Peter, but unsuccessfully. The list of condemnations was adopted, and the name of pope Honorius added to it. Obviously, the council selected only leaders of the heresy, to be condemned by name, and avoided throwing anathemas to those who adopted ambiguous stands (*i.e.* some popes who succeeded Honorius, particularly Vitalian), or simply followed the accepted position of their church (patriarchs Thomas, John, Constantine and Theodore). The condemnation of Honorius did not raise any objection on the part of the Roman legates or of Agatho's successor, St Leo II (682-3).[106] It was reaffirmed

---

[105]*LP* I, pp. 354-365.

[106]Writing back to Constantinople after receiving the Council's *Acts*, pope Leo specifically mentions Honorius, who "instead of giving glory to this apostolic church by teaching apostolic tradition, has tried to subvert the immaculate faith by impious treason" (*hanc apostolicam ecclesiam non apostolicae traditionis doctrina lustravit, sed*

by the Seventh council (787) and repeated by all popes at their consecration until the eleventh century.

The final decree of the council affirmed the two "natural energies" and the two "natural wills" of Christ making it also clear that "the two natural wills are not opposed to each other, as the impious heretics suggested, but the human will follows His divine and all-powerful will, never opposes it, or struggles against it, but is rather submitted to it" (δύο μὲν φυσικὰ θελήματα, οὐχ ὑπενατία, μὴ γένοιτο, καθὼς οἱ ἀσεβεῖς ἔφησαν αἱρετικοί, ἀλλ' ἑπόμενον τὸ ἀνθρώπινον αὐτοῦ θέλημα, καὶ μὴ ἀντιπίπτον, ἢ ἀντιπαλαῖον μᾶλλον μὲν οὖν καὶ ὑποτασσόμενον τῷ θείῳ αὐτοῦ καὶ πανσθενεῖ θελήματι).[107]

The conciliar decree was accepted without further debate. It was clear, however, that the wide support received, for several decades, by the "Monoenergistic" approach to christology reflected its attractiveness to many Eastern circles, who were struggling for centuries with the problem of reconciling Cyrillian views with the Chalcedonian formulation. The ease with which Monoenergism (or Monotheletism) made Chalcedon itself acceptable to many Monophysites in Armenia, Syria and Egypt seems to indicate that it met their concern for preserving the unity of subject in Christ.[108] The formulas of Sergius had also been used in some "Neo-Chalcedonian" circles, notably by patriarch Anastasius I of Antioch (559-70, 593-9), so that the stubborness of his titular successor Macarius in 680-1 may be explained by his fear of betraying a formula which was popular in the church of Antioch, where he hoped to return.

But the real significance of the decisions made in 680-1 lay not in words and formulas, as much as in a vision of the Incarnation, witnessed in the theology of St Maximus. The Maximian synthesis which implied a final legitimization of the Chalcedonian formula of the hypostatic union, as well as the Cyrillian perception of the "divine" destiny of humanity, remained as the ultimate legacy of the seventh century in the history of Christianity.

---

profana proditione immaculam fidem subvertere conatus est), Jaffe-Wattenbach, 2118, PL 96, col 408 B; on the various sources confirming the condemnation of Honorius, see Duchesne, *L'Eglise*, p. 473, note 1.

[107]Mansi XI, col. 655, cf. English tr. of the long decree in NPNF, XIV, pp. 344-6.

[108]Monophysite authors, like Michael the Syrian, consider Maximus as a great heresiarch, and the council of 680-1 as the result of a bribe offered by pope Agatho to emperor Constantine IV (*Chron.*, XI, LL; ed. cit., II, pp. 447-8).

EPILOGUE

The Arab conquest of the Middle East, North Africa and large sections of Spain opened a new chapter in the history of Christendom. The Copts, the Syrian Jacobites, the Armenians, destined to remain for centuries in a state of heroic, but isolated struggle for survival as religious minorities within the vast world of Islam, gradually lost the sense of belonging to a world greater than their own. The same can be said of the powerful, but distant kingdom of Ethiopia. Their long resistance against Chalcedon had understandably left them with bitter memories of the Byzantine empire, although their theology, their carefully preserved liturgical traditions and their spirituality owed much to the period, when they fully shared the life of the universal Church. Their faithfulness to that Tradition, and to a christology which has remained fundamentally Cyrillian, was elucidated by the consensus of modern scholarship beginning in the nineteenth century[1] and culminating in more recent meetings of theologians.[2] Actually, it becomes increasingly embarrassing to use the term "Monophysite" to designate these ancient churches, since the term has acquired a perjorative connotation during centuries of polemics. If we too have used it, it is only for lack of another adequate name, and also because of our conviction, substantiated in this volume, that the term "Monophysite" in itself does not imply a christological heresy: it simply points to an exclusive preference for the Cyrillian formula "one nature incarnate of God the Word." The orthodoxy of that formula—and that of Cyrillian

[1]Cf. for instance, the works of the Russian bishop Porphyry Uspensky *Verouchenie, bogosluzhenie i pravila tserkovnago blagochiniya Egipetskikh khristian (koptov)* ("Doctrine, worship and rules of church order among Egyptian Christians" [Copts]), St Petersburg, 1856, and of I. E. Troitsky, *Izlozhenie very tserkvi Armyanskoy* ("The faith of the Armenian church"), St Petersburg, 1875.

[2]"Unofficial consultation between theologians of Eastern Orthodox and Oriental Orthodox Churches, Aarhus, Denmark, August 11-15, 1964," in GOTR, X, 2, Winter 1964-5; "Papers and Discussions between Eastern Orthodox and Oriental Orthodox Theologians," The Bristol Consultation, July 25-29, 1967, in GOTR, XIII, 2, Fall 1968.

christology in general—was reaffirmed very clearly by the Fifth ecumenical council of 553. The issue between Chalcedonians and Non-Chalcedonians, therefore, lies only in the question whether any formula, even one used by the Great Cyril, can be canonized forever, and whether new issues, such as that of Eutyches in 448, did not require Chalcedonian "development," just as other issues, such as Monoenergism, or Iconoclasm, or any ancient and modern "ism," demand a fresh theological response. Any theology invariably uses imperfect human language, but, within the catholic Church and by the power of the Spirit of Truth, a variety of terminologies may adequately express the one living apostolic tradition. Thus, a necessary and adequate terminological innovation was confirmed at Chalcedon, without any detriment to the fundamental soteriological intuition of St Cyril.

The period of Church history covered in this volume produced not only tragedy and division. It also saw an extraordinary expansion of the Christian faith among the ancient societies and nations of the East, as well as in the midst of the fresh "Barbarian" humanity, which in big waves, swept the territories of the Roman world in the West. It is a great joy to discover today the broad similarity of this Christian movement, unplanned, spontaneous, and largely dependent on a few saintly personalities, in the East and in the West. How similar indeed, and how spiritually close are the stories of impromptu missionaries like St Patrick of Ireland, St Frumentios of Ethiopia, and St Nino of Georgia! How parallel also the activities of Syrian monks in so many countries of the Middle East, and of the Irish monks in the West! Through those examples, and so many others, the study of Christian history discloses the Spirit of a catholic and orthodox, truly united faith of the first centuries.

What is remarkable is that, within this unity of inspiration, faith and ecclesial order were maintained without a binding universal, administrative system. Of course, the empire offered its services, as a unifying structure, and the Church used it, often at the expense of its inner freedom and occasionally falling into the temptation of identifying its spiritual mission with the political goals which are normal for any State to pursue. Indeed, as we have noted in the first chapters, there was a consensus among Christians that the existence of the ideally universal Roman empire as a tool of Christian expansion and welfare was a providential event, which allowed the Christian mission to become truly universal. At no time, however, did Christians concede to the State the right to become the real source of belief, or a criterion of orthodoxy. Examples of Christians admitting the right, and duty, of the emperor, to defend and promote orthodoxy, are as numerous as are the protests against his religious decrees, when they were considered as inadequate.

In contemporary historiography, it is still common to simplify the record by accusing the Byzantine emperors of caesaro-papism, and to condemn the "imperial centuries" of Church history as a shame, a disaster. But the facts are more complicated and the record is mixed. There can be no justification for the mass repressions of religious resistance in Egypt by imperial troops, or for the treatment reserved by Constans II for pope Martin and Maximus the Confessor: the empire certainly deserves full blame for such acts. However, it cannot be denied either that the universal Christian Church needed a center, which would make ecumenical councils possible, encourage encounters of cultures, and translate the "catholic" nature of Christianity into visible, social, historical reality. In those areas, the imperial record is not one of failures only. Byzantium's legacy includes the aspiration for a truly universal Christendom, common to Greeks, Latins, Syrians and Egyptians; a theology, which is not bound by formulas, but acknowledges the orthodoxy of Cyril, Leo, Chalcedon and Maximus; an attempt to humanize Roman Law, by assuming into it love and mercy; an art which succeeded in projecting the eschatological vision of a humanity deified in Christ. None of these achievements can be used as a proof of some divine revelation, sanctioning dogmatically the theocratic ideology of Constantine, Theodosius I, and Justinian. Theirs were human, historical achievements, accepted and "received" by the Church as manifestations of Her unchangeable divino-human Being, but this Being itself was present only in the eschatological reality of the Eucharist, and manifested in the experience of saints.

During the centuries covered in this volume, there already was another, and potentially competing, center of world Christendom, gradually emerging in the "Old Rome." Early Christian tradition enshrined in the New Testament, had already recognized the importance of a spiritual center for all local churches, long before the emergence of a Christian empire. The original apostolic Judeo-Christian community of Jerusalem, the eschatological realization of biblical prophecies, as described in the Book of Acts, and for which St Paul made symbolically important collections in the churches founded by him among the Gentiles, had played this role for the first Christian generation. Could this center be transferred elsewhere after the destruction of Jerusalem by Emepor Titus in AD 70 and the dispersion of the Judeo-Christian community? Without ever formally claiming this legacy from Jerusalem, the church of Rome began very early to stress the importance of its founding by the apostles Peter and Paul. Gradually the emphasis shifted to Peter alone, and the logia of Jesus himself addressed to the one who was "first" among the Twelve, the "Rock" of faith, and the "Shepherd" of Christ's lambs, served to enhance the prestige of Peter's "successor."

The history of the first centuries of Christianity produces no evidence to show that this concept of a "Petrine" succession in Rome entailed, either in the West or in the East, anything but a certain moral authority and prestige. Ecclesiastical centralization around major centers was closely linked to the imperial administrative system, not to the church of Rome. Centralization was enforced much earlier in the East, because the imperial system was stronger in place there than in the West. In the fifth, sixth and seventh centuries, the canonical rights of the Eastern "patriarchs," especially of Constantinople, were clearly set within definite and vast territories, while the Roman bishop could hardly be seen as a "patriarch" at all, since his direct jurisdiction extended only to the "suburbicarian" bishops and, more vaguely, to his "vicars" in Thessalonica and Arles. The rest of Western, Latin Christendom was made up of totally independent churches (Africa, Spain, Gaul, the Celtic dioceses). Nevertheless—perhaps since pope Stephen, or at least since pope Damasus, but even much more plainly, in the fifth century, with St Leo the Great and Gelasius—the Roman bishop defined his role in the universal church as the ultimate doctrinal and disciplinary authority, by virtue of his "Petrine" succession. Such claims and their implications were not clearly understood in most of the West. In the East, they were placed in an "imperial" context and attributed not to Peter's legacy, but to the perennial symbolic status of "Rome" within the still "Roman" empire. Outside of the church in Rome, these claims came to be used explicitly by the British mission, led by St Augustine and Theodore of Tarsus, and by the mission to the Germans, headed by St Boniface. Out of the latter came the Carolingian civilization which accepted the eminence of the "Old Rome," partly in opposition to the tradition of the imperial system centered in Constantinople. This evolution was encouraged, during the centuries of "Byzantine papacy," by the practice adopted by the Eastern emperors to entrust to the Roman bishops the task of maintaining the authority of Roman laws and Roman legitimacy among the Western Barbarians. The concept of the pope, as guardian of *Romanitas*, would eventually be assumed by the emerging medieval papacy.

None of these historical developments, however, can serve as a sufficient explanation for the inner conviction of the Roman church about its unique functions and authority, a conviction which originally lacked realism and was met with disbelief and misunderstanding in most of the Christian world. As a result of the overgrowth of such Roman claims in the ninth and eleventh centuries and the inevitable reaction against it, the schism itself eventually became inevitable.

The ultimate meaning and significance of an universal center cannot be discovered without a reexamination of the historical evidence. Since it is impossible to marshal any unquestionable scriptural, or patristic, or conciliar evidence in favor of the fully structured Roman papacy, the form and location of an universal Christian center, whose usefulness and even necessity cannot really be denied, must be a matter of acceptance and "reception" by the Church. The empire itself played its centralizing role for centuries, because it had been accepted and "received," with reservations and limitations, by the Church, as a human, but legitimate instrument of cohesion and unity. The claims of the Roman church are the result of a different, more subtle and spiritual rationalization. However, in order to be interpreted as an expression of divine guidance for the Church in history, they too must be "received" by a consensus of all local churches. The great Tradition, which has been examined in this volume, accepted the position of Rome, as "first" among the churches without any antagonism. What remained controversial, was not so much the Roman "primacy" itself, but its later forms and implications which came about through historical development. Was this medieval development legitimate? The answer to this question can hardly be found in Scripture, and must therefore be looked for in Tradition. But Tradition, which involves historical change, must also show at least some degree of consistency and continuity especially with the period of the ecumenical councils, when, in spite of problems and tensions, Rome and the East were able to find common criteria to solve the difficulties which stood between them. The study of Church history would be meaning-

less if it did not include a search for consistent and permanent ecclesiological principles, enshrined in Holy Tradition, but frequently hidden
by the "traditions of men." In this sense, Church history is the indis-
pensable tool of any legitimate search for a theology of Christian unity.

INDEX

ATLANTIC OCEAN

NORTH SEA

BALTIC SEA

MEDITERRANEAN SEA

AFRICA

Iona
Armagh
Whitby
Ripon
York
Bangor
Hereford
Hatfield
London
Canterbury

Fontaine
Rheims
Trier
Paris
Troyes
Luxeuil
Tours
Orleans
Auxerre
Poitiers
FRANKISH KINGDOM
Lyon
Clermont
Toulouse
Vienne
ALPS MTS
Milan
Turin
Ferrara
Aquilea
Sirmium
SIRM A
Narbonne
Valence
Vaison
Genoa
Bobbio
Pisa
Ravenna
DALMATIA
ILLY
Agde
Arles
Riez
Gubbio
Nursia
ADRIATIC SEA
Just
PYRENEES MTS
Corsica
Rome
Subiaco
Dyrrachium
MACED
Braga
Zaragossa
Sardinia
Ostia
Mt Cassino
Nola
TYRRENIAN SEA
Toledo
Cagliari
Cordoba
Seville
Carthagena
Lilybaeum
Syracuse
IONIAN SEA
Ceuta
Carthage

Rhine R.
Albis R.
SUEDES MTS
Rhone R.